DEVELOPMENT BETRAYED

Modernity promised control over nature through science, material abundance through superior technology, and effective government through rational social organization. Instead of leading to this promised land it has brought us back to the brink of environmental and cultural disaster. Why has there been this gap between modernity's aspirations and its achievements? *Development Betrayed* offers a powerful answer to this question.

Development, with its unshakeable commitment to the idea of progress, is rooted in modernism and has been betrayed by each of its major tenets. Attempts to control nature have led to the verge of environmental catastrophe. Western technologies have proved inappropriate for the needs of the South, and governments are unable to respond to the crises that have resulted.

Offering a thorough and lively critique of the ideas behind development, Richard Norgaard also offers an alternative coevolutionary paradigm, in which development is portrayed as a coevolution between cultural and ecological systems. Rather than a future with all peoples merging to one best way of knowing and doing things, he envisions a future of a patchwork quilt of cultures with real possibilities for harmony.

Richard Norgaard was environmentalist David Brower's river guide during the flooding of the Glen Canyon on the Colorado River. He earned a PhD in Economics at the University of Chicago before going on to investigate the environmental problems of petroleum development in Alaska, hydroelectric dams in California, pesticide use in modern agriculture, and deforestation in the Amazon. He has been a member of the faculty at the University of California at Berkeley since 1970, where he is currently a Professor of Energy and Resources, and is also a member of the US National Committee for the Scientific Committee on Problems of the Environment.

DEVELOPMENT BETRAYED

The end of progress and a coevolutionary revisioning of the future

Richard B. Norgaard

London and New York

First published 1994
by Routledge
11 New Fetter Lane, London EC4P 4EE

Simultaneously published in the USA and Canada
by Routledge
29 West 35th Street, New York, NY 10001

Typeset in Garamond by
J&L Composition Ltd, Filey, North Yorkshire
Printed and bound in Great Britain by
Mackays of Chatham PLC, Chatham, Kent

British Library Cataloguing in Publication Data
A catalogue record for this book is available from the British Library

Library of Congress Cataloging in Publication Data
has been applied for

ISBN 0–415–06861–4 (hbk)   0–415–06862–2 (pbk)

To all in the past who extended cultural, environmental, and moral expectations into the present;

To my parents, John and Marva Dawn, as well as to David and Anne Brower and Lou and Claire Elliott who empowered me at an early age with their trust, faith, and hopes;

To my teachers, colleagues, and students who challenged my intellectual creativity;

And to my wife, Nancy Rader, to children, Kari and Marc, and to diverse peoples, young and old, around the globe who are revisioning the future with me to assure that it is respectful of life, rich with dignity, and full of meaning again.

CONTENTS

FIGURES AND TABLES

PREFACE

On special occasions, far from academe, I awake to both complete peace and unbounded comprehension. I am watching the early sun descend a sandstone wall in a canyon of the southwestern United States, with my ear to the beach listening to boulders rumbling along the bed of an Alaskan river, awaking from a nap on a slab of talus high in the Colorado Rockies, or lying in a hammock and being soothed by the rush of water along the hull of a small Amazon River freighter. These beautiful moments on awaking come several days after I have ceased my academic efforts to understand and begin to comprehend directly. There are no objects perceived or questions answered, just oneness.

This ultimate beauty is inevitably too soon shattered by a hiking companion ready to move on, the tasks of rafting rivers that deliver the necessary solitude, or the startup of the monotonous beat of the river boat's diesel engine ready to take me deeper into the Amazon. I imagine that these blessed moments of peace and comprehension occurred more frequently for people in the past. Today, they are very special times. And I suspect more and more people never experience them at all.

I write in the face of modernity's incoherence: the wealth amid poverty, the domination amid rhetoric of equality, the rape amid love of people and nature, the noise amid the music. Hope is a prerequisite for constructive thought and action, a moral imperative in the words of my colleague John Harte. I think, write, and teach, and act in my life beyond academe sustained by a hope with no rational basis.

While my search for coherence has led to fewer and fewer answers, I have become increasingly comfortable without them. In place of answers, I have developed an even greater faith in thinking. More importantly, I better understand the importance of sharing. Though this book espouses thinking about development as a coevolutionary process between a social system and its environmental system, I do not think coevolutionary thinking is necessarily correct. I do not think any one way of thinking will ever be right. Indeed, right thinking is a wrong concept. Though I have not pursued the beauty of mathematical reasoning for several decades, I am still attracted to rigorous arguments that appear to be independent and complete. But now my thoughts span too wide a range of problems and stem from too many disciplines. I am well beyond any pretensions of expertise let alone mathematical beauty. Logical, rigorous thinking is essential, but I now recognize that understanding cannot be an individual undertaking. To the extent modern peoples understand the dilemmas of modernity, it is through the sharing of different understandings. And our modern faith in rightness over sharing is the major obstacle to better understanding and the resolution of modernity's environmental problems.

My personal evolution reflects the social and environmental activism and intellectual life for which Berkeley is justly famous. I became who I am because I shared the Glen Canyon with numerous environmentalists and intellectuals before and after the dam choked off the Colorado River in January 1963. My participation as a faculty member at Berkeley in the interdisciplinary graduate groups of Energy and Resources and Latin American Studies have given me exceptional access to the knowledge, experiences, and patterns of thinking of many other faculty and to the personal experiences, unceasing questions, and enthusiasm of students from all around the world and from many academic backgrounds. The university life has provided exceptional opportunities also to live in Brazil, to work for shorter periods throughout the world, and even to function within the culture of the World Bank and other institutions. My interest in environmental epistemology, or more generally how we think we know, has been stimulated by the intellectual diversity on the Berkeley campus, through my work with other cultures, and by the steadfastness of worldview and belief in right thinking among my colleagues in the discipline of my formal training, economics. But even within economics, the most clearly ideologically driven academic discipline, a small space has been provided for an iconoclast. For all of this I am grateful.

ACKNOWLEDGEMENTS

This book has evolved over a very long time period during which many faculty and student colleagues in Berkeley and beyond have entered into valuable discussion, provided specific comments on the text, or directed me to the writing of others. I cannot possibly list all of the people who have contributed to the diverse thoughts I have melded into this book, but hope I have not slighted too many.

Sam Barakat
Thomas Berry
Kenneth Boulding
Daniel Bromley
Barbara Brower
Tim Brown
Ronald Brunner
Ernst Callenbach
Mary E. Clark
Andrew Cohen
Stuart Cowan
Paul Craig
Dilip da Cunha
Herman Daly
Anushka Drescher
Paul and Anne Ehrlich
Arturo Escobar
Philip Fearnside
Peggy Lee Fiedler
Lee Freese

Raul Garcia
Paul Gelles
Vinay Gidwani
Peter Goering
Robert Goodland
Ernst Haas
John Harte
Susanna Hecht
John Holdren
Richard Howarth
Deborah Jensen
Sharad Lele
Patricia Mace
Michael Maniates
Omar Masera
Sandra Moniaga
Monica Moore
Maria Murmis
Kari Norgaard
Thomas O'Brien

Martin O'Connor
Ruth Oscar
Jan Prevetti
Laurel Prevetti
Nancy Rader
Jesse Ribot
Jeff Romm
Alan Sanstad
Richard Sclove
Ben Shaine
Nigel Smith
Shiv Someshwar
Ruth Steiner
Kim Taylor
Peter Taylor
Catherine Taylor
Lori Ann Thrupp
Alan Treffeisen
Ignacio Valero
Michael Warburton

In addition, I wish to thank Alan Jarvis, Social Sciences Editor, for his encouragement, patience, and help, as well as Sean Connolly, Copy Editor; Rory Smith, Desk Editor; and other staff at Routledge for all they contributed toward the completion of the book.

1

THE BETRAYAL OF PROGRESS

I think economic growth is a good thing. It pleases me to see it achieved, it distresses me to witness its failure, especially when the failure is due to misdirected policies. I can see little sense in the romantic argument that happy people in poor countries ought to be left alone. Whether they are happy is irrelevant, for the drive for economic development that causes such turmoil in the poor country is led for the most part by the elites of those countries themselves. The drive for modernization is a fact; there seems to be no turning back.

(Gayl D. Ness 1967: ix)

Modernity promised control over nature through science, material abundance through superior technology, and effective government through rational social organization. Modernity also promised peace and justice through a higher individual morality and superior collective culture to which all, free of material want, would ascend. Modernity, in short, promised to transform the heretofore slow and precarious course of human progress onto a fast track. Belief in progress facilitated Western and westernized patterns of development for several centuries throughout much of the world. The industrial revolution in Europe and then the United States during the nineteenth century began to confirm modernity's promises. On this evidence, faith in progress survived the World War, the Great Depression, and the political turmoil that led to another World War, all in the first half of the twentieth century. At mid-twentieth century, progress somehow still assured peace, equality, and happiness for all. This confidence in the possibilities for progress was rallied in support of an international economic development that would transform the lives of even the most "obdurate" landlord and peasant in the most "backward" reaches of the globe.

Yet during the second half of this century, yesterday's promise, only partly fulfilled:

- fostered material madness;
- accentuated inequality;

1

- imprisoned modernity's devotees in bureaucratic gridlock;
- accelerated the depletion of the stock resources and the degradation of the environment on which progress depends;
- pitted people against people in a multitude of regional wars;
- made political and economic hostages and refugees of a sizeable portion of the global population; and
- took the United States and Soviet Union to the brink of mutual nuclear annihilation.

Accelerating progress through planned development has been the recent project of modernity, yet development has gone seriously awry. The basic tenets around which the modern transformation was conceived and carried out deceived us. Modernism, and its more recent manifestation as development, have betrayed progress.

Progress's betrayal is being exposed in at least three different ways. First, while a few have attained material abundance, resource depletion and environmental degradation now endanger many and threaten the hopes of all to come. Second, the public sectors of capitalist and socialist, of authoritarian and democratic, and of developed and undeveloped nations are powerless. The socialist governments of Eastern Europe and what was the Soviet Union have collapsed, leaving diverse peoples struggling to redefine their cultural, economic, and political systems as this book is being written. Meanwhile, democratic capitalist societies, the presumed economic victors as the century comes to a close, are having increasing difficulty providing education, health care, and housing for their poor and are stymied by a plethora of new intertwined environmental problems and cultural contradictions. We, the progeny of ancestors who followed the modern path, are having ever greater difficulty publicly comprehending the complexity of new social and environmental problems, understanding our collective interest in resolving them, and breaking the bureacuratic deadlock created by the extremes of competing political interests and inadequacies of scientistic reasoning. And third, an increasing number of people are declaring that modernism as culture is specious. The open resurgence of cultural, ethnic, and religious diversity after years of suppression, through brutal repression at worst to voluntary assimilation at best, is perhaps the most challenging exposure of the betrayal.

The betrayal of progress is revealed through our recognition of these problems. As is the nature of a betrayal, we believed in the tenets of modernism while modernity itself was not following the promised course. Modernism betrayed progress by leading us into, preventing us from seeing, and keeping us from addressing interwoven environmental, organizational, and cultural problems.

THE ENVIRONMENTAL CHALLENGE

People have always encountered problems interacting with their environment, but historically the problems were isolated and only affected specific peoples in specific ways. Today, in contrast, we are beginning to perceive that the technologies and social organization that facilitated a fivefold increase in global population during this century are responsible for the environmental degradation, global climate change, and loss of biodiversity which affect all peoples, now and forevermore. On modernity's fast track, the pursuit of trivial materialism by people of the industrialized North will burn up the bulk of the fossil fuels and transform the planet through climate change before basic needs will have been met for many in the South.

The modern project of development has come to a halt in most of the world. Advanced medical technologies are still extending the lives of the rich. But even in the rich countries, more and more children are being born into poverty, living in unsafe environments, and receiving little or no health care. A good case has been made that the Soviet Union's demise was a case of ecocide, of such massive deterioration of the environment and degradation of the work force that it ground to a halt. During the debt crisis in Latin America during the 1980s, living conditions deteriorated, population outgrew sewage treatment facilities, and an epidemic of cholera swept across South America during the early 1990s. Cholera for the first time now appears to have become endemic in the Western hemisphere. Bringing sewage treatment and water treatment systems up to modern standards would cost an estimated $200 billion. While this is a small portion of defense expenditures in South America, to say nothing of North America, the cost of clean water was judged excessive. Scientists are hoping to develop a vaccine so that the poor can better live with the *v. cholerae* that thrives in human excrement.

Recent advances in Western science now offer a good understanding of why development along the present course is unsustainable. The pattern of knowing that provides this understanding, however, also played a key role in the development and implementation of our unsustainable interactions with our environment. And unfortunately, Western science is not so advanced, and probably never will be, as to provide a sufficiently detailed picture of the consequences of continuing on our present course to convince those who still believe in modernity. Nor can Western science provide directions toward a better course. Progress is in limbo.

POLITICAL AND BUREAUCRATIC DEADLOCK

While humanity's environmental crisis instigated this book, the future cannot be addressed without also addressing two additional ways in which progress has been betrayed. The problem ultimately is that environmental crises are crises of social organization and cultural character.

3

The second exposure of the betrayal has manifested itself disparately in different countries. It has not been very well articulated in the public discourse. A very general characterization would be that the effectiveness of our collective action is not on a par with the difficulties of our collective problems. While the peoples of what was the Soviet Union are most notably facing this issue at the close of the twentieth century, the phenomenon is very widespread. Neighborhoods, communities, and other local forms of social organization that give individuals a sense of social identity have declined in importance. Problems that used to be solved within families, through churches, or at the community level have been rediagnosed as systemic problems of modernization demanding the attention of central governments. Partly as a consequence, local, state, and national legislative bodies are hopelessly deadlocked between competing interest groups demanding that a larger piece of the public pie be dedicated to the problems they find most troublesome. Yet given the plethora of temptations and sense of identity now garnered through individual materialism, most people also insist that the public pie must shrink.

The governmental agencies that are still funded are hopelessly stalemated with many problems unsolved. Legislative bodies have expanded the mandates of heretofore single purpose agencies in an effort to meet competing interests and address the complexity of problems. This has in effect passed the political conflicts associated with the interrelatedness of problems on to the agencies. The agencies, however, were established under the pretense that they merely had to uncover the facts, rationally determine solutions, and efficiently implement projects and programs. In addition to having to deal with stronger competing interests, determining rational solutions has become more, rather than less, difficult with the expansion of scientific knowledge, the use of scientific reasoning by special interest groups, and the acceptance of scientistic arguments by the populace at large. The advance of science has answered some questions, but its most important effect has been that it has taught different interests how to ask many far more difficult questions. With each interest group publicly raising the questions that must be answered to justify the solutions advocated by their opponents, public agencies have become bogged down in hopeless searches and justifications for solutions which, if they do not satisfy a bare majority, at least defeat the public's will to continue the search.

Agencies with land use and environmental management responsibilities are having special difficulty. They suffer from analysis paralysis because, typically by legislative mandate, they have been required to use natural science technocratically. Apparently competing political interests are, in fact, synthetically interconnected through a complex, ecological web. The environmental sciences are separate, reductionist ways of acquiring insights into particulars. Grasping at impossible conclusions from futile syntheses of the individual disciplines, the land management agencies have become leading participants in the politicization and degradation of science.

In the industrialized, market economies, private enterprise is providing individual consumers with ever more wondrous and increasingly meaningless choices. The very success of captivating private initiative has created new problems which require collective action. The social costs of private enterprise overlap with the environmental challenges, but this is just the beginning of the problem. An increasing number of people do not fit the jobs that are available in the most developed nations and are appearing on the streets homeless. Others are voluntarily dropping out of modernism's race for material goods. Some are settling for drugs and crime. Some find solace in cult religions. The contradictions of increasingly market-based economies in the less developed nations are at least as great. The number of problems to be solved and the opportunities for channeling the productive power of individual initiative positively have not been greater since the Great Depression. Yet in most market-oriented economies, the public has neither the confidence to assist nor a collective vision to which they might put the market's "invisible hand." On the contrary, nearly all nations are busily trying to obtain more material goods, whatever they may be, by strengthening performance incentives and competing ever more effectively in the global market economy whose direction is even harder to guide.

THE RECULTURALIZATION OF THE GLOBE

The third manner in which modernism and development have betrayed progress is yet more difficult to characterize. The public significance and accepted role of culture, ethnicity, and religion are changing. Modernism kept these differences under control through three strategies. First, to the extent that nations have been politically pluralistic, people have willfully down-played their cultural, ethnic, and religious differences by accepting them simply as differences in values. Second, to the extent that majorities or elite in power have expected all to rise to the same modern beliefs, they have tolerated differences if the recalcitrant group accepts a second class status within the society. Third, the belief in modernism also has justified the repression and extermination of minorities, especially indigenous peoples by colonialists. All three strategies have been used in different proportions, countries, and times. The first denigrates the full social significance of being a person of a particular color, cultural heritage, or religious belief and of associating with others who share the same traits. The second begins to acknowledge the significance but requires those in the group to accept less status within society. The third strategy is morally reprehensible by any standard.

None of modernism's strategies for dealing with cultural diversity is working as well as it did, for better and for worse. The most dramatic

5

response to the Soviet Union's acknowledgment that the Communist party line was open to challenge was a phenomenally rapid, boisterously expressed cultural and ethnic redifferentiation which bolstered local identity while leaving virtually homeless the millions of people forcibly transplaced by the Soviet effort to forge one modern culture. The great melting pot of the United States increasingly resembles a wok of lightly braised ingredients. And Europeans continue to maintain many of their distinctive national traits even though they share a common market, watch American shows on Japanese televisions, and have absorbed a significant influx of non-European political and economic refugees from their former colonies. Most importantly, traditional peoples, north and south, are demanding and beginning to receive a little cultural respect and a chance to effect their own futures. Our recognition of earlier cultures and traditional peoples, however tentative, is an implicit acknowledgment that cultures are more than systems for perpetuating values. We are beginning to accept that culture embodies other ways of knowing, organizing, and interacting with the environment as well.

I am deeply satisfied by this cultural resurgence, growing respect for traditional peoples, and ultimately expanded notion of viable forms of community, knowledge, organization, and technology. The progressive fantasy of all peoples converging upon one highest way of valuing, knowing, organizing, and interacting with their environment was perpetrated by the myths that sustained governments ranging from authoritarian to democratic and from market to socialist. This nightmare is now beginning to mellow. And yet amid this explosion and recognition of heterogeneity, racial and cultural hatred is also on the rise. Differences, at best, make politics more difficult. At worst, they induce the most inhumane types of psychological torture and physical violence in which people engage. I have no idea whether over two hundred nations, especially those with cultural refugees, regional polities, and the global polity at large will have the respect for differences necessary to work out common problems together. A culturally richer world, especially one as crowded and beset with problems as ours is today, requires a new philosophical basis which inherently honors diversity.

This may seem like an excessively elaborate portrayal of the betrayal of progress. The interconnections between environmental crises, stalemated bureaucracies, and cultural resurgence that I have tried to draw are by no means obvious from within the modern world view. The linkages will become clearer with the exploration of a new way of understanding process and structure that leads to a revisioning of the future. Modernism itself, however, must be characterized first.

MODERNISM: KEY TENETS

Modernism consists of a rich panoply of still evolving beliefs which arose with the successes of Western science and political reorganization in Europe and North America during the past three centuries. The three ways through which modernism's betrayal of progress is being exposed correspond to three underlying tenets of modernism which, though they too have been evolving, have retained clear identities. The environmental disasters and social injustices identified in prior critiques of development can be shown to be rooted in these underlying tenets.

The first important tenet of modernism is that Western science steadily advances, constantly produces better and better technologies and ways of organizing, and hence future generations will continually be better off than are current generations. Inherent in this tenet has been the idea that better technologies and social organization facilitate better control over nature, not a better, deeper relationship with nature. Belief in progress has excused people from the moral dilemma of addressing the effects of their decisions on the opportunities for the next generation. Furthermore, underprivileged peoples accepted injustices on the premise that, if they worked hard and did not fight the system, their children had a good chance of being among the privileged. Fewer people believe this now. The widespread acceptance during the 1980s that development has not been sustainable has social as well as environmental roots. The overly simple belief that modernism is the fast track of progress is being rejected. How the course of progress itself will evolve is still unclear.

The second key nexus of beliefs is at the intersection of positivism and monism. Positivism is the belief that values and facts can be kept separate. Monism is the belief that the separate sciences – physics, chemistry, biology; the applied sciences such as agriculture, engineering, and forestry; and the social sciences such as economics – lead to a unique answer when confronting complex problems. These two tenets logically lead to the conclusion that, once legislative bodies establish goals, they can delegate problems to experts to solve. This line of thought has facilitated the development and operation of centralized technocracies. Technocracies would not compete with democracy, in this understanding of science, if social decision-making were only a matter of resolving value questions and values and facts could be separated. It is now clear, however, that experts cannot determine the states of their separate parts of social and environmental systems, let alone how all the parts might cohere. And yet experts in other areas as well as generalists, humanists, and lay people generally are still excluded from participating in most social decision-making. Technocracy, girded by public faith in positivism and monism, has served powerful interests, effectively relegating democratic decision-making to a very limited role.

Third, modernism is also characterized by the belief that cultural differences will fade away as people discover the effectiveness of rational Western culture. During the Renaissance, new ways of thinking about social order, technology, and people's relations to the land, in short a new world view, began to replace the earlier European world view that evolved under the domination of the Catholic Church and through feudal relations. These new ways of perceiving the world and peoples' relations to it, not scientific themselves, were thought to be superior because of their association with the rise of Western science. Having accepted a new world view themselves, Europeans fully expected people of other cultures to see its superiority. Alternatively, those peoples who could not see its superiority were considered hopeless cases who were impeding the progress of the majority to utopia and who therefore could be rightfully suppressed.

All three characterizations of modernism incorporate understandings of, and expectations for, how Western science would work, not simply in theory or in the laboratory where success was indeed manifest, but in social and natural environments. The realization of the persistence and now global nature of environmental problems exposes the fallacy of these beliefs. The acknowledgment that widely different governments are having great difficulty being effective exposes the fallacy of believing that Western science would necessarily lead to an effective social order. The resurgence of cultural diversity exposes the fallacy of believing that all would "rise" to Western rationality. Modernists' expectations that science would provide environmental solutions, rational social organization, and a higher culture to which all would aspire were obviously excessive. Modernists have expected far too much of Western science. To a large extent these expectations were generated by scientists themselves. Yet at the end of the twentieth century, scientists also are disturbed by the differences between how and what they know and the historic perceptions of science that have become institutionalized in our social structure and public expectations. It is the inappropriateness of our historic understandings of and expectations for Western science, not the patterns of thinking and the knowledge Western science has brought us, that are at the root of the betrayal.

We commonly divide the sciences into the natural and the social. Next we note that our natural science knowledge is "hard," that advances in physics, chemistry, and molecular biology have been consistent with our high expectations. In the social sciences, or more generally, in the sciences which try to understand complex systems including ecological systems, our knowledge is "soft," our expectations have not been met. We also acknowledge that the hard sciences have produced the new technologies which work very effectively at one scale – the scope of analysis of physics, chemistry, and molecular biology – and wreak social and ecological havoc at a broader scale when deployed in human environments. We then argue that our problems are due to the weakness of the systemic sciences.

This division of science into disciplines with separate responsibilities promotes irresponsibility. The separate sciences independently take credit for successes and independently blame deficiencies in other realms of knowledge for failures. What is the value of the separate understandings from the physical sciences acquired by analysis under controlled conditions in laboratories, in closed systems, if these understandings cannot be synthesized and extended to work in social and environmental systems without destroying those systems? Our ability to comprehend as a whole is all that matters in the end. Many physicists, morally shaken by the U.S. decision to drop the atomic bomb on Hiroshima, organized to express their concern over the social and ecological consequences of modern technologies. A significant group of biologists are redefining the boundaries between science and policy in response to their growing awareness of the loss of biological diversity. But the division of the sciences has induced incredible irresponsibility among scientists as a whole. If we must have subcategories, we would be much better off if we reminded ourselves that we have unnatural and unsocial sciences, ecological and unecological sciences, and systemic and unsystemic sciences.

As I introduce the general argument, I have deliberately defined modernism to encompass many of the characteristics of both the Western liberal world view and the Western marxist world view. Its use is also consistent with the outlooks of those who favor democratic socialism or totalitarian private enterprise. Obviously there are dimensions in which modern views are very different. But the betrayal of progress is quite insensitive to which of these political and economic dimensions has been important during any particular nation's history. All of the political and economic offspring of modernism share in the betrayal.

Obviously modernism is most important in the West, including, but with different emphases, what was the Soviet Union. Modernism plays an important role in countries that have patterned themselves on the West. It is especially important among the upper classes and urbanized people of Latin America. Modernism is important, albeit frequently as an oppositional, among Islamic fundamentalists. The beliefs characterizing this world view are least important among the rural poor of African countries, in the remoter regions of China, and in half a dozen countries on China's borders. Yet among the elite, especially among the Western-educated elite, modernism is important everywhere.

SUMMARY

This book critiques the dominant role of modern beliefs; it is a critique of the narrowness of formally accepted patterns of thinking in the modern world. Western science figures prominently in this critique, not with respect to how scientists go about trying to understand, but with respect to how society accepts particular scientific ways of understanding and tries to act rationally on these understandings to the exclusion of other ways of knowing, both scientific and traditional. Scientists, in turn, become entangled in science's misuse. Environmental and cultural destruction can be linked to the dominance of these beliefs about science. The particular scientific ways of knowing by themselves are neither bad nor good, but the beliefs which make these ways dominant create both an overdependence on particular ways of understanding and blindspots through the exclusion of other ways of knowing. The myths that guide how individual scientific ways of knowing are translated in public knowledge and action compound the problem. Modern technologies, forms of social organization, value systems, and environments now reflect this inappropriate dominance, excluding alternatives that might be more culturally and environmentally viable.

Critiques of modernity are easy and now numerous. This book, however, develops a coevolutionary explanation of how social and environmental systems change. It is the novelty of the coevolutionary perspective that gives the critique new substance. And it is the coevolutionary perspective that provides the new vision of progress developed in the closing chapters.

2

THE CHALLENGE OF SUSTAINABILITY

It upsets many people even to contemplate the possibility that we are caught up in a social process, not under the control of any human agency. This view of the world may be more difficult to accept than the realization that we are not at the center of the universe and the discovery that we are products of blind natural selection.

(Herbert Kaufman 1981)

Pollution control, population planning, energy conservation, and resource management have been incorporated into national policies during the latter half of the twentieth century. Most nations are not putting sufficient short-run emphasis on these long-term problems, but none outwardly disagree with their importance. Resource exploitation, environmental degradation, and commodity output have been constrained, albeit only moderately, by limiting where production can occur, by investing resources to curb pollution, and by rejecting some technologies outright. Agencies for land use planning, pollution control, and technology regulation have added fresh layers to the bureaucratic onions of both the developed and developing nations.

The call for sustainability that began in the mid-1980s appears rather vague compared to the earlier calls for specific controls. Environmentalists want environmental systems and the diversity of species sustained, a rather broad call for a social movement which has had only specific successes to date. But their call is reinforced by many others who have become disillusioned with the course of development. To put it crassly, consumers want consumption sustained. Workers want jobs sustained. Capitalists and socialists have their "isms," while aristocrats, autocrats, bureaucrats, and technocrats have their "cracies." All are threatened by the decay of global life support systems. No one can publicly advocate unsustainable progress and maintain credibility. Thus sustainability calls to and is being called for by many, from tribal peoples to the most erudite academics, from peasant farmers to agroindustrialists, from denim-clad eco-activists to pinstripe-suited bankers. With the term meaning something different to everyone, the quest for sustainable development is off to a cacophonous start.

As individuals we still have widely different economic positions to protect

11

and different aspirations to achieve. But a surprisingly global "we" realize that the underlying process that has positioned us where we are and fostered our aspirations is unsustainable. With our disparate starting points and interests in the future, this realization is not the same as a consensus on what we should do. But the agreement that things must change makes the close of the twentieth century one of the most fluid and exciting times in history.

Historically, people in industrialized countries have not perceived environmental problems in the same way as people in developing countries. North Americans, because of their cultural history, have tended to glorify nature, to decry its defilement, and to propose "back-to-nature" type solutions. As a consequence of their colonial history, Third World peoples have tended to be much more concerned with the social origins and human consequences of environmental degradation. Northern environmentalists were shocked in 1972 by the positions taken by the South at the U.N. Conference on the Human Environment in Stockholm. Environmental leaders and scientists from North and South have learned from each other since that clash in views through repeated discussions and teamwork in the field. The 1987 report of the World Commission on Environment and Development reflects both views. There is a new synthesis arising among world political leaders as well. Among the populace the differences between North and South are diminishing. Northern workers are becoming more politically active with respect to the dangers of their work and home environments, while Southern peoples are gaining a broader understanding of the importance of ecological systems and processes for economic development. Initially, international agencies such as the World Bank were only pressured by Northern environmentalists. Now they have to respond to pressures from the developing countries themselves. Nevertheless, cultural differences still make communication between North and South on environmental questions very difficult.

Global environmental degradation is perhaps the most blatant challenge to modernity. Yet most scientists and concerned laypeople still interpret the widespread perception that modernity is undermining itself as a mandate for multiple adjustments guided by an expansion in data collection, a more sophisticated use of Western science, more controls on technology, better institutional design, and appeals to existing values. This interpretation of the path to sustainable development calls for the expansion of the domain of modern rationality and intensification of its application. But if modernity is undermining itself, might not its enlargement and strengthening hasten the process? The logic, however, is that development has gone awry because people have not been fully in control. Modernity is failing because, with control over nature only partial and with the social systems not fully rationalized, the project is like a poorly designed space mission, doomed to failure. The challenge of sustainable development is commonly being interpreted as a need for better knowledge and more control, in short, as a challenge to complete the modern agenda.

Following the logic of modernity, an objective of control must be specified. What is to be sustained? With sustainable development meaning different things to different people, many have argued for a rigorous, scientific definition to which all should defer. Beyond the need for a public consensus, development agencies need an operational definition to guide their actions. While the logic of this argument is commendable, sustainable development has eluded numerous attempts to give it a comprehensive, operational definition. Why this is so and what the challenge of sustainable development means for modernity is the subject of this chapter. The first step is to review the challenges of sustainable development as perceived by the environmental scientists who have alerted us to so many dangers.

THE ENVIRONMENTAL SCIENCE PERSPECTIVE

"Horror stories" of environmental destruction are common in the news media. These vignettes, while frequently elaborated by environmental activists and journalists, stress a few facts determined by environmental scientists and demographers. These facts "speak for themselves" in that they inevitably result in highly undesirable if not impossible circumstances for people when extrapolated two to five decades into the future. The complications of how scientists know and the uncertainty of the "facts" are typically not given sufficient attention in the media. Other interest groups then expose the scientific uncertainty to defend business as usual. Policy formulation must acknowledge that we never know perfectly and that every way of knowing has built-in weaknesses. The challenge is to translate the information presented, along with other often conflicting information, into effective plans of action. Consider the following vignettes.

Global climate change is expected to result in an average increase in temperatures of between 1.5 and 4.5 degrees centigrade (2.7 and 8.1 degrees fahrenheit) by the year 2030. Average temperatures during the last ice age were only 5 degrees centigrade lower than now. This change, however, is taking place much faster, putting greater stress on species and ecosystems, to say nothing of people and economic systems. The increase will be greater than average in the middle of continents and toward the poles. There is much more uncertainty about how regional temperatures and precipitation will change. While some animals are fairly mobile and some plants have their seeds dispersed great distances by wind or animals, many species will not be able to find suitable climates fast enough. Furthermore, those that can move are unlikely to find the other species with which they have coevolved able to move with them. And of course, the growth and reproduction periods for *Sequoia sempervirens* and other species will simply be out of phase with the rate of change. The adjustment problems for individuals and families as well as for agricultural,

13

industrial, and urban systems will in many ways be analogous to those of species and their ecosystems.

A 1.5 to 4.5 degree centigrade increase in temperature is expected to produce a sea level rise of 20 to 140 centimeters. A 50 centimeter rise would displace 16 percent of the population of Egypt and a comparable percentage in Bangladesh. Species in coastal ecosystems in many places will be severely stressed by the rapidity of the change.

The depletion of the ozone in the stratosphere by chlorofluorocarbons (CFCs) and other trace gases is resulting in an increase in ultraviolet radiation which will increase skin cancer, affect plant and animal organisms differentially and thereby ecosystems in unknown ways, and through diverse pathways add to the complexity of the dynamics of global climate change. The production of CFCs increased by approximately 50 percent over the past two decades and production in the Third World could result in a continued increase in spite of the agreement (Montreal Protocol) among the existing producing nations. Chlorine atoms from CFCs catalyze the breakdown of ozone in the stratosphere but remain very stable themselves, continuing to act as catalysts until perhaps neutralized by methane. Thus the stock of existing CFCs is expected to deplete ozone through much of the next century. Too little is known about the process of ozone depletion. "Holes" in the ozone layer, for example, were not expected. For the first several years in which holes appeared in the data collected over Antarctica, they were presumed to be observational errors.

In Africa, with still relatively sparse population levels, the productivity of the drylands steadily declined during the 1980s while forests were being cut 17 times faster than they were being replanted. Due to ineffective or exploitive social organization, poor terms of trade, inappropriate technologies, and bad weather, food production did not keep pace with population growth. But the fertility rate, nearly twice that of the rest of the world, will result in a population by the year 2025 roughly equal to the combined populations of Europe and North and South America.

Bangladesh, among the five poorest countries now, is also the most densely populated major country. In 1990 Bangladesh, a country the size of the state of Wisconsin, had a population of approximately 115 million and was growing at 2.5 percent per year. If massive starvation and war are avoided, the U.N. estimates that the population will stabilize at 342 million in the middle to latter years of the twenty-first century. Several hundred thousand died in the hurricane of early 1991, a human disaster associated with a natural event with casualties comparable to the allied war against Iraq in the same period, yet the total population of Bangladesh regained its pre-hurricane numbers at least as fast as relief agencies were able to respond fully to the calamity.

Tropical deforestation continued at a rate of 8 to 12 million hectares per year during the 1980s, converting the land to extremely low productivity uses at best, destroying the land of and introducing diseases to many of the last traditional peoples, and adding significantly to global warming. Estimates of the total number of species on earth increased from around 5 million to around 35 million on investigation of the number of insects in the forest canopy. Estimates of species loss through tropical deforestation vary widely due to the uncertainty over the numbers of species, let alone their characteristics, the rates and patterns of deforestation, and the subsequent environments following deforestation to which some species may adapt. All estimates, however, are shockingly high.

The rate of application of industrially produced nitrogen in agriculture increased approximately 50 percent between 1975 and 1985 even though food production increased only 25 percent (and some of this was through the expansion of agriculture onto new lands). Rates of application have leveled off in the U.S., but a net accumulation of nitrogen in ground water continues and has resulted in poisonings and the loss of domestic water supplies.

The foregoing vignettes are now part of the public consciousness that includes the hazards in the operation of and waste from nuclear power plants, acid deposition and the transformation of lakes and forests, the increase in pesticide poisonings in the developing countries, the inability to reduce significantly the use of toxics in modern agriculture, all pastiched together in our consciousness with visions of duped, perhaps drunk, sea captains sailing among oil spills and styrofoam debris looking for a place to unload a rusty old freighter full of industrial toxics. In quite a few cases we have good numbers with respect to the magnitude of the assaults and in some cases even rough estimates of the likely response of the environmental system. But these measurements are no more systematically integrated than the miscellaneous vignettes that form the public consciousness. Nevertheless, we have a pretty good idea of the general malaise and of why development is unsustainable.

THE CHALLENGE TO SOCIAL ORGANIZATION

Environmental problems are problems of social organization. This fact is frequently portrayed as a problem of our inability to devise social systems which can foresee and control the problems of new technologies. Most people understand that a solution entails people changing how they use technologies and which technologies they use. To be sure, the challenge is too frequently perceived as simply a problem of people needing to invent and adopt more appropriate technologies. Thinking beyond this, most acknowledge that the challenge is to change our organizational structure so that people engage in more environmentally beneficial activities relative to detrimental activities. Unsustainable development, in this context, has resulted from technology outpacing changes in social organization. Incentives and regulations must evolve with technologies.

Neoclassical economists argue that the development and use of inappropriate technologies and the inappropriate use of what could be benign technologies is attributable to poorly defined property rights. If people knew who had the right to do what to whom, and these rights were defined, assigned, and enforced in a socially acceptable way, the private economy could be left to function without government interference. Ethicists argue that individualism has been overstressed in Western society and that people will behave in better ways if those ways are well defined and enforced through social pressure. Lawyers assume that people will always behave in their own interest and argue for more regulations on individual activity, more public monitoring, and the use of police power when the regulations are violated. And marxists argue that technologies are misused because of the social structure, because of the excessive power and short run, narrow interests of capitalists. Their solution is to reorganize society with more equality.

Each of these explanations of the nature of the challenge of sustainable development stress an approach to reorganization. The proponents of each explanation have developed powerful arguments as to why development has been unsustainable and what must be done. Each is an argument that has guided human attempts to reorganize the social order to meet developmental challenges for at least a century. And each is also consistent with modernism, a product of modern economic and political thought.

As a conceptual pluralist, I find each of these explanations of why development has been unsustainable and what needs to be done to make it sustainable quite useful. No doubt solutions will come through various mixes of the mechanisms advocated. At the same time I find these explanations and their implied solutions lacking. As indicated above, none of the explanations or solutions is new. All emphasize social organization vis-à-vis technology without questioning the nature of the science which is critical to the conception and development of the technologies in the first place. Most important, none of the conventional explanations question how we are to perceive what sustainable development really would be so that we can modify existing behavior appropriately, or in the marxist solution, behave correctly after power is distributed more equally.

When we set about trying to define sustainable development, we discover that our ability to conceive what it would really be in an operational sense is very limited. Our constrained ability to define what it would be is due to the limitations of Western science or, for that matter, any other way of

16

knowing of which we are aware. This realization, in turn, suggests why the conventional idea that we need to make our words operational so that we can reorganize will not be effective. The realization also provides an entrée for rethinking the nature of the problem and solution.

DEFINING SUSTAINABLE DEVELOPMENT

Can we define sustainable development? More specifically, can we define it in a way that is operational within the modern world view? Development planners in national and international agencies need such a definition to make decisions about economies and the environment on a day-to-day basis so that development turns out to be sustainable. Developing a workable definition of sustainable development is, in itself, a major challenge to the modern vision. Consider, for example, the following attempts:

> Sustainable development is development that meets the needs of the present without compromising the ability of future generations to meet their own needs.
> (World Commission on Environment and Development 1987: 43)

This definition certainly presents the general idea. It provides a criterion for what sustainable development is, though it makes no attempt to indicate how it is achieved. But even as a criterion, it does not define needs, does not require that needs be efficiently met, and leaves open the possibility that the present generation could live beyond its needs so long as future generations' needs are met. Questions raised by the generality of this first criterion can be reduced, but only by raising other specific questions. For example:

> Sustainable development is . . . a pattern of social and structural economic transformations (i.e. development) which optimizes the economic and other societal benefits available in the present, without jeopardizing the likely potential for similar benefits in the future.
> (Goodland and Ledec 1987: 36)

This criterion says the present generation should get as much as they can so long as future generations can get that much also. Through this wording, efficiency is mandated so that the most possible will be consumed by all. But how much is that and how do we know whether we have exceeded it?

The criterion of Goodland and Ledec deliberately acknowledges that it is acceptable for the types of benefits that future generations receive to be different so long as they are comparable. This is important because the natural and human environment might change considerably with respect to what can be produced but not necessarily be better or worse. Furthermore, tastes can change between generations. But this leads to the difficult problem of how the happiness of different peoples enjoying different things might be compared.

Economists have adopted procedures that implicitly compare gains and losses of different types to different peoples in cost-benefit analyses. These practices, however, stem from procedural agreements worked out within the profession in current institutional settings and have little theoretical basis. We should be concerned about using these approaches because economic reasoning has played an important role in guiding economic development along an unsustainable path, or at least in rationalizing it. There is good reason to suspect that economics, as it evolved within existing institutions, is at the heart of the problem of why development has been unsustainable.

While both of the foregoing criteria rightfully stress people now and in the future, ultimately whether development is sustainable depends on the condition of the environment which present peoples pass on to future peoples. Most researchers discuss the environmental complexities of an operational definition of sustainable development by arguing that some property or combination of properties of the environmental system must be maintained. For example:

> The common use of the word "sustainability" suggests an ability to maintain some activity in the face of stress. . . . We thus define agricultural sustainability as the ability to maintain productivity, whether of a field or farm or nation, in the face of stress or shock.
>
> (Conway and Barbier 1988: 653)

And sometimes definitions of sustainable development include biological, economic, and social systems together:

> To maximize simultaneously the biological system goals (genetic diversity, resilience, biological productivity), economic system goals (satisfaction of basic needs, enhancement of equity, increasing useful goods and services), and social system goals (cultural diversity, institutional sustainability, social justice, participation).
>
> (Barbier 1987: 103)

Unfortunately, it is only possible to maximize one thing at a time. An aggregate of things can be maximized if there is some way to weight them and add them together, some sort of a valuing scheme, so that they become effectively one thing.

The need for a valuing scheme brings the problem of defining sustainable development back to economic reasoning and its problems. Economists take how people value environmental quality and the future as a given. But what if development has not been sustainable because society's value system in the past has put too little weight on the environment and the future? And might not the acceptance now of the idea of sustainable development indicate a shift in values which is incompatible with the economists' approach of taking values as given? To meet our modern need for a scientifically defensible definition of sustainability we enter into a vicious circle of using patterns of thinking which are associated with the unsustainability of development we are trying to avoid.

The challenge of defining sustainable development, however, is much more complicated than this. None of the foregoing definitions is operational within the mandates of existing agencies. In part this is because they are not set within the boundaries of time, space, and activities relevant to the decision making of any agency. The difficulties of deriving an operational definition of sustainable development becomes clearer when the definition is disaggregated to give emphasis to boundaries. Consider the following seven increasingly comprehensive levels of analysis.

First, we can start at the local level and simply ask whether a region's agricultural and industrial practices can continue indefinitely or whether they will destroy the local resource base and environmental system. This first question, or level of analysis, is appropriate for local or regional government. It ignores whether there might be subsidies to the region – whether material and energy inputs are being supplied on net from outside the region.

Second, an operational definition of sustainable development, even at a regional environmental system level, will have to contend with how to weigh the degradation of some aspects of the environment against investments in beneficial environmental transformations and investments in new capital equipment and facilities. Again, economics has procedures for comparing investments and disinvestments, but these approaches can falsely balance, or equate, an investment with a quick payoff against an irreversible environmental degradation. New procedures are needed if the same old unsustainable paths are to be avoided.

Third, even from a regional perspective, we can ask whether the region is dependent upon energy or material inputs from beyond its boundaries. If it is dependent upon external, nonrenewable resources, then we need to know how long the external resources might last given the demand for it by other regions, whether there are local renewable resources which could substitute and be used within the existing structure of the local economy, and whether the external inputs have a long life in the economy as capital or a short life as an immediate input that is used and lost thereafter. If the region is dependent upon external renewable resources, we need to know whether these are being managed in a sustainable manner.

These are very basic questions posed simply at the regional level. Certainly, from an environmental science perspective, materials and energy balances must be considered in any operational definition of sustainable development. Yet keeping track of the diverse flows, especially for multiple regions with complex economies, would be nearly impossible. One of the challenges of sustainable development, as conceived from the perspective of the data needs of environmental management using Western science, would be to devise ways of keeping track of multiple flows without all of the labor force working full time as energy and materials accountants. But this is only the beginning of the problem.

Fourth, real problems arise when we consider things that have few if any physical units of measurement. At the fourth level of sophistication, for example, we might begin to worry whether the region is in some sense culturally sustainable, whether it is contributing as much to the knowledge, organizational, and technological bases of other regions as it is dependent upon them. The optimists in the earlier debate over the limits to growth have always argued that new technologies and a better educated populace compensate for the depletion of resources and the degradation of environments. But how might we determine and keep track of whether this is so or not?

Fifth, the region would want to know whether it has technological and organizational options available to adapt to the climate change and surprises imposed upon it by others.

Sixth, we can extend our questioning beyond the interests of the region alone and also question the extent to which the region is contributing to global climate change, forcing other regions to change their behavior. From a global perspective, this sixth level of questioning is key to addressing the difficulties of the transition from hydrocarbon energy stocks to renewable energy sources while adapting to the complications of global climate change induced by the net oxidation of hydrocarbons during the transition.

Seventh, and last, at the national and international levels, planners would want to inquire of the cultural stability of all the regions in combination. Are they evolving along mutually compatible paths or will they, for example, destroy each other through war?

This line of inquiry has clearly gotten out of hand. There is no way that societies could keep track of all of the flows that are quantifiable, no way that they could make sense out of them if they did, and no way to keep track of the unquantifiable flows at all. Sustainable development cannot be defined operationally.

ORGANIZING FOR SUSTAINABLE DEVELOPMENT

Even though I dismiss the possibility of defining sustainable development operationally, a more sophisticated exploration of the difficulties of organizing for sustainable development is in order.

Both developed and developing economies are already attempting to guide economic activity toward much more limited, well defined ends. Developed nations seem to have already reached their organizational limits trying to insure, for example, that all have minimal health care, that utilities provide electricity at fair prices and plan their future development wisely, and that local land use and environmental standards are met. These and many similar efforts will continue to be necessary as they strive toward sustainable development. Assuring sustainability by extending the modern approach, however, will require, by several orders of magnitude, more data collection, interpretation, planning, political decision-making, and bureaucratic control

The developed countries, famed for their organizational abilities and with the resources to devote to organizing, frequently run into organizational limits. For example, when the energy crisis hit, the United States realized that responsibilities and capabilities related to implementing an energy policy were dispersed between multiple agencies. The leasing of public coal fields and petroleum prospects, regulation of environmental damages and land restoration, regulation of pipelines and gas prices, regulation of utilities, development of hydropower, incentives for conservation, licensing of nuclear power plants, and funding for research were spread between as many agencies. This dispersion of responsibility and ability was thought to hinder the design and implementation of a rational energy policy. Eventually many of the separate units within existing agencies responsible for the different tasks were assembled into a newly formed Department of Energy. By the time this reorganization was effected, however, it became clear that the difficulties of enhancing energy supplies and increasing energy conservation were linked to even broader problems such as developing workable wilderness policies, adapting local building codes to encourage greater energy efficiency, responding to newly recognized environmental problems related to energy such as acid rain and nuclear waste disposal, and amending agricultural policies and research and extension programs to encourage farmers to use less energy. If all of the agencies with jurisdiction ultimately affecting the use and environmental consequences of energy were combined, there would be one and only one agency in the entire government.

One agency would make sense except for the immense difficulties of coordinating everyone to a multitude of tasks. The U.S. federal government can be thought of as one agency under the President. Governments, as well as corporations and other forms of social organization, are divided into smaller units on the assumption that some linkages are thought to be less important than others. By ignoring these less important connections, greater effort can be put on the important linkages. But the relative importance of each linkage changes when problems change. Hence specific crises arise from time to time which can be responded to more effectively by restructuring agencies. But crises mellow out and everything is soon discovered to be connected to everything else with no connection arguably much more important than others. And then new crises arise for which a new agency structure would be optimal, for awhile. Crises are the fortunate times when specific interrelationships are obviously important. The rest of the time, all the interrelationships must be addressed simultaneously in order to avoid the next crisis. And for handling all of the interrelationships simultaneously, no particular agency structure is clearly superior.

Most countries are already pretty well bogged down in an informational, bureaucratic, and political quagmire keeping a visible hand on development to the modest extent they do. Marginal changes in policy now seriously threaten what little social cohesion is left. I find it impossible to think about operational definitions of sustainable development because "operational" implies within existing institutions, or at least along the existing course of institutional development. In my judgment, there is little potential for further refinement of modern social rationality to better respond to our environmental dilemma by increasing the responsibilities of bureaucracies or by redrawing their boundaries of responsibility and lines of coordination.

CONCLUSIONS

It is impossible to define sustainable development in an operational manner in the detail and with the level of control presumed in the logic of modernity. This will become more clear after the critique presented in Chapter 6 of the metaphysical and epistemological beliefs of modernism and in Chapter 12 on knowledge, democracy, and bureaucracy. If the greater control required by sustainability is not likely, what are our options? In the next chapter I develop a coevolutionary explanation of social and environmental change. In Chapter 4, I use the coevolutionary pattern of explanation to frame an environmental history which explains how development became unsustainable. And as the chapters unfold, I develop how we might think about affecting our future again.

3

CHANGE AS A COEVOLUTIONARY PROCESS

[Interesting philosophy] says things like "try thinking of it this way" – or more specifically, "try to ignore the apparently futile traditional questions by substituting the following new and possibly interesting questions."

(Richard Rorty 1989: 9)

The real challenge of sustainability is to reframe the challenge. As conventionally understood, sustainable development contests our competence to predict the consequences of our interactions with nature and taxes our capability to control those interactions so that the old idea of development remains intact yet is sustainable. I trust, however, after elaborating on this framing of the challenge in the previous chapter, that it is clear that this challenge cannot be met. The world is far too complex for us to perceive and establish the conditions for sustainability. Those who – on realizing our limited ability to perceive and control – tout the use of markets fail to realize that the objectives that markets reach depend on the system of property rights underlying their performance. The design of the appropriate system of rights not only requires equivalent prescience but presumes a static world. Indeed, even the elaboration in the last chapter, with all of its complications, never went beyond assuming that societies and environments are static, complex systems.

This chapter initiates the framing of societies and environments as coevolving systems. By stressing complex processes instead of complex structures, the challenge of sustainability emerges anew. The new features and associations of this emerging challenge eventually lead to a revisioning of progress.

THE COEVOLUTION OF PESTS, PESTICIDES, POLITICS, AND POLICY

The pesticide story in the United States during the twentieth century provides an excellent example of the coevolutionary process. Let's first recount key historical details of the interplay between pests, pesticides,

23

politics, and policy with as little coevolutionary language as possible, and then show how the coevolutionary framing puts it into perspective.

Prior to World War II, inorganic compounds such as arsenic, sulfur, and lead were used to control insects and other pests. The Pesticide Act of 1910 protected farmers from ineffective products. The Pure Food and Drug Act of 1906 protected consumers from contamination, and pesticide residues were specifically included in the Food, Drug, and Cosmetic Act of 1938. Regulation was seen as a matter of "truth in advertising," of seeing that farmers were getting useful chemicals and consumers were getting healthy food. The Federal Insecticide, Fungicide, and Rodenticide Act of 1947 expanded the range of products covered, but was still largely designed to facilitate the chemical industry and protect farmers from ineffective products.

The discovery of DDT in 1939, followed by other organochlorine insecticides soon after, and their expanding use after World War II changed the dynamics dramatically. By the early 1950s, the organic insecticides had driven inorganics nearly off the market because the organics were really effective initially. And because they were more effective, they were used on more crops and pests than the inorganics. They were so effective that they set in motion an interacting set of events that proved instrumental to our understanding of environmental problems.

The few insects that survived the application of DDT and other organochlorine pesticides were the individuals among the larger population who were the most resistant to the pesticide. When these surviving individuals reproduced, a high proportion of their offspring carried the genetic traits that favored resistance. Since most insects have many generations per season, the selective pressure of the insecticides on the evolution of resistance in insects was observable over a matter of years. I use evolutionary terminology here because evolution as biologists understand it was precisely the process.

In parallel with the problem of resistance were the problems of secondary pests and resurgence. Secondary pests are other species that can play a similar role, or fill a similar agroecological niche, as the initial pest. Reducing the population of the primary pest through the use of pesticides leaves an unfilled niche for secondary pests to fill. Secondary pests might come from neighboring fields or have been present in the sprayed field but in a phase of their life cycle that made them less susceptible at the time of the spraying. Resurgence also relates to the unfilled niche after spraying. Whatever primary pests are left after spraying have little competition after the demise of their cohorts and hence their populations rebuild, or resurge, rapidly. In the event that spraying has also reduced the predators of pests, or alternative prey of the predators, pest populations return even faster. Ecological language is appropriate here for the dynamics are characteristic of disturbed ecosystems.

The response of agricultural researchers and the chemical industry to the occurrence of greater pest problems after the initial success of organic pesticides was to recommend more frequent and heavier spraying. More pests demand more pesticides. This, of course, made sense for each individual farmer, but compounded the problems of resistance for farmers collectively. And, of course, heavier and more frequent spraying resulted in higher pest management costs, but now there was little choice. Many sensed they were on a "pesticide treadmill," but few could see it or how to get off it.

A few researchers were looking at the situation from an evolutionary and ecosystemic perspective and began to advocate more careful monitoring of pest populations before deciding whether to spray, the use of biological controls, and the collective selection of crop types, planting dates, and other practices to outwit insects. These integrated pest management programs included the use of chemicals, but at significantly lower levels. Some farmers adopted the integrated pest management philosophy of agroecosystem management, but the vast majority of farmers just wanted to kill pests.

The reduced effectiveness of the early organics opened up new opportunities for the chemical industry to introduce new insecticides and many were tried. Organophosphates and carbamates soon proved advantageous because of their higher acute toxicity and lower persistance in the environment. Higher acute toxicity was advantageous in that fewer individuals survived, slowing the evolution of resistance. Concern with the persistence of DDT was building with evidence that DDT, other organophosphates, and the derivative chemicals resulting from breakdown in the environment were affecting insect populations and hence bird populations beyond agriculture. Furthermore, these chemicals were accumulating in the food chain with unknown consequences. Rachel Carson and others stimulated a new environmental consciousness during the 1960s which eventually led to the Federal Environmental Pesticide Control Act (FEPCA) of 1972 with its provisions to protect the environment. Soon after DDT was banned and the elimination and regulation of other chemicals followed during the 1970s.

Organophosphates and carbamates, however, had new problems. Organophosphates such as parathion are deadly to people, carbamates to bees, and farmworkers and bees are essential to agriculture itself. Farmworkers and beekeepers joined environmentalists in the early 1970s in seeking protective regulatory decisions. By the later 1970s, communities in agricultural regions began to complain of illnesses, and agricultural chemicals were found to be accumulating in groundwater used for drinking supplies. The increasing awareness of the effects of pesticides on other species, on workers' health, and on the health of adjacent communities intensified the interest in integrated pest management as an alternative.

The chemical industry's response was slowed by the difficulties of getting new chemicals registered and approved for use under the stricter requirements of FEPCA and the administrative procedures of the Environmental Protection Agency. More testing and registration delays also raised the costs of insecticides. The structure of the industry also changed as smaller chemical companies found they could not operate under the new restrictions, as moderate sized firms merged, and even as some larger ones left the field. Industry slowly responded, however, by providing insecticides that targeted narrower ranges of pests to reduce disrupting beneficial insects and which were much less toxic to people. These chemicals, largely synthetic pyrethroids modeled after some of nature's own insecticides, were far more expensive and their application frequently had to be more carefully timed. While farmers could afford these more expensive alternatives when farm prices were high in the mid-1970s, farm prices dropped significantly in the late 1970s and early 1980s and farmers became desperate. In spite of a long tradition of supporting chemical agriculture, in the 1980s, the U.S. Department of Agriculture initiated a program known as LISA (low input sustainable agriculture), which incorporated much of the philosophy and many of the techniques of integrated pest management.

The use of insecticides in U.S. agriculture is still very high, farmers are trying harder than ever to use them well, and other insect control techniques have been introduced as well. Nevertheless, crop losses to insects are about the same as they were before the use of modern insecticides. But we cannot simply stop using them because our agroecosystems and agroeconomy have been transformed by their use such that they must be used. All parties have suffered from unforeseen consequences of insecticide use which has led to a greater consensus on their environmental, social, and economic implications. If we had been able to foresee the diverse twists and turns of the pesticide story, and the foregoing only includes the most essential details, we would not have started using them in the first place.

We could not, however, have foreseen how the pesticide story unfolded because history is not deterministic; it is not like a missile on a predetermined course or even like a complex machine whose movements can be comprehended and thereafter forever predicted. Nevertheless, the changes that took place can be explained as a process of coevolution.

In biology, coevolution refers to the pattern of evolutionary change of two closely interacting species where the fitness of the genetic traits within each species is largely governed by the dominant genetic traits of the other. Coevolutionary explanations have been given for the shape of the beaks of hummingbirds and of the flowers they feed on, the behavior of bees and the distribution of flowering plants, the biochemical defenses of plants and the immunity of their insect prey, and the characteristics of other interactive species. Note that coevolutionary explanations invoke relationships between entities which affect the evolution of the entities. Entities and relationships are constantly changing, yet they constantly reflect each other, like the flowers and the hummingbirds' beaks. Everything is interlocked, yet everything is changing in accordance with the interlockedness.

Now pests and pesticides can also be thought of as interrelated and

26

coevolving in response to the interrelatedness. Pests evolved resistance in response to pesticides, that is easy to see. But one can just as well argue that pesticides evolved new qualities in response to the evolution of resistance among pests. To be more precise, the distribution of individual insects by different traits shifted toward the trait of greater resistance in response to the application of organophosphates while the distribution of insecticides shifted away from organophosphates in response to the development of resistance. But the traits of pests and pesticides were also affected by pesticide legislation and regulatory decisions, which in turn were certainly affected by the characteristics of pest problems and the types of pesticides used. Pesticide legislation, however, did not evolve in response to pests and pesticides directly, but rather evolved in response to how political interests – environmentalists, laborers, beekeepers, and farmers – were affected by pests and pesticides. Similarly, the demand for integrated pest management evolved in response to all of these. In short, pests, pesticides, politics, policy, the pesticide industry, and integrated pest management evolved in response to changes in each other and in the relationships between them, or more simply, they coevolved. This process is illustrated in Figure 3.1 below.

The coevolutionary process will be elaborated in greater detail in later chapters, but a few things should be noted now. While Figure 3.1 could merely be the description of static relations, of a complex machine, it is

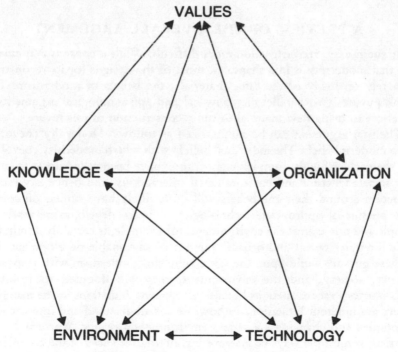

Figure 3.1 The coevolutionary process

coevolutionary because random, or at least totally unforeseeable, introductions occur. Among biological species, the introduction of brand new genetic material through introductions from other ecosystems, genetic drift, and mutations occurs. Similar new chemicals are developed and introduced alongside existing chemicals. Whether these new introductions survive depends on their fitness. In coevolution, fitness is determined by the characteristics of other species or things with which an individual or thing interacts. Coevolutionary processes are not like the dynamics of a machine because the machine does not change. The parts of a machine and the relationships between the parts stay the same. By knowing the parts and relationships of a mechanical system, one can know how the system works. Coevolving systems, on the other hand, have parts and relations which change in unforeseeable ways. At any point in time, it can be described like an ecosystem, but over time it is as unpredictable as the evolution of life itself. Understanding change as coevolution helps us understand why the pesticide story could not have been foretold.

I have been asked many times why I am so entranced by a pattern of thinking that does not facilitate prediction and control. I hope to show how this relatively simple pattern of thinking contrasts with and thereby provides perspective on the pattern of thinking underlying modernity and how it acts as a catalyst for revisioning the future.

A PREVIEW OF THE OVERALL ARGUMENT

Critique is easy, reconstruction more difficult. While a consensus is emerging that modernity is in a shambles, most of the designs for its reconstruction rely on many of the same materials, the beliefs of modernism. This book pursues two parallel metaphysical and epistemological arguments in an effort to bring new material to the reconstruction of our future.

The first argument can be summarized as follows. Modernity coevolved with modern beliefs. The individual beliefs with which modernity coevolved are themselves highly complementary, they have been relied upon to order our social structure and environmental interactions, and hence any reconstruction around the same beliefs will quite likely have similar outcomes. The pursuit of appropriate technologies to make development work for people and not against the environment, for example, is certainly admirable, as is the more recent and broader pursuit of sustainable development. But if these pursuits build upon the same beliefs of modernism with respect to science, society, and the environment, they are doomed to result in unsatisfactory reconstructions because of inherent limitations in the materials. There are inherent limitations in how we can understand and interact with a complex and changing social and environmental reality. Western science consists of multiple ways of interpreting alternative slices of the complexity of reality. These multiple ways are not merging and cannot merge into one coherent whole. Recognition of the conceptual plurality of Western science is a necessary condition for a viable reconstruction. Acknowledging conceptual pluralism, furthermore, opens up possibilities for new materials with which to rebuild. This argument is presented within the dominant, deductive mode of Western thinking even while it exposes the limits of this mode.

The second line of reasoning draws upon, synthesizes, and argues from understandings which have emerged within Western science since Darwin. While evolutionary thought has a formal structure within Western science, the pattern of thinking more broadly interpreted explains and lends legitimacy to other ways of knowing. The traditional knowledge of peoples who have not been Westernized, and what is generally referred to as common sense among those who have, proved fit within the context in which they evolved. Much of the book addresses the meaning of knowledge from a coevolutionary perspective and explores its relations with values, social organization, technology, and the environment. This line of reasoning is inherently synthetic, contrasting with, indeed in contradiction with, the deductive mode of the first line of argument.

The two arguments proceed almost dialectically, first one and then the other with some synthesis along the way. In Chapter 4, "A Coevolutionary Environmental History," I develop an alternative explanation of development that links Western science, resources, and the environment, not in the form of control by one over the others, but as mutually interactive coevolving systems. Western science facilitated the use of coal and petroleum, but the availability and use of these stock hydrocarbons, in turn, helped determine the directions and intensity of effort of Western science. The environmental side-effects of fossil hydrocarbon-fueled agriculture and industry provided a more fertile niche for the environmental sciences. These systems, furthermore, coevolved with modern social order. The pattern of people living in cities, the organization of people to serve multinational industrial enterprises, the centrality of bureaucratic order, and the use of Western science for social decision-making have all coevolved around fossil hydrocarbon-fueled development. This coevolutionary process resulted in considerable concentration of power and material wealth in modern industrial societies which they used to force Westernization on others. Simultaneously, non-westernized peoples sought the same power and material wealth through adoption of modern knowledge, social organization, and technology. Correcting the unsustainability of development is not simply a matter of choosing different technologies for intervening in the environment. The mechanisms of perceiving, choosing, and using technologies are embedded in social structures which are themselves products of modern technologies.

We have great difficulty switching into a coevolutionary framework of thinking because of a strong tradition of believing in progress. Chapter 5,

"The Illusion of Progress," explores the development of Western belief that there is one right way of knowing, that Western science is progressing toward this way, that all peoples will choose to merge to this way of knowing, that with it we will be able to make nature serve human ends, and that, furthermore, one common, right way of knowing will reduce human conflict. These component beliefs in progress became the human components of the agenda of European colonization and now justify international development.

"The Philosophical Roots of the Betrayal," the title of Chapter 6, are atomism, mechanism, monism, universalism, and objectivism. These metaphysical and epistemological beliefs were dominant among scientists and the public in the late nineteenth and early twentieth centuries when many of the relationships between science and social organization were being established. Though no longer held by many scientists, these beliefs are still the basis for public discourse, social organization, and collective decision-making in modern societies. Stemming logically from the philosophical roots of the betrayal have been "Two Maladaptive Determinisms," the title of Chapter 7. The debate between cultural determinists and environmental determinists documents the difficulty of understanding people and nature together. This debate also suggests how difficult it will be for many to adopt a coevolutionary cosmology. The dominance of simple cause and effect explanations are part of the problem. These beliefs help explain why we now perceive development to be biologically and culturally unsustainable. Chapter 8 further elaborates on the roots of coevolutionary thinking in Western science and our understanding of process in the coevolutionary framework. "A Coevolutionary Cosmology," presented in Chapter 9, is radically different from existing conventions.

I bring the two strands of the argument together in Chapter 10, a critique of how liberal Western thought jumps from individualism to globalism with almost no reference to communities and how this has affected our ability to reconstruct the future. This is followed by an application in Chapter 11 of the coevolutionary paradigm to thinking about the design of development in the Amazon. This instrumental use of a paradigm that has heretofore been a cosmological construct provides deeper insight into why modernity has resulted in cultural and environmental degradation. These insights are used, in turn, to explore the social nature of knowledge and critique our limited conception of democracy in Chapter 12, "Democratizing Knowledge." Reinterpreting the nature of knowledge and the processes of attaining it force a rethinking of our social structure in Chapter 13, "Coevolving Discursive Communities." And a parallel rethinking of the global order in Chapter 14, "A Coevolving Cultural Patchwork Quilt." A more detailed preview of these four critical chapters is premature at this time simply because as the argument unfolds it becomes harder and harder to describe in simple terms and familiar concepts. The case, however, is eventually made for radical decentralization, for greater participation in the understanding of and management of human interaction with environmental systems, and greater cultural diversity. The book concludes with Chapter 15, "Progress Revisioned." Since I cannot even describe these later chapters without your first working through the material in the early chapters, it is time to move on to the next chapter.

4

A COEVOLUTIONARY
ENVIRONMENTAL HISTORY

I wouldn't want what I may have said or written to be seen as laying
any claims to totality. I don't try to universalize what I say; conversely,
what I don't say isn't meant to be thereby disqualified as being of no
importance. . . . I like to open up a space of research, try it out, and
then if it doesn't work, try again somewhere else.

(Michel Foucault 1980, in Baynes *et al.* 1987: 101)

The challenge of sustainability will only be met when there is a consensus
on how modernity became unsustainable. This will require a new reading
of history. Heretofore, historians have documented the lives of the rich and
influential, the politics and social change of key periods, and relationships
between science, technology, and progress. We can only learn from the
lessons of history if historians help us see how the factors related to the
situation we now face – the relationships between environmental systems,
knowledge, technology, and social order – contributed to our predicament.
Existing histories assume relations between Western people and the land
which shed little light on, or even deny, what we now see as environmental
problems and cultural failings. This has led to a deliberate effort among
a new group of historians to explicate an environmental history to help
us understand the problems we now face. In this chapter I initiate a
coevolutionary environmental history to explore the nature of the betrayal
of development.

CONVENTIONAL VIEWS OF ENVIRONMENT AND
DEVELOPMENT

Modern explanations of the relationship between development and the
environment have stressed how science and new technologies have facilitated
the discovery of new resources and access to lower grade resources. In these
histories, the environment is viewed as a pool of resource inputs rather than
a complex system that is transformed by development. Science has been the
driving force in the development process as characterized by the schematic

32

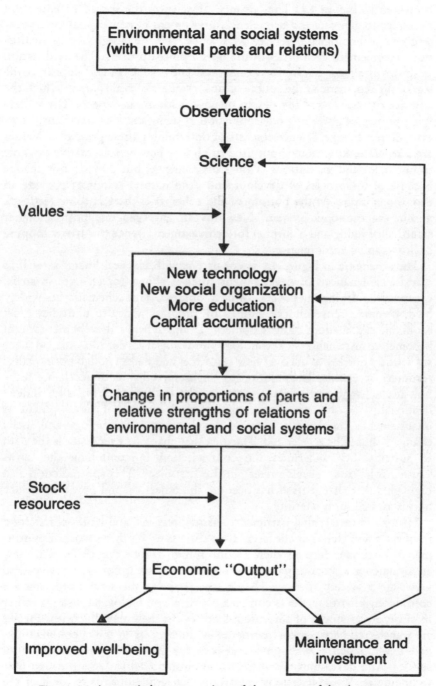

Figure 4.1 A twentieth-century view of the process of development

presented in Figure 4.1. The advance of science, the spread of education necessary to generate and use science, investment in new capital incorporating new technologies generated by science, and the design of new institutions complement each other in the development process. The explanation as drawn is almost linear. Environmental and social systems appear at the top of the schematic as the source of observations of reality upon which the advance of science and the design of new institutions depend. The underlying principles governing environmental systems and social systems, however, do not change. Science consists of determining these principles. Values are a separate, exogenous input used to choose between alternative possible technologies and institutions. Values may change, but they do not change because of the process of development. And natural resources provide an exogenous input. At the bottom of the schematic, there is some feedback within the economic system. New investments generate both a higher standard of living and a surplus for reinvestment, hence the arrow looping back to capital accumulation.

The schematic in Figure 4.1 is consistent with classical liberal as well as marxist explanations of development since it allows for changes in social organization during the process of development. This schematic fits widely held, common-sense understandings of progress and also underlies most economic explanations of development. In this schema, development might become unsustainable if technology and social order do not advance sufficiently quickly to uncover new resources and make enough poor quality resources accessible. The solution to unsustainability is to accelerate technological change and adapt society to these changes. Ironically, indeed irrationally, in this view of environmental history, if development is unsustainable, the driving forces of development – technology and social change – should be accelerated. The idea that changing ever faster is the path to sustainability underlines the contradiction in combining the terms "sustainable" and "development" in the first place. This contradiction also highlights that change itself has become the objective, and now a necessary means as well, of modernity.

Historians researching particular periods, regions, and issues correspond frequently and cluster at conferences to discuss each other's work. Environmental historians formed such a community during the 1970s. The new environmental historians part from the implicit assumptions in conventional views in a variety of ways. Most importantly, the new historians are considering environments as complex physical and biological systems rather than simply as stocks of separate resources. In these new histories, species are transferred between environments in the process of trade, colonization, and development. Development selects for particular characteristics of species. And development transforms environmental systems through new technologies. While science is important, the driving factor in most of the new environmental histories are social forces which have changed the

34

structure of society and hence how people interact with environmental systems. Most importantly, the new environmental historians emphasize the rise, and geographically ever more inclusive network, of markets coupled with the inequities in and increasingly absentee control over resources. In most of the new environmental histories, making development sustainable entails taking control over market forces and divesting control to local peoples or representative governmental bodies.

The new environmental history modifies existing histories driven by a socially neutral, benevolent science mastering nature. The new environmental history is a part of the understanding I am trying to present. On the other hand, another characterization of how modernity unfolded and environmental and social systems transformed will enrich our understanding of the nature of the betrayal. The key features of modernity become even more clear when viewed against an alternative view of history which is markedly different, the perspective of development as a process of coevolution between social and ecological systems.

A COEVOLUTIONARY FRAMEWORK

Conventional environmental histories tend to stress a limited number of exogenous causes, forces from outside the boundaries of the system being analyzed, which determine a limited number of endogenous effects within the system. In Figure 4.1, for example, science, values, and resources can be thought of as exogenous inputs to the interconnected system of technology and social organization which is perceived to change with development. A coevolutionary schematic of development is portrayed in Figure 3.1. It is markedly different from conventional explanations. Rather than having exogenous inputs, everything is symmetrically related to everything else. Nothing is exogenous. The coevolutionary image also diverges radically from the modern world view in that the processes of change are evolutionary instead of deterministic. Furthermore, the nature of each of the subsystems and the relations between them change over time as they evolve.

Imagine that each subsystem of Figure 3.1 – values, knowledge, social organization, technology, and the environment – is composed of different "types" of ways of valuing, knowing, organizing, and doing things. Similarly the environmental subsystem consists of numerous different types of species and other natural characteristics as well as relationships between them. The dominance, or frequency, of each particular type in each subsystem is explained by its fitness with respect to the types of things in the other subsystems. Since the relative importance, or frequency distribution, of types results from selection processes, it is perhaps best to elaborate the process. Imagine a new type is introduced into one of the subsystems. For example, imagine that a new way of understanding, let us call it N for Newtonian, is transferred from Western culture into the knowledge subsystem of a heretofore un-westernized culture. The survival and relative importance of N will depend on the selective pressures from the other subsystems of this culture. If N does not fit, it will not survive in this culture. If N "fits," it will survive. If N fits better than other ways of knowing, it will replace them, or at least reduce their relative importance, and thereby increase its own dominance relative to others. If N survives it begins to put selective pressure on the components of the other subsystems and if N is increasing in dominance, it will exert more and more selective pressure on the relative dominance, or frequency distribution, of components within the other subsystems. With each subsystem applying selective pressure on each of the other subsystems, they all reflect each other.

Environmental subsystems are treated symmetrically with the subsystems of values, knowledge, social organization, and technology in this coevolutionary explanation of history. New technologies exert new selective pressures on species; while transformed environments, in turn, select for different technologies. Similarly, transformed environments select for new ways of understanding environments. I admit that this is an unusual way to think about how people affect environmental systems. Our dominant reaction is to think of people as degrading environments rather than of changing the selective pressures within which species, relationships between species, and other factors prove fit or not. There need not, however, be a contradiction in these ways of thinking. To emphasize coevolutionary processes is not to deny that people directly intervene in and change the characteristics of environments. The coevolutionary perspective merely stresses the next step, how different states of the environment alter the selective pressure and hence the relative dominance of species and relationships between species thereafter.

The modern explanation of history links development to control over nature and to environmental interventions which necessarily reduce the "naturalness" of the environment. The coevolutionary explanation recognizes that many aspects of environmental systems are the result of human intervention over millennia. It emphasizes how nature is social by incorporating how people have put selective pressure on the biosphere. Similarly, it emphasizes how societies are natural. By comparing the two world views, we see more clearly how the division between natural and unnatural is embedded in our modern understanding of nature and development rather than in reality. In the coevolutionary explanation, for example, environmental transformations can both benefit people and be done in a manner which increases species diversity. This combination is difficult to derive starting with a world view which divides the natural and social worlds and assumes that people can only make the natural world less natural.

Development in the modern world view stems from the conscious advance of Western knowledge and its rational application to the design and implementation of better technologies and social organization. The idea of progress and of things getting better, the subject of the next chapter, is implicit in the modern view. In the coevolutionary explanation, knowledge, technologies, and social organization merely change, rather than advance, and the "betterness" of each is only relative to how well it fits with the others and values. Change in the coevolutionary explanation, rather than a process of rational design and improvement, is a process of experimentation, partly conscious, and selection by whether things work or not.

COEVOLUTIONARY DEVELOPMENT POTENTIAL

If development is real, not simply one group exploiting others or this generation living better at the expense of the next, then there must be an inherent potential for development. While economists have extolled the benefits of development, they have given little serious thought as to how development as they have conceived it might actually be possible over the long run. Many natural scientists, meanwhile, have been quick to exploit this weakness and to declare development as presently conceived by economists as a sham.

Natural scientists have a valid point. What economic thought exists on the long term potential for development is either inconsistent with knowledge accumulated in the natural sciences or relies on a yet unidentified source of energy. Both neoclassical and marxist economists have assumed that the potential for continuous development resides in our ability to devise technologies which improve the quality of labor and capital and allow for the continued exploitation of lower and lower quality stock resources. Mining and converting ever lower quality stocks, however, entails more and more work which can only be accomplished with more and more energy simply to maintain current rates of use. Higher rates of use will require even more energy. But the energy sources upon which we now depend are limited. In the absence of alternative sources of energy, the conventional economic explanation defies the second law of thermodynamics.

The coevolutionary pattern of explanation is ideally suited for thinking about process. At the same time, because this pattern of thinking has its roots in the biological sciences, it is unusually amenable to the incorporation of knowledge from the natural sciences. We can be explicit about coevolutionary development potential. It stems from three interrelated phenomena. First, evolution has been a negentropic process. Planet Earth evolved a better order for people until the industrial revolution. This first phenomenon appears to violate the second law of thermodynamics. Because the relations between entropy and development have long confused economists, a thorough elaboration is developed in the bibliographic essay to Chapter 7. Second, the environment improved for people through its coevolution with knowledge, social organization, and technology. Third, additional coevolutionary potential remains.

From a perspective limited to people and Planet Earth, evolution has been a negentropic process. Four and a half billion years ago, Earth did not have the order that allows us to exist today. Whether by chance or by design, life somehow started. Gradually life transformed its own environment. The nitrogen molecules in the atmosphere are thought to be a product of the early anaerobic life forms while oxygen molecules are largely a product of later net plant growth. By evolutionary processes, various species coevolved to form the highly diverse and complex ecosystems of today. The oxygen we breathe, the plants and animals we eat, and the hydrocarbons we tap to fuel our industry are products of biological processes. Even the ordering of minerals improved from a human perspective through various physical processes over eons stemming from solar energy and the gradual cooling of the earth. From a human perspective, entropy on planet earth has decreased.

From simple amoebas to complex vertebrates, life is largely a process of maintaining order, of maintaining the processes of life and the characteristics of particular species. This order is encoded as information in the arrangement of the bases of DNA molecules. Single-celled organisms and tissue cells in higher organisms replicate by a process whereby paired chains in the DNA molecule split, reform their paired parts, and provide the information necessary for reconstructing the characteristics of new cells. Individual cells form and die, but the cell's order lives on and the orderly life processes provided by each cell type continue. Similarly, individuals die but species live on through the sexual reproduction of individuals.

Order, however, is not simply maintained. The diverse gene pools of each species are constantly subjected to the selective pressures of changing biological and, to a lesser extent, physical factors. The fitness of characteristics of individuals within a particular species is constantly redefined as associated species evolve new characteristics. Species are always being pushed into smaller niches or finding it possible to expand into larger niches in accordance with changes in species with which they associate. Long-term changes in global climates also slowly select for individuals with characteristics that help them cope with different temperature and humidity and the associated changes in biota or who can migrate to more suitable climates. Most of this constant adjustment favors individuals with genetic characteristics already represented in the gene pool of the species.

The gene pool independently diversifies. Mutations occur through imperfect DNA replication and DNA damage. A small proportion of these mutations eventually prove fit by facilitating the functioning of the organism in its existing niche or allowing it to expand its niche. In turn, fit mutations change the biotic selective pressures on other species and affect their evolutionary course. The repercussions are unending and, perhaps, not even dampened as they circle outward from the initial change. It is a mistake, however, to put too much emphasis on genetics. Animals, even amoebas, learn. The sensory systems of even the most simple animals enable them to recognize different stimuli. Similarly, the brains of even the less developed species deduce cause and effect and extrapolate experience to new situations. Western thought has emphasized formal knowledge and neglected the innate and informal. The fitness of individuals among animal species, especially the vertebrates, is partly related to the correctness of their perceptions and understandings of reality, of how animals see and interpret diverse physical phenomena and the complex web of life. At the same time, reality has coevolved with animals' perceptions and understandings of reality. Minds and nature reflect a "necessary unity."

Within this coevolutionary process, the well-being of people can improve to the extent that their ways of knowing, social organization, and technologies select for an evolutionary course of the biosphere which complements their values. With this brief introduction of the coevolutionary framework and the nature of the potential for development, let's rethink our environmental history.

COEVOLUTIONARY BEGINNINGS

The Earth's biosphere evolved over some three and a half billion years. It did not just come into being whole and working like an intricate clock. People have been involved in this global evolutionary process for only about three million years, while our primate ancestors have been participating in its evolution for considerably longer. While this is a mere one thousandth of earth's total geophysical history, people have nonetheless put important selective pressures on the evolution of the biosphere during the earth's much shorter biological history. Furthermore, specific characteristics of the primates which were to become people and the early people which were to become people as we know them today were selected according to how well they fit the evolving biological system. People and their environment have coevolved.

While we are well aware today of our impact on the survival of other species, we tend to underestimate the cumulative effect of early people on nature. Hunting and gathering by people put selective pressure on the species hunted and gathered. People in hunting and gathering societies transformed habitats to favor particular game and plant products. At the same time, hunting and gathering selected for effective hunters and gatherers who were more likely to survive and to support a larger number of offspring. While such activities only slightly changed the balance of selective forces in more distant parts of the biosphere, the cumulative effect on the course of evolution may well have been significant. Agriculture has simply been a more deliberate and intensive effort with far more significant impacts. Planting and watering, hand weeding, plowing, flooding, and burning are direct means of favoring productive species, reducing the competition for nutrients by "weeds," and nurturing species that complement each other.

39

Plants support one another by providing shade, by having associated soil microorganisms that fix nitrogen or help other plants absorb mineral nutrients, and by hosting predators of other plant's pests. Later the selective pressure on the biological system was heavily influenced by the agricultural practices of deforesting and clearing land, weeding out some species and encouraging others, selecting the varieties that most consistently produced well, and eventually the practice of irrigation. These environmental transformations facilitated the evolution of some species. Some of them became unable to survive without people. Agriculture, in turn, selected for different perceptive abilities and physical strengths among humans than had hunting and gathering.

Agriculture began between five and ten thousand years ago when there were approximately five million people in the world. Population doubled eight times, increasing to about 1.6 billion people by the middle of the nineteenth century. These eight doublings were only possible through an increase in the effectiveness with which people interacted with their environment. They occurred well before the use of fossil fuels or technologies based on modern science had a significant impact on the ability of most people in the world to obtain food, clothing, and shelter. Although the industrial revolution was underway in Europe and the United States beginning in the mid-nineteenth century, even these more advanced economies were still mostly based on agriculture which did not use fossil fuels.

The coevolutionary paradigm explains the eight doublings in world population, and many more before the beginnings of agriculture, occurring through changes in knowledge, technology, social organization, and the environment. But unlike modern explanations, which emphasize the deliberate accumulation of knowledge and conscious design of technologies, institutions, and environmental transformations, the coevolutionary explanation accounts for change through selection, through trial, error, and the survival of what proves fit. The coevolutionary processes of trial, selection, and survival or not are significantly different from the presumption of knowledge and conscious design.

In the coevolutionary explanation, experiential knowledge, both individual and collective, is maintained in the belief systems of each culture. Experiments with alternative social structure uncovered organizational forms which enhance people's ability to interact with their environment as well as with each other. Simultaneously, people intervene in the environment, and if the environmental response is favorable, they establish myths and forms of social organization to rationalize and encourage the intervention by individuals and thereby to maintain the favorable environmental response. Hence myth and social organization are selected according to their fitness to the environment. At the same time, the fitness of environmental changes are determined in part by whether they fit people's myths and social organization. In this manner, social and environmental systems coevolve such that environmental systems reflect the characteristics of social systems

40

– their knowledge, values, social organization, and technologies – while social systems reflect the characteristics of environmental systems – their mix of species, rates of productivity, spatial and temporal variation, and resilience. The coevolutionary description of development explains why, and to some extent how, everything is related to everything else.

Agriculture has long relied on cultural knowledge for managing ecosystems. People shifted the mix of species toward those they preferred even before agriculture. These shifts in the species mix were not carried out rationally by the standards of Western science. People did not ponder whether their plants were receiving the right amounts of nitrogen or whether the plants that survived the last invasion of pests might have had a biochemical defensive system. People followed diverse practices, acting individually and in groups, because they were a part of a culture which included a myriad of myths about how people should work with each other and the land. And these myths had survived tests of fitness over generations.

Both agroecosystem management and deliberate selective pressure have been culturally learned and reinforced. Individuals learn selection and management techniques from others. Societies maintain and allocate shared resources including fields and water. Appropriate behavior is culturally enforced. Cultural ecologists have shown for traditional societies how values, kinship, customs, rituals, and taboos are related to the maintenance of the society's interaction with its ecosystem. To a large extent culture still guides modern agricultural societies, but modernization has entailed a continual substitution of formal institutions and objective knowledge for culture and cultural knowledge as we commonly think of them.

The process of coevolution was not limited to mutual genetic selection. People survive to a large extent as members of groups. Group success depends on culture: the system of values, beliefs, artifacts, and art forms which sustain social organization and rationalize action. Values and beliefs which fit the ecosystem survive and multiply; less fit ones eventually disappear. And thus cultural traits are selected much like genetic traits. At the same time, cultural values and beliefs influence how people interact with their ecosystem and apply selective pressure on species. Not only have people and their environment coevolved, but social systems and environmental systems have coevolved.

The rise of paddy rice culture in Asia is an instructive example. The land-intensive practice of slash and burn agriculture was gradually abandoned over many centuries as investments were made in dikes, terraces, and water delivery systems for increasingly intensive paddy agriculture. This ecological transformation provided superior weed control and greater nutrient retention. The environmental system modification process, however, was not unilateral. In order to maintain the ecological system in its modified form and to acquire the benefits of modification, individuals changed their behavior and the social system adapted to assist and reinforce appropriate

41

individual behavior. In the case of paddy rice, the benefits from ecological transformation could only be acquired through complex social changes that facilitated property ownership, water management, and labor exchanges.

Neither neoclassical nor marxist theory even addresses, let alone explains, the development associated with the eight doublings in human population during the agricultural revolution. Our understanding of recent history as a process of modernization provides little insight into the bulk of human history before the industrial revolution. Development economists today stress the importance of formal schooling, the adoption of modern technologies, the use of modern inputs in agriculture, the use of energy for transportation and industry, and the importance of market systems for providing appropriate incentives. But for most of the last five thousand to ten thousand years, few workers went to school; tools only improved modestly; very few inputs were applied to agriculture; Western science had not yet provided access to stocks of energy resources, and people were not organized primarily around markets or hierarchical bureaucratic structures. The process of development was different.

THE COEVOLUTION OF MODERN AGRICULTURE

Economic interpretations of Western history typically emphasize the dramatic increase in the productivity of the few individuals still working in agriculture. This increase is generally attributed to a continual decrease in environmental constraints on farmers. The coevolutionary perspective emphasizes the increase in individual task specialization and the increase in the cultural or institutional complexity of maintaining feedback mechanisms between specialized actors within the social system and between the social system and the ecosystem. The coevolutionary view emphasizes an increasingly important, and frequently more complex, interaction between people and their environment.

Western agriculture was once a small-scale, labor-intensive, polycultural, and near-subsistence interaction between social and ecological systems. The systems coevolved to a large-scale, mechanized and energy-intensive, monocultural, commercial farming interaction. This new agricultural interaction is maintained by a highly complex system of farm implement, agrochemical, and seed industries; a highly developed marketing system; and government institutions to generate and disseminate knowledge, develop new inputs, regulate markets, absorb risk, subsidize capital, limit the distributional effects of adjustments, and control environmental and health impacts. The fitness of these agricultural institutions is constantly tested by the ecosystem's responses to the style of farming occurring under their umbrella.

Mechanical innovations preceded and tended to select for chemical technologies which, in turn, reinforced the fitness of mechanical technologies in modern agriculture. Mechanized agricultural production is less expensive in larger units. Increasing returns to scale with mechanization led to larger, monocultural farms. Under monoculture, the farmer became dependent on the success of one or two crops. The increased risk of farming but one or two crops encouraged the development and use of agrochemicals to assure successful production. Quite rapidly, the chemical industry became a powerful economic and political feature of agriculture. The agroecosystem's responses to agrochemicals led to new institutions to regulate pesticides and reduce water pollution from fertilizers. They also led to new research programs in agricultural experiment stations to reduce the farmer's dependence on chemicals. Simultaneously, as fertilizer responsiveness became the most important, almost sole, criterion of fitness in crops, the number of varieties planted drastically reduced. The loss in the diversity of crops planted made agriculture more vulnerable to the arrival or evolution of new crop diseases and pests. The seed industry acquired the responsibility of maintaining, developing, and supplying new varieties as plagues and pests arose from year to year. Thus modernization can be thought of as the coevolution of the research, input supplying, and regulatory sectors to the agroecosystem's responses to new inputs and techniques.

Throughout this coevolutionary process between the technological components of the social system and the ecosystem, there has been a complementary coevolution in the economic organization of agriculture. Many near subsistence, independent farmers supplying to nearly free markets evolved toward a complex form of corporate/state agricultural capitalism. The risks of monoculture averted through the technological coevolution described in the previous paragraph were also avoided through organizational change. Ownership of farmland concentrated into fewer hands as farmers tried to plant additional crops over large areas. Farmers also supported government sponsored crop insurance, subsidies to capital investments, and regulated markets to reduce their financial exposure. Many farmers incorporated to reduce personal risk and increase their access to capital. Large, nonagricultural corporations also bid the highest prices for some farmlands as the uncertainties of agriculture increased. In a few cases corporations, whose primary business was in industry, even operated very large farms. These transformations in economic organization coevolved with the new technologies, ecological responses thereto, and the difficulties of spreading risks, obtaining capital, and operating in a government regulated and supported industry.

Coevolution is a positive feedback process. Crop insurance and regulated markets reduced the risks of monocultural production and made it more attractive, further fueling the practice already induced by mechanization. Larger farms made it more difficult for the "farmer" to manage for the particular nature of each area of his farm, further fueling the use of agrochemicals simply to override the ecosystem. The existence of regulatory systems have facilitated the safer use of toxics while increasing their social acceptability, and perhaps their use, as well.

Today's agricultural ecosystems have soil features, weed dynamics, and insect–crop interactions that reflect coevolution with the social system. Likewise, today's agricultural institutions reflect the vulnerability of disturbed soil to wind and water erosion, the adaptations of insect populations to chemical control, the susceptibility of monocultural systems to variations in weather, and the need to maintain genetic diversity over time.

THE INDUSTRIAL REVOLUTION AND COEVOLUTION OF MODERN SOCIETIES

Since the middle of the nineteenth century, the First World has experienced dramatic improvements in living standards. Since the middle of the twentieth century, the Third World has experienced both rapid population growth and some improvements in living standards. But a century and a half is a short time, and there have only been a little more than two additional doublings, albeit very quick ones, in population since the industrial revolution.

The dramatic increase in material well-being and in the rate of population growth during the past century and a half can also be understood as a process of coevolution. With industrialization, social systems coevolved to facilitate development through the exploitation of coal and petroleum. Social systems no longer coevolved to interact more effectively with environmental systems. To the extent social systems responded to environmental transformations, they were reactionary, belated efforts to prevent excessive damage rather than to enhance new opportunities. Thus the past century can be characterized as social system coevolution on stock resources and the neglect of environmental systems. The era of hydrocarbons drove a wedge between the earlier coevolution of social and ecological systems. Capturing the energy of the sun through ecosystem management became less and less important as Western science facilitated the capture of fossil energy. Social systems coevolved with the expanding number of technologies for using hydrocarbons and only later adopted institutions to correct the detrimental transformations this coevolution entailed for ecosystems and ultimately for people. Hydrocarbons freed societies from immediate environmental constraints but not from ultimate environmental constraints – the limits of the hydrocarbons themselves and of the atmosphere and oceans to absorb carbon dioxide and other greenhouse gases associated with fossil fuel economies. The value systems, knowledge systems, social organization, and technologies of Western and westernized cultures coevolved to fit the opportunities which the exploitation of fossil energy provided. Western and westernized social systems reflect these medium-term opportunities rather than the long-run opportunities of coevolutionary development with renewable resources.

Environmental systems have also coevolved with industrialization, but the nature of the coevolution differs from that experienced during the rise of agriculture. By tapping into fossil hydrocarbons for energy, Western societies freed themselves from many of the complexities of interacting with environmental systems. With an independent energy source providing fertilizers, farmers could avoid the complexities of interplanting crops that were good hosts of nitrogen fixing bacteria with those that were not. Fossil hydrocarbon energy also reduced the cost of obtaining and applying many other inputs – fencing, liming, fungicides, herbicides, and insecticides. Furthermore, inexpensive energy meant crops could be stored for longer periods and transported over greater distances. Thus, over the past century and a half, there have been massive changes in how agriculture is practiced and organized, changes which proved fit because of industrialization. These changes have given people the sense of being free from or having control over nature and being able to consciously design their future. The rapid advances in mining, industry, transportation, and communication complemented this sense of control.

The sense of control facilitated by fossil fuels reinforced the scientific cosmology that had been evolving since Bacon, Galileo, and Newton. Nature was viewed as a giant machine – the metaphor of a watch was commonly used – existing apart from people, whose complexities could be determined by systematic hypothesizing and testing. This view was complemented by discoveries and inventions before fossil fuels energized agriculture and industry. But with the rapid rise of industry and transformation of agriculture during the late nineteenth and early twentieth centuries, people in the First World became almost euphoric about the possibilities of knowing and controlling nature and rationally planning their destinies. Visions of utopias without physical toil or social strife abounded in both the intellectual literature and the popular discourse of the age.

Conventional theories of economic development have been derived from observations while western social systems were coevolving with fossil fuels. Both neoclassical and marxist economic theory explain growth in terms of the accumulation of physical capital and improvements in human ingenuity which enhance our ability to use rationally the earth's resources and to increase the rates of material production. Progress – equated with the advance of Western science, the process of modernization, and material economic growth – drives development in both neoclassical and marxist theories. The progress of Western science and the superiority of Western social organization is embedded in our very conception of economic development. But while we think of the social and technological changes of the past century as having been rationally designed, in fact the number of efforts that have failed suggests that *ex post* selection according to what proves fit has indeed played a strong role. More importantly, many things are not proving fit with Western values over the longer run. The beliefs of

45

modernism have been instrumental in bringing us to the environmental problems, bureaucratic malaise, and cultural repression we now face. The euphoria of control over nature and of overcoming the limitations of historic ways of valuing, knowing, and organizing has given way to despondency. Regardless of whether human life on earth now is more or less precarious, more or less equal, or more or less rewarding than it was a century or two ago, many people are ready for more effective ways of understanding and a new course beyond modernism.

COEVOLUTIONARY ENVIRONMENTAL HISTORY LESSONS

In the coevolutionary paradigm, the environment determines the fitness of how people behave as guided by alternative ways of knowing, forms of social organization, and types of technologies. Yet at the same time, how people know, organize, and use tools determine the fitness of characteristics of an evolving environment. At any point in time, each determines the other. Over time, neither is more important than the other. And depending on genetic mutations, value shifts, technological changes, and social innovations that arise randomly, the evolutionary path is reset for a period until another change occurs. Thus the coevolutionary perspective explains why options are disturbingly limited in the short run; culture has determined environment and environment has determined culture. At each point in time there is a near gridlock of coevolved knowledge, values, technologies, social organization, and natural environment. Yet over the longer run we approach the equally disturbing situation of nothing determining anything, that all will change in unpredictable ways. Where we will be in the future is determined by neither today's culture nor environment alone but by these and a host of unpredictable future factors. Yet come the future, near gridlock will prevail.

Can any lessons be drawn from so encompassing an interpretation of environmental history? Coevolution explains the past well, but by its nature does not predict. It does not give us any stable cause-and-effect relationships by which we can choose between actions to reach desired effects and avoid undesired effects. And yet this weakness is also a virtue. The first and perhaps most important lesson from this understanding of environmental history is that the idea that we could predict how new ways of doing things would affect our environment was and still is a delusion. If history is easily explained in an evolutionary framework, it might be because evolutionary processes really are important. If that is the case, then the ability to predict and control will always be limited. And if this is indeed the case, then the first lesson of a coevolutionary environmental history is that experimentation should be undertaken cautiously on a small scale with as much monitoring of the evolutionary chain of events thereafter as possible.

Massive programs to quickly adopt new ways of knowing, organizing, and doing things are inherently risky. Multiple small experiments are better than a few big ones.

The second lesson is related to the first. Experiments that entail very long time commitments should be avoided. If our ability to foresee the future is limited, then changes that can be undone quickly or will naturally depreciate are preferable. The folly of committing to the management of nuclear wastes for 50,000 years, for example, is clearer from a coevolutionary perspective.

The third lesson is also closely related to the first. Diversity in coevolving systems is inherently good. Without diversity, the coevolutionary process can stagnate. With diversity, systems will more likely survive changes in climate or other external disturbances. The virtues of diversity will be elaborated further in Chapter 14.

The fourth lesson is a mixture of bad news and good news. From the coevolutionary perspective, things really are interconnected and adding a new component, such as a new agency or technology, will not quickly shift how the system behaves. This is simply because the component is likely to be selected out. If the coevolutionary course is going well for people, it is likely to be pretty stable, but the same is true if it is going badly. On the other hand, small changes which do prove fit, i.e. are initially compatible with other components in the system, can still change the coevolutionary course for better or for worse. The question of the rate of coevolutionary change is addressed more fully in the annotations to this chapter, but a coevolutionary environmental history emphasizes how things work by evolutionary, rather than either mechanical or revolutionary, processes.

The fifth lesson is also extremely valuable. The preliminary coevolutionary history outlined in this chapter sheds new light on why the industrial revolution was so important. Prior to the significant exploitation of fossil hydrocarbons, cultures coevolved with ecosystems. With the exploitation of fossil hydrocarbons, cultures coevolved around hydrocarbons, apparently becoming increasingly free of ecosystems for the last century. To a large extent the apparent freedom was due to the long delays between the initial net oxidation of hydrocarbons and the cumulative impacts of their use which we now think are leading to climate change. In any case, modern values, knowledge, organization, and technological systems reflect the availability of fossil hydrocarbons rather than the features needed to interact with and continue to coevolve effectively with ecosystems. The transition to sustainable development will not be easy because of the extent to which hydrocarbons have driven a wedge between cultural evolution and the biosphere.

The coevolutionary environmental history is no more right or wrong than modern explanations. The coevolutionary explanation, however, differs dramatically from modern views. This difference can heighten our understanding of modernism and of the challenges of sustainable development, effective social organization, and cultural diversity. If we had this understanding earlier, modernism's betrayal of development could have been foreseen and avoided. And as we gain this perspective, it may provide the basis for new alternatives for development.

5

THE ILLUSIONS OF PROGRESS

If there were good cause for believing that the earth would be
uninhabitable in AD 2000 or 2100 the doctrine of Progress would lose
its meaning and automatically disappear.

(J. B. Bury 1920)

The idea of progress has had a marked effect on Western culture since the
sixteenth century when historians, philosophers, and scientists began to
question what was then a conventional wisdom. It had been widely held
that humanity was in a perpetual downward spiral. The Church taught that
mankind's descent began when Adam and Eve ate the apple in the Garden
of Eden. Intellectuals dated the fall to the end of Greek philosophy. And
by any objective account, all could see that the last great engineering works
dated to the Roman Empire. While a few thought things were getting better
during the sixteenth century, by the seventeenth century, a strong case could
be made that life on earth had improved slowly over the past few centuries
through the invention of instruments such as the compass, the design of
better boats, the discovery of new continents, and the introduction of exotic
crops to Europe. This realization fused with millenarianism, the Christian
hope for a kingdom of heaven on earth, into the idea of Progress. Thus the
idea that humanity was in an unending downward fall was replaced by a
positive, uplifting sense of both material and moral destiny that has been
central to the identity of Western and westernized peoples to this day.

A positive image of the future facilitates the individual initiative and social
relations we associate with a nontotalitarian society. The idea of progress
has been the key to change – personal, economic, institutional, and political
– in the Western and westernized world. Belief in progress historically
"sugar coated" political conflicts and "greased" the policy process. The
potential for unending debate over this versus that and between one group
and another was attenuated by our faith that shortly all can have both.
Furthermore, hard work was justified in the belief that it would yield faster
advancement to a better life later. There have been, of course, some
contradictory uses of the belief. When ethical conflicts have blocked the

49

course of empires, for example, forging ahead at great human cost has been too easily portrayed as a necessary short run compromise along the long run path to a better world. Nevertheless, a positive image of the future appears to be a very helpful stimulus to individual and collective action with long run benefits and to the maintenance of social relations short of totalitarianism.

The belief in progress is so much a part of modernism, so prevalent in Western private and public discourse, that to openly question modernism is to openly question the idea of progress, tantamount to being a pessimist, giving up, dropping out, and becoming a social misfit. The Western sense of time as history moving forward, onward, or upward is so strong that, even in academe, those who raise questions about Western beliefs in progress are accused of romanticizing the past or of advocating going backward.

The particular positive image of the future, which in the West evolved associations with modernity, however, has several aspects which have already terminated the future for many humanities and is likely to result in an early demise for its perpetrators as well. Three aspects are especially important to the thesis of this book. First, the modern belief in progress was so strong during the nineteenth century that Western and westernized peoples lost much of their sense of responsibility for the earth and for future generations. We believed that progress through Western science would solve everything and thus that responsibility entailed accelerating the advance of science. While this belief is no longer as strong as it has been, it still thwarts responsible environmental management to protect future generations. Given the complexities of global environmental management with development driven by stock hydrocarbon energy, technological optimism hastens humankind's demise. Second, though the Western idea of progress was initially closely associated with religious beliefs, our image of the future today has little if any moral vision. Progress has become vacuous. And third, the Western image of the future has been culturally homogeneous. All people were seen to be progressing to the same highest cultural state. In the modern view of progress, cultural diversity has been seen not only as a temporal phenomenon but as evidence that sufficient progress has not yet occurred. This conception seriously limits the possibilities of humanity attaining its full potential.

Recent history has shown that many of the particulars of the modern image of the future were naive. Environmental degradation threatens future material wealth. Individualism threatens the ethical rules which bind people into societies. Western dominance threatens the few remaining traditional cultures from which new lessons can be drawn. Though the modern idea of progress is seriously battered, there is no alternative positive vision of the future around which people, communities, nations, or international bodies can negotiate day-to-day decisions. And partly as a consequence, stalemates are now the norm at every level of political decision-making. A revisioning of progress is overdue.

A SHORT HISTORY OF THE IDEA OF PROGRESS

The image of the Renaissance as a flowering of artistic expression and scientific advance unknown for a millennium provides the initial template to the modern idea of progress. The great explorations of the world and the establishment of colonial empires added an expanding geopolitical and economic dimension to the framework. The demise of feudal society and the rise of capitalism added socioeconomic transformation to the vision. The continued rise of science, new technologies, and material progress filled in the picture by the latter part of the eighteenth century. While the modern image of progress became ever more elaborate, each embellishment was tied to knowledge: to its absolute increase, spread among the populace, and application in the development of better technologies for exploiting nature, improved products for easier living, and superior institutions for organizing people more rationally.

Progress only gradually replaced Providence. Historically people felt they had little control over their destiny. Floods, droughts, and plagues were acts of God and the misery and death they inflicted were God's will. A new conventional wisdom developed over the centuries that people would continually gain increased mastery over nature through scientific advance. New scientific explanations for natural phenomena replaced appeals to Providence while new technologies brought some measure of control. The natural world could be changed, misery could be reduced, and death could be postponed. By the nineteenth century, people at all levels of Western societies took progress for granted. While Marx found many aspects of the new industrial world repugnant, he was so confident that they would pass that he elevated the modern idea of progress to a law of history.

By the end of the nineteenth century, the public's belief in progress was becoming institutionalized and the term economic development arose. The scheme became grander. In the United States, for example, it was no longer enough for the government to send survey parties West in advance of the settlers, or to provide the incentives for the construction of the great railroad system. It became accepted that government could play a stronger role through the promotion and dissemination of science and technology, direct investment in great public works, and coordination through a benevolent technocracy. The idea of Providence is now considered quaint while the idea of control is so strong in parts of the West that the occurrence of misery or early death are viewed as a matter of social and scientific inadequacy or irresponsibility. Thus the term progress referred to the belief in what was possible while development referred to the conscious process of making it happen. And as technocrats and economists assumed the role of implementing economic development, they also assumed the defense and elaboration of the modern idea of progress.

Belief in progress provided the justification for Westerners to expand the geographical domain of modernity. Helping people of other cultures to progress beyond their backwardness was seen to be good, even if these people did not recognize it. Individuals within non-Western cultures abandoned their culture's belief system, technologies, and associated institutions and adopted Western ways because they too believed in progress. The rhetoric of progress is alive in the public discourse of countries such as Brazil and Thailand where significant improvements in the well-being of many has occurred. Even in countries such as Bangladesh and Vietnam, where development has had little positive impact, faith in progress still fuels hope.

Though the modern idea of progress is still strong in the developed countries, at the close of the twentieth century more and more people are wondering whether they are on a material-well-being treadmill. The initial joy of new purchases is not sustained by use and something more is desired again. Things are short-lived substitutes for the loss of a culture that provided nonmaterial meaning to life. At the same time, many people are also interpreting global environmental change as evidence that to the extent they are living materially well, it is at the expense of the basic needs of their grandchildren. With little or no faith in progress, students are not as motivated in college as were their parents, who studied in the conviction that their struggles would be well rewarded. The dwindling faith in progress makes it more difficult to break the political deadlocks between competing interests because no group is willing to sacrifice their position now in the faith that new opportunities will arise tomorrow.

At the same time, while faith in the modern idea of progress has diminished, our image of a desirable future has been changing. The cultural rediversification taking place in developed countries, the increasing ability of the late-to-become independent nations to identify their own goals, and the rise in respect for indigenous cultures are redefining our vision of the future. The modern conception of progress as the merging of different races, cultures, and nations, advancing together in monotonous synchrony, has lost its glory.

Critiques of Western belief in progress have a long history. An elaboration of these critiques provides deeper insight into the nature of our beliefs, documents the robustness of these beliefs to reasoned attack, and indicates the weak areas that will have to be stronger in any new understanding of progress.

TECHNOLOGICAL OPTIMISM

In North America, at least, the idea of progress has long been countered by doom-sayers arguing that the frontier is closing, resources are running out, and population increases are accelerating the arrival of a miserable ending. Those concerned with the long-run scarcity of resources have goaded the vanguards of progress, economists since World War II, to affirm their faith publicly. Hence economists left and right have argued vociferously that continual improvements in technology will assure long-run resource abundance.

In the late 1940s and early 1950s there was considerable concern in the United States about whether resources in the decades ahead would become scarce due to the incredible rate of use of materials during World War II. In the 1960s, as medicines reduced child mortality rates in the Third World and their populations began to grow rapidly, people in the First World became concerned with the "population bomb". The 1970s started with the first "Earth Day" and the transformation of the American environmental movement from an emphasis on preserving wilderness and wildlife to managing pollutants and protecting human habitats. Soon after, "The Limits to Growth" were modeled on a computer and then the energy crisis generated lines at gas stations and a plethora of studies on energy scarcity. During the 1980s, First World scientists became worried about environmental degradation and the loss of biodiversity in the Third World. By the late 1980s, environmental scientists had alerted the public to the perils of global climate change. European environmental movements have evolved through a similar series of concerns over the past quarter century.

Whether resource scarcity or environmental constraints will ultimately limit progress or not cannot be answered definitively. Certainly, we are constantly experiencing various resource scarcities and environmental constraints in the short run. Certainly the rise and fall in our concerns over particular limits or particular ways of perceiving limits are social phenomena rather than real phenomena. The rise and fall in government programs supporting research, development, and the implementation of solar power from 1975 to 1985, for example, cannot be related to the steady decline in the real stocks of fossil hydrocarbons during this period. Clearly, whenever we ponder ultimate limits, we are dealing with our perceptions of our environment. Yet, though environmental scientists do not have all the facts, they do have very sophisticated perceptions of the nature of resources and environmental systems. The issues they have brought to the public's attention certainly deserve serious consideration.

The public's ability to consider, however, has been seriously distorted by its historic faith in progress. Economists in particular have played to this faith. They have argued that technology will offset all possible resource limits and environmental constraints. Neoclassical economists countered the concern over the rapid rates of population growth in the Third World by arguing that development needed to be accelerated so that these countries would go through the "demographic transition," the term for the decline in the rate of population growth experienced by Europe and the United

States in the latter nineteenth and early twentieth centuries. Neoclassical economists first responded to the concern over environmental degradation in the Third World with the argument that amenities could only be addressed after basic needs were met, so faster development was the solution.

Each of these counter arguments was an extrapolation of past good fortune experienced in the North rather than a fresh analysis of what might lie ahead for the North or the actual conditions in the South. The analyses easily led to arguments that development should be accelerated, rather than undertaken more cautiously, in order to gain the new technologies to offset scarcity or to push through the demographic transition. Playing on the Western belief in progress, economists argued that all problems are due to too little progress.

The marxist response to concerns over resource and environmental limits was somewhat different from the neoclassical but led to similar conclusions. Marxists chided those in the rich countries concerned with population growth among the poor, interpreting the concern as evidence that the rich at best feared that the increasing number of poor would compete with them for resources and that the rich at worst were worried that population growth would accelerate the inevitable revolution and redistribution of power to the working class. Similarly, they argued that Northerners wanted to slow development in the South by imposing environmental controls in order to keep them as underdeveloped suppliers of raw materials and cheap labor. These positions also led marxists to conclude that progress simply needed speeding up so that the social transformations to socialism and then communism would come sooner.

Many people operate on their *belief* that progress will occur through continued technological advance unless *scientifically* proven otherwise. The analyses of environmental scientists have been attacked because their scientific models are not perfectly convincing. This strategy has been used against arguments warning of population growth, resource scarcity, of the loss of biodiversity, and of global climate change. Again let me stress that we cannot know the future. We can only contemplate in as many and as sophisticated ways as we can the social and environmental ramifications over time of our actions today. My concern for the purposes of this chapter is that this collective thinking process continues to be short-circuited by residual, simplistic, beliefs in progress. Because our belief in progress stops us from pursuing some of these important questions prematurely, the chance that we are undertaking foolish activities is far greater than it need be.

Perhaps progress will be limited by our ability to respond to problems, by our ability to be able to develop new technologies and forms of social organization to interact more effectively with our environment. There is increasing evidence that there are social limits to our present course of development.

In its most simple version, progress was thought of as being linear, much as portrayed by the causal chain running down the center of Figure 4.1 in the last chapter. In this vision, better science leads to better technology and more rational social organization and thereby to more material well-being through more effective control of nature. Similarly, both neoclassical and marxist economists have described the stages of social transformation as being linear. These simple images began in Europe, moved and became refined in North America, and were transferred to Third World peoples as they embarked on development after independence. They are still widely held and still invoked in arguments even by those who are well aware of their simplicity.

Even during the nineteenth century, however, it should have been clear that progress was a much more complex process. First, the advance of science required an ever more educated populace to work with the new technologies. The extra time in school took able-bodied young adults out of economic production. Second, the advance of science and technology could no longer simply be left to the few great minds who pursued knowledge for its own sake. Governments began to systematically invest in and establish permanent institutions for science and technology. Third, the increase in material goods production facilitated by new technologies resulted in the depletion of natural resources. Thus science had to be directed to the development of new technologies and social organization to exploit new resources, problems for which earlier science and technology were partially responsible. These three phenomena are illustrated as feedback loops in the otherwise linear image of Figure 4.1.

During the twentieth century we have also learned that many new technologies not only sequentially deplete different qualities of resources but also degrade the environment. This has necessitated further investments in science, technology, and institutions. Furthermore, we have become attuned to how people's values in both Western and westernized cultures have been modified by development and then how these changes, in turn, have affected social organization and the choice of technology. People now recognize that every new technology, even those designed to correct the problems of earlier technologies, bring unforeseen consequences. If we added these additional feedbacks to the picture, Figure 4.1 would be indistinguishable from a plate of spaghetti. This, of course, is much of the problem. Our simple image of development has become lost, and none too soon, in the complex of good, bad, and potentially disastrous things that development, when pursued on the basis of this too simple a vision, has wrought.

Progress in the modern vision cannot possibly continue much longer into the future. Modern progress is intimately linked to our ability to know and manipulate our environment. This requires higher and higher levels of education. Hence more and more adult years are spent going to school. In the United States, the increase in the proportion of adult years spent in higher education between 1870 and 1980 extrapolated out into the future results in all of the adult population attending school all of the time by the year 2062. Perhaps this is a little unrealistic, so imagine that only half of those historically attending school were acquiring skills to generate, work with, and control the side-effects of the new technologies necessary to exploit lower quality resources and more complex environmental processes. With this assumption, 100 percent of the population would still have to be attending school by the year 2086. This, of course, does not leave any time for anyone to do the teaching, undertake the research, use the technologies, or participate in the control of the side effects. Extrapolations, of course, are nothing more than mathematical exercises, but this particular exercise ought to raise doubts in our minds as to the potential for further progress as we have known it.

THE IMBALANCE BETWEEN TECHNOLOGICAL AND CULTURAL PROGRESS

Many have argued that there is an imbalance between the rate of technical progress and the rate of social progress. In this characterization, technological optimism is well founded, but it has been inappropriately coupled with unfounded sociological optimism. New technologies arise faster than we can develop the organizational capability to control their social and environmental side effects. We are devising new types of pollutants far faster than we are developing institutions for their control. Many nations now have the expertise to develop nuclear, chemical, and biological weapons, but it is by no means clear whether even the most developed have been able to devise institutions to reduce the likelihood of war. But the problem is not simply one of uneven rates. New technologies are determining the kinds of social organization that evolve as well as the kinds that must be designed to control and offset technology's effects. Societies, rather than picking and molding technologies according to their values, are being shaped by technology.

There are two ways to correct an imbalance in the rates of change between technology and society. Some argue that we should slow the rate of technological progress to match the slower rate of organizational change. Others argue that technical change cannot be slowed or that we should not slow a good thing, hence we should accelerate our social evolution. The imbalance in rates is well accepted, yet the opposing solutions have effectively cancelled each other out. But emphasizing the rates of change diverts attention from the problem of what progress should be. Framing the imbalance in terms of whether technology is controlling the nature of society or vice versa challenges societies to take control.

The combination of these portrayals of the human dilemma have offset technological optimism to a considerable extent. Yet the residual optimism remains as dangerous as before given the ever higher risks inherent in the increasing intensity and number of ways people are intervening in the biosphere. Thus more and more people are calling for controls over and massive guidance of technology. Yet this control can only be exercised by each society developing a collective sense of self, defining its objectives, and thereby determining what progress is for its people. This leads us into the issue of the moral direction of progress.

THE VACUITY OF PROGRESS

Is progress whatever science and technology makes possible and societies can adapt to? In its original conception, the idea of progress was closely allied with Christian views of moral advance and utopia on earth. Improvements in material well-being confirmed God's beneficence by relieving suffering, made it easier for individuals to fulfill God's will, and facilitated a collective fashioning of the world around Christian beliefs. Progress, however, steadily lost its moral direction over the subsequent centuries. The separation of church and state meant the moral direction of all had to come through people acting individually. Yet the collective vision of a moral future steadily waned. As positivism became the accepted methodology for publicly addressing problems, values, the subjective dimensions of every problem, were downplayed. Under positivism, with all sides arguing that they were only addressing the facts, we lost our ability to speak to values and to integrate them in our individual and collective decision-making. At the same time, the idea that society and its objectives were merely the sum of its individuals and their desires became widely accepted. Furthermore, society did not have to make conscious value choices because the "invisible hand" served everyone's desires as well as possible. And finally, as development succeeded, the preoccupation of individuals with their position on the treadmill of consumerism displaced the remaining sense that progress needed to be subjectively defined. Thus progress has become whatever will be. It is difficult to argue that we need to revision progress because what "it" is steadfastly remains unclear and because its vacuity is shielded by other beliefs – positivism, individualism, the invisible hand, and consumerism – which define the West.

And yet Western people retain a strong sense that something is amiss. As individuals we suffer from "future shock," a loss of continuity with the past, because the rate of introduction of wondrous new products and opportunities far exceed our ability to give them any cultural meaning. Fireplaces and old kitchen stoves evoke a sense of sharing, sustenance, and shelter to those who have grown up with them. Baseboard heaters and microwave ovens do not. Other examples fit other generations and cultures. Our sense of who we are in the grander scheme of things does not evolve as rapidly as technology keeps replacing the things. For similar reasons, we either grossly exaggerate or totally ignore the risks of new technologies because we are unable to develop a reasonable perspective or approach to handling them. We are out of synch with the world in which we live. But again, it is not simply a matter of people being behind the beat of technology, but of technology determining the rhythm with which people are trying to synchronize.

PROGRESS AND THE THIRD WORLD

The belief that progress is vacuous has different roots in developing nations. Disillusion has been nurtured by the disparity in economic well-being between classes of people within nations as well as between nations with different histories. The very term "developing nations" itself has lost much of its meaning. It used to portray a positive image of all nations and all within each nation steadily developing. But while development was envisioned as a smooth process of improvements in well-being, in fact individuals and nations were burdened with wrenching disruptions as they became tied into unstable global markets, as they adopted technologies which redistribute wealth and opportunity, and as they intermittently embarked on and terminated unrealistic development plans. The poorest individuals and nations with the least flexibility and fewest options have not overcome the turmoil sufficiently to find a development track. The difficulties of the poor have also been compounded by the environmental uncertainties of floods, droughts, and agricultural pests. In any case, rather than homogeneous development, differences between nations and between people within nations have been accentuated.

But even the relatively rich, powerful, and successful in the developing world are disillusioned. The Western idea of progress must seem at least somewhat naive to the political leaders and capitalists of Argentina and Brazil, for example. The most powerful people in some of the most successful of developing countries have little control over their destinies. They are helplessly sandwiched between the demands of the International Monetary Fund for fiscally tighter economic policies to insure the repayment of their $100 billion debts and the demands of increasingly vocal populaces distraught by triple-digit inflation, high unemployment, and economies bouncing between boom and bust. Our belief in progress can tolerate an occasionally stumble, but development, in fact, has been chaotic in even the more successful countries.

THE REEMERGENCE OF CULTURAL HETEROGENEITY

Growing doubts about the Western idea of progress has rekindled the cultural diversity that remains in the North. People today, especially people of color, are more likely than at mid-century proudly to accept and live their lives around their cultural background rather than pretend they had none. Cultural diversity, furthermore, has been reinforced in Europe and North America in the latter half of this century through a resurgence of immigrants – political, economic, and intellectual refugees from the colonial empires of old as well as from the former Soviet Union and Eastern Europe. Minorities are now openly demanding control over the evolution of their futures. And people who no longer have cultural roots have looked for other paths and objectives, a search that led to both the healthy consideration and the ridiculous feigning of other cultures. Lastly, cultural redifferentiation is having a major impact on geopolitics.

The fall of the Shah, the reestablishment of Islamic culture in Iran, and the strengthening of Islamic values, understanding, and forms of social organization in a significant portion of the world have also had a profound effect on the old idea of progress. Since Iran's rejection of Western culture, Westerners are less prone to think all cultures will merge. China, also perceived by Westerners as joining the mainstream between the liberalization inspired by Deng Xiaoping in the late 1970s and the crushing of the students in Tiananmen Square in 1989, is once again seen as going its own way. Third World countries continue to define what they mean by development in spite of the homogenizing effects of Western technical assistance, the narrow criteria used to design development projects and to make loans, the rigors of international markets, or the deals struck during the acquisition of armaments from the First World.

PROGRESS AND TRADITIONAL PEOPLES

The decline in our belief in progress as a process of cultural homogenization is perhaps most striking when we consider recent developments in attitudes toward traditional peoples. Historically, peoples who clung to their own cultures were a threat to modern peoples' belief in progress. As that belief has weakened and transformed, other cultures pose less of a threat. This offers some hope that the few remaining non-westernized peoples might have more influence over their own evolution.

Modern people's intolerance has been rooted in the most pure and benevolent of hopes, the idea that humanity was advancing toward both universal values and one right way of knowing. It was thought that with progress, greed and hate would fade away. Harmony would be further assured through a rational social order that respected human rights. Since people of other cultures who resisted being converted to Western values and rationality were clearly not on the path of progress, their demise could be rightfully hastened. Through most of the nineteenth century, Westerners still felt it was acceptable to exterminate cultures in the way of progress. The Soviet Union continued this practice well into the twentieth century.

And people in developing nations today still rationalize the extermination of Amazonian Indians, Timorese, and Tibetans, among others, who get in the way of the dominant culture.

While many non-Western cultures have been destroyed through direct violence and the introduction of disease, many other cultures have met their demise through the loss of a positive vision of their future. Many traditional peoples in the vicinity of westernized peoples have gained respect by shifting cultures. Many of those who did not shift, or shift fast enough, have been driven to alcohol or suffered other difficulties trying to balance between two worlds. The policies of most governments have wavered between benign neglect, forced acculturation, and cultural preservation. This vacillation itself has been as destructive to the self-determination of non-Western peoples and positive evolution of their cultures as the campaigns of violence during the preceding centuries.

Policies still waver, but new trends in attitudes toward indigenous peoples began to emerge in the 1980s. Though Pope John Paul II is constraining choice within the Catholic Church, he has spoken of the beauty of cultural diversity, has visited with indigenous peoples, and has commended some of their religious beliefs, especially their respect for the earth. Nine U.S. Protestant denominations and the United Church of Canada have apologized to indigenous peoples for the past conduct of their missionaries. And Amazon tribal leaders have met with Barber Conable, when he was President of the World Bank, to discuss their futures.

Cultural survival is also being enhanced, as the Western idea of progress wanes, through new interest in the knowledge of other peoples. Western scientists are beginning to look at traditional agricultural systems in order to understand how agroecosystems, management techniques, and cultures can coevolve sustainably. Thus non-Western cultures are beginning to receive respect, albeit still far too little, on their own merits.

This new respect for traditional cultures could be interpreted as evidence of "progress" in the development and acceptance of tolerance, a concept with strong Judeo-Christian roots. Whatever unfolds, does so from something, or progresses from something that was there before. So long as there is a future unfolding from a past, there will be progress. The important thing is which ideas and values advance and which recede in importance. The progress in our respect for non-Western cultures opens up the possibility for a very different and more interesting world than when only Western culture and westernized people were respected.

Direction seems intrinsic to our idea of progress. To move along in some direction suggests an axis with a label. Historically the important axis on which Western societies were expected to progress was Judeo-Christian morality; today it is too often simply gross national product. With a limited number of axes by which progress is deemed to occur, cultural homogeneity is inevitable. To sustain a culturally diverse future, our vision of the future will have to include different trajectories for different cultures.

6

THE PHILOSOPHICAL ROOTS
OF THE BETRAYAL

Interesting philosophy is rarely an examination of the pros and cons
of a thesis. Usually it is, implicitly or explicitly, a contest between an
entrenched vocabulary which has become a nuisance and a half-formed
new vocabulary which vaguely promises great things.

(Richard Rorty 1989: 9)

Many have ventured thoughtful explanations as to why development during
the past century has been so environmentally destructive. Some natural
scientists argue that massive environmental destruction is inevitable when
human populations are expanding exponentially. Others emphasize that far
too many new substances have been introduced into the environment before
determining their impacts on other species let alone ourselves. Economists
argue that producers and consumers behave in a manner that cannot
be sustained because market prices do not include environmental costs.
Moralists argue that people generally are too greedy and shortsighted,
while marxists argue that capitalists are too avaricious and myopic. Every
discipline has a preferred explanation of our environmental crises consistent
with its patterns of thinking. There is no reason to take issue with any of
these explanations rooted in particular disciplines of thought for each
provides insights.

Beyond these disciplinary explanations, however, there are broader
philosophical interpretations of why modernism has led to the degradation
of environmental systems. These arguments also link to the destruction of
cultural systems. Most people believe humans think in a more sophisticated
manner than other species. It seems likely that our way of thinking is related
to other uniquely human characteristics such as how we organize into social
systems and how we transform environmental systems. Thus I argue that
key premises of Western patterns of thinking help explain the cultural and
biological destruction associated with modernism.

I want to make it very clear that I am not addressing the diverse and
contradictory ways in which each of us thinks as individuals. Nor am I
addressing how scientists actually think or how science really progresses. I

61

Table 6.1 Dominant and alternate premises

Dominant Premises	Alternate Premises
Atomism: Systems consist of unchanging parts and are simply the sum of their parts.	*Holism*: Parts cannot be understood apart from their wholes and wholes are different from the sum of their parts.
Mechanism: Relationships between parts are fixed, systems move smoothly from one equilibrium to another, and changes are reversible.	Systems might be mechanical, but they might also be deterministic yet not predictable or smooth because they are chaotic or simply very discontinuous. Systems can also be evolutionary.
Universalism: Diverse, complex phenomena are the result of underlying universal principles which are few in number and unchanging over time and space.	*Contextualism*: Phenomena are contingent upon a large number of factors particular to the time and place. Similar phenomena might well occur in different times and places due to widely different factors.
Objectivism: We can stand apart from what we are trying to understand.	*Subjectivism*: Systems cannot be understood apart from us and our activities, our values, and how we have known and hence acted upon systems in the past.
Monism: Our separate individual ways of understanding complex systems are merging into a coherent whole.	*Pluralism*: Complex systems can only be known through alternate patterns of thinking which are necessarily simplifications of reality. Different patterns are inherently incongruent.

am only addressing the metaphysical and epistemological premises, suppositions, or beliefs underlying the modern world view. These premises, however, are critically important for they determine the bounds of acceptable political discourse as well as the processes of public fact gathering, decision-making, and implementation.

Modernism destroys cultural and biological systems because of five closely interlinked metaphysical and epistemological premises that characterize Western thought. Labeling them with parallel "isms", they are atomism, mechanism, objectivism, universalism, and monism. These five philosophical suppositions address the nature of reality, how people fit into reality, how we can know, and the nature of knowledge. Today these beliefs are implicit to many arguments, but they are quite explicitly expressed in the works of nineteenth-century scientists and social philosophers. Most people now, including the vast majority of scientists, lose little sleep contemplating the ultimate nature of reality or how they think they know. Nevertheless, these key philosophical premises are unconsciously, implicitly, and eclectically invoked in arguments presented in both public and scientific occasions.

Furthermore these premises are implied in the arguments of academics, capitalists, environmentalists, and politicians with diverse and frequently opposing interests. A few people build arguments around these beliefs for strategic purposes, fully cognizant that they are inappropriate to the particular case for which they are utilizing them. This is because the suppositions are so widely embedded in Western institutions that they cannot be questioned. To question publicly these premises is to disempower oneself from effectively working in large organizations, serving as a scientific or technical expert, or publicly engaging in political discourse.

Atomism, mechanism, universalism, objectivism, and monism are not poor philosophical suppositions from which to reason. They have proven to be extremely productive for both Western science and other institutions. The problem is that these beliefs are embedded in our public discourse to the exclusion of other metaphysical and epistemological premises which are more appropriate for understanding the complexities of environmental systems and which are more supportive of cultural pluralism.

THE DOMINANT METAPHYSICAL AND EPISTEMOLOGICAL SUPPOSITIONS

Atomism is the premise that systems consist of parts that do not change and that systems can be thought of as the sum of their parts. This belief is usually traced to the Greek philosophers, especially Democritus who wrote in the fifth century B.C. Chemistry made rapid progress, after centuries of confusion as alchemy, by adhering strictly to the idea of atomism. Atoms in chemical reactions are thought merely to combine, and the compound is thought to be merely the sum of the parts even though entirely new properties emerge when the compound is formed. When reactions are reversed, we think of the atoms as unchanged. Since at least subdisciplines of all of the other natural sciences build upon the principles of chemistry, atomism has proven to be a very powerful metaphysical construct for understanding the natural world.

Atomism as a metaphysical premise has also been very influential in how we understand our social world. Western political philosophy, most notably that which is strongly rooted in the thinking of John Locke (1632–1704), has stressed the individual and characterized societies as the sum of their individuals. Democracy and atomism have been closely associated. Similarly, Western economic thought has stressed individual producers and consumers with supply and demand being the sum of their respective activities.

Atomism also serves us well at an operational level. It facilitates thinking about solving problems as a process of solving separate tasks which, when each is completed, results in the whole being solved. Postal services, for example, treat each letter as a separate problem, bag problems into postal zones, ship bags to separate locations, and so on until the job is done. Similarly, we think of economies as consisting of millions of people working on separate tasks which are connected within businesses and corporations and then through markets. Undertaking each separate task accomplishes the whole, the provision of goods and services. The problem, of course, is that some operations cannot be divided into separate tasks but must be undertaken simultaneously in close coordination. The heart surgeon, anesthesiologist, and staff maintaining and monitoring life supporting equipment must operate around an organic, not atomistic, paradigm.

Mechanism is the premise that the relations between the parts of a system do not change. Oxygen and hydrogen always combine in the same proportions under particular conditions to form water. The planets revolve around the sun, always in accordance with the principles of mechanics. Obviously for these two cases and many more in the natural world, our belief in mechanism is quite reasonable. Mechanical systems behave in a regular manner. Mechanical systems also have the special characteristic of reversibility. Changes can be unchanged; the system can always return to its original state with sufficient additional energy input. Once the regularities of a particular system are known, how the system responds is predictable. And once we can predict the effect of different changes, we can choose to impose the change that will have a desired effect.

The ability to predict and control is so closely tied to our beliefs about science that explanations which have few predictive qualities and hence do not empower people, theories of evolution being the most obvious example, are not thought of as being scientific even by a few, albeit older, philosophers of science.

Universalism is the belief that the parts of systems and the relations between the parts have an underlying nature which is the same everywhere and at all times. Equally importantly, the underlying nature of things and relations are thought to be interpretable by a relatively small number of universal principles. There are many examples where universalism holds. The laws of thermodynamics are few in number, universally true, and underlie and explain many processes. A few principles of chemistry are especially important and widely applicable. Through these principles we know that coal-fired electric generation plants operate the same around the world, with even their minor divergences due to ambient temperature differences explicable by the laws of thermodynamics and the principles of chemistry. Most processes designed by people, industrial processes especially, operate the same across time and space. Agriculture, of course, is an extremely important exception. Each crop variety is sensitive to the local characteristics of soils, climate, and pests – factors whose effects on agriculture cannot be explained by a few basic principles. Western agricultural scientists and industry experts, however, have strived to reduce this local sensitivity as much as possible by developing industrially produced inputs to override the natural factors and by developing crop varieties which respond to produced inputs. Thus universalism seems to be a common property at the level of basic physical processes but not for complex systems. Our belief in universalism, moreover, makes it a management goal in our interactions with more complex systems.

Objectivism is the belief that natural and social systems can be understood and acted upon objectively, as if people can understand and act and not be a part of the system they are understanding and changing. Science is about unchanging, real objects and the relations between them which can be known "objectively". Science addresses, for example, the qualities of insects and the relations between them. The knowledge acquired through science is not supposed to be tainted by our subjective feelings about creepy crawly things. Holding to objectivism, moreover, means the behavior of the insects is not thought to be affected by the presence or activities of the scientist studying them. Objectivism is a reasonable supposition for physics, though there are some notable difficulties even here, and becomes increasingly unrealistic as it becomes more difficult for the scientists to isolate themselves from the systems they are studying.

Objectivism includes the premise that it is possible to comprehend reality as if it did not include ourselves and that reality can be known independently of our values. Western science is widely believed to be objective in the sense that it is commonly thought to be only concerned with the facts about reality apart from how people value different things. When this supposed quality is extended to beliefs about the use of science in public decision-making, objectivism is frequently referred to as positivism. Of the five philosophical beliefs, objectivism or positivism is the only one which is explicitly invoked in public discourse today. It is typically invoked when a speaker wants to convince an audience that her or his arguments only deal with the facts and hence are immutable reality.

The belief that science is value-free and that reality can be understood as if people are apart from reality is very important to our Western conception of science. The belief makes some sense for the knowledge we have acquired of parts of systems under controlled laboratory conditions, but the belief loses its context when this knowledge is then put into practice under uncontrolled conditions beyond the laboratory. When people cannot be isolated from the system under study, this belief lacks even this initial footing as well as a basis in practice. And lastly, there is good reason to believe that our values affect our choice of patterns of thinking for interpreting systems. While this is especially so for the social sciences, there is good evidence for this in the natural sciences as well.

Monism is the belief that there is one best way of understanding systems. Alternatively, monism is the belief that there is only one best way for knowing any particular system and that the multiple ways of comprehending different systems fit, or will fit as science progresses, into a coherent whole of understanding. Monism denies the possibility of multiple right and contradictory answers stemming from alternative ways of thinking about the same problem. If there are alternative ways of thinking about something, at least the answers must be congruent. And if two paths of thinking result in different or incongruent answers, one path must be wrong or science has not progressed sufficiently for us to understand how they fit together. Monism as a premise is supported by the consistencies between much of physics, chemistry, and microbiology. But scientific debates over the complexities of social and environmental systems are frequently fueled by excessive belief in monism in areas where there is little evidence to support the premise.

Let me emphasize again that these metaphysical and epistemological premises proved extremely effective well into the twentieth century. Physics and chemistry were enormously successful in establishing the characteristics of basic units of nature and in determining universal relations between units. The biological sciences, including their application in agriculture, and the environmental sciences, including their application in engineering, have drawn heavily upon physics and chemistry. The use of this knowledge in the design of industrial processes and manufacture of products, in the manufacture of chemicals and machines to enhance agricultural productivity, and to produce ever more novel consumer goods has transformed the lives of almost everyone. Most of the technologies we use were developed through the aid of these philosophical premises.

These metaphysical and epistemological suppositions, however, are not well suited for thinking about complex systems, especially systems which include people. Yet they have become so embedded in the rules of Western political discourse and organizational behavior that alternative philosophical premises which would help us understand complex systems as well as support cultural pluralism have not been tolerated. How Western social rationality became so constrained and the implications of these constraints deserves further elaboration.

WESTERN SOCIAL RATIONALITY

Early Western scientists set out to understand a static world as God had created it. They envisioned the acquisition of knowledge as a process whereby individual minds investigated nature's parts, or atoms, and processes, or mechanics. The mind was thought of as an independent entity that perceives and interprets. Asking questions, thinking, and acting were thought neither to influence the underlying principles which govern nature nor to affect the mind itself. Like the mind, nature also just was. Thus people and the natural world were juxtaposed in the Western world view. The idea of objectivity stems from this static juxtaposition.

Scientific knowledge of atomistic parts and mechanistic relations could be used to develop technologies to adjust the relative numbers of the parts and the relative strengths of the relations. Through these adjustments, people could transform nature to have the properties and behave in a manner more consistent with desired objectives. Objectivism meant that human action did not change the underlying nature of parts or relations. With unchanging parts and relations, knowledge could be presumed to be universal over time. Furthermore, differences in natural and social systems across regions could also be thought of as differences in the proportions of parts and strengths of relations. Thus the idea of underlying universal truths could be maintained across diverse environments and cultures.

This atomistic-mechanistic view of knowledge and its use is illustrated in Figure 6.1. Note that this diagram is a simplification of Figure 4.1. The major difference is that the line of causation, the process of development in the earlier diagram, is looped back on itself. The barrier drawn between the changing proportions of the parts and strengths of the relations and the nature of the parts and relations is a key aspect of the epistemological stance. No such barrier, of course, exists between the reality from which we draw theories and design technologies and the reality we affect through our social organization and technologies.

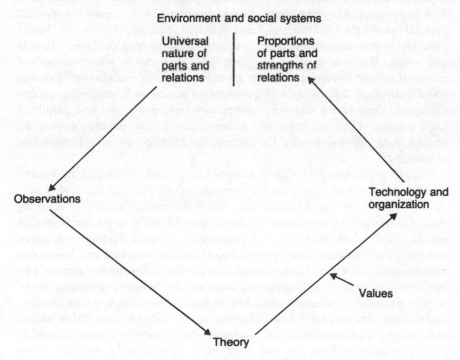

Figure 6.1 A Newtonian world view of science and action

The adoption of this metaphysical and epistemological stance in the public sphere traces up through many political philosophers and social movements. Certainly one of the stronger tracings stems from the positivist philosophy espoused by Auguste Comte between 1825 and 1850. Comte extended Newton's mechanical framework to social systems, stressed the importance of values but took them as given and apart from his framework. As a product of his times, his thinking complemented that of many others pursuing similar lines. Comte, however, was the most prolific and outspoken. He coined the terms positivism and sociology. He and his many followers truly believed that social systems could be understood by the methods of Western science, that the consequences of alternative courses of action could be predicted, and that people could then rationally choose between courses according to that which they valued most. He clearly envisioned that science, by serving the process of social decision-making, would free society from the irrationalities of established religions and the tyranny of arbitrary power. His philosophy of positivism integrated science and social processes and replaced existing religious authority and raw political power. Comte literally thought of positivism as a superior religion, one that could be more benevolent by effectively linking science, individual values, and social action.

The foregoing attributes of positivism shaped the modern world view. The process of adopting these views, however, was somewhat erratic. Natural scientists, technocrats, and market-oriented economists found positivist beliefs very compatible. It is interesting to note that while Comte and other Western intellectuals then and now have always espoused universal enlightenment, positivism gives the currently enlightened a special social authority. As the role of government in the industrializing nations expanded, drew upon scientific information and expertise, and patterned itself on the scientific approach, rational positivism reigned as implicit official state religion during the twentieth century much as Comte had envisioned.

Though positivism was eagerly accepted as a social philosophy by natural scientists, technocrats, and market-oriented economists, it has had a very stormy history within the social sciences themselves. Patterns of thinking that emphasized the importance of history and local context are rooted in beliefs which clash with rational positivism. Only a minority of social scientists today believe that facts and values can be separated and hence that rational positivism is an adequate basis for public philosophy. Since rational positivism is well institutionalized and widely believed publicly, social science patterns of thought, and hence social scientists working in their professional capacity, have little influence in governments. Natural scientists, technocrats, and neoclassical economists participate as professionals in public decision-making because they have more readily accepted these publicly dominant epistemological and metaphysical beliefs and reinforced them through their mode of participation. Change seems unlikely until other combinations of philosophical beliefs acquire sufficient public acceptance to compete with positivism.

Neoclassical economics as used in capitalist countries and the analogous optimization techniques used in socialist countries, both to guide and to rationalize public decision-making, epitomize the modern world view. Early economists explicitly acknowledged their philosophical debt to Isaac Newton while the mathematizers of economics – Cournot, Jevons, Pareto, and Walras – formalized economics along the mechanistic models of Newton. The neoclassical model is atomistic in the assumption that land, labor, and capital are separate components, like individual atoms. They are combined during the production of goods and services and are only related to each other through their relative values determined in exchange. Neoclassical economics is mechanistic in its assumption that economic systems can operate in equilibrium at any position along a continuum and move back and forth between positions. If more labor becomes available, the economic system adjusts so that more labor intensive goods are produced and are sold at lower prices relative to capital intensive goods, the returns to labor fall, and the returns to capital increase. If the quantity of labor returns to its previous level, the economy produces the previous mix of goods at the same prices and the earnings of labor and capital return to their previous levels. Economists, with few exceptions, construct atomistic-mechanistic models of economies characterized by a range of stable equilibria and the reversibility of system changes.

Thus economics incorporated atomism and mechanism, the two most productive assumptions of Western natural science. The parts of the economy as well as the relations between the parts do not change their characteristics. The only thing that changes in the basic economic world view is the relative numbers of different parts and the relative strengths of different relations. The imaginary barrier of Figure 6.1 is clearly in place. The economists' knowledge of the economic system can be used to change the relative numbers and strengths in order to make it behave in a manner better suited to our objective values without changing the characteristics of the parts and relations themselves. Under this construct, the theories of economics about the parts and relations still hold even after using the theories to intervene in the economy.

Partly because these metaphysical and epistemological beliefs were especially productive for science during the later nineteenth and early twentieth centuries, the public became thoroughly enamored of science and the ways in which science seemed to insure progress. This public support led governments to promote science actively. And along with this came the adoption of scientific procedures and criteria in administrative decision-making. It was quite natural that the metaphysical and epistemological beliefs widely held at the time by scientists and the public became tightly embedded in our public institutions. These beliefs, however, now underlie many of the crises of modernism.

WESTERN PUBLIC RATIONALITY AND THE CRISES OF MODERNISM

The five metaphysical and epistemological beliefs underlying modern rationality are rarely the basis for thought and action by individuals, families, and small groups. Today, the most innovative scientists and most successful entrepreneurs do not rely solely on these premises. Yet these suppositions are the only ones which are *publicly* held acceptable for use in *public* discourse and decision-making. The challenges of sustained human interaction with the biosphere require a public response. But arguments for environmental action that are rooted in other philosophical premises are weeded out of the public dialogue. Recreating an understanding of society that is greater than the sum of its individuals and re-imaging the future so that we do not all end up as identical, inhuman consumers choking in a polluted world requires a new public response. Let me argue that we have failed to respond adequately to date because the five publicly held philosophical postulates underlying modernism are inappropriate to the task.

By publicly agreeing to atomism, we accept that problems can be divided into parts. We have become so effective at dividing and conquering that problems that can be treated in this manner are no longer problems. For this reason, the critical problems that dominate the agenda of modernism today do not have the property of separability. Affluence, environmental degradation, and the health problems of the industrial countries must be understood as one problem. Global climate change, acid rain, and the accumulation of toxics cannot be treated apart from the high rates of use of energy and materials for industrial production and transport associated with Western opulence. Similarly poverty and environmental degradation in the poor countries must be seen as one problem. Poverty cannot be solved without better environmental management and better environmental management cannot be attained without the managers of the land receiving a fair return. Whole systems must be addressed. But our public belief in atomism legitimates the position of those who argue that fixing the parts is sufficient as well as the position of those who argue that fixing the parts has not been effective in the past and that thus nothing can be done.

By publicly agreeing to mechanism, we accept as a basic premise that it is possible to predict how systems will respond to different stimuli and hence to make them behave as we see fit. But we repeatedly delude ourselves when we act on the premise that ecosystems and societies are analogous to mechanical systems. Our remedies do not lead to new equilibrium solutions we prefer. On the contrary, new problems with new relationships between

70

them evolve with every step we take. Automobiles solved the problems of horse transportation, but brand new, unforeseen problems – rapid urban growth, freeways, the loss of community, air pollution, spills from oil tankers, and global climate change – with complicated relationships between them evolved to take the place of the old problems and relationships.

The consequences of mechanistic premises when dealing with systems which are better understood as coevolving deserves elaboration. In the case of pest control, for example, the mechanical world view simply has insecticides reducing the population of insects to a preferred new equilibrium level. The coevolutionary perspective, however, also alerts us to the fact that the pesticide exerts selective pressure on the insect population. Those individual insects which are more resistant to the insecticide are more likely to survive and have offspring. Since insects have offspring frequently, resistance to the insecticide develops within the population remarkably quickly. The evolution of resistance, in turn, results in selective pressure against the original insecticide in favor of new insecticides for which this population of insects has not yet acquired resistance. The coevolutionary process can go back and forth without reaching an equilibrium. The mechanical view gives the impression that the insecticide provides an easy solution. The coevolutionary view indicates that the use of insecticides will change the path of coevolution in a manner which may be better, but may be worse.

The destruction of cultural systems is also facilitated through overdependence on a mechanical world view. When new technologies, values, types of knowledge, and ways of organizing are accepted by or imposed on cultures, the mechanical view of cultures assumes simply that a new cultural equilibrium will be reached. The original traits and relationships that define the culture are presumed to remain intact after a new introduction, only the relative frequency of the traits and strengths of the relationships are presumed to change. From a coevolutionary perspective, however, one expects that some aspects of the culture will be selected out and driven to extinction and that underlying cultural relationships will be forever changed. Cultural systems are always evolving, of course, but if changes are introduced with the expectations generated by a mechanical understanding of systems, the rate of cultural change will be faster and the types of changes will in fact be quite unexpected.

The process of cultural transformation is also illustrative. Consider the introduction of a fertilizer-responsive rice into a traditional culture. From the mechanical perspective, this is seen simply as an additional technical option among those available to farmers. Old varieties are presumed always to exist. A socially enlightened mechanical view accepts that the adoption of the responsive rice will depend on social organization and cultural values. The mechanical world view, however, does not foresee that if the new rice is adopted that it will select in favor of the form of social organization that is most favorable to it. For example, a fertilizer-responsive rice requires the purchase of fertilizer. This fact favors those who plant for the market over those who plant for subsistence. Thus the introduction of the new rice creates the situation where a coevolution process favors market social organization and the supporting individualist values.

To be sure, good things as well as bad have not been foreseen in the past from the mechanistic perspective. Yet the bad at the end of the twentieth century look bad indeed. I contend that the process of delusion illustrated above is occurring repeatedly across the spectrum of public decisions, to the extent that this, among other philosophical explanations, is a significant "cause" of the crises of modernism. Given the consequences of global climate change and the loss of biodiversity as well as our renewed interest in the importance of maintaining cultural systems and diversity, it seems unduly risky to speed ahead with only the mechanical world view to guide us in public decisions.

The errors generated by assuming mechanism are compounded by assuming objectivism. People and how they think, organize, and value things are clearly a part of the coevolutionary process in both of the foregoing examples. People's mechanical perception of insect control and of the introduction of a new rice variety is obviously critical to the coevolutionary path that is initiated in each case. Changes in technical options on the farm select for social organization and values as the coevolutionary process unfolds. To premise that people are apart from the natural processes they seek to modify is to put on a blindfold voluntarily.

To assume atomism and mechanism is to assume the existence of the barrier in Figure 6.1, which somehow isolates the reality on which we derive our knowledge from the reality on which we act. The existence of this imaginary barrier in our public understanding of science and its absence in reality provides an epistemological explanation of why development has been unsustainable. Action changes the nature of parts and relations, typically in an irreversible manner. The introduction of totally new parts – agrichemicals and industrial wastes into ecosystems and televisions and fax machines into social systems – create brand new relations. Basing action on science girded by false beliefs in universals, in unchanging parts and relations, continually results in "unforeseen" changes in social and environmental systems. Thus the unsustainability of past development has an epistemological explanation.

By publicly agreeing to universalism, we also accept that phenomena in widely different places and times can be understood through the application of a few simple principles. To the extent that universal principles do apply, then problems, once these principles are known, are not complex or difficult to solve. Furthermore, since the principles are universally true, explanations can be determined and solutions devised from afar. Being close to a system, such as an agroecosystem or a group of traditional peoples, and knowing intimate details has no special advantage for if scientific principles are universal and few in number only a few critical facts must be known. Thus universalism, or at least belief in universalism, promotes management from afar, centralization, and large-scale, factory-like operations with many laborers and few who monitor, think, and manage. Of course, to the extent universalism is inappropriate but we erroneously think it is appropriate, mistakes are made.

By publicly agreeing to monism, we end up arbitrarily throwing out answers which conflict with established knowledge but which may be just as good and reliable. Different ways of understanding complex systems yield different insights. But if we publicly believe that there is only one best way of understanding any given system, then the understanding that can be gained from multiple insights is forgone. Alternative lines of reasoning utilizing different types of information are eliminated from the rational calculus of technocratic agencies when they prove incongruent with dominant patterns and premises. At the level of political discourse, a greater diversity of arguments is entertained. But the work of politicians has been reduced, due to our limited vision of the role of politics, by passing problems on to agencies delegated to resolve problems scientifically. The paucity of ways of understanding at this level leads us to make mistakes which could have been foreseen and prevented.

By publicly agreeing to monism we have no public basis for utilizing the knowledge of other cultures. Acupuncture, for example, has been used effectively in Asia for centuries. Because this knowledge is inconsistent with Western medical understanding, its practice has been severely restricted in the West until relatively recently. Acupuncture is still largely unavailable in hospitals because the management of hospitals is dominated by Western doctors. Last but not least, by publicly agreeing to monism we are unable to look upon cultures with different knowledge systems as equals. This disrespect for other cultures hastens cultural narrowing.

CONCLUSIONS

The characteristics of our environmental difficulties have been identified differently by biologists, climatologists, demographers, economists, geologists, and on through the alphabet. While each of their explanations provides insight, each fails to identify how progress driven by science has gone astray. The metaphysical and epistemological suppositions of the modern world view explain the environmental side of the betrayal quite simply. They are common to most disciplines. Furthermore, these same beliefs underlie the cultural destruction associated with modernism.

In Chapter 5 on the idea of progress, I argued that people developed excessive expectations for Western science with respect to the possibilities for designing rational social systems. Our inability to meet these expectations is also rooted in our excessive reliance on particular metaphysical and epistemological premises which are inappropriate for understanding complex systems, especially complex systems with the "understander" inside of them. A more appropriate cosmology is elaborated in Chapter 9. But first we have a chapter on the problems of deterministic thinking and then a chapter further elaborating the coevolutionary process.

7

TWO MALADAPTIVE
DETERMINISMS

Our theories . . . are rays of light, which illuminate a part of the target, leaving the rest in darkness. . . . It is obvious that a theory which is to perform this function satisfactorily must be well chosen; otherwise it will illumine the wrong things. Further, since it is a changing world that we are studying, a theory which illumines the right things at one time may illumine the wrong things at another.

(John R. Hicks 1981: 232)

Western understanding has been greatly enriched by the myriad of details uncovered through the advance of the separate disciplines of Western science. We know far more than our forbears knew about the decay rate of different nuclear wastes, the opportunities to transform solar radiation into electricity, how pesticide resistance develops among malaria-bearing mosquitoes, and how to develop new medicines. We also know more about how social and economic systems work, though the rate of their evolution means that much of this knowledge is obsolete soon after we have grasped it. The issue at this point, however, is that the details of our separate knowledges do not fit into a coherent understanding of how people relate to nature and how this relationship can be improved. A more integrated understanding is necessarily imbedded in our thinking as we make personal, day-to-day decisions and is absolutely essential when we make public decisions about whether to invest in solar or nuclear power technologies or chemical or ecological agricultural technologies. While science has progressed dramatically with respect to details, it has progressed little at an integrated level of understanding, and for such understanding, we still rely on other ways of knowing.

Among those other ways of knowing, people typically fall into one of two categories when pondering the complexities of our relation to nature and their implications for action. People in the first category rely on the supposition that environmental factors ultimately determine what people can and cannot do. People in this group, the environmental determinists, emphasize the individual facts we have learned about nature by studying it apart from people. Taking nature as "given and fixed", they argue that people must learn to conform to her laws. They cite all of the surprising and unfortunate side effects of our attempts to manipulate nature as evidence of their position. People in the second group assume we are learning how to manipulate nature to do our will and that any problems we experience in doing so today will be overcome by the advance of science sufficiently soon to avoid any ultimate catastrophes. People in this group, the cultural determinists, cite the long history of successful technologies, the corresponding improvements experienced in the well-being of people in the industrial nations, and our ability to overcome problems thus far.

Cultural determinists certainly have more faith in progress than environmental determinists. Historically, however, even environmental determinists had high hopes. Some think rapid progress through broader use of science is our only hope. Environmental determinists see, of course, a different sort of progress, a different interpretation of science, as necessary to our survival. Thus belief in progress through Western science is not the fundamental nature of this division in thinking, hence this additional chapter. From a coevolutionary perspective, both of these determinisms are too simple, together they explain and justify everything and nothing, while their juxtaposition has resulted in a stalemate in Western, and now global, thinking.

HISTORICAL BACKGROUND

Environmental determinists have emphasized that particular environments force people to behave in predetermined ways and that people are similar in comparable environments. Cultural determinists have argued roughly the opposite, that people transform, and thereby determine, their environments and that cultures are surprisingly varied within similar environments. While many scholars have tried to synthesize the two lines of reasoning into a more sophisticated explanation of the relationships between people and their environment, members of each school of thought have had a strong proclivity toward their respective simple, extreme positions. Environmental problems continue to accumulate in part because of the effort wasted in unproductive battles between these two positions.

Europeans were fascinated by the variety of peoples and environments they began to "discover" in the fifteenth century and colonized thereafter. They readily observed that some patterns of behavior and forms of social organization were peculiar to particular environments. Indeed, explorers, conquerors, and traders from earlier dominant groups had made similar observations for millennia. Cold climates required people to protect themselves from the cold. Dry climates required people to protect and ration water. Mountainous environments made trade difficult even between adjacent villages, while marine environments facilitated trade between continents.

Fertile valleys support dense populations and hierarchical social orders. Sterile deserts do not. These environmental factors are given and determine culture.

From these simple observations, more elaborate explanations developed. The demands of the environment on individuals led to social organization that complemented adaptive individual behavior. And the physical and biological phenomena that determined how individuals behave and how societies organize then directly influenced the development of the personalities of individuals and cultural traits of societies. For example, those tropical environments which were relatively benign and biologically complex were thought to encourage individual ingenuity and a social order that facilitated specialization. Harsh climates induced both individual hardiness and social structures that encouraged saving and sharing. Highly productive environments supporting dense populations also favored individual tolerance for living closely with others. Surplus production favored the rise of class-based societies with disparate work loads and wealth. Ease of travel promoted entrepreneurial talents and social organization that facilitated the accumulation of commercial capital and trade. For centuries, people have readily found convincing empirical support for environmental determinism. Some things clearly are determined by the environment, and the extensions of the obvious have strong intuitive appeal. And yet clearly much of the evidence comes from selectively observing a very complex world.

Cultural determinism, in contrast, is rooted more in people's understanding of history as well as in geographical observation. Advances in technology, while slower in ages past, were well documented. People knew that they had more control over their environment than their distant ancestors. Tree stumps where there were no longer trees and other indicators of past environments also provided strong evidence that people determined their environments and that cultures developed independently of environmental factors. Cross-cultural evidence, or geography, also bolstered the argument. The daily activities of Europeans differed dramatically from those of American Indians even though the natural environments of the two groups were surprisingly similar. They differed because their cultures, including their knowledge and technology, led them to do different things. The people of Java, the Congo, and the Amazon lived very different lives even though they all lived in tropical rainforests. More importantly, the Javanese completely transformed their environment to intricately terraced rice paddies. And the complex social order, finely tuned behavior, and highly developed art of Java are completely different from the order, behavior, and art of the Amazon or Congo. Thus culture is culturally determined and imprints on the environment.

Both environmental and cultural determinism are pervasive in modern thinking, albeit mostly in their more tempered forms. Environmental possibilism, one of the moderated versions, argues that the environment does not exactly determine behavior and culture, but it does determine the range of possible behaviors and cultures. The environment rules out some activities and requires others, and this results in much commonality in individual behavior and in cultures across similar environments even while other features vary. The nature of the environment does not determine everything. Environmental probalists argue that while anything may be possible, some behavioral and cultural characteristics are much more probable depending on the environment. Both of these softer positions still argue that the paths of causation go in one direction, or are far more important in one direction, than in the other. Neither school of thought recognizes and emphasizes the complex maze of reciprocal causation between environment and culture.

AN IDEOLOGICAL DEADLOCK

The two opposing determinisms are maladaptive. As set and separate patterns of thought, they obscure our understanding of the current human predicament more than they help. The continued separateness of these understandings and the way in which the debate between the adherents of these two schools of thought has evolved has closed off further evolution in our understanding.

Each determinism is in many ways correct since causation clearly runs as each school indicates, because it runs both ways. Both being correct would not be a problem if the adherents to each were not so determined to be protagonists, each endlessly defending their position and refusing to acknowledge the validity of the other. Donella and Dennis Meadows, for example, argued "The Limits to Growth" in the early 1970s by constructing a systems model which was largely environmentally deterministic. Cultural determinists counter-argued that the supposed limits would easily be breached if the model had been constructed with sufficient learning, technological innovation, and market feedbacks to encourage substitution to new materials. Neither side conceded the validity of the other's arguments, they never joined forces, and no one built a better model to explore the policy implications of a more sophisticated point of view. As a consequence, very little learning occurred.

Cultural determinists were also enraged, and to some extent rightly so, when Konrad Lorenz in the 1960s and E. O. Wilson in the 1970s argued that behavioral and sociological traits in species, including humans, are genetically encoded and become dominant through natural selection. To argue that behavior and social organization are the way they are because they proved fit and that they are genetically encoded and unchangeable over generations contradicts our Western sense of free will and of individual and social responsibility. The sociobiology debate stimulated both Lorenz and Wilson to develop coevolutionary syntheses of the reciprocal selection processes between culture and genetic traits. Nevertheless, the protagonists have, to this day, kept right on attacking Lorenz's and Wilson's initial explorations, failing to acknowledge that these same scholars subsequently developed resolutions to the debate. Once again the rigidity of the positions of most participants has prevented further research and the discourse from proceeding toward more sophisticated understanding.

Cultural determinists have also stimulated the rage of environmental determinists. Julian Simon, for example, argued in his "The Ultimate Resource" that our ability to think has resulted in better and better interactions with our environment. Since the advances in knowledge uncovered by one person can be used by all, having more thinking people on the earth will result in even faster improvements. Simon, of course, was updating the Western idea of progress with a pronatal twist and extrapolating past successes across all peoples and out into the future. Environmental determinists quickly responded that Simon's scenario entailed great leaps of faith and unlimited energy from unidentified sources with no mention of how their side-effects were to be managed.

While social scientists have resisted all tyranny by natural law, natural scientists are split. Some constantly remind us of resource and environmental limits. Others see technology overcoming practical limits for some time to come. Respected scientists in each camp have vehemently claimed that their arguments are scientific and that charlatans in the other camp are purveying "hogwash". The debate has stifled the development of social norms, environmental laws, and administrative regulations.

Within the general realm of environmental determinism, two other distinct maladaptive determinisms lurk: mechanistic determinism and entropic determinism. These two patterns of thought also impede the acceptance of new ways of understanding and in particular a coevolutionary way of understanding. Mechanistic determinism is rooted in an atomistic-mechanistic interpretation of the natural world. Entropic determinism follows from a misinterpretation of the second law of thermodynamics. These are explored in the bibliographic essay to this chapter.

CONCLUSIONS

It is unproductive to debate over whether cultural determinism or environmental determinism is correct, to argue over whether "natural science is making anything possible" or "the world will go to hell in a hand basket if we do not obey nature's law", or even if we do. But the importance of these patterns of thought as separate views cannot be overemphasized. The deep antagonism between the schools should not be dismissed as silly from the coevolutionary vantage. The division and hostility between these positions document that questions of environment, resources, and development over the long run clearly need a new frame in which a new consensus can emerge, one which I hope will use both Western and indigenous knowledges more fully. The deadlock between these ideologies has prevented the political mobilization necessary to set out on a new course. We need to move beyond these deadlocks.

It is probably very important to keep in mind that the debates between academics of alternative mechanistic-deterministic mindsets are not purely differences in how individuals think but are the result of how differences are reinforced within cultures, especially intellectual communities. The identity of most academics is predominantly with respect to the beliefs of those within the discipline he or she was trained and continues to associate. Few academics participate extensively in other communities in which the dominant epistemological beliefs are different from their own. Academics are rarely exposed to alternative intellectual cultures thriving on their very own campuses due to the disciplinary structure of modern universities. Hence when they do encounter well-stated arguments from a different mindset, especially when it is receiving public attention, they deny that it is scientific. The ferocity of their reaction reflects the threat other ways of thinking pose to their own sense of identity. Academics, of course, represent the extreme, but all socialized peoples garner a sense of identity in the particular ways in which they were socialized. Formal education, of course, is the dominant socialization of modernity. Less disciplinary socialization would certainly help.

The conflicts between environmental and cultural determinism are resolved very simply by interpreting social and ecological systems as the outcome of a coevolutionary process. But the coevolutionary view I develop in this book is certainly not the first attempt at a synthesis.

8

THE COEVOLUTIONARY
PROCESS ELABORATED

Thinking of the changes in social and environmental systems over time as a process of coevolution acknowledges that cultures affect which environmental features prove fit and that environments affect which cultural features prove fit. In this sense, coevolution accepts both environmental determinism and cultural determinism while recasting them as a selection process. Merely accepting both lines of causation eliminates the worst of the maladaptive characteristics of the two deterministic schools of thought.

The coevolutionary explanation of change, however, goes beyond interactive determinism. As an evolutionary theory, it builds on the idea that species and other system components have a variety of traits that are context-specific and change over time rather than some supposed universal characteristics. The distribution of traits, moreover, does not reproduce itself perfectly. Imperfect DNA replication results in new traits in biological species, most of which do not prove fit, but a few of which do. Furthermore, the distribution of traits can become more diverse through introductions of new traits through migration of individuals from other areas and less diverse through extinctions. And the relative dominance of any particular trait is constantly changing according to changing criteria of fitness which, in turn, depend on the relative dominance of the characteristics of other system components. For these reasons, coevolutionary thinking is really different from cause and effect or deterministic thinking. Those who must think deterministically even to begin to understand the coevolutionary process might first simply think of several deterministic processes with mutual feedbacks, both positive and negative, between the components, and then expand this simple model to include statistical or random properties, the introduction of new components, a hierarchical nature, and regional contextuality.

While accepting the possibility of processes being coevolutionary circumvents the maladaptive determinisms discussed in the last chapter, it raises new problems. As a different pattern of thinking, it stimulates new questions and answers. Disappointment awaits those who insist that the old questions are the ones that must still be answered, or that the answers must indicate which preconceived line of thinking is correct. Only new questions, new insights, possibly new answers, and certainly new directions of query are indicated.

COEVOLUTIONARY EXPLANATIONS

The terms to coevolve and coevolution refer to an ongoing positive feedback between components of evolving systems. A digression on the term "feedback" as it has been used since the development of cybernetics is appropriate at this point. We are accustomed to negative-feedback systems. The most popular example is that of a room thermostat which sends a signal to the furnace to turn on when the room cools down and, when the furnace warms the room to the desired temperature, it sends a signal to the furnace to turn off. Negative feedbacks keep systems in equilibrium. The thermostat informs the furnace how to keep the room at a constant temperature. The mechanical models of the Newtonian world view, including those of neoclassical economics, must have negative feedbacks so that when a change occurs the models find a new equilibrium.

Now imagine what would happen if the thermostat gives the opposite signal. Imagine that as the room warms up, the thermostat directs the furnace to put out even more heat. Then as the room becomes hotter and hotter, the furnace roars ever more effectively, the room becomes hotter and hotter while the thermostat continues to inform the furnace to try even harder. This would be a positive feedback. Positive feedbacks are self-amplifying, explosively driving some variable in the model to infinity or implosively to zero. Thus, just as negative feedbacks bring systems into equilibrium, positive feedbacks lead to disequilibrium. As thinkers and designers, systems that either "blow up" or "pop" are disturbing, hence we avoid systems with positive feedbacks like the plague. Negative-feedback mechanical systems facilitate prediction and prescription, thereby empowering their users, like neoclassical economists, with a special authority. And yet, as convenient as negative-feedback models are for understanding and design, the natural and social processes and their interactions that we observe clearly do not lead to equilibrium conditions. New identifiable states of nature and society arise and yet keep on changing, but only rarely blow up or pop. Such ongoing change in isolated systems, or of systems which are under a nearly constant influence from an outside force such as the sun, can only be explained in terms of positive feedbacks. Coevolutionary processes can go on indefinitely because they have this positive feedback feature though coevolving systems may also reach equilibria.

Simple cause-and-effect relationships require an external cause to get an effect. Mechanical systems consisting of many cause-and-effect relationships which work in negative feedback also need an external cause to initiate change. When an external cause initiates change, the change occurs and stops. In a single relationship, the effect occurs. In mechanical systems, a single external cause perturbs the system and then it returns to its old equilibrium, while an ongoing external change will shift it to a new equilibrium. In each case, renewed change can only occur with a new external, or exogenous, cause. The dependence of simple cause and effect and mechanical systems on exogenous causes can be pretty limiting. When ecosystems are defined to include all of the interesting variables, from where else can causes arise to instigate mechanistic change? When changes in the system, rather than the nature of its structure or a particular state of the system are of interest, one does not want to always appeal to external forces for an explanation. Indeed, such explanations are not explanations at all. While Newtonian thinking has helped us understand systems and change, it has some obvious limitations with respect to understanding the ongoing, nonequilibrium changes we observe with no apparent direction by an external force. Indeed, mechanistic framings have led researchers to try to correlate changes in the sun's radiation with diverse events on earth. Coevolutionary models of systems, on the other hand, can readily be thought of as providing their own change from within, or endogenously.

On rereading Darwin, one finds clear evidence that he was well aware that the evolutionary changes of species are affected by the characteristics of other species as much as by the characteristics of the physical environment. Nevertheless, the simple explanation of the evolutionary process that species ever so gradually evolve to better fit a niche within a fixed physical environment dominates our public understanding. In this rendition, the evolutionary process is slow and directional. The emphasis on the gradual and slow rate of evolution is hard to explain in retrospect. The paleontologists uncovering the fossil record certainly had a geologist's sense of time, the cumulative changes they observed at the time seemed to be small given the overall periods of time involved, hence on *average* they were slow. And since no one had seen evolution in their lifetime, the process must have been slow. The directionality of evolution was clear since the physical niche is given. The gradualist explanation has been so effective in conveying the idea of evolution in the classroom and to the public generally that it has overridden our deeper understandings of the process. This common, simple explanation rules to such an extent that biologists themselves sometimes have to be reminded that our understanding of evolution was always more complex and has also evolved dramatically over the past three decades.

When species evolve in response to changes in each other rather than a predetermined physical niche, all evolutionary direction is lost. Furthermore, when the selective forces themselves change, evolution and extinction are likely to occur at very uneven rates. Thus the dominant view among evolutionary theorists now is that groups of interacting species, at different times and places, have periods during which they share many characteristics which fit together. During these periods when traits have evolved such that they can be thought of as, metaphorically speaking, locked together, evolutionary change is slow. Locked together, the characteristics of each species in the group reflects the characteristics of the other species in the group. When locked, evolutionary change continues slowly. Periods of rapid evolution among a group of species, and changes in the composition of the group, can be initiated by the introduction of a genetic trait or species from another area or by a mutation in one species which proves fit. As the group becomes "unlocked", criteria for fitness change significantly, and with new selection criteria, evolution can occur more rapidly. Whatever the source, the new fit characteristic of species, or the loss of characteristics or whole species, puts new selective pressures on the other species. When these new selective pressures are sufficient that they unlock the interactive fitness of the group, evolutionary change can be fast. Thus evolution is now thought of as occurring at widely varying rates, and sometimes quite quickly.

With more emphasis on coevolutionary processes, the directionality of evolution is no longer determined by a steady advance toward perfect fitness with an unchanging environment. Species are no longer thought to get better and better at anything. And contrary to the publicly held understanding, changes in the physical environment are important explanatory variables in evolutionary history. The ash from volcanoes or the dust raised by a crashing meteor is thought to have darkened the sky and induced a climate change that led to the extinction of dinosaurs. At various times of the world's biological history, species numbers have declined significantly, and it was usually the more complex species that suffered the most. The popular association of evolution and progress, due no doubt to the relative late arrival of people as well as the tendency of recent peoples to equate history with progress, is not substantiated by the historical record using numeric criteria, and certainly not from the subjective vantage of dinosaurs.

Though both ecology and evolution arose out of what was known as natural history in the last century, they specialized along separate paths for much of this century. Evolutionary thought became dominated by advances in our knowledge of genetics beginning in the 1920s, while ecology retained strong ties to field investigations and a desire to understand whole systems. The time periods with which the two disciplines work can also be wildly different. With the rise of coevolutionary thinking, however, the two disciplines are sharing more common ground. Coevolution explains how the relations between species which make up ecosystems evolve while the interactions between species within ecosystems explains which selective forces are affecting the evolution of each species. This complementarity means that our comprehension of evolution is becoming intimately tied to our understanding of ecology.

Ecological thinking focuses on the interactions of species within ecosystems. In some cases, geographical features define ecosystems. Oceans define terrestrial island ecosystems. But to a large extent, an ecosystem is a mental construct of the discipline. Ecosystem boundaries vary depending on whether one is studying microbes, ants, or elephants even when they are all in the same geographic region. Ecologists think of the globe as a patchwork quilt of ecosystems or as a hierarchical patchwork of ecosystems given how boundaries are affected by the particular species or variable of interest. Thus it is typically less than discreet to ask an ecological researcher or practitioner where she or he thinks one ecosystem ends and another begins.

For the same reasons that ecosystems are ultimately ill-defined, the boundaries of the coevolutionary process cannot be predetermined. The mutual selection processes between particular flowers and hummingbirds can clearly be very important and sufficient to explain many features of the two. These selection processes are certainly more important than those between, for example, soil microbes and hummingbirds. Yet if the flower is coevolving with the soil microbes, the hummingbird is probably also to some extent as well and this process, for some trait, may prove critical. Other definitional problems abound. Birds which winter in habitats far from those in which they spend their summers can affect the evolutionary course of species within two ecosystems. But since the bird is a product of both ecosystems, are not the distant ecosystems themselves in some sense coevolving? Time may affect the definition of the boundaries of analysis as well. Islands are easily thought of as ecosystems in which coevolution occurs. The introduction of species from beyond the island, even if a rare event in the coevolutionary process, forces a wider boundary when longer time periods are being considered. The boundary problem is not trivial, and there are no perfect ways of contending with it.

I have repeatedly stressed in earlier chapters that while mechanical mental constructs of reality assume independent, unchanging parts and fixed relations between them, coevolutionary constructs assume evolving parts and relations. The foregoing discussion of coevolutionary explanations adds the following key concepts. First, coevolution explains how species in ecosystems so obviously fit together without having been designed. Second, mechanical models of systems incorporate negative feedbacks which bring the system back to equilibrium after a change while coevolving systems can keep on changing. Third, coevolving systems need no external driving mechanism. And fourth, the boundaries of coevolutionary systems are inherently more difficult to stipulate because parts and relations are co-evolving and changing their boundaries. In addition, different time scales are important for different clusters of species due to widely different reproductive periods and hence possible rates of coevolution.

THE GENETICS OF THE COEVOLUTIONARY PROCESS

From simple amoebae to complex vertebrates, life is largely a process of maintaining order, of maintaining the processes of life and the characteristics of particular species. This order is encoded as information in the arrangement of the bases of DNA molecules. Single-celled organisms and tissue cells in higher organisms replicate by a process whereby paired chains in the DNA molecule split, reform their paired parts, and provide the information necessary for reconstructing the characteristics of new cells. Individual cells form and die, but the cell's order lives on and the orderly processes provided by each cell type continue. Similarly, individuals die but species live on through the sexual reproduction of individuals.

Ironically, out of this process of maintaining order, the process of coevolutionary change arises. Within any given population of interbreeding individuals of a species, there are variations in genetic characteristics, or genotypes. The gene pool of a population is the size and distribution, or relative frequency, of different genotypes of these interbreeding individuals. The frequency of genotypes within a gene pool is determined by biological and physical selective pressures which affect the likelihood of survival of offspring of different genotypes. Since these selective pressures themselves change, the gene pool is constantly changing. The fitness of individuals with different genetic characteristics among closely coevolving species is constantly redefined as each species evolves new characteristics and applies new selection criteria on the others. Species are constantly finding that their niche is becoming more or less competitive or more or less complementary according to changes in species with which they associate. Long-term changes in climate also slowly select for individuals that can cope with different temperature and humidity and the associated changes in biota or who can migrate to more suitable climates. Most of this constant adjustment favors individuals with genetic characteristics already represented in the gene pool of the species.

The gene pool of a species, however, also diversifies independently. Mutations occur through imperfect DNA replication and DNA damage. A small proportion of these mutations eventually prove fit by facilitating the functioning of the organism within its existing niche, within existing selection criteria, allowing it to expand its numbers or to change to a more advantageous niche. In turn, fit mutations within one species change the selective pressures on other species and affect their evolutionary course. The gene pool of a particular population of a species can also diversify through the introduction of genes brought with individuals who migrate from other populations and thereby affect the species' evolutionary course and that of other species with which it coevolves. The repercussions are unending, perhaps dampened, and perhaps not, as they circle outward from the instigating change.

Our understanding of coevolution is deeply rooted in our understanding of genetics. For this reason for many individuals, evolutionary processes are genetic processes. Much of the reaction against sociobiology was rooted in this sense of inseparability between evolution and genetics. Evolutionary and coevolutionary models, or patterns of thinking, however, need not be limited to biology any more than Newtonian mechanical patterns of thinking need be limited to the motions of the planets around the sun. Sociobiologists advanced the idea that cultural systems had units analogous to genetic traits which were passed from generation to generation so long as they were not selected out. Opponents laughed at the idea, arguing that cultures had nothing like genes at all. To their way of thinking, genes were real; the supposed analogs in cultures were products of the imagination. Their arguments are nonsense. And the best way to point this out is to note that the idea of genes is a mental construct which has changed dramatically over time. In a final one sentence summary of the history of the gene to 1966, E. A. Carlson notes:

> The gene has been considered to be an undefined unit, a unit-character, a unit factor, a factor, an abstract point on a recombination map, a three-dimensional segment of an anaphase chromosome, a linear segment of an interphase chromosome, a sac of genomere, a series of linear sub-genes, a spherical unit defined by target theory, a dynamic functional quantity of one specific unit, a pseudoallele, a specific chromosome segment subject to a position effect, a rearrangement within a continuous chromosome molecule, a cistron within which fine structure can be demonstrated, and a linear segment of nucleic acid specifying a structural or regulatory product.
> (E. A. Carlson 1966, quoted in Burian 1985)

The fact that we have not known, and to some extent still do not know, what genes "really" are, however, neither prevented the rise of the formal discipline of genetics in academe nor kept the extensive use of the term in biological discourse from being extremely effective in enhancing our understanding of how the distribution of traits are passed from generation to generation and how the distribution changes. Genes are no more or less real or, apparently, definable than types of ways of valuing, ways of knowing, ways of organizing or ways of doing things. The coevolutionary pattern of thinking is a mental construct whose application can be broadened.

THE ROLE OF PERCEIVING, LEARNING, AND UNDERSTANDING

Let me stress again that evolutionary thinking has been constrained as much as aided by our understanding of genetics. Within genetics, much of the early research was conducted with fruit flies and other species which breed quickly. As a consequence, one shortcoming has been that behavior, especially informed behavior, had not been incorporated into our understanding of biological evolution before the sociobiology debate that began in the 1970s. Animals perceive, learn, and understand. The sensory systems of even the most simple animals enable them to recognize different stimuli. Similarly, the brains of even the less developed species deduce cause and effect and extrapolate experience to new situations. Furthermore, Western thought on thinking has emphasized formal knowledge and neglected the innate and informal. For these reasons, little attention has been given to perceiving, learning, and understanding among other species and their role in evolution. Only a few evolutionists have given much consideration to the interplay between minds and nature in the evolutionary process. We have emphasized fitness in the context of a slowly changing physical environment, and more recently in the context of a coevolving biological system. But we have not given sufficient attention to how perceiving, learning, and knowing have been intertwined in the coevolutionary process from somewhere near the beginning. The fitness of animal species, especially the vertebrates, is partly related to the correctness of their perceptions and understandings of reality, of how animals see and interpret diverse physical phenomena and the complex web of life. At the same time, reality has coevolved with animals' perceptions and understandings of reality. The environmental reality of the hunted is the perceptions and understandings of the hunter and *vice versa*. Minds and nature reflect a "necessary unity".

Animals not only perceive, learn, and understand, but do so together. Ants, wolves, and humans, among others, have learned to live in social groups. In the ants, social roles have become genetically encoded. For wolves and people, culture is undoubtedly the primary repository. Though the social linkages are dramatically different in each social group, each share a common feature. The survival of individuals and hence the species now depends on their social behavior. Cultures, like gene pools, evolve through random change and selection. Cultural adaptations survive if they make the culture more fit. Information with considerable survival value becomes incorporated in culture – in the myths, rituals, and peer pressures – in ways which individuals do not understand or even sense. It is well to remember, however, that cultural fitness also depends on genetic characteristics, while genetic fitness depends on culture.

THE COEVOLUTION OF ENVIRONMENT AND HUMAN CULTURE

Our understanding of coevolved systems, of how relations between the parts of systems can affect the evolution of those parts and the system overall, acquired through the development of coevolutionary thinking in biology can also enrich how we think about social and ecological systems. Coevolution explains how social and environmental systems can fit together and reflect each other without having been designed. It also indicates how change can occur endogenously, without direction, and at uneven rates. Coevolution also gives us insights into how systems of coevolving species mutually affect each other. These explanatory properties are very attractive for thinking about how cultural systems and ecological systems interrelate over time.

Our biosphere evolved over some three and a half billion years. It did not just come into being whole and working like an intricate clock. People have been involved in this global evolutionary process for only about three million years, while our primate ancestors have been participating in its evolution for considerably longer. While this is a mere one thousandth of earth's total geophysical history, people have nonetheless put important selective pressures on the evolution of the biosphere during the earth's shorter biological history. Furthermore, the primates which were to become people and the early people which were to become present people were selected according to how well they fit the evolving biological system. People and their environment have coevolved.

While we are well aware today of our devasting, negative impact on other species, we tend to underestimate the cumulative effect of early people on nature. Hunting and gathering by people put selective pressure on the species hunted and gathered. People in hunting and gathering societies transformed habitats to favor particular game and plant products. At the same time, hunting and gathering selected for effective hunters and gatherers who were more likely to survive and to support a larger number of offspring. While such activities only slightly changed the balance of selective forces in more distant parts of the biosphere, the cumulative effect on the course of evolution may well have been significant. Agriculture has been a more deliberate and intensive effort with far more significant impacts than hunting and gathering. Planting and watering, hand weeding, plowing, flooding, and burning are direct means of favoring productive species, reducing the competition for nutrients by "weeds," and nurturing species that complement each other. Plants support one another by providing shade, by having associated soil microorganisms that fix nitrogen or help other plants absorb mineral nutrients, and by hosting predators of other plant's pests. Later the selective pressure on the biological system was heavily influenced by the agricultural practices of deforesting and clearing land, weeding out some species and encouraging others, selecting the varieties that most consistently produced well, enriching soil, and eventually irrigating. These environmental transformations facilitated the evolution of species unable to survive without people. Agriculture, in turn, selected for different perceptive abilities and physical strengths among humans than had hunting and gathering.

Agriculture has long relied on cultural knowledge for ecosystem management. People shifted the mix of species toward those they preferred even before agriculture. These shifts in the species mix were not carried out rationally by the standards of Western science. People did not ponder whether their plants were receiving the right amounts of nitrogen or whether the plants that survived the last invasion of pests might have had a biochemical defensive system. People followed diverse practices, acting individually and in groups, because they were a part of a culture which included a myriad of myths about how people should work with each other and the land. And these myths had survived tests of fitness over generations.

Both agroecosystem management and deliberate selective pressure have been culturally learned and reinforced. Individuals learn selection and management techniques from others. Society maintains and allocates shared resources including fields and water. Appropriate behavior is culturally enforced. Cultural ecologists have shown for traditional societies how values, kinship, customs, rituals, and taboos are related to the maintenance of the society's interaction with its ecosystem. To a large extent culture still guides modern agricultural societies, but modernization has entailed a continual substitution of formal institutions and objective knowledge for culture and cultural knowledge as we commonly think of them.

The process of coevolution was not limited to mutual genetic selection. People survive to a large extent as members of groups. Group success depends on culture: the system of values, beliefs, artifacts, and artforms which sustain social organization and rationalize action. Values and beliefs which fit the ecosystem survive and multiply; less fit ones eventually disappear. And thus cultural traits are selected much like genetic traits. At the same time, cultural values and beliefs influence how people interact with their ecosystem and apply selective pressure on species. Not only have people and their environment coevolved, but social systems and environmental systems have coevolved.

Through this process, the world can be thought of as having become a patchwork quilt of loosely interconnected, coevolving social and ecological systems. Within each patch the ecological system evolved in response to cultural pressures and tended to reflect the values, world view, and social organization of local peoples. At the same time, the cultural system in each patch evolved in response to selection for fitness with respect to the ecosystem and hence tended to reflect the fertility, species composition, stability, and management options presented by the ecosystem. The reflections of each system in the other also evolved. Through this process, each patch took on unique characteristics particular to the random biological and cultural mutations of the patch. In this world view, what can be known is particular rather than universal. Universal truths still exist with respect to physical and chemical processes, but the diversity of complex biological and social systems that can be built upon these universal processes are unlimited.

At the same time, some environmental factors such as climate and topography have been the same across patches. These common macro factors lead to some similarities that can be found between patches. Similarly, in some regions and times, cultural beliefs and social organization brought aspects of social unity across patches. Buddhism spread from India across much of Asia, affecting people's perception of nature forever after. Various Chinese dynasties brought parallel, connected social organization to vast areas. These environmental and social constancies led to some nearly universal phenomena across the patches. Generalizations can always be made. But the coevolutionary view helps us comprehend how the loose connectedness between people and their cultures assured uniqueness between patches.

One of the most notable features of the evolving patchwork quilt is that the changing values and beliefs, or the cultural knowledge, in each patch were in some sense "right". They had not only survived to date but were a part of the template to the process of the evolution of other species, to the selection of genetic traits of people, and to the selection of social order. Similarly, the social organization in each patch was "right" for it affected the fitness of emerging values and beliefs, the genetic fitness of people, and the characteristics of other species. Cultural knowledge, social organization, and biological characteristics play active roles as part of the template to each other's evolution. This intrinsic or internal "rightness" associated with evolutionary explanations is typically very disturbing in Western culture where things are, on the one hand, objectively understood and, on the other, subjectively evaluated according to an external value system. Social Darwinism, a late nineteenth- and early twentieth-century school of thought, was appropriately criticized for simply justifying the status quo. "Rightness" necessarily has different meanings in different conceptual frameworks.

The coevolving of parts and relations can be portrayed at any level of complexity. The coevolution of the ecological system, values, knowledge, social organization, and technology has been illustrated in earlier chapters. This world view is distinctly different from the dominant Western view of a "natural" world that just is, minds that just perceive and acquire objective knowledge, and societies organized to utilize knowledge rationally to exploit resources, and to correct the environmental catastrophes this view creates.

9

A COEVOLUTIONARY COSMOLOGY

> The debate on choice of frameworks is not a matter of appealing to
> some higher standard of rationality, some algorithm for choosing the
> most rational from among competing systems of beliefs; it is a choice
> of how one wants to live one's life.
>
> (Paul A. Roth 1987: 244–45)

The coevolutionary cosmology developed in this chapter is very different
from the modern portrayal of the underlying nature of the world. One
might think of this alternative construction of the cosmos as being the polar
opposite of the dominant framing in that it stresses basic properties which
are systematically different from the modern cosmology. Presenting the two
constructions in terms of opposite poles, however, presumes there is a meta
position from which one can perceive that the modern and a coevolutionary
cosmology are at juxtaposed ends of the same globe. This would require a
perspective on perspectives, a cosmology of cosmologies, a way of getting
out of our own representations. Since the idea of cosmology alerts us to the
importance of looking for representations, it must presume we can comprehend representations, hence there must be representations of representations,
and we find ourselves moving from the inside out of a set of nested Chinese
boxes. Indeed, the principle of conceptual pluralism in my coevolutionary
cosmology starts us in this direction and thereby identifies a whole host of
new issues.

The modern portrayal represents the cosmos as being made up of parts –
subatomic particles, atoms, molecules and on to inanimate structures and
living organisms – constructed on and relating to each other according to a
finite number of principles which people can come to understand through
detached observation. The coevolutionary construction I frame in this
chapter, on the other hand, starts at a more aggregate level and includes
people and how we know from within the cosmos. The coevolutionary
cosmology that follows builds upon six principles. First, people are within
and affect both the state and the evolution of the cosmos we are trying to
understand. Second, how we understand the cosmos determines how we

affect the system; how we know selects for properties of the evolving system we try to know. Third is the principle of conceptual pluralism. Different ways of knowing different aspects of the cosmos are really different and unlikely to merge into a coherent understanding of the whole. We must contend with multiple ways of understanding and disparate insights. It is naive to presume that syntheses are possible. Fourth, people understand collectively; we are dependent on other people and how we are organized socially for much of what we know. Fifth, parts and relations within systems are historically contingent. And sixth, phenomena within systems of higher levels of complexity are contextual. No doubt others think from within coevolutionary cosmologies constructed upon principles stated somewhat differently, perhaps with a little less overlap and hence redundancy, but this set gets us started.

Note that the principles themselves repeatedly refer to the cosmos as a whole, to the cosmos as a system rather than to fundamental parts. Furthermore, the cosmos includes people and how we know. Unlike the modern cosmology which derives from a perspective appropriate for experimental tinkering with mechanical systems under controlled conditions, this coevolutionary cosmology is derived for the world in which we live. The principles appropriate to experimental physical sciences were adopted by, or forced upon, all scientists and applied as well to the logic of public policy-making. The six principles of the coevolutionary cosmology not only complement the broader argument of this book that development is a process of coevolution, but also complement the understandings and working environments of most people better than modern cosmology.

Nevertheless, even though a coevolutionary cosmology fits our world of experience better than the modern, people are still strongly imprinted by the modern construction of the cosmos, have difficulty accepting coevolutionary explanations of social and environmental history, and resist using this perspective. It is difficult to comprehend a new portrayal when our minds are unconsciously rooted in a cosmology that is inherently at odds with the new construction. Making the dominant epistemology and its relation to cosmology explicit in Chapter 6 and a new cosmology explicit in this chapter might facilitate acceptance of coevolutionary representations. Whether or not a coevolutionary cosmology gains acceptance, an exploration of its principles sheds further light on the nature of modernity and its alternatives.

ENDOGENOUS ACTION AND KNOWLEDGE

The first two principles of my coevolutionary cosmology are fairly obvious yet strangely lacking in the Western world view. First, clearly, we are a part of the system we are trying to understand, hence what we do affects the system we are trying to understand. The observer and the observed are interrelated. We cannot be objective in the sense that a laboratory scientist can observe a physical process or chemical reaction without being a part of the process. For the world beyond the laboratory, the world in which we live, we are constantly interacting with that which we are trying to observe and understand. Few people have the opportunity, for example, to observe the interactions of people and their environment through a one way window and then to explain and redirect the interactions from an objective position. Even if we could observe and direct from an objective stance, the patterns of explanation we choose to use derive from our participation in social and environmental systems somewhere. There is no neutral, objective position.

Many people recognize that how we understand is largely determined by the cultural system we are within, or at least the systems we have been in over the past. Development experts from the North, if they do not acknowledge it themselves, will be quickly informed by those in the South that their understandings are rooted in the social systems, physical environments, and development experience of the already industrialized nations of largely European peoples. Economic explanations are frequently ventured in modern social systems because modern people are accustomed to economic logic. Economists, of course, are more likely to venture economic explanations, while ecologists, having spent more time among other ecologists, are more likely to use ecological explanations. And I spend much of my professional life in meetings mediating between economists and ecologists, and occasionally between people from the North and the South, where members from each group are concerned that the understanding of those in the other is certainly incomplete and probably wrong. People readily attribute the reasoning of those on a different end of the political spectrum to their political position, effectively accusing them of blindly accepting an ideology. From a coevolutionary perspective, the reasoning of each of us simply is affected by the social and environmental systems in which we have evolved and become comfortable. Ideological accusations can thus be significantly reduced while, at the same time, ideology can be generally accepted within a broader frame.

The second cosmological principle of this coevolutionary cosmology, however, attributes causality in the other direction. How we reason affects the social and environmental systems in which we evolve. How we understand agricultural systems, for example, affects our agricultural decisions and thereby affects both the agroecosystem and agri*culture* which we were originally trying to understand in order to decide. The first principle alone generates a spiral with an unknown trajectory. Since we are inside of our systems, our decisions affect the state of the systems from a mechanical perspective and the evolution of the systems from a coevolutionary perspective. The direction of the spiral depends on the nature of the discord between our knowledge and the "true" state of the system at the time of the decision.

The important point is that how we know affects the subsequent state of the system and how it continues to evolve.

Accepting that how we know both is within the system we are trying to understand and affects the system we are trying to understand identifies an important new issue. In a truly mechanical world where the nature of parts and relations remain fixed but their relative proportions and strengths change, how we know and the state of the system could reach an equilibrium or a stable cycle. But to the extent we live in a world of coevolving parts and relations, understandings must necessarily keep evolving, replacing themselves, to keep up with the cosmos that our understandings are changing. Coevolutionary change also occurs because of innovations and through the introduction of other values, organization, and technology from other places. Such introductions also select for new dominant understandings, but new knowledge itself is certainly a dominant source of system evolution selecting for yet newer knowledge. This means there is no absolute knowledge, for knowledge only has meaning relative to how well it explains the state, dynamics, and evolution of a system. Similarly, there is no meaning to the idea that knowledge accumulates.

This view of the nature of knowledge and our interactions with systems helps explain why there are always new problems needing new solutions. It is not simply the case, as is often argued, that we are constantly generating new problems because we cannot foresee all of the consequences of our actions. To foresee all of the consequences of coevolution would require knowledge of a cosmos yet to exist. The rest of the principles highlight why such foresight is effectively impossible. But note an important point before we move on. By including ourselves, what we do, and how we decide to do it within a coevolutionary cosmology, the distinction between cosmology and epistemology becomes moot. The cosmos we wish to know and the epistemes by which we try to know it are interactive.

In the dominant cosmology, scientific knowledge and the principles of interacting with complex systems are timeless. In a coevolving cosmos, learning about and adjusting interactions with complex systems is an ongoing, adaptive process. As we acquire understanding and intervene with newly acquired concepts of management, we change the coevolutionary path of the system, making our new insights and management concepts obsolete. Adaptive environmental management, and thereby dispensing with fixed management rules, is necessary. To the extent the cosmos is best understood as coevolving, fixed property rules, such as rights to pollute, will eventually contribute to environmental problems and unsustainability.

CONCEPTUAL PLURALISM

The third principle would fall into the category of epistemology if this were still a separate realm. Our understanding of complex systems is necessarily based on multiple incongruent ways of knowing. Environmental systems, for example, can be thought of as consisting of biological systems – the systems of interacting living organisms – and physical systems – the systems made up of hydrological cycles, ocean currents, regional to global climate cycles, etc. The two systems, of course, interact. Ecologists have multiple ways of simplifying their understanding of ecological systems into formal, tractable models: energetics, food webs, biogeochemical cycles, population biology, community ecology, hierarchy theory, and coevolution among others. Each conceptual pattern leaves out different parts of biological systems, differs with respect to the nature of relationships between the parts, and has different interfaces between the biological and physical systems. Similarly physical scientists understand different subdivisions of physical systems through different patterns of reasoning.

Most people, including scientists, still believe that our multiple ways of understanding different aspects of ecosystems can be merged into one coherent view. Many while trying to work within this belief, however, become disillusioned by the incongruencies of data when they are trying to assess a larger environmental picture. This disillusion is typically expressed as an absence of appropriate data. But data are associated with particular, tractable models. Data appropriate to a model of population dynamics are rarely appropriate to coevolutionary, community, energetics, or hierarchy models. Some types of data are associated with more than one model, but the time period and geographic scale of the data frequently do not match or, when they do, the interpretation of the data through the different models frequently conflicts. A typical reaction is that more data must be needed. But the problem is not simply a matter of a lack of data. Nor is it simply a matter of different agencies or scientists collecting data in different seasons, averaging them over different periods, or collecting at different "ideal" locations because they are pursuing different ideals. The problem, rather, is that data sets are incomparable because they have been collected in the context of incomparable models of different aspects of systems and only have meaning in the context of their respective models.

Many environmental policy debates center on the difficulties of interpreting the state of the environment from multiple data sets, the difficulties of determining the ways in which people affect the state, the difficulties of assessing the effects of alternative human interactions, and the difficulties of understanding the effectiveness of policies to get people to behave differently. Certainly, some of the contention occurs because individual models at each level of analysis are not proven, and in some sense can never be proven. The principle of conceptual pluralism, however, identifies a problem which is less well recognized, the incommensurability of multiple models. Contention and contradictions occur in environmental debates because our multiple models do not fit into a single coherent understanding. For complex systems – organismal, ecological, environmental, and social systems – our understandings are not merging. Conceptual pluralism is what we have.

96

The case for acknowledging conceptual pluralism is not an argument for using just any framework of analysis. On the contrary, recognizing conceptual pluralism should heighten our awareness of the structure and assumptions of diverse conceptual frameworks through appreciation of their differences. For narrow, well-defined questions, the most suitable framework is typically somewhat predetermined. Analysts, however, repeatedly ignore how the framework with which they are accustomed and are supposedly most familiar contains assumptions that preclude pursuit of other questions. Economists, for example, have tried to determine whether resources are scarce in the long run using models which assume that private resource allocators are already informed of the nature of resource scarcity and acting in accordance with this information. Attempts to extend patterns of reasoning to fit new circumstances frequently lead to an abuse of the underlying assumptions and logics of the patterns of reasoning. Conceptual pluralism acknowledges the limits, and hence the appropriateness, of specific patterns of reasoning to specific questions.

To accept conceptual pluralism is to accept multiple insights and the inherent inability of science to describe complex systems consistently, to predict how they might behave, or to prescribe how to make them behave in another way. If science as it is conventionally understood provides fragmented, incomplete insights at best, whatever understandings we have of whole systems are synthesized by some other process than what has heretofore been understood as science. This leads us directly to the fourth principle of my coevolutionary cosmology.

THE COLLECTIVE NATURE OF UNDERSTANDING

The pace and timing of the acceptance of ideas within academic disciplines is a sociological phenomenon. Science is beginning to be understood as a social process in another sense. The directions in which knowledge accumulates, and is forgotten, depends on social organization as influenced by people's needs and the relative power of interest groups. Research on weather, for example, has been most influenced by the needs of farmers and airlines. Weather monitoring and meteorological institutions were designed to meet the needs of these interest groups. The state of our knowledge about weather reflects the questions asked and the structure of the institutions, right down to the location of weather stations. As we try to grapple with the new questions of global climate change, we discover significant gaps in our knowledge that are directly attributable to how meteorology was funded and directed.

It is also becoming clear that science has gone beyond being a process of individual researchers using equipment made in their own laboratories. Scientists in most fields during the latter half of the twentieth century work in increasingly larger teams, relying on increasingly complex equipment designed by others. Furthermore, scientists incorporate information generated by the experiments of other scientists in the interpretation of the results of their own experiments. As experiments become more complex and expensive to undertake, findings from one study are more likely to be incorporated into interpretations of other experiments without sufficient replication of the first experiments by the next scientists. Scientists rely on each other more and more. It is increasingly well recognized that our understanding of complex systems is based on the work of multiple scientists, that no one scientist understands the whole.

Yet another social aspect of science is beginning to be recognized. The various individual agencies with environmental management responsibilities in the United States, for example, were initially constructed around, recruit from, and interact with members from particular individual environmental sciences around which they consequently evolve. The U.S. Department of Fish and Game and the U.S. Bureau of Reclamation were established to solve different problems which were separately conceived through biological and hydrological paradigms respectively. The agencies are staffed with wildlife managers and water engineers who perceive the world, collect and interpret data, and communicate with each other within their agencies with the assistance of their respective patterns of thought. Not only are environmental data collected through agencies initiated under different paradigms, but the individuals within the agencies, and in some sense the organizations as a whole, acquire experiential knowledge which is bounded by the initial conceptions of problems and initial training of the experts within the agencies and the professional community with which they interact. Agencies can be thought of as being connected to "epistemic communities" with which they learn and as being unable to adopt new paradigms independently of them. The agricultural and forestry schools and research programs of the Land Grant universities in the United States, for example, train the bulk of agricultural and forestry technocrats in federal and state departments of agriculture and provide them with the latest scientific findings throughout their careers. The technocrats, in turn, strongly influence the direction and funding of the universities' research programs, locking the two in an epistemic community that has only recently begun to look at modern agriculture critically.

Many have disparagingly acknowledged the rigidities in how organizations and their epistemic communities learn and know, but to the extent this is a fact, there is no reason to decry it. While typically constrained in its diversity, the experiential knowledge of organizations can still be more than the sum of the knowledges of the individual scientists in the organization and can exhibit an organizational "common sense" that is essential to the agency's performance. It is very difficult to conceive of how societies could be structured to manage their interactions with the environment without divisions occurring along patterns of thinking. The difficulty is clear in my own attempt to address this issue with the suggestion of "coevolving discursive communities" in Chapter 13.

There is yet another difference with the dominant cosmology, for it implicitly presumes the cosmos is observed and comprehended by an individual mind. To be sure, modern science acknowledges that no mind can make all of the observations or comprehend all that is known, but it assumes this is simply due to the limited power of individual minds to observe and hold all of the knowledge from a multitude of fields. Following the notion that systems are the sum of their parts, the dominant cosmology implicitly assumes knowledge consists of additive things. Conceptual pluralism stresses that our separate knowledges are not additive. Thinking of science as a social process identifies the importance of how people, organizations, and ways of knowing interact.

Accepting that our separate ways of knowing in the individual disciplines do not merge to a coherent whole, and accepting that no person can absorb all knowledge, leaves us with the problem of how we derive collective understandings of complex systems. Clearly, if the patterns of thinking and knowledges from our separate disciplines do not cohere, our knowledge of complex systems must necessarily lack coherence, the logical rigor associated with Western science. And yet societies somehow arrive at understandings which are sufficiently publicly accepted to form the basis of collective decision-making. We intervene in ecosystems all of the time based on some sort of understanding, right or wrong. If we were more aware of the nature of our understanding, perhaps we could use it more effectively.

My coevolutionary cosmology accepts that scientists from different disciplines, and ultimately the public at large, acquire a collective understanding of complex systems through engaging in extended discourse until sufficient consensus is acquired to facilitate decision-making. Science as a social process in this sense entails scientists entering into discourse, debating and rethinking each others' understandings, and approaching an interpretive consensus about the key properties of the system they are trying to understand. There are four key aspects of this social process of understanding complex systems. First, the discourse occurs among scientists of different disciplines who do not share a common pattern of thinking. Second, the needs and interest groups served by this process of understanding complex systems are different than those served by the individual sciences. Conflicts develop, not simply due to different patterns of thinking, but also due to differences of opinion over what was important in the first place within the individual sciences, between the cultures of the individual sciences, between interest groups associated with the individual sciences, and between interest groups concerned with the larger representation. Third, these understandings of complex systems can only be tested by history, and then under poorly controlled conditions. And fourth, how we should design experiments before they are run is a matter of intense public interest because of the irreversibility of the experiments and the risks entailed. Understanding the global climate system and the effect of greenhouse gases is the ultimate example. Thus the public necessarily becomes involved in the social processes of understanding larger, complex systems. For all of these reasons, the social processes of understanding the integrated cosmos that is emerging today are significantly different than those associated with understanding the parts of the cosmos structured by modernity.

A CONTINGENT, CONTEXTUAL, COEVOLVING COSMOS

The fifth and sixth principles with respect to the contingent nature of historical events and the contextual nature of parts within systems are closely interrelated to each other and coevolutionary explanations of process. These terms are so tightly bound to a coevolutionary portrayal of the cosmos that they are inseparable. Similarly, they are diametrically opposed to the modern portrayal of the cosmos as being made up of parts with underlying universal characteristics and interrelated by underlying universal patterns. In a coevolving cosmos, parts can only be understood in the context of the particular systems in which they are embedded, and history unfolds event by event according to the chance convergence of particular conditions at particular times.

Systems just are. History just is. The parts of a coevolving cosmos can only be understood in the context of whole systems because parts coevolve in the context of wholes. This, of course, is clearly self-referential, but circularity is necessarily blatant in any fundamental representation. Systems might have been constructed very differently and histories might have unfolded very differently under only slightly different starting conditions. Systems and histories can be thought of as the products of numerous "rolls of the dice" wherein a single different roll among many along the way can dramatically change the systems' structure or the direction of history. This aspect of the alternative cosmology is especially frustrating because, with each system and period of history being different from another, there are no principles to simplify learning, other than the principles of the coevolutionary cosmology itself. We can describe the unfolding of events in terms of preceding contingent events and describe each part of each system in the context of the wholes, but there are no principles by which to predict on the basis of one part or event the nature of the next. Without predictive power, there is no basis for prescription in the sense we understand prediction and prescription from the modern framing of the cosmos.

FURTHER IMPLICATIONS

This coevolutionary cosmology follows directly from the portrayal of the interconnections and coevolution between values, knowledge, organization, technology, and the environment. The foregoing elaboration stresses that we are inside the cosmos and the multiple ways we know are inside of the cosmos. This blurs the distinction between cosmology and epistemology. A further elaboration would point out that our values are also within the cosmos as are our ways of organizing, types of technologies, and of course environmental systems. The portrayal thus far refers to systems within the cosmos without stipulating whether they are natural or social systems. Elaborating the cosmology beyond knowledge systems would also blur the customary distinctions between cosmology and moral philosophy, political philosophy, and even technology.

Let me initiate an elaboration that will be developed further in the later chapters that revision the future. We design social systems in accordance with how we think we know. Our environmental management agencies are structured to collect data and manage systems within established disciplinary boundaries while the boundaries of the disciplines themselves coevolve with the needs and understandings of working agencies. Increasingly, economic criteria are being added to the procedures of bureaucratic decision-making reflecting our rising faith in economic rationality and the politics of constraining public decisions by economic criteria. How we know, in short, affects how we organize, which, in turn, affects how organizations learn and the information available to individuals and other organizations. To a considerable extent, the evidence to date suggests that the coevolution of modern knowledge and social structure has been a process of locking in, of mutual reinforcement of organizational structure and patterns of thinking, rather than a process of continually breaking out and redefining. Against this process, we must acknowledge that environmentalism has seriously challenged this order and that cultural pluralism may unlock it yet.

There is the possibility that monism, or universalism, might be dropped from the modern portrayal of the underlying nature of the cosmos without the other aspects of the portrayal being discarded simultaneously. The logic and evidence against monism is now quite persuasive. In any case, conceptual pluralism is an especially key concept of this book and deserves some concluding observations.

CONCLUSIONS

Conceptual pluralism requires that most, or at least the dominant, participants in the process of learning and deciding:

1 be conscious of their own conceptual frameworks,
2 be conscious of the advantages and disadvantages of the frameworks used by others, and
3 be tolerant of the use of different frameworks used by others.

Some participants might also be adept at using different theories as indicated by the circumstances.

Conceptual pluralism entails a contradiction. It requires the acceptance even of methodologies that are at odds not only with a coevolutionary cosmology but with pluralism itself. Pluralists must be able to work with monists or in situations where monism is required. Logical positivism, for example, assumes monism and denies that how we think affects cultural and ecological systems. Yet logical positivism is necessary because modern people still perceive science in terms of objective, universal truths. To a large extent modern societies are organized to act on science presented from this, and only this, methodological stance. Until the illogic of logical positivism is better known throughout modern societies, the use of logical positivist arguments will be justified in certain circumstances. Hopefully, the conscious use of logical positivist arguments will also incorporate warnings of its dangers. In any case, pluralists must be able to work with logical positivists until pluralism is broadly accepted.

Pluralism makes sense. We must address the complex interplay of global economies and local interests, sophisticated technologies and human frailties, environmental systems and social controls on their use, and limited resources. Clearly there is not one best, let alone all-encompassing, perspective for understanding and managing problems of the complexity we now face. Arguments that are adamantly presented initially as right thinking are frequently better developed a decade later in a pluralist frame.

Pluralism prevents brash action. Those who are accustomed to "one right way of thinking" will point out that the practice of conceptual pluralism will lead to multiple "answers" and no clear course of action. In fact, science only gives insights into complex issues. It is easy to suffer the delusion that the insight of a particular method is the answer when no other methods have been tried to provide other insights. Single method/answer delusions lead to brash action which are likely to subsequently prove to be mistakes. Also, people who only think one way are susceptible to twisted, deliberately distorted arguments in those areas for which their pattern of thinking is least adequate. The multiple insights of multiple methods constantly remind us of the complexity of social and ecological systems and the difficulties of taking action.

Conceptual pluralism promotes participation and decentralization. Any given framework is better understood by, more appreciated by, or results in answers which are more advantageous to some people than others. Any framework that has been highly elaborated to stretch its usefulness can only be understood by a few who are well informed of its technical details. The use of a single framework, without modification for regional differences, facilitates control from a single center of analysis. Thus the use of a single framework disenfranchises or disqualifies the majority, facilitates the tyranny of technocrats, and encourages centralization. Openness to multiple frames of analysis is a prerequisite to democracy and local control.

Broader, less well-defined questions can only be pursued through multiple, overlapping analyses, extensive discussion between diverse experts and the people directly affected, and judgment. If we accept that there is not a comprehensive right way of predicting the future consequences of our choices, we will more likely make decisions sequentially in relatively small increments, build monitoring and learning into every program of change, and be adaptive. At the same time, overviews of where we are and where we are trying to get to are extremely important for providing criteria for selecting individual steps.

Pluralism can help sustain biological and cultural diversity. The adoption of Western forms of knowing, technological intervention, and social organization has reduced both cultural and biological diversity. Yet to a considerable extent, ecosystems are still different because the selective pressures applied by people have been different due to differences in how people have thought about nature. Similarly, cultural diversity still exists because of the diversity in ways of thinking. Conscious conceptual diversity will facilitate the return of the patchwork quilt, complementing coordinated effort where needed. If we hold to the belief that knowledge consists of universal laws with universal applicability, we will apply it accordingly and destroy the diversity in the cultural and ecological systems we are trying to sustain.

10

COEVOLUTIONARY LESSONS
FROM THE AMAZON

The Amazon is an unusual place to turn to initiate the constructive final chapters of this book. Everyone has heard the horror stories of development failure and environmental destruction. What constructive lessons can be learned? My own understanding of the interrelations between social and environmental problems and development evolved rapidly and took diverse new directions through my encounters with development in the tropical rainforests of the Brazilian Amazon. I was working with the Ford Foundation on resources and the environment issues during 1978 and 1979. This was nearly a decade too early to attract much interest in environmental issues in Brazil, but an ideal time to observe the development process. I found that both marxist and market explanations facilitated my observations and illuminated some of the reasons development efforts had failed in the Amazon for nearly four centuries. And yet, neither marxist nor market explanations addressed the systemic nature of particular ecosystems, let alone the complexities of tropical rainforests. This led me to develop my own coevolutionary perspective through reading tropical ecology and cultural ecology. In fact, the book you are reading was originally going to be about the Amazon and the coevolutionary perspective alone. But once having learned a coevolutionary pattern of thinking, my own understanding began to coevolve with more and more patterns of thinking, disciplinary literatures, and issues. Hence the sweeping nature of the book. Though my understanding and concerns continued to broaden beyond the tropcial rainforest, I returned to the Amazon during the 1980s in different capacities, including that of a Northern environmental imperialist to negotiate a World Bank Amazon policy loan to Brazil. I regret that this chapter provides my sole example of how a coevolutionary framework can be used to understand better a real ecosystem and social system.

Agricultural development can be thought of as a coevolutionary process between a social system and an ecological system. People's agricultural activities put selective pressure on components of the ecosystem while the ecosystem's characteristics select for individual action and social organization. When these mutual selective processes are complementary and beneficial

104

to people, either fortuitously or by design, agricultural development is underway. The agricultural interventions and elaborate systems of social organization and technology that have been imposed on the Amazon, however, tend to "break down" rather quickly to technologies and social systems reminiscent of those of the indigenous peoples. This chapter applies the coevolutionary pattern of thinking to identify why the social systems that Westerners have tried to match with the environmental system of the Amazon have resulted in the collapse of both social structures and the environment. Coevolutionary thinking also identifies characteristics of social systems which might lead to a process of selection between social and ecological systems which would be beneficial for people. On the surface, this chapter is about the Amazon, but the deeper message is about modernity.

Assuming development is a coevolutionary process negates development planning as it has been understood. One cannot plan that which coevolves. Yet one might still use an understanding of development as a coevolutionary process to try to identify the boundaries of the initial conditions from which coevolutionary development might unfold. This chapter identifies why the social systems which have been imported into the Amazon have instigated coevolutionary "undevelopment" and asks what characteristics social systems might need to instigate development in the Amazon ecosystem. Thus I demonstrate that a coevolutionary analysis can have some predictive and prescriptive capacity even though it is not as amenable to prediction and prescription as analyses derived from models which assume systems are atomistic and mechanistic. While metaphysical and epistemological issues still arise, this chapter gets closer to the ground, to a level at which societies and development experts try to design and implement plans.

This analysis of the difficulties of developing the Amazon also gives a better understanding of the nature of modern agriculture in temperate zones. The Amazon ecosystem has very few stocks to buffer or delay unwanted outcomes whereas temperate agroecosystems have buffers in the form of stocks of soil which hold nutrients and water. In the temperate zone, furthermore, these good properties are complemented by technologies, the use of fertilizers and irrigation water from afar, which make these qualities even less essential. As a consequence, the time and spatial scales on which malfunctioning between the social and ecological systems and subsequent coevolution occur are vastly different in the two agricultural systems. This and other insights stem from an investigation that necessarily goes into some detail.

ECOLOGICAL AND SOCIAL SYSTEMS IN THE AMAZON

Descriptions of environmental destruction in the Amazon have an exotic appeal, spread rapidly, and are difficult for most people to verify. In fact, the Amazon tropical rainforests are not the "lungs of the earth", only a small part of the Amazon has gone from a "green hell" to a "red desert", and only a fraction of that is made up of lateritic soil that turns into brick when exposed to the sun. Nevertheless, environmental transformation is an extremely serious problem. Historically the transformation has been from species-rich virgin forest to agricultural crops using swidden (slash and burn) techniques for three to five years, and then a fairly rapid recovery to less species-rich secondary forest. Government-supported efforts during the 1970s to introduce people without land from beyond the Amazon into the jungle in planned colonization programs attempted to break the swidden pattern of cultivation and establish permanent agriculture. A few of these efforts succeeded where the soils are unusually good. Most have failed. Government-subsidized schemes to promote cattle ranching in the Brazilian Amazon began in the 1960s and were dramatically accelerated during the 1970s. Cattle ranchers cleared the forest using bulldozers, disturbing and compacting the soil. Repeated burning to keep weedy tree species out, further compaction of the soil by the hooves of the cattle over a five- to fifteen-year period, and the large size of the cattle pastures effectively prevented reforestation by natural processes. Through these development schemes, species and whole subsystems were lost before plans to reserve and manage species were ever developed and implemented.

More importantly, and still less popularly known, the environmental transformations in the name of development have rarely been successful for people. Interactions between Amazon ecosystems and the modern social systems that have been imposed on the Amazon are usually mutually destructive. Much of the problem has been that portions of modern social systems have been extended into the Amazon to exploit resources. Those people who are effecting the extension identify with the dominant social system and, in any case, are totally incapable of adapting the responses of the dominant system to their experiences with the responses of the Amazon ecosystem.

Our understanding of agricultural development is rooted largely in the successful experiences of the temperate zones and of irrigated agriculture in the tropics where mixed vegetation systems are converted to monocultural systems. Following this approach, the Amazon vegetation system, at best, has been a short term convert and then only with considerable coercion. Wet tropical rainforest systems are renowned for their incredible species diversity and rapid vegetation regrowth. With respect to the social system, agricultural development usually entails permanent settlements; individual task specialization; and a hierarchy of institutions to assign property and manage communal resources, coordinate tasks, facilitate the exchange of goods and services, and perpetuate technical knowledge and social order. Until the recent organized and subsidized development efforts, both Indians and the rural descendants of past settlement attempts have been remarkably mobile; have individually combined multiple crop and shifting agricultural practices with hunting, fishing, and the gathering of fruits and nuts; and have had relatively little social structure beyond the family. Agricultural coevolution generally has been a process whereby the ecosystem becomes increasingly less complex and the social system becomes increasingly more complex. In the Amazon, the process of coevolution seems to "climax" with swidden agriculture.

At an earlier time it was acceptable for colonialists and later development planners to generalize about the failure of people to develop sophisticated social systems and industrial technologies in the humid tropics by invoking the enervating effects of heat, excessive rainfall, poor soils, and debilitating diseases. These environmental explanations proved to be too simple on further examination. At about the same time, the success of the Marshall Plan that facilitated the rebuilding of Europe after World War II encouraged a blind faith among academics and policy makers in the idea that development was possible for all social systems and ecosystems through central planning and capital and technology transfers. Thus, though environmental determinism with respect to the tropics maintained an unresolved predominance among the public at large, development efforts in the tropics were initiated on a new note of optimism. The situation has reversed in recent times. The public tends to believe that development for all is a reasonable hope while academics and policy makers, after four decades of effort, are discouraged by their inability to predict in advance which general policies or specific projects might indeed lead to development, by the increased disparity between rich and poor, and by ongoing social and political instability even where material productivity has increased. The increased evidence of environmental destruction associated with development during the 1980s added to the concerns. Thus this chapter uses coevolutionary thinking to determine whether it provides practical insights for development in the Amazon.

Much of the social structure in the Amazon today, especially in the isolated river towns, is an artifact of the *aviamento* system of property rights and social relations. Because this social system is unusual by modern standards and because it supported an extractive economy for more than a century, it deserves careful consideration. Coevolutionary explanations are inherently historical. The Portuguese Crown assigned to specific individuals the sole rights both to the products that could be collected from the natural forest and to trade within large regions typically demarcated by watersheds. Given that almost all transportation was along the rivers, this system of property allowed particular individuals to control all trade on their watersheds and earn a monopoly profit, or extract the surplus from any labor, on economic activities in the region involving trade. The word *aviamento*, in fact, means to dispatch or send and only these individuals had the right to dispatch materials up or down the river past their posts at the junction of large rivers with the Amazon or its major tributaries. The Grand Para and Maranhao Company in Belem near the mouth of the Amazon River handled all materials coming from and going to the rest of Brazil and Europe. The influence of this social system is still strongly felt in the remote river towns.

Those with trading rights up river from Belem established traders at various regional outposts along the rivers who, in turn, recruited Indians and peasants to collect mostly spices and nuts but also latex, particular woods, and some hides. Collectors were assigned gathering areas along and back from the rivers. Though these rights were only weakly enforced, they provided some incentives for long term management over short term exploitation. Collectors, however, were obligated to sell what they collected from the jungle to official traders and only official traders had products to sell from the outside. By paying low prices for collected goods and charging high prices for goods imported into the Amazon, traders drove collectors into debt bondage. In the absence of any other police force, the trading companies also assumed enforcement responsibilities. It is rather discouraging to acknowledge that of all the Westernized social systems tried in the Amazon ecosystem, *aviamento* – an exploitive and authoritarian system by most standards – proved fit longer than any other Western social system and aspects of this system continue to prove fit.

In 1843 Charles Goodyear took out a patent on a vulcanization process for latex, which gave this extractive good from the Amazon many more uses in the industrialized world. By the 1850s, more pliable, more elastic, and more durable products began to appear on the market. Through other new processes, latex could be easily molded into useful shapes and then transformed into ebonite, a solid black plastic-like material. Solid rubber tires appeared in the 1870s followed by the invention of the pneumatic tire by John Dunlop in 1888. With the appearance of the automobile, demand for latex began to soar. Thus exports of latex from the Amazon increased from 156 tons in 1830 to almost 35,000 tons by 1910, approximately doubling each decade. The number of people employed in the exploitation of rubber increased from less than 2000 to more than 100,000.

Aviamento facilitated this dramatic increase in output. The exploiters built grand opera houses in Manaus and Belem with the surplus they extracted from the workers who in turn extracted the latex from the trees. But rubber's reign was short lived. The Amazon lost the market to Malaysia where the British developed rubber trees in plantations. Latex prices dropped 80 percent between 1910 and 1920 largely because on a plantation tappers only had a 10-meter walk from tree to tree. In the natural jungle, distances varied from 50 and 200 meters between trees on a typical rubber collection trail. Prices decreased 60 percent from their already low price in the subsequent decade due to the Great Depression. As prices declined, young adults abandoned the system and eventually many in the older generations left as well. And yet many stayed on the land, tapping small quantities of latex for the market and engaging in subsistence agriculture. The descendants of those who stayed still live along the river and populate the river towns of the Amazon today. Much of the class structure still descends from the social relations established under *aviamento*.

THE COEVOLUTIONARY FRAMEWORK

If agricultural interactions between the ecosystem and social system are mutually compatible, then sustained agriculture is possible. If there are positive mutual responses or feedbacks between the systems on net over time, coevolutionary change is taking place. If these positive feedbacks result in a coevolution that favors people, coevolutionary agricultural development is taking place. Coevolutionary agricultural development is most easily envisaged when there is a surplus above maintenance needs in the two systems that is deliberately or fortuitously invested in the establishment of new interactions such that conditions for people improve. Maintenance needs frequently shift with coevolution from the ecosystem to the social system. In modern agricultural systems, for example, soil fertility is typically maintained through deliberate application of industrial produced fertilizers by farmers rather than through complementary, almost management free, relationships between plants and nitrogen-fixing bacteria. The extra cost of investing in and maintaining new feedback mechanisms through the social system must be deducted from the gross surplus of any new interaction between the systems. A net surplus, and hence the possibility for coevolution, may develop through:

1 exogenous changes in the ecosystem which are favorable to people,
2 new knowledge about how to interact with an ecosystem,
3 a subsidy from (or the removal of a transfer to) another region, or
4 a redistribution of power in the social system.

With coevolution toward modern agriculture, the social system typically assumes the complementary activities and regulatory functions previously endogenous to the ecosystem. Modern agriculture almost always involves reducing the number of species in the ecosystem, typically lowering the combined efficiency of nutrient cycling, higher but less stable rates of production, and low biomass stocks relative to the ecosystem before modern agriculture. As people push ecosystems to meet their own needs, they often intervene in some of the nutrient cycles and disturb equilibriating mechanisms which had previously evolved in the system. Fertilizing and the management of legumes to replace lost nutrient cycles, weed control to offset successional processes, and insect control to compensate for displaced equilibriating mechanisms such as pest predators will probably have to be introduced. These new activities within the social system are costs because they involve manual labor, managerial effort, knowledge acquisition, and the diversion of natural resources that might otherwise have been consumed beyond agriculture. Ecosystem transformation does not necessarily entail people assuming some of the regulatory feedbacks that were previously endogenous to the ecosystem, but modern transformations of ecosystems have had this characteristic. This phenomenon has caused difficulties in that the people who have individually or collectively initiated the transformation do not immediately recognize the need to provide feedback mechanisms, may not experience all of the consequences themselves of not providing the feedback, and those who do experience the repercussions are rarely organized appropriately to assume the responsibility. In any case, either the costs of assuming the feedback for the ecosystem or the costs of continued ecosystem change in the absence of people assuming the regulatory function must be considered.

Whether coevolutionary changes are beneficial on net depends on people's values. And inevitably when speaking of people's values, one asks how people and their different values are counted. Social evaluation has exasperated moral philosophers and policy analysts for centuries even when they assume people do not change when social systems change. In the coevolutionary model, with everything evolving in response to everything else and with values internal rather than external to the model, the problem becomes impossible. People's values change and the distribution of power changes as social organization coevolves. Whether there is a net benefit and whether a new interaction between transformed social and ecological systems will be interpreted as coevolutionary development depends on the values of the groups involved, the distribution between these groups of the positive and negative effects of the new interaction, and the historical and new distribution of power between the groups. Analogous interactive opportunities with respect to the ecosystem for two societies with similar overall capabilities might be chosen by one society and shunned by the other because of differences in either their power structures or values. The coevolutionary explanation of agricultural development is no more value-free than any other model. It can be, however, more explicit about values since their changes are also incorporated in the model.

POSSIBLE SOCIAL SYSTEM ADAPTATIONS

The tropical rainforest ecosystem has three especially important characteristics:

1 the unperturbed natural system has an unusually large number of different species,
2 the recovery path of the system after a perturbation is not easily predicted, and
3 the productivity per unit area of species of interest to people, and to modern economies in particular, is especially low.

This division of characteristics and the individual descriptions are rooted in modern ways of thinking about and interacting with ecosystems. Indigenous peoples of the Amazon would probably think of their own ecosystem quite differently even if they had also been exposed to the corn, soybean, and wheat fields of the American midwest or the redwood forests of California. The coevolutionary paradigm at least helps us understand the roots and limitations of our analysis, something repeatedly overlooked by modern agriculturalists in developing countries.

The key characteristics reflect that modern science is better at taxonomy than at principles of ecosystem dynamics. We think in terms of species diversity rather than axioms of ecosystem interaction because taxonomy is more advanced than ecology. The number of linkages in an ecosystem typically increases more than proportionately with the number of parts. This increased complexity makes system behavior even more difficult to understand in the tropics than in the temperate zone. The problems of predicting how the ecosystem will respond to agricultural intervention and the low and uncertain economic yield people obtain are specific to the particular technologies used. Technologies, in turn, are partially rooted in scientific understanding. Thus, the following characterizations of the ecosystem are bound up in the broader explanations of why coevolution has stopped with swidden agriculture in the Amazon. The coevolutionary model helps us see the inevitable circularity in our reasoning.

The Amazon ecosystem is amazingly heterogeneous. There are up to 50 species of trees per hectare; 235 species of woody plants; more species of butterflies in a single locality than in all of the United States, and approximately 2,000 species of fish in the river system. Some evolutionists have argued that the relative climatic stability during the Ice Age and the low seasonal variability of the tropical rainforest provided a relative continuity which may have allowed for the greater species diversity, niche specialization, and interdependence. Climatic variability in the temperate zones may prevent such specialization and interdependence since variability requires a wider range of behavior and less interdependence to survive. Others have argued that the heterogeneity may be due to differential disturbance, for example through fire induced by lightning or by people, in relatively small areas or patches and low rates of species movement from one patch to another. In the tropical rainforest ecosystem, seeds are transported by animals rather than wind, limiting their rate of disbursement, and there are few migratory species or even species which roam great distances. Since only one disturbance per patch could set it off on a new coevolutionary path, the differential disturbance and climatic continuity hypotheses are mutually compatible.

In any case, this ecological richness presents an organizational challenge for social systems. The maintenance needs of a social system interacting with a heterogeneous ecosystem are higher because managing, harvesting, shipping, processing, inventorying, marketing, and preparing for consumption numerous different species entails forgoing economies of scale, especially in the utilization of information. Management and extraction technologies developed in the less-diverse ecosystems of the temperate zone are not well suited to the Amazon. Neither fish meal nor wood pulp can be readily made from a wide and varying mix of species with existing technologies. The exploitation of high-valued species alone is thwarted by the physical presence of so many low-valued species and interdependencies between species including niche competition. Little current research is appropriate for improving existing approaches developed by Indians for interacting in a diverse ecosystem.

The unpredictability of the ecosystem response to agricultural technologies stems from a combination of factors. *First*, with a greater number of species with their greater niche specificity, the number of possible disturbances to the system is larger. While in the temperate zone, logging usually entails removing the dominant tree species from the ecosystem, in the tropical rainforest, logging may remove one or more of a large variety of species. The number of possible disturbances and hence ecosystem responses is greater. With the same absolute knowledge of how temperate forests and tropical rainforest behave, the tropical rainforest is always surprising us. Subtle differences in people's activities will more likely be critical to some species resulting in a different perturbation and recovery path. *Second*, although weather variations are smaller in the tropical rainforest than in the temperate zone, weather still affects the dynamics of the ecosystem and thereby people's activities. The greater niche specificity makes the dynamics of individual species and hence the system as a whole very sensitive to small changes.

Third, variations in the flows in the tropical rainforest ecosystem are not ameliorated by buffer stocks. The soils are very porous and do not hold water, making plants very dependent on the regularity of rainfall. What irregularities there are in the rainfall have greater impacts on individual species and the dynamics of the ecosystem than in the temperate zone. Similarly, there are almost no stocks of nutrients in the soil so that plants are dependent on each other to host nitrogen-fixing bacteria and microbial life which help them absorb minerals. This brings us to the *fourth* reason for the unpredictability of the system. The sequence and distribution of flora and fauna are more determined by species interaction. In the major ecosystems in the temperate zone, seed pollination and dissemination are typically performed by wind – a largely exogenous and predictable factor. For the tropical rainforest and the swidden plots within them, pollination and dissemination are almost always carried out by fauna whose populations and behavior themselves vary with agricultural intervention.

These ecosystem-response uncertainties present partially avoidable risks to agriculturalists. Individual farmers can increase the likelihood of successful interaction by acquiring and utilizing more information about ecosystem

112

responses, by forgoing economies of scale and diversifying their activities, and by insuring against risks through formal institutions or informal bonds between relatives and neighbors. For society, interaction with success comparable to that in the temperate zones requires, for the same level of well-being, better developed education, extension, and agroecosystem management systems and more sophisticated risk-sharing institutions. These social responses to uncertainty take up whatever surplus would otherwise be available for investments in further agricultural coevolution.

The low economic productivity of the tropical rainforest is largely associated with crops that require even flows of nutrients from stocks in the soil. In the temperate zone, the soil system acts as a reservoir of organic material, essential minerals, and water. In the tropics, organic matter quickly decays in the year-round warmth, and minerals leach away with the high rainfall. These losses are prevented in the native vegetation system by a rapid recycling of the nutrients back into the standing biomass. A superficial mat of fine roots captures a high percentage of nutrients from litter soon after leaves fall and decay. Plants which have not evolved in this setting are typically ill suited to this system of nutrient recycling. In addition, the soils that have evolved in the tropical rainforest have very little organic matter or other water retentive characteristics. For this reason, introduced species typically also suffer from lack of water in the soil during the few months of the year when evapotranspiration exceeds rainfall. Furthermore, introduced species are typically not adapted to the low pH of the soil and suffer from associated aluminum and iron toxicities. Due to the unsuitability of introduced species, their productivity is typically low and uncertain compared with how they perform in their native environments.

TECHNOLOGICAL OPTIONS AND SOCIAL SYSTEM CHARACTERISTICS

Technological options seem to fall into five categories:

1 highgrading the most valuable natural species,
2 swidden or slash and burn agricultural systems,
3 use of perennials, mimicking some of the features of the rainforest ecosystem,
4 overriding the ecosystem with energy-intensive modern agricultural technologies, and
5 utilization of the floodplain.

Each of these options and combinations of them have been utilized in the Amazon. Their potentials for achieving coevolution vary with respect to both their likelihood of success and the paths of change open to the social system.

Historically, highgrading has been the predominant technology of westernized peoples. Highgrading consists of removing the very best, i.e. most valuable, from a broad mix of species. Over the past four centuries, certain species of trees, turtles, alligators, spotted cats, and, more recently fish have been exploited to levels so low that it is no longer profitable to harvest them and frequently to levels so low that they are in danger of becoming extinct. Individuals did not own these species and no western system of social organization has ever been established in the Amazon to protect adequately and collectively manage species. Hence, those species which have an economic value, typically from external markets, suffer the "tragedy of the commons." From an ecological perspective, the term "highgrading" differs from exploitation per se in that it incorporates a mixed-species view of the world and the competition of unexploited species for the niches of the exploited. From a social perspective, highgrading requires little social organization which is fitting since the spatial density of economic activity is very low, matching the low areal density of the species highgraded. Exploitation to extinction, or at least local extinction, is very likely in this combined ecological and social setting because of the low areal density of the collectors and their prey, the great numbers of species, and the near absence of distinct seasonal behavior make the assignment and enforcement of property rights or regulation by a society costly. The river turtle is a partial exception. The major predation strategy by people – capturing mature turtles, eggs, and young at nesting sites – is controlled with some success because the turtles congregate and use the same small number of beaches for nesting at predictable times of the year. Though predation is easy, control of predation is also easy. Highgrading, almost by definition, might initiate but cannot sustain coevolutionary development. There are conceivable combinations of species reproduction strategies, predation techniques, market demand conditions, and property assignment or regulatory costs such that highgrading might lead to species management and coevolutionary development rather than to an unregulated low-level equilibrium or extinction. Highgrading and an unfavorable species mix have not occurred in two cases of special interest: natural rubber trees tapped for latex and Brazil nut exploitation. The establishment of *aviamento* at the time the products from these species became especially valued and heavily exploited may have been critical to the protection of these species.

Hunting, fishing, and gathering have always been supplemented by some agriculture. The only widely successful agricultural technique in the Amazon has been slash and burn, or swidden, wherein a hectare or two of the forest is cleared, the fallen trees allowed to dry before they are burned, and then annual crops are planted for two to four years. The productivity of the system for introduced crops is temporarily increased through the transfer of nutrients from the forest biomass into the soil in the form of ash. Crop yields decline each year as the fertility from the ashes is leached away and as the reinvading succession vegetation competes for nutrients, water, and sunlight. The farmer can fight this succession process with a machete or through intermediate burns, but native species increasingly out-compete agricultural crops in the ever less fertile soil. Both productivity and predictability are relatively high initially when soil fertility is relatively high and competing natural vegetation is nearly absent. Rice is typically grown the first year because it requires more nutrients and does not compete well with intruders. As vegetation encroaches and soil fertility declines, beans and then eventually cassava are planted. But the productivity and predictability continue to decline and within a few years the clearing is abandoned. Farmers typically clear plots each year and hence are managing plots at all stages all of the time. This, combined with the practice of intermixing crops on plots, reduces risk. Land in swidden production provides reasonable yields, but land is typically only in production 10–30 percent of the time. Thus, the overall productivity of the land remains low.

Multicrop swidden agriculture combined with fishing, hunting, and gathering has provided adequate subsistence returns for many people. Between 1940 and 1960, the population of the Brazilian Amazon grew at 2 percent per year. These years – from the time the rural population stabilized after the collapse of the rubber economy until the emergence of active Amazon development policies – were a period during which the region was little affected by national policies or external trade. Swidden agriculture works. It can be a sustainable system and could be promoted throughout the Amazon to support a significant total population. The problem with swidden agriculture, however, is that further coevolution may not be possible within short-term planning horizons for two reasons.

First, with low areal productivity, distances between individual households are great. Distance impedes the delivery of education, agricultural information, and health care to individuals while impeding the individual's participation in politics and policy formation. With respect to economic participation in a social system, the costs of overcoming distance reduce the gains from trade and, therefore, the gains from specialization. Since farmers receive a residual of market prices after transport costs, prices received by farmers tend to vary more than market prices since transportation costs are relatively fixed. Distance also reduces the opportunities for farmers to share risk. Low productivity and the production of food primarily for subsistence result in a very low marketable surplus per unit area. This makes it difficult to justify the good roads and adequate storage facilities needed to enhance the returns to producers that would stimulate a larger marketable surplus. The unfortunate positive feedbacks here are clear. Long distances, poor transportation, and poor storage conditions account for the low prices actually received by farmers and for the high losses in product – 37 percent in the case of rice in the mid-1970s on the Transamazon Highway – between production and local markets.

Second, the existing stock of scientific agricultural information, modes of thinking about agricultural technologies, and experience with rural development systems are heavily biased toward continuous cultivation practices and relatively dense settlement. While agricultural researchers no longer simply think of swidden as backward and destructive, little knowledge has been acquired about the system and little research is being undertaken. While upland rice and cassava account for the vast majority of land in food crops in the Brazilian Amazon, almost no research has been undertaken on these crops under the swidden conditions of typical farms. A valuable aspect of the coevolutionary view is that it emphasizes that development is a continuous process, largely building on the past, rather than a discontinuous process with wholesale implantations of technologies and social systems. Swidden agriculture may have the greatest potential for coevolution in the tropical rainforest, but the knowledge base must be improved. In at least some areas, experimentation with social infrastructure complementary to swidden agriculture rather than with continuous cropping is needed.

Perennials predominate in the natural forest system, perennial crops provide better competition against the processes of succession, and several perennial crops – pepper and cacao in particular – thrive in Amazon soils. Many have argued that a perennial crop agricultural system would be a successful transformation of the tropical rainforest ecosystem because crops with characteristics similar to the natural vegetation will require less energy, materials, and human effort to maintain. However, because perennial crops usually have very little subsistence food value, coevolution must extend to distant markets. This necessitates a more highly developed social system for credit, marketing, storage, and transportation of products as well as the supply of foods for those who manage perennials to eat. Unfortunately, all of these social systems features have proven difficult and costly to maintain in the Amazon.

Perennials are less sensitive to environmental factors, but the economic risks of environmentally related damage to perennials can be greater because all future harvests are at stake. When cacao, pepper, and rubber are grown in plantations, they are subject to attack by fungi that can halt economic production. In addition, due to the sensitivity of the prices of perennial crops to variations in the demand for these crops, market prices can fluctuate dramatically. Changes in production in the Amazon alone have affected the stability of international prices of cacao and pepper. Nevertheless, perennials can play a very important supplementary role in agricultural development. Nuts and fruits can be valuable sources of protein and vitamins. Trees provide protection to the soil and other crops from sun and driving rain. Nutrient recycling can also be enhanced with trees through various symbiotic relationships. Nevertheless, for perennials to serve a key role in development, the social system needs more sophisticated risk sharing, price forecasting, and planning and regulatory components than does a social system at the same level of well-being in the temperate zone.

Overriding the processes of the rainforest ecosystem with industrially produced fertilizers and pesticides is also a possibility. With sufficient energy, the heterogenous rainforest can be made to behave like the monocultural systems we associate with agriculture in the temperate zones. Sufficient energy needs to be transferred to the ecosystem in the form of fertilizers, calcium, and herbicides in an appropriate manner. Appropriate fertilization practices, however, are complicated due to high rates of leaching; high soil acidity; aluminum and sometimes iron toxicities; and phosphorous, calcium, and micronutrient deficiencies. Moreover, the cultivars that respond best to fertilizers tend to be more susceptible to the wide variety of pests in the tropics. Hence, better pest management is necessary to protect the productivity gains. Because strategies for pest management have not been well developed, using pesticides is more likely to trigger pest resurgence and outbreaks of secondary pests in Amazonia, similar to those experienced in other developing regions. The unforeseen consequences of intervention deter, if not defeat, the energy-intensive approach. Like that for perennials, this approach requires well developed markets for both inputs and for outputs and an education and extension system to generate and maintain special entrepreneurial and ecosystem managerial skills. Uncertain energy prices and national programs to reduce energy dependence also make this approach less likely to prove fit.

Much of the floodplain in the Amazon has heavy, reasonably fertile soils that appear well suited for cultivating paddy rice and perhaps other crops. With diking and draining, at least two crops of irrigated rice can be grown per year with a fairly consistent annual production of between five and eight times the yield per area of upland rice and with much greater and more certain returns to farmers. Furthermore, unlike swidden systems, production can take place year after year, increasing the productivity per area to 20 to 40 times that of production on the upland areas. Weed management and efficient nutrient usage are handled largely through water control. Energy for pumping and draining irrigation water might be tapped from the adjacent river channels using in-stream turbines or waterwheels. The high productivity per unit area would facilitate the provision of social services while good access to river transportation further enhances net returns. The intensification of paddy production in Asia documents that the technology is highly malleable. Paddy rice can be cultivated under widely different combinations of labor, capital, material inputs, and managerial skill. Thus coevolution from a wide variety of initial conditions and along many paths appears to be possible.

Floodplain development, however, also has its costs. The floodplain is the most productive natural habitat now for fish and timber. It supports much of the existing subsistence agriculture. Rivers, of course, have flood plains for good reason, and as the floodplain became increasingly occupied with paddy, flooding would be greater elsewhere. While conflicts between these uses and paddy rice development would be minimal in the beginning, an institution for coordinating floodplain development would eventually have to be incorporated into the social system.

TRANSACTIONS COSTS

Until only recently, both political and economic theory assumed a frictionless world in which people learned, organized, agreed upon solutions, and implemented them at no cost. This vision followed from Newton's mechanics. It ignores the costs of knowledge, information, and skill acquisition, decision-making, contracting, and enforcement. One does not have to look very hard at the industrialized economies to see that most people are engaged in learning, thinking, contracting, and enforcement . . . after they have spent an hour or more just trying to get to school or work. We still envision people's labor as consisting of physically tilling soil and crafting products whereas in fact few are employed in these jobs. Furthermore, farm managers, workers in the service sector, and to some extent industrial workers – including those in agriculture – now spend much of their life going to school and making decisions. Economists have referred to the friction in market transactions – the costs of information, contracting, and enforcement – as transaction costs. For lack of a better alternative word, I will expand the meaning of transactions costs to include the costs of making social systems function generally, including the costs of interacting effectively with the complex and changing conditions of the environment.

In this context, let me make a series of interrelated hypotheses. The level or intensity of transactions necessary for maintaining social systems that interact with tropical rainforest ecosystems effectively and sustainably is comparable to that now experienced by northern nations grappling with the social and environmental consequences of industrialization. For development to succeed in the Amazon or anywhere else, the returns from interacting with the ecosystem must be sufficient to cover the transactions costs, leaving a surplus for further investment in change. Swidden agriculture, hunting, and gathering as traditionally practiced supports a minimally necessary social structure but leaves little or no surplus for change. It is not clear if there is another technology, though paddy rice is an excellent candidate, which will support the necessary transactions and leave a surplus. Development efforts have failed to date because of the level of transactions necessary. The productivity of the technologies initiated in the Amazon have been grossly overestimated while their transactions costs have been underestimated. Transactions costs, in short, limit development.

In the Amazon, transactions costs are high because of the diversity of the ecosystem, the heterogeneity of the older social systems still surviving, the multiplicity of objectives of the different peoples trying to influence development, and the paucity of knowledge with respect to compatible technologies and forms of social organization. The blame for development failure in the Amazon has been put on specific components of these factors. But development failure can be generalized as being the consequences of ineffective interactions between the social and ecological systems and net losses due to the high transactions costs of devising and maintaining feedbacks within the social system and between the social system and ecosystem.

The quantity, variety, and intricacy of agroenvironmental decisions contribute to high transactions costs. The information component, especially, is high due to ecosystem complexity and the costs of overcoming distance to collect information in the field or to communicate information between extension personnel, agriculturalists, and workers. High transactions costs reduce the optimum intensity of management and, thereby, productivity per unit area. High information collection and transmittal costs encourage labor-intensive activities, such as forest clearing and planting more area, rather than management-intensive activities based on better information. The resulting dispersion of settlement and economic activity compounds the transactions costs problem by increasing the costs associated with distance. Over the longer run, lower productivity per unit area accentuates transactions costs because distance interferes with the accumulation of skills, information, and communication ability through schooling and extension programs.

Transactions costs are also high in the Amazon due to the cultural diversity of the social system. The Indians, peasants, and landed classes are vastly different. Since the concerted effort to populate the Amazon beginning in the late 1960s, peasants from outside the Amazon, bureaucrats loyal to state and federal capitals, technocrats, capitalists and their bankers, and multinational corporate representatives have joined the population mix. Coevolution is limited by the communication costs associated with the transmittal of technical information and the formulation of development policies, both private and public.

For example, in the Amazon as elsewhere, agricultural extension agents work more easily with educated farmers. The transactions costs of disseminating information and reaching and keeping agreements are lower because the cultural barriers are lower. The more educated farmers tend to have more capital to purchase the equipment and supplies advocated by extension agents trained in modern techniques. Frequently these farmers are closer to markets or live near the best roads and are more easily visited by extension agents. These advantages increase as extension agents, pleased to see new techniques put into practice, spend more time with the successful farmers. The other side of this success story, however, is that the farmers who need more help in fact receive less than a proportionate share. Initial disparities in wealth, experience, and education were significantly exaggerated among the colonists along the Transamazon Highway. Such increasing disparities are contrary to the egalitarian objectives of colonization and increase the transactions costs of political participation and public policy formulation by creating more diverse needs and greater cultural barriers to communication.

THE BUREAUCRATIC JUNGLE

In light of the diverse areal and temporal complexities of interacting with the tropical ecosystem, minimal social superstructure beyond those making decisions in the field is needed to keep transactions costs low. Development in the Amazon, however, has been overseen by a maze of agencies headquartered in capital and industrial cities. This bureaucratic jungle has added to the complications of farmers and others interacting with the ecological jungle. Political, administrative, and corporate power is concentrated in capitals such as Brasilia and industrial cities such as Sao Paulo, far removed from the Amazon. The public servants enmeshed in development decisions located in the Amazon and corporate field managers have limited authority to respond to changes in the field. At the same time, they are saddled with unrealistic work plans drawn up by bureaucrats or corporate officials who may never have been in the Amazon and understand little about its social and ecological systems. Transactions costs are even higher to the extent that international development agencies, multinational banks, and multinational corporations have joined the effort to spur development. Central control can be efficient where there are economies of scale in the gathering and disseminating of information and where there are interdependencies between regions or activities. In a diverse, complex and uncertain ecosystem with relatively few interconnections between activities in other regions, decisions cannot be efficiently mandated from afar. In the Amazon, there is greater justification for the decentralization of economic and political power so that the local social system can respond opportunely to the intricate and varying nature of the ecosystem. From the perspective of those in national capitals, industrial cities, and international centers, centralization is justified, not on efficiency grounds, but by their desire to control and obtain returns from the capital and talent they are transferring to the Amazon. The coevolutionary perspective highlights the transactions costs of the interrelations between social and ecological systems and complements existing arguments for endogenously directed and controlled development.

IMPLICATIONS FOR THE REVISIONING OF PROGRESS

The coevolutionary interpretation of development failure in the Amazon helps document the broader coevolutionary perspective on the past and the future explored in the now more general book. Attempts to predict, direct, and control development based on presumably universal concepts of how development occurs that have been held by Westerners have been a resounding failure in the Amazon. Traditional knowledge has repeatedly proven more reliable. It is also clear that the surviving social systems in the Amazon coevolved with the ecological system. Attempts to link the Amazon economy to the global economy or to the international development process have repeatedly resulted in ecosystem degradation and eventually the collapse of local social systems. All of this supports the revisioning of progress as a process of economic and cultural divergence toward a patchwork quilt of coevolving cultures and its associated coevolutionary cosmology.

The significance of these findings for changing the structure and processes of Western and westernized societies are explored in greater detail in Chapter 12 on the democratization of progressivism. But first, the consequences of individualism are explored.

11

THE TYRANNY OF LIBERAL INDIVIDUALISM

One of the most important lessons that can be drawn from the Amazon is that social systems and ecosystems *should* coevolve. They should be allowed to coevolve locally and regionally rather than be overridden through the imposition of external value, knowledge, organizational, and technological systems. Such impositions are likely to lead to both social and environmental disasters. For cultural and natural systems to coevolve on a regional scale, cohesion within the region and separation from other regions are necessary. Communities, cultures, and bioregions are social structures for which system cohesion and separation are understood to be required. But these commonly understood terms are at the mercy of two currently more dominant concepts, individualism and globalism. Dominated by individualism and globalism, communities, cultures, and bioregions little influence either conscious social design or unconscious social evolution.

Western social philosophy starts with the individual and leaps to the national and on to the global. We are intellectually impoverished in our public discourse when it comes to thinking about communities. The historical biases of Western social philosophy are apparent today in "me first" materialism and in the globalization of the world economy. The premises of Western social theory are apparent among dying rural communities which are unneeded for the support of modern agriculture; in the faces of the unemployed in rusting industrial communities after manufacturing capital has moved to developing countries where wages are low and employment benefits few; in the social and environmental disasters of central Third World cities which have grown incredibly rapidly; and in the expansion from the commercial centers of shopping malls and individual homes across the landscape of North America and increasingly in other places as well.

The dominant, modern conception of people and of social relationships posits individuals as having assets – material resources, talents, votes, and even love – that they trade with each other. People exist as individuals, have preferences as individuals, and hold discrete, tradeable assets. People and things are separate; they can be reduced to atomistic parts. People choose

122

to exchange, according to the economic logic of exchange relations, when doing so improves their happiness. Thus modifying social systems to facilitate exchange is seen as the way to improve individual well-being and thereby well-being overall. And to a large extent social relations have coevolved with this atomistic-mechanistic understanding of social relations. Across what have been widely different cultural groups and ecological systems, economies, indeed social systems in every dimension, are interpreted by modern peoples as merely mechanisms for exchange between individuals. The global penetration and dominance of this modern conception of people, things, and social systems has increased individualist values, selecting against the social values associated with nonexchange relations. Liberal individualism, excessive emphasis on exchange relations, and globalization have led progress astray.

Earlier chapters emphasized how popularly held beliefs are associated with the rise of natural science over the past four hundred years, and how these historic beliefs select for ways of organizing and doing things which cause environmental problems and impede our coevolution with environmental systems. This chapter documents how beliefs associated with the history of Western social philosophy over a similar period impede coevolution at a community level.

LIBERAL INDIVIDUALISM

At least since John Locke's treatises of the seventeenth century, individualism has been central to the dominant Western constructs of social and moral philosophy. In the wake of the bitter religious conflicts and costly social turmoil of the Thirty Years War, philosophers found it safer to abstract from cultural realities and began to construct arguments with respect to the nature of social systems and moral obligations based on the nature of individuals. People were presumed to have innate traits entirely apart from their cultures which dictated the terms of social organization. This treatment of individuals was reinforced by the success of atomism in the natural sciences and the rise of science, especially the work of Newton, in the same period. The philosophical fabrication of individualism, in turn, became the basis for economic thought, from classical to neoclassical economic theory and to the politics of economic liberalism.

Tolerance and the freedom to choose are very much a part of modern liberal rhetoric. But it has been a tolerance for individual deviation and for the freedom of individuals to choose. Individuals banding together in communities and choosing within a cultural system of understanding, values, and social pressures is portrayed as oppressive. Even one's preferences are portrayed, at least in economic theory, as being independent of one's culture or social association. In the name of liberalism, modern peoples have pressured each other, as well as modernizing peoples, to choose independently of whatever cultural heritages they may have. In the face of the material and other choices offered by modernity, the cultures of all but the strongest or most isolated of peoples have broken down. Through its emphasis on individualism, modernity is culturally disrespectful, even while respecting individual differences.

Ultimately, however, people are only different because of the values and ways of knowing they share as members of different cultures. Western respect for the individual, in short, breaks down the cultures which make individuals different. And the resulting identity crises of individuals is typically assuaged through consumerism, thereby both validating the materialism and importance of exchange and further bolstering liberal individualism with a positive feedback.

ECONOMIC EXCHANGE

The preeminence of exchange in our understanding of social systems is also rooted in liberal individualism. The theory of exchange is very straightforward. Economists reason that if a chooser chooses, it is because it is to the chooser's advantage, for a chooser would not choose to do something that would be disadvantageous. And if two choosers choose to enter into an exchange, it is because it makes each of them better off. This logic – with a few caveats about choosers being fully informed and bearing all of the costs and receiving all of the benefits of their own decisions – is the basis of market economics. The logic of free choice now dominates most economic discussions, indeed most modern discussions of social organization, from the local to the global. And the logic is impeccable.

Economists, in keeping with a three-hundred-year tradition in Western philosophy, however, have always assumed that choosers are individuals, or perhaps corporations. Choosers are not families, not communities, not people within bioregions, not cultural groups, not even nations. Any choices these other social units may themselves deem reasonable are interpreted in the understanding of economic liberalism as constraints on the free choice of individuals and barriers to trade.

But why should not families, or communities, or cultures, or nations be free to choose? Why should collective choice not be an option? Nations should be free to choose whether particular types of trade are advantageous to the nation or not. There is nothing in the logic of free choice or free trade that says the choosers or traders must be individuals. Indeed, the two conditions underlying the logic – that choosers be fully informed and bear all of the costs and receive all of the benefits of their decisions – frequently justify decision-making by larger social units. The logic of exchange does not relieve the tension between the interests of individuals and the interests of the whole.

There is a long history of economic thought on when the invisible hand fails to align private interest with public interest. Nevertheless, economists as a profession remain solid advocates of free trade among individuals first and worry about the public consequences later. Neoclassical economics accepts the assumption of liberal individualism on the presumption that, in general, Adam Smith's invisible hand does work.

There is, however, another explanation for the economic profession's stance. The logic of economics does not yield unique answers when more than one social unit might express an interest in choosing. Without a single answer, economics cannot be used technocratically to deduce what society should do. Economists seem to have agreed informally to refer only to individuals and corporations as choosers because it allows them to fulfill their progressive, à la Auguste Comte, econocratic role. There is no reason that economic logic cannot complement democratic, rather than technocratic, decision-making. It is important to realize, however, that the way economic reasoning would complement democracy would be entirely inconsistent with the culture of the discipline of economics that has coevolved with the progressive, technocratic strand of Western thought and the forms of capitalism with limited democracy that this strand supports. As econocrats, they perceive themselves as informing politicians and the public and as being given the power to implement political decisions in finer detail. As participants in the democratic process, they would have no more power than many others with particular ways of thinking that would help the democratic process work through a complex question.

In fact, of course, nations repeatedly choose to constrain trade because they do not always find trade in their national interest. Economists typically counter that nations do not really behave in their national interest because decisions are not made sufficiently democratically or equitably or knowledgeably. But economists are arguing from a position that denies the whole idea that social units might be more than the sum of their parts. There is a cynical dishonesty to their plea that social groups are not what they should be when argued from a perspective that denies the essence of social groups at all.

Even among the quite democratic, equitable, and informed Scandinavian countries, individuals are not free to trade as they please. With greater respect for groups as decision-making units, more groups might become like the Amish in the United States and establish cultural barriers. Some nations would no doubt choose near complete isolation, much as Bhutan, China, Japan, Myanmar (Burma), and Tanzania have chosen at various times. Barriers need not go up simply to protect culture. Communities that are not culturally distinct traditionally from other communities may logically choose to regulate how they relate with the rest of the world in order to protect their environment or their health. A community that chooses to have a viable agricultural sector without the use of pesticides, for example, might restrict or tax the importation of cheaper foods produced with the use of pesticides elsewhere in order to assure their own viability. Barriers for a large variety of reasons may be appropriate depending on the desires of the groups choosing. At the same time, it is important to acknowledge that cultural choice and differences, or at least the maintenance of differences, rely on barriers. Groups – be they families, communities, or nations – only have significance to the extent that they can act and maintain themselves as a group, and this means some sorts of barriers are essential.

The logic of exchange combined with the implicit assumption that only individuals should be free to choose has been used to break down cultural barriers around the world. Exchange makes everyone better off. The benefits of exchange are quick and immediately visible. On the other hand, the decline of culture is slow, the importance of its decline is difficult to assess, and the connections between exchange and the weakening of cultures are not obvious. With the loss of cultural identity, reinforcing one's identity through material consumption becomes a more viable option. With the loss of recognizing oneself as a member of a group, collective action becomes more difficult, further strengthening market relations and the need to use market approaches to solve social problems. These positive feedbacks may be weak, but when culture is identified with traditions of the past and people have faith in modern progress, there has, until the recent decline in faith in modern progress, been little to counteract this positive feedback process. And this process has weakened the cohesiveness and ability of groups – families, neighborhoods, communities, states, and nations as well as academic, cultural, environmental, political, religious, and other organizations – to act collectively. Perhaps the only saving grace has been that corporations have suffered the same fate.

RISK AND THE GLOBAL VILLAGE

The past two centuries of development have transformed what was a coevolving mosaic of traditional farming systems into a global economy based on modern technologies. The adoption of Western knowledge and technologies selected for complementary social organization and values, setting disparate cultures on convergent paths. The logic of exchange has been misused to rationalize the process that is portrayed as both inevitable and a sign of progress. Progressives, playing with romantic rhetoric, sometimes refer to the emergence of a global village.

Perhaps villages can be scaled up to a global level, but the global market system that has been emerging over the past few centuries performs few of the functions of a village. This is because the theory of exchange at the level it is invoked in public discourse pays too little attention to risk and almost none to the ways ecosystems function.

Agriculture is the most important example. Agroecosystems that were unique to particular cultures and ecosystems also merged in the process of globalization. Under the selective pressure from common cropping, fertilization, and pest control practices of modern agriculture, crop varieties, soil characteristics, and plant-pest interactions are increasingly alike within trade-determined growing regions of the world. Furthermore, the technologies employed and the economic and institutional sectors which support them are becoming more nearly identical. The mechanistic grid of universal truths developed by Western science has boldly overlayed the elaborate mosaic of traditional agricultural systems with simple, repeated patterns linked by markets. And the spread of liberal individualism facilitated the convergence of coevolutionary processes.

One of the most important aspects of the convergence from many traditional agroecosystems to the modern global agroecosystem has been a shift in the nature of risk and its management. The vagaries of production have long been recognized as critical to thinking about agricultural systems. Traditional and modern agroeconomic worlds have some risks in common. Variations in the conditions of production occur for both due to changes in weather, the introduction or evolution of new crop pests and diseases, and the occurrence of war. There are also differences. In the traditional world, for example, illness can reduce the availability of labor for local agricultural activities. In the global agricultural economy, regional production conditions can vary significantly with changes in exchange rates, the introduction of new technologies, and changes in national agricultural policies. Differences in the nature of risk and the means of managing risk in traditional and modern agroecosystems help explain the breakdown of cultural and biological systems.

In the traditional world, uncertainty for agriculturalists largely stemmed from "natural" causes: weather, pests, and diseases. I use the word "natural" fully cognizant, of course, of how environments have coevolved with people. In the modern world, changes in crop prices and in agricultural, environmental, and trade policies cause more uncertainty than the weather for most farmers. To a considerable extent, the adoption of modern technologies and institutions to reduce "natural" risks for individual farmers has resulted in new forms of risks and a shift of risk to larger groups and future peoples. The transformation in the interplay between the nature of risk and its management make it impossible to construct a simple taxonomy appropriate for the two agroeconomic worlds.

Though some of the natural risks have been the same in both agroeconomic worlds, the manifestation of these risks and methods of avoidance have differed. Crop pests and disease, for example, were a constant problem in the traditional world, but to the extent they were constant, they were not risks. They were fairly constant because traditional agroecosystems were typically connected to larger natural ecosystems. Pests flowed from the natural ecosystem to the agroecosystem, but predators of the pests also flowed just as readily. When soils depleted or weeds became excessive, mulching materials could be collected from the natural system. In short, the natural system buffered, or provided materials which could be used to buffer, the variations in the agroecosystem.

To the extent that pests and disease, as well as weather variability, reduce the productivity of food species independently, risk can be reduced simply by taking advantage of the law of large numbers. Thus each producer reduced risks by planting multiple crops and varieties in different micro-environments at different times of the year. By planting or using species with negative covariances, or by diversifying management strategies to encourage negative covariances, traditional peoples also spread their risk in ideal portfolios.

A portfolio approach to risk management cannot be practiced generation after generation, however, if diversity is not maintained. By planting diverse crops in diverse environments, by varying production strategies, and by bringing new strains into their fields from the natural environment, each producer helped maintain genetic diversity. There are instances where the genetic diversity of crops increased under traditional practice. As suggested in the previous section, the genetic diversity of species along the fuzzy boundaries of the mosaic was increased through the selective pressure of hunting, gathering, and modest management.

The important point is that within the coevolving mosaic of traditional agriculture, people avoided risk through more diverse interaction with their ecological system. This managed interaction lowered individual and collective risk and, furthermore, sustained or enhanced options for future generations to avoid risk. Anthropologists have also documented how individual risk was also reduced through sharing between individuals. Knowledge of these risk sharing mechanisms is critical to our understanding of traditional social organization.

The situation for modern agroeconomic systems is rather different from that for traditional ones. With large areas planted in one crop, modern farmers are especially vulnerable to weather, pests, and disease. But pest and disease losses are reduced in the short run through the use of chemicals and the planting of resistant species. The expansion of irrigated agriculture has reduced losses due to the vagaries of weather. Modern technologies modify the environment, overriding ecological processes and environmental constraints to increase yield and reduce risk rather than working with the ecological and environmental system.

Modern farmers still use the law of large numbers and portfolio theory to reduce risk. The law, however, is exercised through the use of future markets, the purchase of crop insurance, and the management of capital assets – frequently beyond agriculture – rather than through crop diversification. The perceived gains from specialization in production have reduced real options for risk management on the farm and driven farmers to spread their risk through the use of financial markets and government agricultural programs.

Food production objectives vary little in either the traditional or the modern world because nutritional needs are nearly constant and tastes change only slowly. Whenever individuals in the traditional world produced some crops in quantities greater than their own needs, they exchanged goods with each other, whether through sharing or through markets. In the traditional world, individual producers in a group or region found the same crops and products in demand each year. The relative value of crops or price levels *ex post* certainly varied tremendously according to the success of the harvest due to variations in local production conditions. In some cases these variations were ameliorated through trade with other regions experiencing offsetting deficits and surpluses. But *ex ante* prices, the prices that influence planting and management decisions, were relatively constant from year to year. In the global economy, however, *ex ante* prices vary considerably, directing local producers to plant in response to variations in past and expected output elsewhere. *Ex post* prices in the global agroeconomy, however, have probably been closer to *ex ante* than in traditional agroeconomies.

The transformation from the coevolving mosaic has occurred in part because individuals and societies perceive that risk can be reduced through participation in the market. Money invested in financial markets is typically less perishable than agricultural commodities. Money saved from selling surplus production in good years can be used for purchasing food through global markets in bad years. This reasoning encourages specialization by individuals and even nations in those crops that they can produce with the highest value on the average. Thus while efficiency on a global scale may be increased in the process of expanding the scope of the market, global risk also may increase. Globally, no one senses the risk which relatively self-sufficient communities reduced through a portfolio approach to crop selection and management. Global markets need a global agency to oversee whether the overall mix of crops being produced makes for a low risk portfolio and to encourage a safer mix. No such agency exists today.

In the global agroeconomy, poor crop yields in some locations are offset by good yields in others. To the extent they are not, speculators hold the least perishable crops, typically grains, in anticipation of a globally bad year. If speculators have held too little, the economy adjusts. Economists envision economies as mechanical systems that freely shift along a continuum of stable equilibria. When the production of a crop is down in one country due to poor rains, the price of the crop rises, inducing farmers around the world to bring more land into production in this crop and to farm existing land more intensively. Workers, tools, and land shift from the production of other crops to the production of the affected crop. Higher wages and land rents for production of the affected crop induce the shift. When production in the afflicted area returns to normal, the rest of the world returns to its old equilibrium.

In the idealized world of economic theory, speculation and adjustments to exogenous change maximize economic well-being. With all producers adjusting best to compensate for the failure of one crop in one country, the impact of the failure is minimized. The adjustment processes keep aggregate well-being as close to the undisturbed maximum as possible. Hence the global economy has less variation than it would if the adjustments did not take place, though perhaps not less than would be possible if individual producers and nations were not specializing and using the market to offset their own risk.

Ironically, this process of reducing risk for the whole increases the amount of change for individual producers with respect to who produces what and with which capital and land. Variation in global agricultural production is reduced through increased variability in prices and hence local production responses by individuals. The global agricultural economy, furthermore, is tightly linked to global resource markets, industry, and the flow of capital. Domestic agricultural prices not only respond to changes in the success of agriculture in far away places but reflect, through variations in the exchange rate, global changes in the prices of natural resources, industrial goods and capital as well.

The increasing local uncertainties induced by fluctuations in agricultural prices as the global agroeconomy becomes more interdependent are not foreseen by farmers individually deciding to tie into the global system. Nations must eventually respond to the uncertainties with food price policies, trade and currency controls, capital loss write-offs against income taxes, unemployment insurance, and other institutions to buffer the impact on farmers of the global mechanism for reducing uncertainties in food supplies overall.

With the evolution of complex social institutions to monitor and attempt to regulate the side-effects of modern technologies and the gyrations of global agricultural prices, changes in the management and the political use of institutions themselves have become a major source of uncertainty. Changes in environmental regulations or trade policies can become critical. A president's decision to allow or forbid the sale of wheat to a foreign adversary is as critical and unpredictable for the wheat farmer as the path of a passing hailstorm. In most countries, agricultural credit and price policies change from year to year. Monetary policies affect the exchange rate and hence the prices of crops sold in international markets. Modern farmers must follow the interplay between economic and institutional changes as closely as traditional farmers followed the dynamics of pests, predators, and weather. Indeed, it is fair to say that the traditional farmer gave most of his attention to interacting with the complexities of the agroecosystem while the modern farmer must dedicate an increasing, and in many situations now dominant, share of his attention to interacting with the complexities of the global economy and institutional system.

In summary, risk and its management are ultimately a problem of production since food consumption, especially in poor countries, can vary little. Risk management in traditional agroeconomies dealt with risk as a problem of production in a manner that maintained risk management options for the future. To the extent risk management in modern agriculture is through production rather than pooling and financial asset management, it relies on technologies that override problems in the short run while creating more problems in the long run. Science, of course, is presumed to be waiting in the wings for yet another rescue, and yet each rescue heretofore has entailed another round of unforeseen risks.

Second, individuals and groups can pool their risks, but pooling depends on the risks being different between individuals and nations and works even better if risks are negatively correlated. With the demise of the coevolving mosaic and the trend toward one modern, global culture, the differences in uncertainties on which pooling depends have been reduced dramatically. Furthermore, there are few different peoples, crops, and technologies to bring into the market over whom and which to further spread risk. The global agroeconomy has reached out and spread risks to the whole globe short of China.

The vast majority of the literature on risk in agriculture has concentrated on individual behavior and the design of institutions to reduce economic uncertainty to the individual. The influence of the larger transformations in the global economy, however, have not been investigated with respect to resource conservation. In the context of existing economic theory about how global production, speculation, and future markets work, there should be little variation in either agricultural input or output prices. Clearly, the perceptions of how markets guide producers, speculators, and the designers of new institutions are blind to the larger picture.

SOCIAL VALUES, INTERCONNECTANCE, AND THE MYTH OF CHOICE

The modern portrayal of social systems as the sum of the interactions of autonomous individuals responding to their individual values denies interconnections between peoples and nature and thereby both the existence of and need for social and environmental values. Ironically, though there are no public ethics in this portrayal, the inadequacies and dominance of the portrayal makes such ethics all the more essential. By portraying the individual as an independent entity, a dichotomy is drawn between the individual and the group. The emphasis on individual choice makes social choice an exception. The modern stress on the individual sets up the conflict between acting in one's own interest and acting in the common interest.

Individualism, choice, and the need for public ethics and commitment to the common good are inseparable artifacts of atomism.

This inseparability can perhaps best be demonstrated by portraying what it would be like to be truly conscious of interconnectance. Imagine yourself in a traditional culture of a limited number of people interacting fairly directly with nature. You realize a multiplicity of interconnectances. Nothing exists in and of itself, everything is interrelated. You fully realize you are embedded in a family that extends out to the community and that everything you do affects and is affected by everything each of the other members do. Things – tools, seeds, and the land – furthermore are also bundled. Everything goes in circles, is reciprocal, not in the sense of exchange and the trade flow diagrams of economics, but in the sense of physics and the conservation of matter and energy. Things do not simply come or go for they are always doing both, like nutrients coming from and returning to nature, like life and death are one. Furthermore, you live in a system that is evolving. You sense how today unfolded from many yesterdays and how each action in some sense determines the future, making you and what you do inseparable from the past and the future.

When truly conscious of interconnectance, one realizes that the whole Western construct of choice, of weighing options, and of conflict between the individual and the group follows from the premise of atomism and individualism. In a truly interconnected world, clear choices cannot be perceived. The outcome of any decision depends on numerous unforesee-able, linked vicissitudes and the actions taken by others and extends indefinitely into the future, to be borne by one's fellow beings and descendants forever. To the extent that earlier cultures were more conscious of interconnectance than Western peoples, especially after the Renaissance, it is easy to see how they settled into patterns of behavior that seemed to work and then followed them in humble deference to the unknowable. Individuals who did not follow traditions, furthermore, in fact did create problems and were rightly chastised or even driven out of the group. Novel situations of course arose for which no tradition could be followed. But traditional cultures are known to be rich in stories describing complex relations. Individuals who were more adept at choosing between the application of different interconnectance stories under novel situations were regarded as wise and suitable to be leaders.

Though the behavior of people within cultures seems to indicate preferences, behaviors in traditional cultures express little. People living in a highly interconnected cosmos for which traditional behaviors have been established are merely doing what has to be done.

This portrayal suggests how much of modern values are linked to the premises of individualism and atomism. The whole field of ethics assumes choices are possible, and this assumes separability. And clearly positivism, the idea that values can be kept separate from facts, makes no sense at all when one is really conscious of interrelatedness.

All of this sheds light on modernity's madness. While atomism and individualism were always stronger in Western cultures than in most others, organic understandings of systems and the sense of belonging to a community were reinforced by churches and the social structure. The community ethic needed to counteract the unfortunate consequences of individualism were reproduced from generation to generation in relative balance. The Renaissance, then, was a watershed after which atomistic-mechanistic understandings of systems and individualism became increasingly strong, reinforced by the success of technologies based on Western science and social structures increasingly based on exchange. Conversely, organismic understandings and commitment to community thereafter were less and less effective in reproducing themselves from one generation to the next and steadily declined. Thus today, we are left with the tyranny of liberal individualism.

FEMINISM

Western social structure is currently being most effectively challenged by women addressing the differential status of men and the ways in which men dominate women. The vast majority of feminists are simply striving for gender equality within the framework of liberal individualism, avoiding questioning modernity itself. Nevertheless, a large number of feminists are exploring explanations for inequality. On discovering the roots of inequality in Western philosophy, these feminists are beginning to question modernity itself.

Some feminists now argue, for example, that a Newtonian world view contradicts what have historically been very primal experiences of women and what for the majority are still extremely important: child carrying, bearing, and nursing. The subsequent family and household roles of women in most cultures have entailed more coordination, sharing, and supporting than have the roles of men. Women are more likely to view themselves as living in a partnership with their spouse, children, relatives, and neighbors. Thus women would naturally view the world more organically or holistically than men. There are, of course, exceptions.

Many have pondered the extent to which this general juxtapostion in world views is biological or cultural. Child bearing is biological, hormonal balances influence affection and aggression and are now thought to affect development as well, and cognitive differences are now recognized. And yet cultural factors are certainly extremely important. Males and females receive different cues based on their gender from everyone they encounter and clearly perceive the relative availability of different roles for which they can prepare and in which they can play in society. The extent, however, that this contrast in world views is due to in-born differences or divergences between how men and women are incorporated into societies cannot be determined. Biological and cultural factors have coevolved over generations and are ultimately inseparable. To ask the question is to think reductionistically, like a man.

Regardless of the divergences in the coevolution of biological and cultural factors for men and women, in fact, men and atomistic thinking dominate in Western science and Western science drives modernity. Both men and women now argue that atomistic-mechanistic thinking is more rational than the thinking practiced by women. Reductionistic thinking is certainly more decisive in that it supports prediction and control. The dominant premises of modernity, including universalism and monism, provide the methods by which men perceive, influence the design of, and dominate from within both natural and social systems. The use of Western science, furthermore, has become institutionalized, making what are thought of as feminine patterns of thinking inappropriate in public discourse, indeed, even contrary to the law. From a coevolutionary perspective, the dominant world view, men's dominance over women and nature, liberal individualism, and environmental systems have all coevolved.

In light of the earlier discussion on interconnectance, it is interesting to note that women are typically described as being more subjective. To many people this term implies that women are concerned more with values than facts, more with who is affected than with the intricacies of resources and technologies. The term subjective, however, also implies connectedness, an inability to separate oneself out as an individual apart from other individuals, apart from the subject whether another person or the environment. To be subjective is to find oneself integral with other people and nature. In this sense, being subjective is not a matter of values, and as noted earlier, is unlikely to be so since much of our understanding of choice and values is associated with atomism. Being subjective is having a systemic, and perhaps coevolutionary, cosmos.

In any case, whether or not reductionist reasoning is more rational, in fact, depends on the underlying nature of the cosmos. If things really are interconnected tightly, or if the social and environmental problems we are now experiencing are related to tight interconnectance, then there is nothing superior about reductionist reasoning for solving what are now recognized as the problems of modernity. The first step of reductionist reasoning is to ignore as much connectance as possible, to treat mutual causation as one-way causation, or to assume mutual feedbacks are negative and equilibrating. Holistic thinking may be indecisive, romantic, ineffective, value-laden, and naive by dominant epistemological standards, but at least it does not commit one to fallacious answers and imprudent decisions. The prediction and control of atomistic-mechanistic-universalist-monist reasoning are illusory, create problems, and prevent modern peoples from finding solutions.

Ecofeminists find the social issues of feminism and the ethical and world view issues of environmentalism inseparable. Exploring the connections, philosophical ecofeminists are finding strong correlations between the cosmologies of women, naturalists, and traditional peoples. They too are reading Western philosophers and scientists who are examining the implications of evolutionary and other nonequilibirum, nonreductionist models of systems.

CONCLUSIONS

Liberal individualism and globalism, or at least their dominance, facilitate a culturally disrespectful world, a world in which group association of any kind is irrational. Shifting from an atomistic-mechanistic understanding of structure and process which complements individualism and exchange to conceptual pluralism which includes a coevolutionary understanding of process could play a key role in giving groups and cultures new legitimacy. To move in the direction of the coevolutionary patchwork quilt of cultures elaborated in Chapter 13, or at least a peaceful one, all peoples would have to allow other peoples to form and behave as cultural groups. This key, initiating premise may not seem especially radical at first. But it means that the tyranny of liberal individualism would have to be tempered. This is radical. Western individualism formed a very important role in freeing people from the arbitrary power of church and state. Individual rights to justice, personal protection, and property in some forms will still be needed. At the same time, community must be recognized again.

We are trapped by the templates of our minds, or more specifically by the dominance of too few templates, which pattern our choices with respect to social organization. Additional templates are our best hope. Understanding coevolution as process provides an additional template. Existing templates, however, also need to be enriched. The next chapter begins a revisioning of how the future could be. This revisioning builds on the only institution beyond the market which enjoys widespread support, the institution of democracy, which could be seriously enriched by understanding it as a process of group learning and understanding. This enrichment, in turn, gives groups new meaning.

12

DEMOCRATIZING KNOWLEDGE

> Knowledge and skill present an interesting problem. There is surely a limit to what any individual can learn or learn to do. A group, however, seems to remove the limit by specialization; but specialization calls for co-ordination, which is undoubtedly subject to increasing cost.
>
> (Frank H. Knight 1930, cited in 1956: 187)

Economist Frank Knight stumbled upon an important principle of social organization. While individuals are limited in the number of skills and types of knowledge they can learn, societies can do more and know more than any individual through having individuals specialize in particular skills and types of knowledge. But there must be ways of coordinating these individual skills and knowledge, and such mechanisms themselves require time and effort on everyone's part as well as people who specialize in coordination. One coordinating pathway links two people, three people require three pathways, four people require six, and five people require ten. By this reasoning, with skills or knowledge distributed between n people, the costs of coordination increase at the rate of $n(n-1)/2$, or exponentially, with specialization.

Social theorists frequently come across this principle. Yet even though coordination is the essence of social organization, this principle is not a part of modern wisdom and must constantly be rediscovered anew. Key premises of Western political philosophy keep us from thinking about, in effect blind us from seeing, the coordinating mechanisms upon which modern societies depend.

Markets, of course, are well recognized as coordinating mechanisms. However, the dominant portrayal of this mechanism is that it is an "invisible hand," working entirely passively, still leaving people independent. With a history of extensive opportunities to farm and initiate small businesses on a moving frontier, the people of the United States in some ways were shielded from the harsh realities of markets and social power. The metaphor of the market as an invisible hand fit the U.S. experience relatively better than for people in Europe or those under colonial rule. But by the 1920s, many in the United States had clearly seen a visible organizing hand. Corporate coordination – managers on the assembly line, executives in office suites, procurers of land and resources, directors in smoke-filled board rooms, and bankers beyond – coordinated people during the twentieth century at least as much as markets. The quote from Frank Knight continues with the plaintive words: "In the United States, the increasing proportion of the population which the census shows to be earning their living by telling others what to do is already a theme for viewers-with-alarm." American social theorists, from right to left, have documented the transition from the time when the vast majority of people in the United States worked on relatively small farms and in modest farming communities to when the majority experienced big city life working as laborers in large industries or as paper-pushers, the ultimate coordinators, in corporations and bureaucracies. From the late nineteenth and through much of the twentieth century, this transformation was a topic of Western political discourse. At the end of the twentieth century, however, the metaphor of the "invisible hand" is once again keeping people in the United States from addressing structure and power, this time clearly inappropriately and for reasons less than obvious. For reasons equally difficult to understand, the myth reigns throughout Western political economic discourse, as if the majority of modern peoples were self-employed and responding to markets rather than reporting to work in large, bureaucratically-administered organizations in which coordination is the essence of work itself.

My own demythologizing of this transition in previous chapters, while not denying the marxist explanations for the existence of hierarchy and power, stresses how the dominance of our beliefs in individualism and markets has weakened our sense of community and our ability to respond collectively to unfavorable environmental and cultural changes. Frank Knight's quote indicates considerations beyond markets are in order for he also noted that specialized knowledge, as well as skills, need coordination. In keeping with the epistemological orientation of this book, this chapter focuses on this concern.

Modern philosophy and social theory are nearly as poorly developed as popular consciousness with respect to how specialized knowledges are coordinated. Western epistemological premises account for much of this deficiency. Atomism presumes nature can be understood as consisting of parts. Having long believed in the unity of knowledge, modern peoples see disciplinary understandings of the parts as partial reflections of one whole reality. Furthermore, objectivism includes the idea that each objective thinker would reach the same answer, a myth that leads to the conclusion that it makes no difference who does the thinking. So long as separate understandings held by different people of different parts of reality are thought to naturally fit together into a unified whole, no mechanisms for the coordination of separate understandings are thought to be needed. Thus the Western premises of atomism, monism, and objectivism shield us from acknowledging the existence of the mechanisms by which societies actually coordinate separate understandings. Operating in the midst of maladaptive beliefs, the coordinating mechanisms which must necessarily exist are not well adapted. And when these unrecognized, maladaptive mechanisms conflict with recognized social mechanisms, the conflicts are poorly interpreted. Thus, for example, we only dimly perceive and weakly address the friction between how we make science work and democratic decision-making.

However intuitive the separation of fact and value and the unity of knowledge may have been in earlier times, few who think very seriously about Western knowledge believe in objectivism, monism, and atomism today. These premises of Western thought exist as myths, and whichever interests they may have served after it became clear by mid-century that science did not actually progress in accordance with them, the myths are clearly maladaptive now. Indeed, by looking into the complications of coordinating separate understandings, we see not only how the processes of collective understanding and decision-making need to change, the subject of this chapter, but also how the ways we structure communities to facilitate these collective processes need to change, the subject of the next.

A BRIEF RETURN TO THE BUREAUCRATIC JUNGLE

There is no better way to acquire social insight than to participate in a different yet westernized culture, observe its peculiarities, and then discover that the absurdities which were difficult to rationalize were simply exaggerations of modernity's shortcomings. Working on development and environment issues in Brazil not only facilitated my interpreting development as a coevolutionary process but initiated my queries into the relationships between bureaucracy and Western beliefs about knowledge, in short, about social structure, social processes, and epistemology.

The development of the Brazilian tropical rainforests from the late 1960s through the late 1980s was largely planned in and administered from the capital in Brasilia, far from the Amazon. During my first year in the Amazon in 1978, I repeatedly heard complaints from lower-level bureaucrats in the field. The evolution of Amazon development through experience, or "learning by doing," was not possible. Field administrators could neither alter the development plans themselves nor send adequate signals back to Brasilia as to why and how the plans should be modified. Belief in the initial plans and rationales – rooted in development theory, experience in the South of Brazil, and a few, inadequate scientific studies in the Amazon – was so complete among planners in Brasilia that information from the field that contradicted the plans was not believed. Thus mistakes, such as the provision of credit to colonists only for the planting of inappropriate strains of rice, were repeated until the colonists went broke. And when the folly was complete, still nothing was learned. Wholly new development plans and rationales were synthesized from theoretical arguments and sparse data which, if used selectively, supported them. An acceleration of the subsidization of deforestation for corporate cattle ranching, for example, was the "rational" planners' response to the failure of agricultural colonization projects.

During my second year in Brazil, I had the opportunity to serve in Brasilia on an Amazon planning team myself. I soon discovered that only a few of the team members had ever been to the Amazon beyond the limits of its two major cities, Belem and Manaus. Indeed, only one other team member, of about twenty total, had more experience on the ground in the Amazon than me, and I had only worked in Brazil for a year. More frustrating still, almost none of the other team members felt it would be appropriate to visit the major areas in which development had been encouraged in order to learn first hand what had gone wrong or to visit any new areas we might propose for development to assess their suitability directly. Nearly all thought a new, improved plan could be derived in Brasilia through a better application of theory to existing maps, data, and reports derived by others in the field, though much of the primary material also lacked ground truthing. To me, it was obvious that we should check, discuss, and fit together the bits and pieces of knowledge derived by others in the context of what we could see in the field and what people with field experience could tell us. For the rest of the team, more elaborate theories and a more thorough investigation of the bits and pieces of recorded knowledge would naturally fit into a coherent understanding from which a new plan would flow. As I explored this difference in perceptions, the words they chose to justify staying in Brasilia also indicated that going out into the field and working with people with experience was not only unnecessary but also beneath their dignity. People in the field were expected to follow plans, not participate in their making.

At the time I realized that our different positions were rooted in cultures with different degrees and styles of class structure. Being a planner or bureaucrat in Brasilia conveyed more and higher class than I had anticipated. In view of the fact that the most powerful people with whom the members of the Amazon planning team interacted were development planners from the North, they might rationalize that they were near the top of the only mountain. And I had also heard that bureaucrats who had lost favor along the climb to the top were assigned to the field. Still, I was not prepared to accept the idea that class not only entailed being powerful but also entailed being right.

The impracticality of thinking that the bits and pieces of information we had would fit together without pondering their fit in the field continued to astound me. The U.S. planning teams with which I had been associated earlier in Alaska, for example, continuously relied on ground-truthing and people with field experience. And yet I had to admit that books on scientific method, then and now, as well as books on planning at the time were silent on what was obviously a critical part of the process of applying science that had evolved in the North. And even though participation is now much touted in the planning process, theory as to why ground truthing and participation might facilitate the application of science is still weak and informal. The relationships between knowledge, beliefs about science, social organization, and collective decision-making have haunted me ever since this experience in Brasilia.

DEVELOPED COUNTRY DILEMMAS

Coordinating different, partial environmental understandings in the over-developed countries is also encountering increasing difficulties which can readily be seen as political in their underlying nature. Global climate change is an obvious case. The difficulties of resolving and coordinating under-standings between scientists has delayed collective action, especially by the United States, putting all the biosphere and humanity at risk. Multiple scientists are involved in the development of our understanding of climate change because no one scientist can understand all of the pathways through which it occurs and by which its ramifications affect us. Atmospheric physicists, climatologists, oceanographers, combustion engineers, soil scientists, biologists, silviculturalists, and economists, among others, are trying to fit their understandings together. Yet coherence is inherently impossible for the knowledges of the scientists from separate disciplines cover different variables, different spatial scales, and different time scales. And multiple, incongruent patterns of thinking are being used. Concern stems both from what mechanical models of global physical processes indicate might happen to climate and from what evolutionary models of bio-logical systems indicate might happen to ecosystems and species. Physical and biological phenomena are mutually interactive. The survival of tree species after warming affects the albedo of the earth and the degradation of organic matter in soil through warming releases further greenhouse gases and thereby feedback on the physical processes of climate change. And yet the mechanical models used to model the physical aspects of climate change do not cohere with the evolutionary models that give biologists insights about which species might move to suitable areas as climate changes, how and the extent to which species might recombine into functioning ecosystems, and which species, types of ecosystems, and ecosystem func-tions will be lost forever. Big computer models force scientists to integrate models and data, help them explore feedbacks, and help illustrate the problem. But deeper understanding is coming through a collective synthesis between the scientists themselves, through sharing and consensus building founded on a slowly increasing mutual trust in each other's knowledge and its implications. In short, our understanding of complex problems necessarily comes through a social process of consensus.

At the same time, contention and deep questioning are the only safeguards against a false consensus. These safeguards themselves, however, make open sharing and a collective understanding difficult to achieve. Scientists trying to comprehend climate change, for example, have serious differences in their understandings which need to be aired and resolved. And yet, some differences are matters of judgment rather than science, rooted in different hopes for technological salvation, different interests in material and environmental objectives, and different levels of concern for the long run. The process of consensus building, in short, is unavoidably a political process if only because different world views can prevent scientific consensus. People with different world views couch their arguments in scientific terms. And people who do not agree with the direction the consensus may be taking, argue that there is not a scientific basis for the consensus.

With the future of humanity at stake, contention rooted in misunderstandings of the nature of collective understanding, on not realizing the necessity for, and nature of, processes to coordinate separate knowledges, needs to be reduced as much as possible. And yet we have little basis for even thinking about how disciplinary science, values, coordinating understanding, social structure, and collective action fit together. How should a scientific community be defined; what proportion of scientists constitutes a reasonable consensus; how can a consensus be facilitated with minimal cost; what are the best ways to minimize the chances of a false consensus; and how are the tensions between scientific consensus, administrative, democratic, and legal processes going to be structurally and procedurally resolved?

Local environmental problems challenge the coordination of diverse understandings as well. The choice of technologies to treat waste and the siting of treatment facilities and disposal areas, for example, raise a panoply of issues. Experts with diverse scientific backgrounds become involved from agencies responsible for air and water quality, public health, and land use. Scientists representing and responding to the regulations of local, state, and federal agencies, scientists brought in as consultants to these agencies, and experts from special interest groups representing industry, land development, or environmental organizations are all involved. Waste disposal raises issues beyond the community's boundaries such as: why does modern packaging result in so much waste, why are modern products so short-lived, and how come so much is either toxic or long-lived as waste? Similarly the community will ask why it has to accept waste from beyond its boundaries while seeking ways to export its own waste elsewhere. If the community ever works its way through these contentious questions, it must digest a maze of information about the possibilities for sorting waste, the different types of air pollution and solid waste associated with alternative processing techniques, the geological suitability of different disposal sites, the implications for exposure during waste transport to alternative sites, and last but by no means least, in whose backyard the facilities are to be sited.

The problem of selecting waste disposal processes and sites is not simply one of scientific complexity which an Einstein could understand given access to the knowledge of the separate experts. The experts, when asked to provide answers, are silent on questions laypeople are fully capable of asking, do not link phenomena they have good reason to suspect are interconnected, provide conflicting information, and present information in ranges that conflate the natural variability of the numbers in question and the limits of scientific knowledge. Some of these discrepancies can be resolved through additional research, but further research is also likely to lead to more questions and meanwhile garbage is piling up. Integrating scientific incongruities into administrative and democratic procedures at city, county, state, and federal governmental levels obviously further compounds the difficulties of the process.

Environmental activists, empowered by broad public concern, have forged innovative pathways through political, administrative, and legal systems to resolve social conflicts. One consequence of this success is that legislative bodies have responded by requiring agencies to incorporate citizen participation in environmental decision-making from the beginning. While citizens initially saw participation as a way to inform experts in the agencies of their concerns, the experts initially saw it as an opportunity to provide the facts to people they viewed as overly concerned and under informed. Environmental activists saw the requirements for participation as a way of getting new scientific information onto the political agenda. Activists, however, also saw participation as a way of deterring projects, and perhaps even defeating them, through analysis paralysis. After two decades of very mixed experience from these disparate expectations, constructive approaches are beginning to evolve at the local level. With sufficient experience or through effective mediators, local participants are finding that success requires assuming the responsibility to listen better, to become informed, to work with people with different understandings and objectives, and to patiently involve bureaucrats in other administrative jurisdictions within their locally synthesized, richer, collective comprehension of problems and solutions. The success stories, however, are the exception. Theoretical explanations of successful coordinating efforts to hasten the coevolution of more effective social organization and processes generally are much needed.

THE LEGACY OF PROGRESSIVE BUREAUCRACIES

Much of the difficulty in reaching collective understandings of complex environmental and social problems is rooted in modern beliefs about science, social structure, and public decision-making which were codified in the design and influenced the evolution of progressive institutions. The term progressive in this context refers to the progressive movement in the latter half of the nineteenth century that advocated strong governmental agencies staffed by experts to accelerate development. This use of the term follows the writings of Auguste Comte, who argued that societies could avoid many of the absurdities of politics, including the defense of the status quo, through the use of scientifically trained experts who advise legislatures on the best way to do things and to whom legislatures, after setting broad goals, would delegate responsibilities for final policy design and implementation. Scientists, being on the vanguard of the new rather than stuck in the traditions of the past, have been seen from the progressive view as forward-looking and catalytic to the unfolding of progress.

Comte's vision of progressive institutions and processes justified the fledgling technocracies that had begun to evolve in Europe and the United States during the nineteenth century and patterned the design and evolution of major institutions such as the Department of Agriculture after the Civil War in the United States. Progressive agencies seemed especially suited for the complexities of managing natural resources. The Forest Service, Army Corps of Engineers, and Bureau of Reclamation in the United States and analogous institutions in other countries developed into major agencies and key instruments of development. Progressive institutions were well established by the end of the nineteenth century in the overdeveloped North and installed during the second half of the twentieth century in the underdeveloped South.

Agricultural, forest, and water experts undertook research, extended their knowledge to farmers, planned major projects and sought funding from the legislative branch, and carried projects out. Most progressive bureaucracies, or technocracies, have been structured like the military, their relationship to the executive branch and legislature has been very similar to that of the military, some of the agencies have been closely associated with the military, and uniforms were, and in some cases still are, common. The legislative branch controlled the "purse strings," but so long as efforts were sufficiently distributed between legislators' districts, the purse remained open and experts guided development. Federal agencies were typically the first to be designed along progressive reasoning and were very successful in attracting the limited available scientific talent in the early years. State agencies followed less successfully, and, even today, poor states in the North have only weak technocratic agencies. Because of the initial shortage of experts, the military structure, and the presumption that scientific truths are universal, progressive institutions favored decision-making from capital cities by strong central institutions.

The historically dominant, now mythical, premises of Western science – atomism, mechanism, universalism, objectivism, and monism – have facilitated the structural design of progressive institutions and the processes by which they work. The division of problems and their assignment to separate agencies with distinct types of expertise is clearly rooted in Western adherence to atomism. Environmental problems and cultural conflicts arise, however, precisely because they cut across the areas of expertise of agricultural, fisheries, forestry, and water agencies. If Western faith in monism had a basis in reality, coordination would be no problem, the sciences would naturally fit together. Coordinating the knowledges of experts in specialized agencies is now recognized, however, as a fundamental difficulty. The expectation that experts could inform politics of the consequences of alternative projects and policies is based on Western faith that processes are mechanical and predictable. But environmental politics is stymied precisely because how the future unfolds is now seen as complex and unpredictable. Political choices must be made using criteria other than a weighing of expected benefits and costs of mechanically predicted, patently unlikely, futures. And lastly, strong, centralized progressive institutions have been rationalized by the premise that scientific truths are universal. But while the first and second laws of physics are universal, even hydrological principles more sophisticated than "water runs downhill" have to be applied with care depending on the context. While a few environmentalists tout universal principles of ecosystem management, these are rooted in a few, too simple ideas developed by early naturalists rather than the far richer, but less generalizable knowledge, of biologists today. While general guiding principles help frame environmental management thinking, most universal management rules reflect physics envy rather than contemporary biology.

Perhaps more importantly, the idea that science could inform politics has always been characterized as scientists being able to predict the consequences of alternative actions so that politicians could choose between them. This has rarely proven to be the case. Scientists have typically argued that they need a stronger base of knowledge generated through research and more scientists in their agencies to accurately predict the dynamics of complex systems. But the increase in knowledge and in the number of scientifically trained people has not improved predictive capacity. As our understanding of chaotic systems and coevolving systems grows, however, the plea for more of the same falls on increasingly deaf ears. We have not yet, however, devised an alternative understanding of how science can serve society and are stuck with a legacy of technocratic agencies whose design and mode of operating do not fit our richer understanding of systems.

The progressivism in this political-scientific sense that became embedded in resource and environmental technocracies has favored decision-making by the scientifically trained rather than the demos or their elected representatives, running counter to the ideal of democracy. The stronger role for scientists and technocrats is frequently justified on the basis that they are merely dealing with the facts; value decisions are still made by legislative bodies or the polity at large. But the facts at hand reflect the course scientific inquiry has pursued which, in turn, reflects the questions deemed important within earlier world views and the choices made by scientists and their funders. Progressivism, furthermore, delegitimizes traditional, including intuitive, ways of knowing and local knowledge. And given the domination of science and technology by men, the implications of the adoption of progressive institutions for gender and power are clear.

Political progressives, as opposed to political conservatives, have historically favored progressive, in the political-scientific sense, institutions without deeply questioning how they disempowered people. At the same time, with the populace largely disempowered, progressive institutions eventually came under the influence of those with economic clout, largely political conservatives with little interest in changing a social structure that had served them well. The agencies are largely staffed by well-intentioned experts, frustrated by the contradictions between the hopes of Auguste Comte and the realities of political power. The dedication of agency staff and political progressives who support them, nonetheless, is framed by the social structure that exists. However socially concerned, only a few see the contradictions between the empowerment of scientists, progressive institutional structures, and democracy.

LIBERAL DEMOCRACY

In the liberal understanding of democracy, and in this case this pretty much means modern understanding, democracy is a matter of adding up votes to see which interest, or which set of values, dominates. People are preferences with votes. Democracy is simply a matter of addition. People may organize as political groups, but this is to form a nucleus of workers to get a question on the ballot, to stimulate voters to vote, or similar matter. Groups have also been portrayed, and to a considerable extent rightly so, as traders of votes. The economic logic of exchange works for votes as well as for market goods. By trading votes, people can give up a vote for something they do not feel strongly about for someone else's promise to vote for something they do feel strongly about. Exchanging votes is an extremely difficult process for individuals alone, while trading votes between groups as a block is more nearly feasible. Political groups form because of the logic of exchange.

And yet ultimately, in the logic of liberal individualism, voting itself makes no sense. There is very little reason to study the issues on the ballot and go to the polls when one's vote is highly unlikely to make a difference. As liberal individualism and exchange become increasingly manifest mind-sets, fewer and fewer people indeed appear at the polls. This, in turn, reinforces the role of technocratic decision-making. In the end, liberal democracy as a process of simply exchanging and adding votes becomes a growing tangle of contradictions.

Not only does our understanding of science not include the coordination of separate knowledges, but our understanding of democracy also no longer speaks to how we collectively know. Democracy, both in popular understanding and in political theory, is a collective process of decision-making. The demos, or people, decide. To be a democracy is to have certain social relations. People need to be politically equal, must have access to information, and must accept the obligation to inform themselves and participate in decision-making. Democracy also carries with it the image of people exchanging information through democratic debate, but this is typically portrayed as a process of dissemination. Each individual learns more and hence is better able to be an informed voter, but society knows no more than it did before.

Modern societies mix democratic and delegated authority. The perceived advantages and disadvantages of democracy for making decisions relative to delegating authority to technocrats in progressive agencies depends on the nature of the problem, and modern societies are presumed to allocate different types of decisions to the mechanisms they best fit. Democracy and bureaucracy access different types of knowledge more easily, and which mechanism is best may hinge on this access to knowledge. But in Western political discourse, when an issue entails unusual knowledge, the need for experts is simply invoked. Knowledge, in short, is taken as given, something which resides within individuals as technocrats or as voters, but more so in technocrats than voters. So if questions are complicated, it is presumed that experts should at least frame the choices. Technocrats also may need better information, but if it cannot be obtained through the sharing of knowledge between technocrats, it is presumed to be generated through research.

The important point is this. Neither our understanding of the sharing of information that takes place through democracy nor our understanding of the similar processes of sharing information that occur between technocrats within and between agencies acknowledges the possibility that shared information can become more than the separate parts. In many cases, for the information to even be useful, it must become more than the separate parts. Processes of dialogue and the sense of obligation to participate in the exchange of ideas, processes, and obligations associated with democracy – whether among scientists, among voters, or among both – are not understood to contribute to the better knowledge necessary for informed decision-making. Similarly, our understanding of societies and communities, of social structure and dynamics, does not incorporate the fact that some knowledge can only come through social or community processes that synthesize separate knowledges into something greater than the parts. With rare exceptions, even social theorists have not addressed the learning that occurs through the coordinating of separate knowledges to reach collective understanding before collective decision-making can be truly informed.

KNOWING AS A SOCIAL PROCESS

The fact that knowing must be a social process whenever separate disciplinary understandings must be merged needs further elaboration. The implications of this fact for our conception of social organization are especially important.

Our Western image of rationality assumes a single individual who observes environmental and social realities, deduces universal truths, and then develops new products or manages environmental and social systems to better meet human needs. Alternatively, objectivity entails the notion that any individual objectively addressing the same facts would reach the same conclusions. The important point is that science as an activity of an individual mind is a dominant image. Yet clearly science itself and its application in the development of products or management of systems have been collective activities, divided among many minds, acting through many social organizations.

In contrast to the common emphasis on the incorporation of science into products, let us consider its use in the management of environmental and social systems. No single individual has ever collected and interpreted all environmental and social data and used it to manage environmental and social systems. Individual scientists have been dependent on other scientists for the equipment they use; for field, laboratory, and computer support; and subsequently for the application of science through management. More important than this vertical dependence, for complex environmental problems, which are necessarily social problems as well, the data of individual scientists are only meaningful in the context of the interpretation of data collected by others, including social scientists. Typically these other scientists have been in completely different institutions collecting and interpreting data for completely different purposes. Knowing has necessarily been a social process. Not recognizing it as such, however, makes the process more difficult than it might be.

The dominant premises of Western science have selected against organizational experiments which would facilitate the social process. The various individual environmental agencies, for example, are closely tied to particular disciplines. Each agency has recruited personnel from, has interacted with people from, and consequently evolved around particular environmental sciences. Personnel within each agency and the people with whom agency personnel most frequently interact form an "epistemic community," a group of like-minded people who reinforce each other's like-mindedness. The U.S. Department of Fish and Game and the U.S. Bureau of Reclamation, for example, were established to solve different problems, which were separately conceived through biological and hydrological paradigms respectively. The agencies have been staffed with wildlife managers and water engineers respectively who perceive the environment, collect and interpret data, and have communicated within their agencies with the assistance of their respective patterns of thought. Experts in both agencies have been looking at the same streams, but looking at them very differently. Not only have the environmental data collected through the two agencies been screened by different paradigms, but the individuals within the agencies, and in some sense the organizations as a whole, have acquired experiential knowledge which has been bounded by the initial conceptions of problems, the initial training of the experts within the agencies, and the professional community with which they have interacted.

Agencies are so much a part of their epistemic communities that they can only learn along with their epistemic communities. This makes change difficult, but, to the extent it is a fact, there is no reason to decry it. It is very difficult to conceive of how societies could be structured to manage peoples' interaction with the environment without divisions occurring along patterns of thinking or patterns of thinking crystallizing within social divisions. Openly and consciously recognizing how specialization affects social organization and acknowledging how specialized knowledges must be coordinated, however, would certainly facilitate knowing as a social process.

The process of coordinating specialized understandings has consisted of scientists from separate agencies along with scientists from universities and nongovernmental organizations engaging in a discourse around the interpretation of an environmental problem. Such discourses are difficult, however, for members of different scientific communities have communicated very poorly with each other because their respective data and experiential knowledge have been rooted in incommensurable patterns of thinking. They may have wanted, especially as individual scientists, to solve problems jointly between their mutual realms of knowledge. Legislators even have mandated agencies to work together on problems. But the barriers have been real; the patterns of thinking really are incommensurable. Coming from different epistemic communities, they have different ways of knowing. These scientific barriers have been in addition to the difficulties of agency cooperation associated with battles over power or confusion with respect to authority. The data of the different agencies and their scientists simply cannot be processed through a common if-this-then-do-that model. There have been, of course, cases where individual scientists in different agencies put their heads together and reached collective environmental interpretations. Their collective explanations along with their associated management judgments, however, have been difficult to communicate to higher levels in their respective agencies because their explanations do not fit the data and patterns of thinking to which higher level, usually older and more experienced, managers in the separate agencies have grown accustomed. Collective understandings have also fallen apart as problems became more broadly conceived and additional scientists from other agencies with other patterns of thinking began to participate in the collective judgment. As the social process broadens, it becomes increasingly difficult to reach a consensus interpretation.

Indeed, a mutual understanding of the complexities of the problem originally identified may never be reached and yet a consensus might well be reached on acceptable strategies to avoid the problem. The global agreement to reduce and eventually eliminate the use of CFCs which breakdown the ozone layer are an excellent example. The 1987 decision to reduce the use of CFCs, the Montreal Protocol, was reached before scientists had a mutually agreed upon understanding of how CFCs disturb the ozone layer and the rate at which the disturbance was occurring. Scientists, in fact, originally dismissed their own data indicating a breakdown, interpreting it as an aberration in their data because they lacked an explanation of the process. As explanations of the process began to develop, the relationships between quantities of CFCs, the timing of their release to the atmosphere, and the timing and extent of disturbance to the ozone layer were still unknown. Nevertheless, scientists did come to a collective judgment that it was wise, given the costs of alternatives to ozone-depleting CFCs, to phase out their use. They had enough information to judge that the problem was probably serious and they were able to reach a consensus on a strategy to avoid the problem. Consensus on avoidance strategies may well be more common than consensus on the causes of and best ways to manage problems. In the early 1990s, the extent of the disturbance was found to be much greater than had been expected.

It is important to stress that the data of the scientists from different disciplines and agencies have not been aggregated and that the joint explanations reached between the scientists have not been realized through a meta model. Consensus interpretations or avoidance strategies have been reached on the basis of judgment. Such an approach is indefensible within the dominant premises of how Western science is supposed to work. The idea of objective reasoning carries with it the idea that no matter who carries out the reasoning, they will reach the same conclusion. Judgments are inconsistent with objectivity. The use of judgment by scientists also conflicts with progressive understandings that legislative bodies make the necessary value judgments that set priorities and that agencies make strictly technical decisions based on scientifically defensible understandings. The scientists' judgments need not be tainted by personal values, though to some extent they inevitably will be, to be judgments. All decisions made by agencies have an aspect of scientific judgment, but the importance and complexities of the environmental problems perceived at the end of the twentieth century are putting this process of judgment in the spotlight.

Widespread belief in the dominant premises of Western science and understanding of rationality as an individual rather than a collective phenomenon have resulted in a difficult dynamic. Scientists, acting individually or as agents for larger groups, have been able to "exit" the consensus-forming process, declaring it unscientific, and thereby reducing and maybe eliminating the possibility of a consensus interpretation or avoidance strategy. Indeed, such declarations and exits have frequently slowed or derailed the process. If a superior rival interpretation is in the making outside the current consensus group, or no interpretation is better than a bad one in the works, the publicly announced exits of individual experts may be beneficial. Better and beneficial, however, have no independent, objective bases. Criticism during the consensual process by a scientist participating at the center of the process or by a well known outsider gains instant scientific and public attention. Scientists are trained to be critical, though there are also strong peer pressures to think alike. It is difficult to judge the extent to which "exiting" or critique are motivated by differences in scientific understanding, differences in values, or by desires for public recognition. And the more socially complex the problem, the more likely it is that some scientist or interest group will find it advantageous to expose the coordinating process as unscientific by appealing to our outdated publicly held beliefs about how science is supposed to work.

KNOWING, LEARNING, AND DEMOCRACY

Understanding knowing as a social process raises critical questions about who should participate in the process. Ideally, under the epistemological and metaphysical tenets of modernity, a democratic society would consist of equally broadly and highly educated people, each fully qualified to understand all dimensions of every complex issue. The accentuation of specialization and increasing importance of superior intelligence and education during the twentieth century has forced a steady, pragmatic retreat from this ideal. It has become accepted that it is simply inefficient for everyone to understand and participate in the resolution of every complex issue. To the extent that differences in intelligence and education have increasingly circumscribed participation, many among the brighter and more educated have felt a special obligation to work in the public interest. And the positivist myth has been maintained in part because it reduces the conflict between elitism and the popular participation associated with Western democratic ideals. These pragmatic escapes, however, have hidden more than resolved the tension between the current use of science in the policy process and democracy. *Intelligentsia oblige* has been weak at best. And positivism has only been adhered to for lack of an alternative.

Acknowledging that understanding complex problems is necessarily a social process compounds these existing tensions between science and democracy. If knowing is necessarily a social process, then how should it operate vis-à-vis democracy? Should the process be open to all or limited to those with PhDs in relevant areas? In the individual sciences, discourse has clearly been almost strictly internal within scientific communities.

During the rare occasions when the public has become aware of debates among, for example, geologists or ecologists, it has looked upon them as curiosities. The discourses over global climate change, nuclear waste disposal, or the importance of biodiversity to future generations, however, have been inherently more interesting, of concern, and open to the public. Inevitably, because of the scope of environmental problems and the myriad of ways in which environmental systems interact with social systems, environmental discourses among scientists address the life styles of the masses. Environmental science discourses, in short, have proven to be about things that people are intensely interested in from a variety of perspectives. It seems inevitable that scientists from both industry and public interest groups would not only become involved in these discourses but take leading roles. Environmental discourses have been more politicized than other scientific discourses because they have been much more likely to address how we organize and what we do, rather than simply minor differences in techniques used in particular activities.

While science is presumed to expand systematically, scientists know very well that research findings depend on the path taken and "rabbit trails" pursued along the way. Similarly, to the extent that knowing is a social process, what is eventually known is determined by the nature of that process. What becomes known is not predetermined. Who participates and how they are allowed to participate determines the types of questions raised, information brought to the discourse, and judgments made and encouraged upon others to make. The participants and process determine the product. Technical solutions and avoidance strategies have been historically dominant because the process was left to technicians. As scientists entered the fray, the myths of how science is supposed to work influenced the process, mostly delaying consensus on anything. The rise of biological thinking introduced new information and new patterns of reasoning. And increased public participation brought problem specification closer to the concerns of people who do not report to work in university or government laboratories.

This leads to the inevitable question of whether collective understanding might be more effectively achieved under some other combination of structures, procedures, and participants than has evolved to date. Should scientists working for government agencies or universities, for example, have greater voice than those more clearly working for special interests? At what point should the public deem an agreement to have been reached even though some scientists and interests continue to disagree? In short, should the boundaries and rules of the process be formally discussed and institutionalized?

The process of reaching collective understanding is, in fact, rapidly evolving. Nongovernmental environmental organizations have added more and more scientists to their staffs and engaged ever more actively in the process of collective understanding. Citizen participation in local and regional planning processes is now well recognized, both North and South, though effective practice has yet to evolve. There is still considerable tension between participation and legislatively delegated authority. With participation mixing democratic-like procedures into the processes of administrative agencies which are themselves responsible to democratically elected officials, public lines of deciding become crossed.

Nongovernmental organizations have had a major impact on the international development discourse. The definition of development goals and strategies used to be firmly in the hands of international development agencies and their epistemic communities of agricultural scientists, engineers, and economists. Development was largely framed in terms of technical possibilities and economic efficiency, as a matter of making "the pie" grow as fast as possible. Tension over the distribution of the benefits of economic development, or how "the pie" is divided, have long been felt within the agencies and their epistemic communities. But serious concern for the environment and the sustainability of development, for women, for traditional peoples, for the incorporation of traditional knowledge, for cultural diversity, and for civil rights and justice have been forced upon the international development agencies, their national counterparts, and their epistemic communities by nongovernmental organizations. These are neither concerns over how to speed development nor over how what development has wrought should be divided. These are concerns over whether development experts know pie from cow paddy.

At the same time, discourses on politics and economics, narrowly defined, have become less open rather than more. The evolution of the role of economists in the public discourse in Western societies provides an ominous warning. In the United States until World War II, economics was a matter widely discussed by educated laypeople. From World War II until well into the 1960s, economists in the public sector began to dominate as econocrats, following the tenets of progressivism. For a short period in the 1970s, interest group pluralism molded their role, and economists were allowed, even encouraged, to champion different interest groups by making their economic arguments as strong as possible. Beginning in the 1980s, however, economists in government and in academe were expected to defend market reasoning, indeed ideology, *per se*. Economic reasoning has been used in a power struggle against other types of reasoning for the determination of policy rather than used in a cooperative search for a deeper collective synthesis. The roles of economists in other industrialized countries have never been so closely patterned, but market ideology became more expected in Europe and Japan during the 1980s as well. In international development agencies and in less developed countries, economists are even more ideological and less effective in contributing to a collective understanding. Economics has become more a matter for experts and less participatory with other disciplines and the public than ever before. During the 1980s and well into the 1990s, economists at the International Monetary Fund nearly dictated how developing economies should be restructured, while economists at the World Bank refrained from preparing development loans until such restructuring was well underway.

DEMOCRATIZING PROGRESS

Progress, heretofore, has been in the hands of experts at best, market forces at worst, and only recently, though distorted by false expectations, in the hands of the public. Progressive institutions disempower the vast majority of individuals and, as designed and operating under modern premises of Western science, simply cannot address complex problems effectively. Markets, on the other hand, empower people to reach the goals they can reach as individuals but disempower individuals in their efforts to reach goals which require collective action. Both markets and progressive institutions disempower communities. Given the increasingly obvious vacuity of the modern vision of progress, it is difficult to understand why the general sense of malaise at the end of the twentieth century is not even more serious than it is.

This book has emphasized the advantages of understanding change as a coevolutionary process, while this particular chapter has emphasized how the understanding of complex systems must be a collective process. This does not leave me in a strong position to individually design better social structures and processes. And yet new visions are sorely needed, and I intend to suggest some initial steps that might lead to the coevolution of societies in fruitful directions.

Let me ground my appeal in the old but still evolving idea of democracy. One cannot facilitate the evolution of new visions of the future completely from scratch, and the idea of democracy carries with it several powerful suppositions about individuals and societies with which many people agree in principle. While some of the ideals of democracy have been well developed for millennia, the ideals continue to evolve, the definition of the demos in particular. The right of women to vote was granted in England as recently as 1918, in Switzerland in 1971. At the same time, many of democracy's widely touted principles of equality have been eroded through an excessive delegation of authority to markets and bureaucracies. Yet the ideals of democracy remain an important part of modern consciousness, available, with some refreshening, for envisioning a better future.

Democracy conveys the ideal of political equality, the vision of open public debate and sharing of knowledge, and the understanding that each person is obligated to stay informed of public issues and to participate in public decision-making. Democracy also connotes, albeit far too weakly, the understanding that the sharing of knowledge – like the sharing of skills, food, and love – can combine to more than the sum of the parts. While all of the ideals need strengthening in practice, the association of democracy with collective knowing needs elaboration as an ideal. With this strengthening, democracy has even more powerful implications for structuring and sustaining communities.

How scientists coordinate their separate understandings determines the collective understanding reached. Science as a social process could be restructured in a variety of ways. Personally, though I think there are more than simply my values in this preference, I would favor a more democratic structure. I think a good case can be made that science would work much better if scientists assumed the ideals and obligations of democracy in their work as scientists. Scientists from each of the disciplines would have to recognize the equality of the different disciplines, acknowledging that each has important information to contribute to the whole. Scientists would be obliged to stay abreast of the understandings of the sciences around them. Each scientist would be obliged to participate in the sharing of knowledge and the building of the collective understandings necessary to work with or to avoid complex problems. Being a scientist would be much less a matter of being an individual expert and much more a matter of being a member of a democratic community. Science would work better if it were democratized, not, for the purpose of this argument, in the sense that it would be open to all, but in the sense that the democratic ideals of community and process and their associated obligations form a superior foundation for coordinating specialized knowledge into something greater than the parts.

Karl Popper argued that science needs "open societies" wherein scientists could freely question other scientists to assure the quality of science, to affect its direction, and to see that it served the public interest. Popper also acknowledged that scientists who were not experts in the field they were questioning as well as lay people could productively participate in the open, questioning exchange he advocated. Popper argued that science was superior in democratic countries relative to totalitarian societies precisely because of the difference in their openness. He worried about the rise of bureaucracy and bureaucratically directed science in democratic countries.

Popper was addressing the control of science, however, not its process. Popper presumed that scientists naturally questioned each other's work and, if left to themselves, would assure its quality if not its applicability. Three decades of research on the sociology of science since the work of Thomas Kuhn documents how scientists group in ways to avoid questioning. And Popper, trained and constantly thinking in terms of physics, only questioned a few of the dominant beliefs about science and rarely explored the difficulties of bringing separate knowledges together into collective understandings.

Clearly my preference for inculcating stronger democratic ideals and obligations among scientists to facilitate the coordinating process reflects my values. Fortunately, it reflects the values of many others as well. In part because the vast majority of scientists already hold democratic ideals and some sense of obligation, there is also considerable evidence that science does work well under more egalitarian circumstances where each scientist feels she or he is a part of a community working together on a problem. And there is considerable evidence that scientific efforts within authoritarian structures do not work well. Perhaps the best general evidence is that scientific enterprises within hierarchical institutions, whether military, bureaucratic, or corporate, tend to be more democratically structured than their host institution.

I am only suggesting, at this stage of the argument merely planting the seed, that the scientific community put a conscious and greater emphasis on the importance of democracy within science in the process of training and promotion. Dropping the myth of monism and adopting a conscious conceptual pluralism would complement a greater emphasis on democracy. So long as monism is taught or implied, coordination, hence democracy within science, serves no functional purpose beyond the good feelings of working together. Consciously teaching conceptual pluralism would heighten respect for how sciences differ, the ways in which their contributions are special, and the need to integrate them through a social process.

Democratizing science is an important seed to plant. Western science will maintain its preeminent status and remain the center for conserving, modifying, and disseminating knowledge for the foreseeable future. The culture of science permeates modern institutions, so democratizing science will affect the behavior of experts and their use of knowledge throughout society. At the same time, it will be very difficult to democratize science without democratizing the institutions in which scientists and technicians work throughout society. This seed would do better in more fertile soil, the soil of fully democratized societies, but single seeds can also lead to trees that split open rocks and create fertile soil around them.

Beyond science, unfortunately, the difficulties increase dramatically. Power and property are relatively minor issues within science; they are major beyond science. Progressive institutions have been delegated authority by democratic institutions. How can these progressive institutions now be democratic in their interactions with the public? The distribution of property between rich and poor affects how markets determine what is made and how. How can the ways in which markets affect progress be democratized?

And yet progressive institutions are evolving in response to the difficulties of addressing environmental complexities. Old boundaries are constantly being crossed as experts in the agencies have been forced to interact with each other, with experts from nongovernmental organizations, and with the public at large. As experts gain a better understanding of knowing as a social process and of the complementarities between democracy and science, the direction of coevolution may become more clear, the rate more rapid. Similarly, as the public begins to understand knowing as a social process and assumes the obligations of becoming informed and participating, the process may work better and better.

To a large extent, centralized progressive institutions were effective historically because they were able to impose their decisions on communities. Local politics have long been portrayed as parochial, and to some extent rightly so. Overriding local interests, however, has resulted in an antagonistic relationship between progressive institutions and local governments and has also disempowered communities, making them increasingly less able to organize and take care of themselves over time. As a consequence, local participation often takes the form of obstruction, the most powerful mode of action remaining for alienated, disempowered actors. Democratizing science, the historic authority behind progressive institutions, may help undo the bad history and empower communities. Democracy as a way of knowing could also revitalize participation and interaction at the community level, empowering local peoples, and making communities more effective in their interaction with centralized progressive institutions. Less centralization would also help, and that is the topic of the next chapter.

Markets will also remain dominant institutions for the foreseeable future. But in spite of the free market rhetoric of economists and the interests their rhetoric supports, the rights and responsibilities of economic actors have always been subject to redefinitions by legislatures, agencies, and courts, and through changes in social norms. Democratizing progress, by giving new strength to communities and establishing new relations between communities and governmental agencies would affect the evolution of markets over time as well.

There will probably still be important roles for scientists in higher levels of government in the resolution of local and regional environmental problems, but their *modus operandi* would probably shift from analysts to facilitators. Analysts try to determine the correct answer, or a portion of the correct answer, and impose it on the process. Scientific facilitators would join the social process of learning at the community or regional level, bringing insights from the resolutions of environmental problems they had facilitated in the past, bringing and providing an initial interpretation of data and studies, helping participants in the process clarify their own contributions, and helping in the search for resolutions between conflicting positions. Such scientists would serve as model participants, demonstrating how an effective person teaches, learns, resolves problems, and communicates. And these skills need to be taught, as well as linked to the concept of science as a social process, at all levels of education so that they can be further cultivated throughout life by those who enter into the process.

The democratization of progress, facilitated by the acceptance of a coevolutionary cosmology would probably also entail decentralization. The next chapter argues that, due to the contextuality of environmental problems, solutions need to be formulated and implemented more at a local level than they have been in the past. People collectively need to decide more

156

locally, and when they delegate authority, it should be delegated as locally as possible. Progressive beliefs favored more centralization than has proven desirable, both from the perspective of managing the contextuality of environmental problems and from the perspective of maintaining viable, politically functional communities.

No doubt many will respond that these ideas are wildly impractical because democratic processes are so time intensive. I do not question the time-intensiveness of democracy. But is it any more impractical than having millions of technocrats pushing papers in hundreds of agencies, each looking at a part of the problem, each submitting their own conclusions with respect to the whole to a technocratic battle? Much of this absurdity could be reduced if conceptual pluralism and knowing as a social process were accepted, but democracy too would be less contentious and wasteful of people's time if these premises were widely acepted. Most importantly, with the acceptance of these more appropriate premises, technocracy looses legitimacy while democracy gains validity.

CONCLUSIONS

Western and westernized societies – whether capitalist or socialist, democratic or authoritarian – increasingly sanctioned technocrats during the nineteenth and first half of the twentieth century to combine shared values, beliefs, and knowledge and act on behalf of the public. This authorization of agricultural scientists, engineers, foresters, planners, and eventually economists was rooted in a common vision of progress and a common faith in how science and technology could accelerate development. The international discourse on sustainable development, however, challenges that common faith and vision of progress and challenges the shared assumptions, understandings, and rationalizations that evolved while experts reigned through progressive institutions.

This chapter presents the case for democratizing progress. In the future I envision, the decline in respect for Western science would be reversed through the practice of a science consistent with its nature as a social process. Respect for other ways of knowing would also be enhanced. With the acceptance of conceptual pluralism, people with different understandings, including different understandings reached through Western science, would reach a consensus with respect to action through open democratic discourse rather than through the closed, and ultimately unscientific, processes inherent in Comte's progressivism. These transformations derive from the coevolutionary cosmology developed in Chapter 9 and, furthermore, would facilitate the coevolutionary patchwork quilt elaborated in Chapter 14. This revitalization of democracy and relegitimization of the diversity of knowledges, in turn, both requires and to some extent would naturally result in a restructuring of social hierarchies, generally toward decentralization, the topic of the next chapter.

13

COEVOLVING DISCURSIVE COMMUNITIES

If man is not to do more harm than good in his efforts to improve the social order, he will have to learn that in this, as in all other fields where essential complexity of an organized kind prevails, he cannot acquire the full knowledge which would make mastery of the events possible. He will therefore have to use what knowledge he can achieve, not to shape the results as the craftsman shapes his handiwork, but rather to cultivate, in the manner in which the gardener does this for his plants. There is danger in the exuberant feeling of ever growing power which the advance of the physical sciences has engendered and which tempts man to try, "dizzy with success," to use a characteristic phrase of early communism, to subject not only our natural but also our human environment to the control of a human will. The recognition of the insuperable limits to his knowledge ought indeed to teach the student of society a lesson of humility which should guard him against becoming an accomplice in men's fatal striving to control society – a striving which makes him not only a tyrant over his fellows, but which may well make him the destroyer of a civilization which no brain has designed but which has grown from the free efforts of millions of individuals.

(Frederich August von Hayek 1974)

Western social philosophy glorifies the individual, Western science revels in the particular, and yet the two together have facilitated the construction of an organized complexity that has expanded its influence across cultural and ecological boundaries. Positive feedback loops between technologies, institutions, and environments drive the complexity ever further beyond control, moving in directions exactly opposite to what modernity has exalted and learned. This geographic expansion and consciously escalated complexity produce an ever-increasing disassociation between people and the social and environmental consequences of their actions. Conversely, the social and environmental conditions within which each person lives are the increasingly disassociated products of trillions of actions taken by billions

158

of people elsewhere. The illusion of individual freedom reigns largely because we are blind to our interconnectedness. We do not see how our options reflect the forbearance of our forebears, how our actions affect each other around the globe, and how our extravagance constrains our descendants. Cause and effect are unconnected because our knowledge stresses fragments rather than connections, parts rather than systems. The illusion is also sustained because our social philosophy blinds us to the importance of community and the advantages of geographically and temporally restraining our impacts. This contradiction between what modernity celebrates and the transformations it has wrought are rationalized by blind faith that the economy is managed by an "invisible hand" and blind faith that natural and social systems can be mechanistically interpreted and controlled through manipulating their parts. And the future of humankind, as well as that for millions of other species, rests on the resolution of the contradiction, the replacement of these myths with premises which will sustain, rather than dissipate, human creativity.

System structure seems to be critically important to the understanding of this contradiction and the revisioning of the future. More specifically, I think the importance of community, the spatial patterns for clustering people, and social hierarchy, must be reconsidered. By questioning the spatial and hierarchical nature of our social structure, this chapter complements the previous one on democracy. Democracy works better with smaller communities with less hierarchy while democracy can help flatten hierarchy and reduce the need for technocratic intervention from central governments.

ANOTHER LESSON FROM THE AMAZON

Let me again highlight events from the Amazon to emphasize key issues. By the early 1970s, development planners had gone beyond single-project planning to integrated planning. Dams to store water contribute little to development without irrigation canals to distribute the water, and irrigation canals contribute little without appropriate crops, trained farmers, credit, storage, and transport to market. Furthermore, sustained productivity required extension agents to continually deliver new information about agricultural practices, better schools to educate the next generation, and medical delivery systems to keep everyone fit and productive. For the Amazon, the planners in Brasilia saw that such services would be difficult to deliver if colonists were widely dispersed on their separate plots. They tried to solve this problem by building the colonists' homes together on the main roads in small communities so that extension agents, health care workers, and school buses would not have to spend all their time wandering down side roads to find the colonists. The central planners saw the importance of communities but only from their perspective, as a way of facilitating the delivery of services from central governments. But the new planned communities had no evolved, internal basis for their existence. Consequently they collapsed, taking the planned benefits of integrated development with them, as each colonist family found it more convenient to live on the land they farmed.

From on high in the Brazilian social hierarchy, planners in Brasilia remain frustrated with their inability to manage the development of the Amazon. While a chain of command seems to be in place, rarely does it get signals to the field. And when signals reach the field, the response is rarely that which is expected in Brasilia.

Communities have long been important in the older settlements along the rivers of the Amazon for quite a different reason. These riverine communities have evolved into nearly independent, small social systems, connected by an occasional boat from Manaus or Belem. They are exploitive, like most Latin American social systems, yet functional nonetheless. Market, credit, schooling, health care, and religious institutions have largely been supported internally. None have been impressive by developed country standards, all have reflected the class structures and traditional values of the communities, but to the extent they continue to exist, it is because sufficient people in each community find it advantageous to keep them working. These existing communities have long concentrated people for the convenient delivery of services from central governments. What these communities have found advantageous, however, has been at odds with the ideas of the central planners, being cultures apart, and consequently little assistance has flowed from Brasilia to the riverine communities.

The development the planners' had perceived as possible was not realized for a variety of reasons elaborated more fully in Chapter 10. The new communities, having been designed to respond to development signals from Brasilia, in fact self-destructed for lack of internal cohesion and the ability to respond to the ecosystem. Older communities have responded better to the signals from the ecosystem around them but have been unresponsive to the development signals from Brasilia. The inability in the case of the Amazon to form sustainable interactions between ecosystems, local communities, and the Western vision of progress coordinated through a hierarchical command based in Brasilia mirrors the larger problem modernity faces in matching social and environmental systems at different scales.

PLACE, SCALE, AND HIERARCHY IN SOCIAL AND ENVIRONMENTAL SYSTEMS

The trouble with the environmental and social problems facing modern peoples is that they are systemic. Problems that can be analyzed and solved independently of a large number of complicating factors have been pretty well solved. Or more precisely, distinct problems have been solved. Too frequently, however, the solution has merely "distanced" the problem from the individual, affecting all in a variety of subtle ways through complex social and environmental pathways. Societies have sought to correct the detrimental effects of distancing associated with modern technologies and expanding markets through local, state, and national governments. A weak international governance occurs through the United Nations system and through multilateral agreements reached by national governments. Each of these governmental levels is organized into separate bureaucracies on the assumption that problems occur in discrete categories as problems of forests, soil, water, urban pollution, or public health. Environmental problems, however, rarely reduce to these categories and only rarely fit the boundaries of existing levels of government.

Consider, for example, the difficulties of resolving the conflicts associated with a reservoir proposed on a river that flows between two states. Imagine the reservoir would affect forest use, water supplies, flood control, fisheries, recreation, and the use of highways. Numerous local and state agencies from each state would have jurisdiction over these issues, making coordination between them difficult. Finding solutions would be even more difficult when decisions reached locally within the state agencies must be approved in the respective capitals. In the capital cities, legislators and bureaucrats would try to see that the solution conforms to state policies which may not be especially appropriate, or even applicable, to the particular problems at hand. Resolution can become even more difficult when the national government becomes involved.

The geographical nesting of local, state, national, and international governance evolved in the context of the historical problems of providing defense, negotiating peace, managing money and banking, maintaining schools, building transportation systems, enforcing and interpreting laws, and supporting research. These functions fit the geographical nesting of existing governance structures reasonably well. But now we face new problems which do not geographically nest.

The boundaries, or scale, of ecosystems depend on which type of biologist is asking which questions. Ecologists speak of ecosystems as if they had boundaries, and they assume boundaries for purposes of research, but in fact systems are interconnected. Species in forest ecosystems generally interact more with each other than they do with species in prairie ecosystems, but some species interact across the boundaries of the two systems. How then might one argue that one ecosystem has a larger scale than the other? How we think about scale clearly depends on what we think is important. Soil microbiologists assume ecosystems have smaller scale than do marine ecologists. A tropical rainforest may be divisible into quite small areas for the purposes of modeling and predicting the behavior of leaf cutter ants but must consist of larger areas to study howler monkeys. The study of fish in the Amazon would concentrate on riverine ecosystems which, though relatively small in total area, cut across large areas and multiple ecosystems as defined by ecologists asking different questions. For ornithologists, the term ecosystem becomes moot. Many individual birds, especially migratory birds, divide their time between areas other biologists commonly refer to as different ecosystems.

Governance for the purposes of managing different environmental problems must be as flexible as ecologists' definition of ecosystems for asking different questions. The fact that nature cannot be characterized as being made up of independent systems means that governance structures to manage a particular problem in a region, where the region is defined by the problem, will have to overlap with governance structures established to manage another problem which shares some of the same geographic area but not all of it. Precisely because of the difficulties that result when governmental boundaries and hierarchies do not mesh with environmental problems and systems, higher level governments have delegated authority to regional organizations specifically established to resolve the problems. These, however, are but a few exceptions to a structure which should be far more flexible. Environmental problem-solving is moving in the right direction, but such overlaps in the existing hierarchical structure present serious administrative problems. The way we conceptualize governance geographically needs to change so that what are now seen as administrative anomalies become accepted solutions.

The hierarchical structure of government itself is also much of the problem. Kenneth Boulding provides us with the image of "a bureaucracy is a hierarchy of wastebaskets." At the base of the bureaucracy, experts working on particular problems at the local level understand problems in great detail. The experts know, however, that their superiors, the administrators in the local offices, will not have the time or the training to digest all the experts have learned. Thus, as the experts prepare their reports, much of their knowledge ends up in the wastebasket. The administrators at the local level, in turn, report to their superiors in the regional office, knowing full well that they cannot pass on all that they know and leave much in the wastebasket again as they write their own reports. And so it goes up the chain of command to the head of the agency, the secretary of the department, and on to the president, until almost all of the information and insights are in numerous wastebaskets of the bureaucracy. At each level, administrators are aware of less and less, selected according to what those below thought they should and could communicate without having it end up in the wastebasket at the next level, until we reach the top where nobody knows anything. Though increasingly uninformed at each level, administrators at each level can delay, reframe, or veto resolutions that seem reasonable at the local level. In theory, bureaucrats at higher levels of the bureaucracy might only screen or modify plans made at lower levels to assure that regional and national interests were represented, but in fact objectives, criteria, and procedures emanate from legislators, executives, and high-level bureaucrats to those at lower levels, and proposals are constantly screened to see that they meet these.

There is little evidence that natural systems are hierarchical in any way comparable to social systems. Natural historians have left us with a hierarchical image of plants at the bottom, herbivores in the middle grazing on the plants, and carnivores living near the top, with man, and I am being gender-specific here out of sarcasm, at the very top. This portrayal of the food chain, however, conveniently ignores the insects and bacteria which daily feed off the "higher" animals, the nitrogen and other nutrients from waste that carnivores provide plants, and the fact that all get consumed in the end. Only people deny their return to the web of life by cremating or embalming their dead.

Even if nature were hierarchical, social and biological hierarchies would have no congruence. It is amusing to picture how environmental problems might be better resolved if executives at the peak of administrative hierarchies managed top predators, upper-level managers worked with carnivores, leaving the middle-level bureaucrats and experts in the field to deal with herbivores and plants. Obviously a nonsensical idea, but perhaps because the image is obviously silly, it helps convey why our regular attempts to mesh "flat" environmental systems with hierarchical social systems do not work. Social hierarchy impedes the meshing of social and ecological systems.

Where social hierarchy makes no sense, flattening the social structure will leave less information in waste baskets. Eliminating hierarchy which serves no functional purpose will also concentrate decision-making where knowledge, destiny, agreement, responsibility, implementation, and enforcement are shared. I have a strong sense that the only way that geographically flexible, flat governance structures will be able to replace the present technocracy will be through the trust and understanding that comes with stronger communities. Smaller, stronger communities would complement an expansion of democracy and help overcome the drive for individualism and its consequent problems discussed earlier.

OPENING ARGUMENTS ON COMMUNITY

Western peoples, myself included, have difficulty thinking about communities because we have had so little practice through formal education and social discourse. As a consequence, some opening statements are necessary to clear the stage of the banalities that pass for serious thought and to set the stage for later arguments.

First, I do not accept the premise that more emphasis on the local means less emphasis on the global. Many of those with whom I have explored this issue jump into this false either/or dichotomy. More emphasis needs to be put on both the local and the global, and if emphasis is in short supply, less should be put on individualism. I also suspect that for environmental issues, governance at the national level is less critical than at the local, regional, and global levels.

Second, community need not be coupled with the local any more than individualism is tied to the local. We need to understand the importance of communities and learn how to make communities help us accomplish our goals in ways analogous to how individualism has guided our structure and direction during the past four hundred years. We need to strengthen both local and global communities. My concept of community includes a large variety of ways people associate. Many communities will cut across other communities, like the riverine ecosystems of the Amazon.

Third, when we think of communities, we tend to think of structures but should in fact be thinking much more about processes. Some processes strengthen community, others should be avoided because they weaken community. Communities as structures cannot be maintained when inappropriate processes are in place. The reference in the opening quotation by von Hayek to gardeners is highly appropriate. Gardens as structures only exist through the constant process of gardening. It is in this sense that the previous chapter on the expansion of our understanding of democracy is critical.

Fourth, I admit that allegiance to communities is a major source of conflict, that communities are not always symbiotic. With confusion over whether and how the promises of modernity can be captured in what was the Soviet Union as well as in much of the global South, ethnic identification and violence between groups are increasing. I fail to see, however, how not acknowledging and not thinking seriously about communities will help people overcome intolerance between communities. Western social philosophy resorted to individualism out of desperation during the insanity of the Thirty Years War (1618–1648) that raged between adherents to Catholicism and Protestantism. Philosophers during this period denied community, imagined social systems as made up of rational, self-interested individuals, constructed acommunal systems on this image, ignored communal phenomena, and left modern peoples with few means for better managing communities and relations between them.

Fifth, and lastly, I acknowledge that my own ability to enter into a discourse on community is sorely undeveloped, in part for lack of others with whom I have been able to share more than banalities. But I know of no solution other than to keep trying to work past this deprivation together.

A COEVOLVING PATCHWORK QUILT OF DISCURSIVE COMMUNITIES

For a century and a half, social systems have coevolved around modern technologies fueled by fossil hydrocarbons. Ecological systems have been overridden by fossil hydrocarbon energy and chemicals and their own coevolution thereby affected. Neither system has coevolved in response to direct signals from the other. Modern technologies fueled by fossil hydrocarbons have temporarily allowed modern culture to expand beyond the boundaries of any particular ecosystem. As a consequence, however, modern societies know no ecosystems and are poorly organized to perceive and respond to their signals. The development of the Amazon, dependent on working with the intricacies of the Amazon ecosystem, could neither be comprehended nor directed from Brasilia. Similarly, making farming more sustainable in multiple ecosystems across the United States and Europe cannot be conceived and directed from Washington, D.C., or Brussels. We think of the biological world, at least historically, as having had distinct ecosystems. Historically, cultural systems tended to work within particular ecological boundaries. Though environments historically coevolved with societies, boundaries remained relatively stable. The Western vision of progress has the same best knowledge, social organization, and technologies being used across ecosystems with interactions between peoples occurring around the globe without barriers. In the process of fulfilling this vision, people have become less and less able to interact in viable communities and to respond to signals from ecosystems. We need to recluster the interactions between people by changing technologies and social organization to increase interconnections within clusters and reduce the interconnections beyond in order to better match social clusters with ecosystems.

Matching people to environments would require increasing local community responsibility and reducing organizational linkages to central governments. Existing technological connections across ecosystems, such as to distant oilfields and to the climate of all through the release of greenhouse gases, also need to be reduced by shifting to technologies which do not have or do not require distant linkages. Reducing existing distant linkages in order to create tighter clusters alone, however, would be insufficient. Local communities also must evolve the ability to interpret and respond to feedbacks from the ecosystems with which they are interacting. Monitoring and research activities, now primarily undertaken by state and national governments, also need to be undertaken at the local community level. The field experience and observations of farmers and other laypeople, largely ignored heretofore, need to be shared and transformed into community knowledge, along with existing formal means of knowing, and transformed into community responses. The challenge is to evolve social systems which perceive responses from the ecosystem, interpret those responses constructively, and respond effectively. When the ecosystem is changing in a manner which is detrimental, a moderating, negative feedback from the community is needed, and when the ecosystem is changing in a way that is beneficial, a supporting, positive feedback is needed.

Since ecosystems are constantly changing, the kinds of signals they send constantly change. This means communities need to be adaptive by maintaining an openness to new types of signals, an openness to new interpretations, and an openness to changing their own organization in order to provide a beneficial response. To be adaptive and continue to coevolve with their environments implies that communities need to maintain diversity in their abilities to perceive, interpret, organize, and adopt rules for behavior and to be able to switch smoothly between them.

I think these arguments mean that communities need to be relatively small. Hierarchical organization with its associated rules, justifications, and information lost in wastebaskets seems more likely the greater the number of people in a community. Communities first and foremost must have sufficiently few members for communication to work effectively. At the same time, since communities need to be defined in relation to environmental problems and since environmental problems overlap, communities will need to overlap. Furthermore, some distant interconnections between social and environmental systems will continue to occur and require a response at larger, even global, levels. These will require some form of encompassing communities, comparable to national and global governance, for an adequate response. Figure 13.1 provides a visual representation.

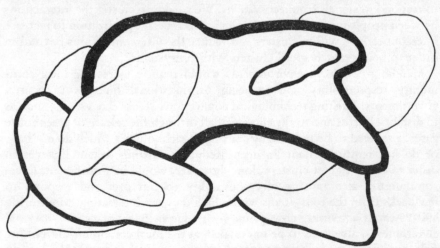

Figure 13.1 Overlapping discursive communities

MORE QUESTIONS THAN ANSWERS

The image of a coevolving patchwork quilt of discursive communities is in sharp contrast to the fixed, nesting structures of largely technocratic governance currently in vogue. The contrast raises numerous questions. What kinds of communities, small enough to behave as communities, might both overlap and encompass other communities across geographical scales? How can communities be small yet some of them be encompassing? Confronted with incongruities between social and environmental systems from the local to the global, with increasing awareness of the global, how can one say that more emphasis on community would be better? Communities, certainly overlapping communities, must communicate between themselves as well. What would be the forum for negotiations between communities and how will agreements be formalized? How will the boundary conflicts between evolving communities be resolved? How will the ever changing decisions, little more than changing discursive under-standings, of coevolving communities be relayed to the populace at large? How would coevolving decisions be enforced? How would this affect the role of a separate judiciary, and how would its jurisdiction be determined in a consciously coevolving social system? What would be the nature of jurisprudence in a society set on adaptive change where precedent would be recognized as the problem rather than the supposed basis of jurisprudence?

Some will no doubt argue that I am being irresponsible to even suggest another vision of social organization with so many major questions left unanswered. My first defense is that I cannot possibly fill in the details myself and the only way for me to participate in the collective process of revisioning the future is to communicate my thoughts. Knowing as a social process cannot possibly meet the standards of responsibility set by those who think of it as an individual process. My second defense is that the questions raised by the contrast between my vision and the current structure have always been there, like the sounds of trees that have fallen in a previously unvisited woods. Few have entered the forest that one finds on thinking about the coevolution of knowledge, social organization, and technology to ask why modern social systems work so poorly with environmental systems. The questions one asks from within this forest are as much a problem for the current social structure as they are for the vision, for they also help identify why our current social system is not working.

REPRESENTATION

Let me suggest one step toward a solution, the more extensive use of an important feature of our present social structure. Clearly, all people cannot take the time to participate directly in all of the many communities, and, if they could, regional, national, and global communities would have far too many participants. Communities made up of representatives, sometimes randomly selected, sometimes self-selected, might be a solution. Just as people have an obligation today to serve on juries when randomly selected, people in the future might assume the obligation to work as a member of a community composed of randomly and self-selected delegates from other areas for the purposes of formulating responses to shared environmental interconnections.

This solution runs counter to the ideal that democracy means everyone should be able to vote on every decision that affects them, with voting on representatives being a poor second-best solution. Of course, this ideal has almost always led to the second-best solution in practice. The alternative I am suggesting would result in most of the populace participating in governance much of the time, perhaps as much, for example, as one day a week for thirty weeks of the year. Rich, middle class, and poor in the industrialized countries now contribute roughly this much time working to support our current technocratic analysis paralysis through taxes. It would be more democratic to contribute to one's governance directly. Certainly if people participated in their governance, they would have more of a sense of community and would be more likely to adjust their behavior as capitalists, entrepreneurs, laborers, and consumers accordingly, easing problems directly and reducing the conflicts that make implementation and enforcement difficult. Alienation would be reduced also, further facilitating people's ability to share understandings, reach agreements, and adhere to them. By assuming more responsibility ourselves rather than delegating so much of it to technocrats, democracy would be enhanced while distancing would be lessened.

Contrary to the current practice of electing representatives, I am deliberately suggesting randomly and self-selected delegates for several reasons. First, there would be plenty of opportunity for everyone to participate and everyone would be expected to participate. With nearly everyone involved in some way, the only issue would be who serves in which communities. Second, I envision a sufficient number of communities that the number of elections and difficulties of numerous people campaigning for election to their preferred community would be quite unmanageable. Third, the lives, boundaries, and tasks of the communities would be constantly evolving, further compounding any election process. Fourth, current experience indicates that elected representatives can be too beholden to special interests, even more beholden than are the whole people behind those special interests themselves. Electing representatives may play a role in a structure of coevolving communicative communities, but I think the case is strong that elections as a process of selection should not dominate.

Idealistic as this vision of governance may seem, modern societies are already moving in this direction. Top scientists regularly get together as members of self-selected groups, as draftees to committees of national academies, and as appointees to panels reporting to legislative bodies in order to resolve conflicting evidence and suggest less risky strategies on behalf of other scientists and the public. Commissions made up of unpaid citizens are being used increasingly to analyze environmental and social problems and suggest solutions. Ad hoc groups of businessmen, environmentalists, and labor leaders are coming together to formulate solutions where technocrats and legislators have failed. Formal dispute resolution outside of government is becoming increasingly accepted among contesting parties. Major, highly bureaucratized development organizations are finding ways to cooperate with nongovernmental organizations. Nongovernmental organizations are abandoning formal political arenas and working with each other on problems directly.

International communities are forming across national boundaries to work on tropical deforestation, climate change, biodiversity, cultural survival, and environmental justice, as well as a whole range of additional problems which are predominantly economic and social in character. These informal communities and their spokespeople are in many cases far more informed than governments and their representatives, are better able to work with the complexities at hand, and are working out solutions between them and encouraging governments to go along with them. Facsimile machines and electronic mail, as well as lower telephone rates, have facilitated direct communication between people in nonhierarchical communities far more than they have helped technocrats who still have to communicate through hierarchical channels. The United Nations Conference on Environment and Development in Rio de Janeiro in June 1992 had an official, parallel Earth Summit of representatives from nongovernmental organizations who worked toward more comprehensive and integrative proposals than the official government delegates.

Serving on a jury, commission, or special panel carries social obligations. Jurors and commissioners serve as representatives of the public and are given strict instructions to guide their judgment to reduce personal biases. Yet individual interpretation of the evidence and weighing of values are necessary and accepted in the process, for if the instructions were sufficiently complete, only one judge or scientist would be needed to reach the right verdict or answer. While the processes of juries and commissions are quite nebulous by the mythical standards of Western science, evidence and arguments typically are thoroughly questioned yet at the same time, a judgment is typically reached. While scientific panels tend toward elitism, I find the combined intellectual and moral environment when I serve on juries and commissions to be far richer and more stimulating than my daily interactions in the realms of science, markets, bureaucracies, or politics. Service in the coevolving discursive communities of the future needs this environment of moral obligation and intellectual inquiry.

Even this modest suggestion leaves key questions unanswered. How, for example, will the random selection system be run and excess volunteers redirected? As a coevolutionist I am in a quandary. I could design a more specific future to give a more convincing image, but to design is to defy my notion of process. New cognizance of the interrelations between social and environmental systems and expanded thinking about democracy, epistemology, and social organization, however, can only further favor and accelerate this evolutionary trend toward informal organization. This trend has occurred in spite of the dominance of conventional philosophical premises. The cosmological and epistemological arguments developed throughout this book provide better rationales for the changes that are occurring. A shift toward coevolutionary cosmology, conceptual pluralism, and understanding learning as a social process will help select against technocratic social organization supported by atomism, mechanism, objectivism, monism, and universalism.

IMPLICATIONS FOR TECHNOLOGY

The vast majority of distant linkages through environmental systems are directly attributable to the use of fossil hydrocarbons, and fossil hydrocarbons account for a large share of distant economic linkages as well. Global environmental feedbacks are forcing the global community to address climate change. The global economic linkages related to hydrocarbons have justified massive defense expenditures and atrocious wars. These distant linkages need to be reduced. Locally, fossil hydrocarbons are used to override rather than work with agroecosystems. Clearly, if communities are to be more responsive to the signals from ecosystems, they will have to use technologies which help people work with ecosystems rather than dominate them.

Many in the current environmental debate argue that most of our problems can be solved by using energy more efficiently, recycling more effectively, and avoiding obviously stupid things like trying to make tropical rainforests behave like cattle pastures. And to a large extent, the technofixers are correct. For them, however, the shift in technologies advocated in the foregoing paragraph would be sufficient, the emphasis of this book on knowledge and social organization superfluous. Technofixers rarely ask how current inefficiencies and inappropriate technologies came to dominate. When one sees the process as having been coevolutionary, one sees that technologies, social organization, ways of knowing, and values need to change together. A consciousness of the types of knowledge and social organization that might combine into a sustainable future will enhance, indeed facilitate, the selection of technologies for a more sustainable coevolution.

RECIPROCITY AS A GUIDING PRINCIPLE

Improving interconnections through coevolving discursive communities and reducing distant connections by selecting appropriate technologies will solve many of modernity's problems. Nevertheless, so long as human behavior is predominantly motivated by the objective of acquiring more material possessions than one's neighbor, the prospects for the future are probably dim. No other species has net acquisition as an objective. Even pack rats are famous for their behavior of leaving a token gift when they carry off a shiny human artifact to their nest. Anthropologists have long noted how acts of giving and being given to play a larger role than the material goods themselves in nonmodern cultures. People are understood to be in reciprocal, not exchange, relations with each other and with nature. Exchange entails bargaining and both parties sensing that they are better off after the exchange and that it is what was exchanged that has made them happier. Reciprocity entails a sense that whatever is given will return, in some form, through some mechanism, someday, if not to you, then to your kin or descendants. In such a system, one would only give to others or nature that which one finds valuable and would want back again. Until people again sense that they are in a closed, circular system, they will continue to live under the illusion that they can acquire materials on net from each other and from the environment in exchange for that which they do not want. No wonder we "give" pollutants to nature. To be in a community is to be inside in a great circle. The cultural rules of reciprocity assure that the old, weak, and temporarily unfortunate receive as needed. No welfare bureaucracy is required. We need a sense of being in a community with nature. The idea of reciprocity facilitates that sense.

Again, many in the current environmental discourse argue that greed is the whole problem. If people's values were different, they argue, material consumption would decrease, different technologies would be preferred, and the social structure would change. And again, I agree, but hasten to add that social structures that have been envisioned are more likely to emerge, and to emerge faster, than ones that have not.

CONCLUSIONS

Individualism has proven to be a form of escapism, of distancing, of disbursing problems on to others and into the future. In this sense, I am merely arguing that the emphases modern peoples have put on individualism, on society being merely the sum of individuals and hence on democracy as simple vote counting, on the invisible hand, and on objectivity, individual rationality, and thereby on technocracy – all of these characteristics of modernity and more – are the source of many of our problems. I see community in juxtaposition to the beliefs associated with individualism. We need to become much more sophisticated in our understanding and use of social *systems* at all scales and start thinking, pretty much from a clean slate, about how social systems interrelate with environmental systems. Few now see how we have been moving toward a coevolving patchwork quilt of discursive communities. The idea that such a social structure might have a viable future probably seems absurd to most, but this says more about our inability to think about social systems as systems at all than about whether the image has merit.

14

A COEVOLVING CULTURAL PATCHWORK QUILT

The cultural imperialism of the European and North American vision of progress is being openly, and increasingly violently, challenged around the globe. The people of the former Soviet Union are reclaiming their diverse cultural identities and challenging the very ends Marx and his devotees assumed were both good and inevitable. Islamic peoples, spanning from northwestern Africa to southeastern Asia, are formulating their own images of their future and are insisting that these images have a respected place in a larger global order. Asian, Black, and Mexican Americans in the United States, while certainly growing more impatient over disparities in economic opportunity, are also taking more pride in their cultural identities and putting less emphasis on equality. It is difficult to integrate into a mainstream which is bifurcating into multiple rivulets. People in lower-income classes in Western industrialized nations are both less patiently awaiting their share of material progress and, at the same time, questioning the whole idea. And the indigenous peoples that have not been eliminated by Western colonization and development in the New World as well as the remaining tribal peoples in Asia are demanding new respect and the opportunity to define their own futures. There is no contradiction in wanting the fruits of progress if they are real and questioning whether the fruits are not really artificial. In spite of middle-class material madness during the final decades of the twentieth century, the Western idea of progress has changed from a powerful agent of global bonding to a contradictory combination of an irritant, a fog blocking our vision, and a stimulus to new thought.

People, North and South, are interpreting the economically patchy, culturally calamitous, and environmentally destructive way history has unfolded with decidedly mixed feelings. The modern vision – of all peoples understanding and respecting each other, living in peace and harmony, cooperatively coaxing more material wealth from the earth – certainly has lofty, idealistic tones. Until recently, however, few saw how this paragon of human harmony was based on cultural homogenization rather than greater love. Similarly, the absence of material want was based on the presumption that humankind could control nature rather than a concern for how social and environmental systems might work in partnership. Many have benefitted from the fact that the pre-modern patchwork quilt of cultures, though severely repressed, continued to evolve on its own. Westerners have long bemoaned further cultural homogenization, albeit mostly out of fear of losing the variety of cuisine, literature, music, and art they themselves enjoy. More recently, however, modern peoples have looked to the remaining differences between peoples for new perspectives on their own difficulties. We are beginning to look at other cultures as repositories of technologies and ways of organizing which might help us work better with nature. And yet, though we are becoming vaguely aware of the importance of cultural diversity, we are neither able to understand nor prepared to work constructively with the reculturalization that is currently underway. On the contrary, we are shocked by the rapidity with which diverse peoples are asserting their cultural separateness and group superiority, frequently with a vengeance. With the demise in faith in progress and the cultural patchwork quilt reasserting itself, we need an image of the future which incorporates and supports, rather than denies, heterogeneity. To argue that the modern project of homogenization is only temporarily stalled is likely to lead to further cultural violence, individual grief, and associated environmental mismanagement, resource waste, and ecoterrorism.

As the twentieth century comes to a close, competition over the path to progress appears naive in light of our new awareness of the environmental consequences of modernity and a reawakening of cultural differences. We did not perceive these problems sooner because we still expected history to unfold progressively. For decades we have been blind to what was really happening, merely being able to see that material progress for the vast majority of the earth's peoples was taking much longer than expected. The modern idea of cultural convergence on the scientifically best way of controlling nature denies the existence of the very problems this view has created. Trying to understand the present with the image of culturally converging progress in our minds has been like trying to find snakes in a jungle when we think they look and behave like monkeys. We need a new model of the directions history has taken us to better perceive the interactions between people and their environment, to fully comprehend cultural differences, and to guide both to a better shared future.

Coevolution is a process. Yet our understanding of process is intimately linked to our understanding of the possible. Thus one contribution of a coevolutionary explanation of development is that it facilitates a new image of how the future could unfold, opening our understanding to new and possibly desirable futures. Consider the following prospect.

Imagine a coevolving patchwork quilt of different cultures. Instead of accepting how modernization is reducing cultural differences to the vacuity of global mass production and individual materialism, we could strive to live constructively within different cultures while respecting and learning from differences between cultures. Today more and more peoples are competing for the same resources and assaulting the environment with the same "best" technologies to produce the same consumer products. Imagine instead a mosaic of cultures depending on different resources and environmental services through the use of different technologies and forms of social organization to produce products for consumers who across cultures had quite different ideas about what they might want. Imagine, instead of a tightly linked global market economy, a loosely connected network of bioregional, cultural economies. And, as opposed to so many peoples entangled in public and corporate bureaucracies, imagine more differentiated forms of social organization with a greater variety of roles between them and with broader opportunities for individual talents to flower. We can hope that the overlapping discursive communities explored in the last chapter would find a place in many of the cultural patches, but not all. The image of a patchwork quilt of cultures follows logically from a coevolutionary conceptualization of process and the importance of diversity. It provides a basis for moving toward a constructive, differentiated future.

I hope that the image of the globe as a mosaic of coevolving social and ecological systems is beginning to take shape in your mind. Though it is still new in my own, let me try to embellish your imagination a little. To ease the transition, think of it as an enrichment of many of the early moral objectives historically incorporated in the idea of progress, a clear replacement of the idea of merging, and a way off the material treadmill on which the furthest progressed are stuck.

In one sense, this new image draws upon our view of the past. Historically, people were more isolated; different peoples worked the land differently; and the coevolutions of social systems with their environmental systems were driven more by factors inside the local culture than outside. Cultures reflected their landscapes and landscapes reflected their cultures. Some social and environmental systems coevolved to extinction, to such environmental degradation that the social system could no longer be supported, or vice versa, while others thrived through mutually supportive interactions for millennia. The diversity of coevolving systems, however, assured that at least some of them would respond favorably to an occasional harsh environmental surprise as well as adapt to long term environmental changes.

Let's make sure, however, that we agree that we are not talking about multiple areas of isolated peoples. Historically, goods, services, knowledge, and technologies were exchanged between distant as well as between nearby cultures. They should still be exchanged in the future. Historically, people moved from place to place and a few should still be able to do so. The coevolutionary framework, however, shifts the emphasis from the exchange of material goods and flows of opportunistic capital in a single global economic culture to flows between cultural systems. And the emphasis shifts from flows of materials to flows of values, ways of thinking, technologies, ways of organizing people, and natural genetic material. Do not think of these flows, however, as mundane economic exchanges typical of modern trade. Take an ecological and evolutionary approach. Think of the occasional flows as providing new natural and social genetic material to the coevolutionary process in each system. Do not think of them simply as something which adds to consumption or productive capacity. If the newly introduced value, way of thinking, technology, way of organizing, or species proves fit, it will subsequently affect the fitness of other components in the system and thereby change the coevolutionary path of the system, cultural and biological.

Introductions of products, technologies, values, understandings, and ways of organizing into one cultural system from another have been important throughout history. It is critical to keep in mind, however, that their importance has also been related to the historic separateness of cultural systems and the relative rarity of introductions. If systems were not somewhat separate, they would be the same and there would be nothing new to introduce. Ever since we have thought of cultural interactions either in simple economic terms or as a part of the process of progressive cultural merging, we have missed an important thing about transfers between cultures. By admitting how flows between cultures affect the coevolutionary process, we admit that cultures might find it advantageous to regulate such flows to maintain their culture or to affect how it coevolves. Thus, though this coevolutionary image of the future is not about isolated cultures, by acknowledging the importance of cultures and thinking of them as coevolving systems, we find ourselves arguing against complete freedom of exchange, against the highly interconnected, global economic grid of modernity.

Biologists find themselves in a similar position arguing for the control of introduced species whenever and wherever possible. Since somewhere near the beginning of life, species, or the same species with new genetic material, have crossed into ecosystems they previously had not occupied, forever after affecting the coevolutionary unfolding. Introduced species and genetic material have been important to the construction of ecosystems, in some sense more important than mutations. And when new material proves fit, the short and long-term outcomes are unknown. Sometimes the complexity of the ecosystem is enhanced when new species are introduced. Frequently the introduction displaces other species that have coevolved together, and the system suffers a partial collapse to a less complex and less diverse system. People began facilitating introductions through their travels and trade from our earliest beginnings, accelerating the natural process of introductions into ecosystems. The movement of people from Asia to the Western Hemisphere where Siberia and Alaska once joined was itself a major introduction which transformed New World ecosystems. But as the frequency of travel and trade increased and became more thorough, the biological world, like the cultural world, began to be tyrannized by a relatively few species that out-compete indigenous varieties, reducing ecosystems to mere skeletons of their former selves, and then dominating them. Because of excessive exchange, controlling exotic species has become a basic tenet of bioreserve management. Biologists, however, have had about as much success in getting exotics out of "natural" ecosystems as agriculturalists have had in eliminating introduced pests, or China has had in eliminating the heretical ideas of Western culture. But at least with less travel and trade, the rate of introductions might slow to more tolerable levels.

By now you should be feeling rather uncomfortable with all of this talk of barriers between people and the idea that communities and cultures might choose to go their separate ways. It is directly counter to our progressive image. I admit some discomfort, much as I do on reading Robert Frost's poem on how good fences make good neighbors. Should not mutual respect make barriers less necessary, understanding break them down, and love overcome them? And yet each of these conventional wisdoms presumes the existence of barriers in the first place. Might there be an appropriate level of cultural identity? Most importantly, the demise of barriers during the twentieth century has been due to homogenization, not the triumph of the good human values of cultural respect, understanding, and love. Ironically, for these moral virtues to triumph and remain triumphant, barriers must have some level of a sustaining force.

I am not advocating that all existing barriers should be strengthened and any new ones approved. Nor am I denying that global institutions for managing global problems like climate change can be forgotten. I am arguing, albeit beyond my cultural base of understanding, that the nature of the opposing forces of cultural differentiation and homogenization need to be understood in the more culturally heterogeneous world to which we are rapidly returning. Cooperation between groups needs to be rooted more firmly in the nature of shared problems and rely less on rhetoric about our all being one humanity. With the full demise of the idea that we are progressing to one best way of feeling, knowing, behaving, and interacting with nature, cultural barriers of different levels and kinds selected by people as members of different groups cannot be looked upon simply as being perverse.

Today, all countries are pretty much coevolving around Western science and fossil hydrocarbons. All countries are applying similar commercial fertilizers and pesticides on similar crops, for only the most productive techniques and inputs will compete on the international market. Sustainability would be enhanced if the differences between the development styles of different countries were greater. If our vision shifts to a patchwork quilt of coevolving economies rather than one modern global economy, inter-connectedness would have to be reduced, self-sufficiency would have to be increased, and different technologies and forms of social organization would have to be tried. Certainly these changes would reduce material well-being in the short run. But with more experimentation, all countries could learn about the range of viable alternatives much faster. Good ideas could still be transferred from patch to patch, country to country, and if they prove fit, could enhance the lives of more people. In the longer run, new styles of development would evolve. With cultural differentiation and new interest in community life, material preferences would diversify between cultural patches and the rewards of cultural participation and community life would reduce pressures to consume. With greater differentiation between development styles, countries would put different selective pressures on their environments and thereby reduce the loss of biodiversity. With different countries coevolving along different courses, humankind would not have all of its eggs in one basket.

The image of a coevolutionary patchwork quilt will only have a significant impact if it becomes widely accepted. The image may never become more specific. A coevolutionary patchwork quilt is a pretty vague idea, and yet it is already as specific as the idea of progress. No definition of progress exists in any operational sense. Even without an operating definition of progress, Western peoples nonetheless incorporated it into their political discourse and made decisions for several centuries in its name in the understanding that it was occurring. Modernism somehow "worked" without an operational definition of progress, the meaning of progress kept changing as it was invoked by different political interests over time, but the way it worked consistently led to environmental and cultural destruction. A coevolutionary patchwork quilt should be a more constructive shared image of and for the future.

The coevolutionary paradigm provides a new basis for thinking about diversity. The image of a coevolving patchwork quilt starts with cultural and biological diversity and can be elaborated to show how these can facilitate sustainability. With this image, cultural diversity would have a stronger basis for survival than it does relying merely on tolerance, or vague respect, as supported by some aspects of most religions. It is inherently an image with different and changing axes on which different societies might progress. With this image, the protection and enhancement of biological diversity would be rooted in more than a philosophy of environmental preservation.

Cultural diversity was possible historically because cultures had more space, people from different cultures were less frequently bumping into each other, technologies of war were not so devastating, and societies were less economically dependent on each other's resources, labor, and technology. Yet even under these relatively favorable conditions, some societies culturally dominated or physically destroyed others. Even if societies become less economically interdependent, it would be impossible to maintain cultural diversity under current population levels and technologies without some common values and common understandings between cultures. A shared understanding of the benefits of diversity and a collective vision of the future as a coevolving patchwork quilt could contribute to such a common vision to make diversity sustainable. Such an understanding would complement existing do-unto-others-as-you-would-have-them-do-unto-you moral philosophies. Whereas the modern idea of progress as cultural merging undercuts this basic rule of reciprocity, an image of the future as a coevolving patchwork quilt would bolster it.

Yet it is by no means clear that the image of a coevolving patchwork quilt of communities and cultures could be commonly held. One of the reasons communities and cultures have been antagonistic is because the sense of identity provided by holding particular beliefs as a member of a group is threatened by the existence of other people finding equally strong senses of identity as members of other groups. Thus, though it may be possible for people to understand how they benefit over the long run from the existence of cultural differences, this may not be sufficient even under the best of circumstances. Moral development with respect to cultural tolerance and respect will still undoubtedly be necessary.

Good will and understanding of the long-term benefits of diversity need only lapse occasionally or be absent from a few cultures for the whole patchwork quilt to be destroyed. For this reason, some form of united oversight and police power would still unfortunately be necessary to intervene when one or more cultures became militarily aggressive, economically domineering, or ecologically destructive. Similarly, while cultural diversity is to be respected, this does not mean that cultures are free to do whatever they might choose so long as it does not affect other cultures. Particular practices such as female infanticide, slavery, and other forms of inhumanity should not be tolerated. The nature of the global contract, means of social pressure across cultures, organization of an overseeing global agency, and governance of the police power will be difficult to define. Perhaps it could evolve from the United Nations organization we have today. Some of its qualities that are now perceived as weaknesses could be strengths in a coevolving patchwork quilt future. Whatever global institutions emerge, they will have to be based on a sufficiently commonly shared understanding of global order and values to determine when order and values are being violated.

We need to share something comparable to Adam Smith's metaphor of the "invisible hand" to rally our organizational proclivity while setting us on a sustainable course. I must confess that the image of a coevolving patchwork quilt of cultures seems an implausible image in an age of international competition. On the other hand, two centuries ago, the idea that economies were guided by an "invisible hand" must have seemed pretty incongruous, during the rise of scientific enlightenment and in the age of economic mercantilism.

A coevolutionary patchwork quilt provides an alternative image of the future, but it is by no means an ideal construct. In contrast to the utopian literature of the nineteenth and early twentieth centuries, the coevolutionary vision does not lead to arguments about how a quicker, firmer step to the march of history will result in a moral, meaningful, and materially cornucopian world. Utopianism is consistent with the idea of progress; truly alternative understandings of process and images of the future cannot be utopian in nature. Indeed, quite to the contrary, with reculturization running in defiance of the residual image of progress and without a broadly accepted philosophical basis for diversity, the future is likely to be even more violent – for individuals, cultures, and the environment – than the past.

The challenge of sustainable development is to derive a viable image of the future, to change the vocabulary of our political discourse, and thereby the decisions we make so that a patchwork of coevolutions of social organization, knowledge, technology, values, and ecosystems is sustainable. The image developed in this chapter builds on a trend – the process of reculturization and a closely related, though less blatantly obvious, reconsideration of the relationships between individuals and their communities. These phenomena defy basic tenets underlying the modern, progressive image. Furthermore I argue, or at least allude to the possibility, that reculturization is a move in a viable direction, that it could support a biologically diverse, environmentally sustainable future.

15

PROGRESS REVISIONED

Having participated in, or permitted, the construction of an environment in which scientific laws come to the fore, both materially, in technological products, and spiritually, in the ideas that are allowed to guide major decisions, we, scientists as well as the common citizens of Western civilization, are subjected to their rule. But social conditions change and science changes with them. Nineteenth century science denied the advantages of cultural plurality; twentieth century science, chastened by a series of rather upsetting revolutions and urged on by sociologists and anthropologists, recognizes them. The same scientists, philosophers, politicians who support science change science by this very support and they change the world with it. This world is not a static entity populated by thinking ants who, crawling all over its crevices, gradually discover its features without affecting them in any way. It is a dynamic and multifaced entity which affects and reflects the activity of its explorers. It was once a world full of gods; it then became a drab material world and it will, hopefully, change further into a more peaceful world where matter and life, thought and feelings, innovation and tradition collaborate for the benefit of all.

(Paul Feyerabend 1987)

Every culture has a life story explaining the creation of the heavens and the earth, a narrative that positions the mountains, streams, and great oceans, an account of relations between plants and animals and people and gods. Most of these great stories nebulously intertwine people and animals and their associated gods. The people of the American Northwest tell a story of their descent from ravens, or is it a raven-like god, or the raven's god. In many great stories, people have previous and subsequent incarnations as animals. There are multiple spirits identified with different animals and plants with whom one should maintain a relation of reciprocity. Earth and life relate in occasionally imaginative ways. One Indian life story has the earth riding on a platform on the back of an elephant which is riding on a turtle. People, animals, water, and earth intertwine and circle about without

181

clear beginnings or endings. The Sufi stories of Arabia, Persia, and Turkey teasingly transform mystic, ascetic people-dervishes into animate as well as inanimate forms bringing us toward intimacy with both our oneness and other worlds and a nothingness beyond. Shared life stories place people in their physical and biological surroundings, connect them to their ancestors and descendants, remind them of their obligations and vulnerability, and escort their daily thoughts and behavior.

Judeo-Christian-Islamic religions introduced a life story wherein the earth, plant and animal life, and people were created separately and sequentially following what came to be interpreted as a grand design. A single God came to be interpreted as having given people dominion over all. It is an atomistic and hierarchical story with clear dominance and vague responsibility. As a life story, it lacks the interdependent, unpredictable, circular, and leveling relations of other great stories of life. After the creation, Western people saw themselves as "in charge" rather than constantly intertwining and circling in a system beyond their control. To be sure, God could always intervene, but the Judeo-Christian-Islamic God would only do so to set the system on course again, not to teasingly meddle in its daily affairs. Western philosophers took this story several steps further by imagining people and how they perceived and thought as outside of the world over which they had dominion, much like God was imagined. In this imaging, God's grand design awaited the advance of human knowledge. To facilitate human prediction and control, the joint authors of the Western narrative assumed universal underlying mechanical relations between parts throughout nature. As creation stories go, modernity's narrative reduced life to a gigantic machine that would eventually be subject to man's control. And the machine consisted of parts and linkages which did not change, lacked being and becoming, and neither thought nor felt. To be sure, people still marveled at nature and the wonders of life. The Sufi tradition remains fully intermingled with Islam. A romantic trend persists among some philosophers, natural historians, writers, and artists. Yet biology still advances largely by using the analogy of a machine of lifeless parts. And economics, whether neoclassical or marxist, addresses the accumulation of material things rather than the interconnectedness of people in human communities and nature.

As the modern creation story evolved, it became a moving hierarchy, racing through time. Knowledge and material well-being improved but the hierarchical structure of people within industrialized nations and of nations North and South remained the same with the formally knowledgeable on the cutting edge, most just struggling to keep up, and others clearly dropping out. Belief in progress through science severed people from their ancestors and descendants. Forebears were portrayed as materially impoverished, uninformed, boors, while descendants were depicted as inevitably living in a wonderworld beyond current people's comprehension.

And unlike any life story heretofore, history unfolded through a ceaseless advance of technology as scientists steadily cracked God's grand design. Posterity no longer depended on the forbearance of forebears' thinking ahead. Modern people's position with respect to others furthermore was reduced to differences in scientific sophistication and material wealth. Not surprisingly, Darwin's theory of evolution was popularized as a substantiation of progress and hierarchy and the superiority of Western culture over others.

The story guided individual behavior and promoted collective action in the West for three centuries. The appearance of progress accelerated with marvelous inventions entertaining and eventually enriching the elite, transforming the lives of farmers and urban workers, and eventually bringing the wonders of technology into the homes, indeed garages, of the poor as well. The sharing of the life story allowed the West to relax its colonial domination over the rest of the world as the promise of more for all united cultures in a global development effort that facilitated greater apparent unity among different peoples than ever before. Science continued to drive this globally shared life story, assuring and seemingly providing better technologies for controlling nature, superior ways of organizing people, improved methods of deducing truth, and rational practices for resolving conflicts.

The coevolving natural and cultural worlds, however, became pauperized by the selective forces of modernity's progressive, mechanical, hierarchical life story. Looking back from the end of the twentieth century, we can now see how relatively minor differences over the best way to rationally organize people combined with personal and national egos and marred the century with world, regional, civil, and ethnic wars as well as costly arms races. While non-Western cultures gained a new shared vision, a new life story, they also lost self-respect and traditional values, knowledge, and technologies disappeared in the process. All became distanced from each other as communities broke down and people became insulated by a complex web of market forces. While the new life story promised much in the future, it left most people, North and South, with an inferior status relative to the more scientifically informed. Poor countries became enmeshed in technological and financial imperialism, human creativity became trapped in bureaucratic social structures driven by instrumental rationality, and within these entanglements, men dominated women by assuming the guardianship of rational thought, scientific knowledge, and its supporting enterprise.

And nature in the end did not succumb but became despoiled, sullied, temperamental, ever less bountiful, ever less creative, and with all harmony with humanity lost. Radioactive materials with half-lives of thousands of years contaminated the earth; toxics entered groundwater aquifers with cleansing periods of centuries. Nature no more thrived through attempts at control and being treated as nonbeings than people did. As great life stories

183

go, the West's story promoted dying over becoming, death over being, species by species.

Material madness distracted all from the impersonality of their lives and the cultural and environmental decay around them. But materialism, the temporal evidence of progress itself, derived from coevolving around the depletion of the stock of fossil hydrocarbons rather than the current flows of energy from the sun captured by ecosystems. Population increased dramatically, seriously compounding the difficulties of balancing nature's energy flows and organic manifestations with human needs. Ways of knowing, organizing, and doing things were selected to complement the use of petroleum and coal while these storehouses of nature's productivity past were being consumed, their oxidation reversing hundreds of millions of years of biogeophysical accumulation and transformation. Greenhouse gases associated with this process of net oxidation wrapped the globe in a warm blanket, initiated a further oxidation of soil and vegetative hydrocarbons, and transformed the radiative balances between ice, snow, vegetative cover, and clouds.

Adam Smith created the most powerful metaphor in history when he described how individuals responding in their own interest to market incentives behave in the public interest "as if guided by an invisible hand." For nearly two hundred years this metaphor has been an important element in the modern political discourse. While it has been used in different ways by various political groups, from the perspective of thinking about sustainable development we can see that how it facilitated not asking difficult questions, not collecting and processing reams of data, and not addressing the big questions about where the hand is taking us. We have no alternative vision to guide us. Yet even without an alternative vision, already we are able to see how those who still believe in the invisible hand do so out of desperation.

The poorest among the poor regions – Haiti and Somalia, much of Ethiopia, and other parts of Africa – dropped out of the race for progress within decades of joining it and have been left on the wayside, ethnic groups pitted against ethnic groups to control the remaining social order and natural resources, their people starving, and with no viable life story of their own to dampen the travesty or with which to set another course. Vietnam, Laos, Cambodia, and Afghanistan may have neither a cultural nor environmental basis on which to enter the race again even as their chance to do so politically seems ever more possible. Numerous poor countries are having increasing difficulty suppressing their ethnic differences through national governments dedicated to development that refuses to manifest itself as promised. The Soviet Union, the real surprise, was the first major power to collapse while diligently pursuing modernity's great life story. Its adaptation of the modern story of progress disempowered people's creativity and initiative in a bureaucratic leviathan, wasted soil in drastic efforts to modernize agriculture, and polluted water and air to accelerate industrial development, each to the breaking point. Democratic, market-oriented nations have interpreted this as a victory for their adaptation of the Western story, not realizing that the differences in versions only amount to how quickly the breaking point is reached.

While the race within European and North American countries, Japan, and the newly industrialized economies continues, many find the path to progress is fading, modernity's life story becoming increasingly mute. Whatever gains there may be from new technologies are being consumed by technocratic agencies and their expert consultants, ever expanding in contentious battle, striving to best contain the unforeseen detrimental social and environmental consequences of technical innovations and global economic interconnectedness. But the connections are increasingly distant from individuals who specialize in increasingly fractured particular tasks and ways of thinking. Problems at the local level are interconnected with the global economy, while the global economy and global environmental problems are beyond the reach of people. Experts have more and more to worry about while the masses are increasingly disempowered. The truly hopeless have dropped out, some merely hungry and homeless, others deranged on drugs, but they plague the system both out of necessity and at will. More and more effort goes into trying to gain control over the positive feedbacks reverberating between technologies, institutions, and the environment on the one hand and the parallel feedbacks accelerating despair and adverse social behavior on the other. Economists are still interpreting these expanding efforts at damage control as a contribution to gross national product in the "service" sector. But obviously, while one might personally improve one's status by becoming an environmental expert, lawyer, policeman, psychologist, or social worker, these are economic costs of a system in its death throes.

Those in power still appeal to the myth of progress to defend a disintegrating social and natural order, not to establish new healthy relations between peoples and their environments. The old image of progress through control is still rallied, for lack of an alternative, clouding our vision at a time when a clearly new, richer image of the construction and interaction of social and environmental orders is desperately needed. The combination of problems is all the more dangerous in a world of modern military technology, of global economic interdependence, with the ease of ecoterrorism, and with some eight times as many people as there were when the modern project was initiated. With the idea of progress rapidly fading, the need for an effective, constructive shared image of the future has never been greater.

There are many critiques of modernity argued from within the tangle of the existing story, playing modern contentions against each other, noting the contradictions between the great story and how history unfolded. Most critics advocate only minor adjustments in the current version of the story.

185

Some are simply arguing that we need to lower our expectations with respect to the possibilities for rational social organization and control over the environment. Some are arguing that we need to bring the rates of technological and cultural change into balance by slowing the former or accelerating the latter. Some are trying to repatch religion into the narrative without editing the materialist story line. Indeed, some hawk religion as a path to material success. Environmentalists are trying to save specific habitats at a time when all ecosystems are threatened by global climate change. Bioregionalists have not found a way to shelter communities from the tyranny of the global economy. While some feminists are envisioning just, meaningful, sustainable lives, most women are compelled by their circumstances to seek equal access to the existing cultural and ecological disaster. To too great an extent, the numerous groups challenging modernity are revisioning only different parts of the modern project.

An effective reimaging of the future is not simply a list of agreed upon objectives, a description of a better world. To be effective, the reimaging of the future must also explain the mistakes of the past and indicate the path to the new objectives. In short, modern peoples need a more elaborate, less mechanical line to their life story. The great story that evolved in Europe from the renaissance through the reformation both explained the failures of the past and justified the new course. While that story line eventually led the West astray, the next story line nevertheless will also have to fulfill the same function, explain the past and indicate a way forward.

What is becoming ever more clear, in short, is the importance of a shared understanding of process. In retrospect, though the modern vision was about change, what progress would attain was always vague while the understanding of the process of attainment – of science and its application to technology, social organization, and public discourse – was elaborated, implemented, and appeared to be confirmed. The hope for progress grew during the eighteenth century as the educated public marvelled in the beauty of Newtonian mechanics. The process was confirmed to all during the nineteenth century with the coming of steam power and the mechanical age that followed. An incomplete story of science in the great story of life became ever better elaborated. While a few aspects of the vision of modern progress are questioned today, by and large the vision, however nebulous, is still intact. Our doubts are with respect to the process, not the prospect; whether there is a path, not the beauty of the peak. For wherever humanity is going in the future, a shared understanding of process is needed in the present.

And the process, modernity's story line, is Western science, not as it actually is at the end of the twentieth century, but as it was presented to the public in the great story told during the second half of the last and first half of this century. It is this immature, expurgated, truncated account of science that became embodied in the structure of institutions and the canons of public discourse that still rule today. It is the mechanical world view of prediction and control; the atomistic assumption that whole problems can be solved in parts; the idea that people, their values, and their patterns of thinking stand apart from reality; the premise of universality; and the presumption that the separate parts of science would surely fit together. Though Western science in fact has far more diverse foundations, these story elements formed a readily coherent package that complemented the vision of progress and thus seemed to define the path. At the same time, atomistic science disempowered people by reducing them to being experts in finely divided fields, leaving only the most wildly visionary and foolishly brave trying to comprehend the whole.

And yet, the most interesting developments of scientific thought during the past century should have modified the great story's promise of people overcoming their earthly bounds, the promise of becoming as objective and rootless as the Judeo-Christian God. Western science is less and less about levering a mechanical world. Evolutionary theory, thermodynamics, quantum mechanics, cybernetics, game theory, and explorations of chaos among others, even statistics, have changed philosophers' and scientists' understanding of processes and the possible. While each of these should have changed modernity's life story, their significances were distorted with their incorporation. Through much of the twentieth century, futurists invoked the rudiments of evolutionary thinking to falsely bolster the same progressive world view, to paint grand visions of progression from the primordial ooze to primitive man and on to man the comprehender and master of the wonders of the universe. Philosophers, however, now understand the diversity of ways science explains, the division between the sciences and humanities are no longer so clear, and once again there is hope for the natural and cultural richness of life. However, the great life story that politicians, policy makers, working scientists, and bureaucrats still appeal to remains lifeless.

Coevolution is a different explanation of process that could become an integral thread in the fabric of a new great life story for Western and westernized peoples. A coevolutionary cosmology provides a basis for explaining how history unfolded by highlighting how the exploitation of fossil hydrocarbons drove a wedge between the coevolution of social and ecological systems. It would not, however, inform us how to get back on the track toward the modern vision of progress. Process and product cannot be independent. The modern explanation of process stresses a cultural merging to universally accepted knowledge, values, ways of organizing, and best technologies. The modern story fosters global homogenization, centralization, and a hierarchy of experts. The coevolutionary explanation of process, on the other hand, admits, helps us see, lends legitimacy to, and identifies the advantages of a diversity of ways of knowing, valuing, organizing, and doing things. A coevolutionary story line would stress the relatedness of all beings as well as physical processes and the interdependence of values and patterns of thinking with the unfolding of life. A coevolutionary story line would complement a vision of diversity, sharing, and richness. It offers hope for a joint venture between people and between people and nature while emphasizing that the future is both unknowable and risky.

Our visions of how the future could be are closely linked to our understandings of process. However, the linkage runs deeper than simply our ability to envision an alternative future to which we might aspire. How we understand relationships between social and environmental systems affects how we choose to behave individually and how we organize to behave collectively and thereby the forces and selective pressures we put on environmental and cultural systems. How we participate in the unfolding of the future depends on the understandings we hold. If we cling to atomistic-mechanistic explanations of parts and processes which, in fact, are better understood as coevolutionary, our behavior defies reality, selects against possible futures we might prefer, and will eventually be our demise.

Western science needs a new narrative for its own survival with dignity. Five hundred years ago, based on the hypothesis of a relationship between bad blood and disease, blood-letting was commonly practiced. We know today that the hypothesis had some basis but that the cure lacked a systemic view of the body. And taken to an extreme, as it occasionally was, death by blood-letting is certain. Scientists today are proud to claim that whatever social and environmental travesties might be associated with modern technologies, science has extended and made life easier and richer. Western science in some sense must be correct and powerful. We have the joy and practicality of getting around in automobiles, for example. Perhaps so. But in what sense is it anymore correct and powerful than five hundred years ago? Putting knowledge from controlled laboratory experiments into open social and environmental systems, is little different from blood-letting. Our automobiles are contributing to the greenhouse gases which are overheating the globe. Science as implemented within the current life story fails to address science's lack of understanding of a grander system with longer reaction times, and is letting the blood of all together in the process. Science, of course, detected the greenhouse problem and helps me advocate a new life story, but science as it still chooses to think of itself is narrower than a life story.

As I bring this book to a close, let me draw on the words of Thomas Berry, Passionist priest, cultural historian, and most respectful scholar of the great stories of the world.

> We have lost contact with our Story, with the Great Story and that is why the instructions being given to me by the moon and the wind and the clover was to tell the story to remind us all what is happening and where we must look for guidance. For we can come together, all the

peoples of earth and all the various members of the great earth community, only in the Great Story, the story of the universe.

For there is no community without a community story, no earth community without the earth story, and no universe without the universe story. These three constitute the Great Story. Without this story the various forces of the planet become mutually destructive rather than mutually coherent.

We need to listen to each other's way of telling the Great Story. But first we in the west, with our newly developed capacity to listen to the universe through our vast telescopes and to hear the sounds of the universe as these come to us from the beginning of time and over some billions of years, we need really to listen to this story as our own special way of understanding and participating in the Great Story.

Whenever we forget our story we become confused. But the winds and the rivers and the mountains, they never become confused. We must go to them constantly to be reminded of the great story, for every being in the universe is what it is only through its participation in the story. We are resensitized whenever we listen to what they are telling us. Long ago they told us that we must be guided by a reverence and a restraint in our relations with the larger community of life, that we must respect the powers of the surrounding universe, that only through a sensitive insertion of ourselves into the great celebration of the earth community can we expect the support of the earth community. If we violate the integrity of this community we will die.

(Berry 1991: 19–20)

We cannot abandon the life story we had, but we can let it live and grow again. We can break beyond the atomistic-mechanistic views of Newton and incorporate the newer understandings about systems uncovered by Western science and new thinking from philosophy which leaves people and their ideas in those systems, abandoning the hope of finding a few universal truths and accepting our own history in the unfolding of reality. We can incorporate the wondrous complexities our new science is documenting into the revitalized story. And we can replant the new story in a reinterpreted religious soil.

The coevolutionary cosmology can contribute to this revisioning. It once again places us and how we think inside a great life story among the animals and plants with whom we share the mountains and valleys, rivers and oceans. The coevolutionary cosmology stresses the communal nature of knowing, making social life a process of sharing rather than of vote counting and enforcement, or of technocrats determining right answers and controlling our lives. It emphasizes the beauty of participating in and sustaining a coevolutionary unfolding rather than the individual glory of power and material accumulation. It values both nature and people. It draws upon recent advances in Western science as well as upon Western values which have withstood the test of time. And most importantly, it gives legitimacy to and a philosophy for interacting with the plurality of evolving human cultures and their distinct yet changing life stories. This framing can contribute to the process of revisioning progress, transforming the image to once again nourish the diverse wonders and universal dignity of being, becoming, and sharing.

BIBLIOGRAPHIC ESSAYS

CHAPTER 1

In order to extend my argument to a broader audience, I have not interrupted the flow of my argument with notes and references. A few chapters refer to specific scholars, but many do not. As a scholar, I realize that my peers will find this omission unforgivable. At the same time, the scholarly style we know today evolved with the practice of specialization and writing to the few within one's specialty. It is simply not possible duly to credit sources when writing at a broad philosophical level across the fields of the natural and social sciences as they apply to the last four centuries of history. For this reason, I have prepared separate bibliographic essays for readers who wish to know more about the general literature from which I have drawn, the specific sources I found most useful, and how I think I have learned from the ideas of others.

Even while relying on bibliographic essays, I have had a major bibliographic difficulty. This book contributes to a large and diverse literature on postmodernity, complements an interesting literature on paradigm change, and parallels some of the ideas developing in the ecofeminist literature. And yet I cite these literatures least well.

Postmodern writers, coming from a variety of disciplines, are bound by their awareness of how grossly different the present turned out to be as compared to the historical expectations of people, one and more generations ago, when what we now know as the present was the future. Modernity as an era in human history differed from others in large part because of people's expectations for the future, and particularly expectations of change rather than continuity. Modernity promised a merging of cultures around a science which would master nature and rationalize social organization. For generations, Western and westernized peoples lived and behaved in accordance with this expectation. This vision was elaborated very effectively by Auguste Comte in the middle of the nineteenth century (Comte, *A General View of Positivism*, 1848). Comte also coined the term "sociology," the discipline which formed most strongly around these expectations. And for this reason, sociologists are among the most surprised and hence prolific postmodernists.

The literature on grand and not-so-grand theories of modernity and post-modernity is large and impressive, but it addresses issues quite different from those I confront. To a large extent, this is because sociologists trying to paint the big picture have traditionally hung their canvas far from the issues that drive my own thinking: resources and the environment and the reculturization processes that have arisen over the past few decades. Leading thinkers in the 1970s such as Daniel Bell (*The Coming of Post-Industrial Society: A Venture in Social Forecasting*, 1973), for example, extrapolated the increasing importance of science, information, and technocratic order and predicted a diminution of concern over resource and environmental issues. Immanuel Wallerstein (*The Modern World System*, 1974) addressed how the capitalist world system controls resources, but, even in his most recent work, he barely acknowledges the difficulties the "world system" has encountered managing the environment and keeping environmentally driven social movements from affecting the political agenda. Recent volumes of papers on modernity and postmodernity suggest, with a few exceptions, that the big picture is still hung in its old location (Martin Albrow and Elizabeth King (eds), *Globalization, Knowledge, and Society*, 1990; Mike Featherstone (ed.), *Global Culture: Nationalism, Globalization, and Modernity*, 1990; and Bryan S. Turner (ed.), *Theories of Modernity and Postmodernity*, 1990). Richard Falk ("Religion and Politics: Verging on the Post Modern," 1988) provides a political analysis of the resurgence of religion, both fundamentalist and progressive, and its role in national politics – from Iran to Nicaragua to the United States. He attributes the resurgence to the inability of either the state or the church, as compromised under modernism, even to address the meaning of the nuclear arms race, mass poverty, and ecological collapse.

Within the postmodern literature, nevertheless, there are many works that complement my ideas. Jean-François Lyotard provides an intriguing explanation of postmodernity that complements my own concern with how the contradictions between beliefs about science and the actual workings of science undercut the legitimacy of science and hence of modernity itself (*The Postmodern Condition: A Report on Knowledge*, 1984). Lyotard, however, never mentions the difficulties modern science faces with postmodern perceptions of and solutions to environmental problems. An excellent compendium of philosophical thought on postmodernity, similarly void of references to environmental problems and the resurgence of non-Western cultures, has been assembled by Kenneth Baynes, James Bohman, and Thomas McCarthy (*After Philosophy: End or Transformation?*, 1987). Philosophers are busily addressing what comes after "truth," and in the process address many issues related to my own final chapters on knowledge and social order. Peter Schwartz and James Oglivy ("The Emergent Paradigm: Changing Patterns of Thought and Belief," 1979) argue that people are escaping the philosophical premises of modernity, beginning to comprehend complexity through multiple patterns of thought, and moving toward what they call hetarchy, a system of interactive systems of values and patterns of explanation which still retain hierarchy within any one system, but no one system dominates. Fred Buttel's presidential address to the Rural Sociological Society ("Environmentalism: Origins, Processes, and Implications for Rural Social Change," 1991) elaborates on how environmental and other new social movements are emerging in the communal void left in the transition from social democracy to neoconservativism around the world during the 1980s. Niklas Luhmann (*Ecological Communication*, 1989) building on Jürgen Habermas (*The Theory of Communicative Action*, 1984, 1987) reportrays society as an evolving, ecological or cybernetic system, constantly evolving new "species" of information gatherers and signallers to keep the system from crashing as new social and environmental problems arise. Niklas Luhmann interprets society as an ecological system which evolves new corrective mechanisms.

While I share many of the realizations of postmodernists, I also differ from them in two ways. First, I do not share their intellectual surprise. The writings of postmodern sociologists tend to be driven by the contradictions between the disciplinary expectations they acquired in college and a reality they have come to know since. Postmodern philosophers are retracing the history of the idea of truth, for the idea of knowing the truth was critical to the modern project, and trying to foresee what comes next. On the other hand, I am driven by a personal environmental experience which occurred early in my adulthood. The dissonance between the promises of modernity, what was taken as truth, and the reality I knew were galvanized into my very essence as a young adult and helped determine my course as a young scholar. While in my late teens, I knew and guided others through one of the most beautiful places on earth, the Glen Canyon of the Colorado River in south central Utah. On January 21, 1963, the Bureau of Reclamation closed the tunnels which had diverted the Colorado around the dam they had been building for a decade and the canyon began to recede under Lake Powell. Knowing this travesty was coming and watching it being carried out fueled my efforts over the subsequent three decades to try to understand the links between Western philosophy, science, and the transformation of social and environmental systems.

Second, by my reading, the vast majority of postmodernists, preoccupied as they are with the discrepancies between expectations and reality, are hesitant to raise new expectations, to participate actively in the revisioning of the future. In this book I not only try to explain why the discrepancies have arisen but also bravely build on my explanation a possible new vision of the future.

The postmodernist literature has many points of access. For a historical view by a philosopher contributing to a revisioning of the future, I recommend Stephen Toulmin (*Cosmopolis: The Hidden Agenda of Modernity*, 1990). Among social theorists, you can do no better than Anthony Giddens (*The Consequences of Modernity*, 1990). A variety of perspectives from sociology can be found in a volume edited by Stephen Crook, Jan Pakulski, and Malcolm Waters (*Postmodernization: Change in Advanced Society*, 1992).

There is a second literature that complements this book, but to which I also pay too little attention. While I document how coevolutionary thinking differs from Newtonian thinking, I dwell little on how my ideas differ from those of others, such as Fritjof Capra (*The Turning Point: Science, Society, and the Rising Culture*, 1982), who also have argued that we are shifting away from a Newtonian world view.

A third literature also has parallel strands. Some feminist critiques of modernity and feminist revisionings of the future parallel my own. While their starting points are different, they cover many of the same issues, and not entirely coincidently. As in the case of the postmodernist writers, drawing the parallels between our efforts would be unwieldy.

The vast majority of feminists in industrialized countries are pleading for equality with men, for equal access to and process within the existing system. A few women, however, are arguing for change. Among the social critics, most are arguing for ways in which the progress modernity promised might finally be delivered. While I do not support patriarchy, I think these feminists are identifying only a small part of the betrayal of development. Ecofeminists, however, are critiquing modernity and revisioning the future through biological-organismic understandings of process rather than mechanical-industrial ones. Northern ecofeminists are joined by a larger proportion of the women in the nonindustrialized nations who are able and willing to speak out. Together they are rejecting modernity's false promises and misguided strategies, reclaiming their own histories, and combining them with environmental understandings of personal to global predicaments. While I have arrived at my understanding through a different process, I share many views with ecofeminists. Their use of biological metaphors and concern with hierarchy and control complement my own. The ecofeminist literature can readily be accessed through a volume edited by Irene Diamond and Gloria Feman Orenstein (*Reweaving the World: The Emergence of Ecofeminism*, 1990). Among particular ecofeminists, the philosophical remapping undertaken by Karen J. Warren most closely parallels my own explorations ("Feminism and Ecology: Making Connections," 1987; "The Power and Promise of Ecological Feminism," 1990).

All this is an elaborate prelude to saying simply that one of my greater disappointments while writing this book was the realization that I could not acknowledge the numerous ways in which my efforts relate to and complement the postmodern, paradigm shift, and ecofeminist literatures. While my work in the end connects quite closely to each of these literatures, I learned through different experiences and built upon those experiences through different academic literatures. This book documents my path to a broadly shared place and shared effort with ecofeminsts in revisioning. Beyond the foregoing passages and references, however, I only occasionally document the sharing.

Now, to return to the style of the bibliographic essays more generally. I have made some effort to see that the essays flow like terse reviews of the literature rather than as a series of disconnected footnotes. The major problem has been with the synthetic nature of the whole book. Many references have guided me at many points along the way, but are only mentioned in one or, at most, two of the essays to avoid excessive duplication. Similarly, I say by no means enough about each work to acknowledge fully its usefulness to me or its possible usefulness to other scholars. The essays merely mention the parts, or my interpretations thereof, that support or relate to a portion of a complex argument. I provide by no means adequate, overall summaries of my references. Furthermore, scholars familiar with particular fields through which I have wandered will find that the works that I have read are not always the most important ones. The thoroughness and quality of the essays also vary. This is not an apologia. The bibliographic essays were more difficult to prepare than simple citations or extensive footnotes and provide far better access for the general reader to the diverse histories of thought on which I draw than do standard approaches of documentation.

Let me also remind readers of the extensive number of people I listed in the acknowledgments. Thorough documentation would entail noting how they guided me to specific sources, provided me with new insights from works I had already read, entered into discourses from which new insights and syntheses followed, and encouraged me to elaborate specific ideas further. Documenting the role of the many people who have interacted with me would have made footnotes altogether excessive and distracting. Much of this book is an elaboration of how learning and knowing is a social process. Documenting that process by the bibliographic standards of earlier understandings of process is impossible. The elaborate acknowledgments and the bibliographic essays suggest the coevolution of my own thought while facilitating access to material by my readers without sacrificing the readability of the text, indeed without sacrificing the very creative process of writing itself.

CHAPTER 2

The World Commission on Environment and Development (WCED) was established by the United Nations General Assembly in 1983 to share perceptions of the problems of environment and development between both rich and poor nations, investigate mechanisms of cooperation, and propose long term strategies. The Commission held hearings around the world and prepared a final report (WCED, *Our Common Future*, 1987). This report, more than any other prior document, reflects the remarkable consensus that development has gone astray, presents the diversity of environmental concerns and perspectives of developed and developing societies, and documents the inadequacy of our national and international institutions for responding to these concerns. Environmentalists will find the proposed strategies inadequate, neither neoclassical nor marxist economic and political theorists will be satisfied with the analysis, and both Northerners and Southerners will be irritated by the shifting finger of blame. The commission did not reach a unified view of the problems. Quite appropriately they included a diversity of views. Most importantly, through hearings and the report, the WCED changed and marked the change in the content and complexity of global political discourse. The elaborate process of preparing for the United Nations Conference on Environment and Development held in Rio de Janeiro, Brazil in June 1992 validated a change in the process of the discourse by formalizing the role of nongovernmental organizations.

Third World perspectives on environment and development are quite varied. Traditional peoples tend to equate land with life itself rather than with political power or economic productivity (Archibold et al., "Culturas Indigenas y Areas Protegidas en Centro America," 1985). Most religions also treat land holistically (see, for example, Krishna Chaitanya, "A Profounder Ecology: The Hindu View of Man and Nature," 1983). Some interesting alternative visions of what development could be, emphasizing cultural and environmental rather than material well-being, build on non-Western traditions (Rajni Kothari, "Environment and Alternative Development," 1979–80). Northern environmentalists frequently find their interests and views to be compatible, even complementary, with those of traditional peoples and of peoples whose lives are guided more by religion than opportunities for material gain (McNeely and Pitt, Culture and Conservation, 1985; Mahdav Gadgil, "Culture, Perceptions and Attitudes to the Environment," 1987). Third World peoples also find Northern environmentalists' concern with wilderness and preservation to be incompatible with a holistic view of people and the environment (Ramachandra Guha, "Radical American Environmentalism and Wilderness Preservation: A Third World Critique," 1989). Westernized Third World people, especially Latin Americans, tend to see environmental issues in terms of power and productivity, marxist and neoclassical perceptions respectively (Ramachandra Guha, "Ideological Trends in Indian Environmentalism," 1988; Pablo Gutman, "Teoria Economica y Problematica Ambiental: Un Dialogo Dificil," 1985; Sunkel and Leal, "Economics and Environment in a Developmental Perspective," 1986; Arturo Escobar with Lori Ann Thrupp, "The Unsustainable Paradigm of Sustainable Development: The Challenge by Social Movements," 1990).

Northern environmentalists still falsely tend to think that Third and Fourth World peoples lack an environmental philosophy; Southern development planners still think Northern environmentalists are too motivated by their wilderness philosophies and love for cute, fuzzy animals; but since the 1980s the environmental discourse between North and South has enlarged the understanding of both.

The brief summaries of the ways in which development is unsustainable were drawn from data and descriptions presented in an environmental yearbook of the World Resources Institute (1988). The exception is the numbers on the loss of species which came from articles on biological diversity by distinguished authors edited by E. O. Wilson (1988). These vignettes of environmental disaster are only presented to document the scale and time periods over which dramatic changes are taking place. Gus Speth ("Can the World be Saved," 1989) has drawn up a similar, more elaborate vignette for carbon dioxide and toxics. The numbers are approximate in such short elaborations, but certainly adequate to incite action in my judgment.

Environmentalism has been transformed by an increasing awareness of global environmental problems, yet ecology as a science is only gradually moving from ecosystem specific thinking toward global thinking. While individual articles on particular aspects of global ecology have long existed, books on global ecology are only now beginning to appear. The U.S. National Academy of Sciences presents an excellent summary of global ecological understanding (Cheryl Simon Silver with Ruth S. DeFries, One Earth, One Future: Our Changing Global Environment, 1990). Mitchell B. Rambler, Lynn Margulis, and René Fester (Global Ecology:

195

Towards a Science of the Biosphere, 1989) have assembled a challenging, if not comprehensive, set of articles by leading thinkers.

There was a burst of articles at the end of the 1980s dedicated to giving sustainable development an operational meaning. In the text I argued that an operational definition was not possible within the modern understanding of knowledge and social organization. The attempts to do so, however, are contributing to the political discourse that will redefine how we think and organize. Since this is a key theme of the book, little more need be said now. Much of the literature addresses whether and how past concepts associated with development have changed. Chief among these is the concept of development as growth in material output, whether sustainable development means sustainable growth, and whether sustained material growth is physically possible. Between the basic needs of a rapidly increasing population of very poor people and the problems of global climate change, the idea of development as sustained increase in material well-being is an artifact of a now unfit faith in progress.

My understanding of the sustainable development literature has been most influenced by reading the following works: Edward Barbier, 1987; Becky Brown *et al.*, 1987; William C. Clark and R. E. Munn (eds), 1986; Gordon Conway, 1985; Herman Daly, 1989; John Dixon and Louise Fallon, 1989; Robert Goodland and George Ledec, 1987; Sharad Lele, 1989 and 1991; John Pezzey, 1989; Michael Redclift, 1984 and 1987; Douglas D. Southgate and John F. Disinger (eds), 1987; and R. Kerry Turner (ed.), 1988.

The idea of sustainable development is clearly affecting the political discourse and the way decisions are made already, even though the term is not operationally definable. Each of the international development agencies has been under severe political pressure to reform so that they do not support unsustainable development. The World Bank, for example, created an environmental policy department and an environmental unit in each of its four area divisions in 1987 in response to political pressure from U.S. and European environmentalists channeled through the U.S. Congress to the U.S. delegate to the Bank's Board of Governors (World Bank, 1987 and 1989; Phillipe Le Prestre, 1989). The preponderance of environmental discussion at economic summit meetings, beginning with that held in Toronto in 1988 and then gaining priority during the Paris meeting in 1989, indicates that environmental issues will dominate the agenda of foreign relations for the rest of the century. Industrial pollution, worker health and safety, the control of nuclear power, the management of nuclear waste, and the loss of access to subsidized Soviet oil play extremely important roles in the deliberations over the reconstruction of eastern Europe.

CHAPTER 3

The coevolutionary way of understanding has its roots in biology and results from the interplay of ecological and evolutionary processes. The term coevolution was coined by Paul Ehrlich and Peter Raven as recently as 1964 ("Butterflies and Plants: A Study in Coevolution"). Reviewing the kinds of plants eaten by butterfly larvae around the world, they found these plants tend to have secondary chemicals which are nonessential for the plants' own growth but apparently have been retained in the process of selection because they reduce attack by butterfly larvae. In turn, butterfly larvae have been selected for resistance to the same chemicals. The idea of coevolution, however, was not strictly new. Many evolutionists have long realized that a species' environment consists largely of other species. Charles Darwin, for example, noted in 1859 "Thus I can understand how a flower and a bee might slowly become, either simultaneously or one after the other, modified and adapted in the most perfect manner to each other" (quoted in Futuyma and Slatkin, 1983: 3). Though biologists knew the environment of species was to a large extent other species, evolutionists only began seriously to incorporate ecology in their thinking after 1964 (Herbert G. Baker and Paul D. Hurd, "Intrafloral Ecology," 1968; Matthew Nitecki (ed.), *Coevolution*, 1983; Douglas J. Futuyma and Montgomery Slatkin, *Coevolution*, 1983).

Once evolutionists recognize ecosystem relations and ecologists recognize evolutionary processes, everything is connected to everything else across species and through time. This expansion in thinking complements existing understandings, developed earlier largely through the study of natural history, that ecosystems were tightly interconnected and species ideally suited for each other (Aldo Leopold, *A Sand County Almanac*, 1949). But this expansion in thinking also confounded existing understandings both within evolutionary thought – such as whether coevolution might be so comprehensive that the term evolution is simply superseded, and within ecological thought – such as the interpretation of mimicry and mutualism. In response, evolutionary biologists have attempted to assert alternative rigid taxonomies of definitions to help untangle the myriad of natural processes and resulting types of relationships. Pair-wise coevolution has been strictly defined to mean that a trait of one species has evolved in response to a trait of another species, which trait itself has evolved in response to the trait in the first. Diffuse coevolution refers to the particular trait of one species evolving in response to a trait or group of traits in other species. Since multiple pair-wise and diffuse coevolutionary processes are no doubt always taking place, the study of coevolution ultimately consists of looking at evolution as a coevolutionary process and documenting relatively specific and strong coevolutionary relationships (Futuyma and Slatkin, 1983: 1–13). In this sense, coevolution is a frame of mind. It will be further elaborated throughout the book.

I was introduced to the pesticide story when, shortly after I joined the University of California in 1970, Robert van den Bosch sought me out to work on the economics of integrated pest management. "Van," a professor in Berkeley's Division of Biological Control, was an inspiring academic and tireless crusader who influenced many around the world. Through his influence and that of Professors Ray Smith and Carl Huffaker, more staid but equally influential academics and reformers, I soon found myself on an advisory committee of the President's Council of Environmental Quality, the advisory committee of a nationwide research effort, undertaking research myself, and then on a committee of the National Academy of Sciences. Being enmeshed in the science and politics of pests and pesticides early in my academic career critically influenced its evolution thereafter. Van tells the pesticide story as he saw it (*The Pesticide Conspiracy*, 1978). John Perkins provides an excellent history of the biology and politics of pesticides with an emphasis on the boll weevil eradication story (*Insects, Experts, and the Insecticide Crisis: The Quest for New Pest Management Strategies*, 1982). Christopher Bosso tests political theory against the story (*Pesticides and Politics: The Life Cycle of a Public Issue*, 1987). Timothy H. Brown helped me put the pesticide story into coevolutionary form ("The Evolution of Pesticide Policy," 1991).

There is a parallel, equally fascinating, story in the coevolution of microbes, the transmission of microbial infections, antibiotics, and microbial resistance well elaborated in a series of articles in *Science* (see: Cohen, Mitchell L., 1992; Bloom, Barry R. and Christopher J. L. Murray, 1992; Neu, Harold C., 1992; and Krause, Richard M., 1992).

CHAPTER 4

Though my sweeping presentation of human and environmental history as a coevolutionary process needs elaborate support, in this essay I will do little more than describe the rise of environmental history as a field and then introduce a few key references to the coevolutionary framework and my sources for agricultural history. The development of thinking about social and environmental systems and the historical setting of the coevolutionary framework will be elaborated thoroughly as the book progresses.

Since the early 1970s, there has been an identifiable group of scholars who label themselves environmental historians. Given their varied styles, they are, at first, most easily described as historians who are not writing on the political development of nations; the lives of great, or at least powerful, leaders; or the wonders of scientific and technological progress. Environmental historians emphasize how people have transformed their environments through conquering and suppressing indigenous cultures, how species that evolved in one ecosystem can affect another, how technologies that evolved in one culture and ecosystem can affect other cultures and ecosystems, how the adoption of new technologies unmatched by new social institutions can transform environments, and how the modern social and economic institutions which distance people from the land end up transforming environments. Equally importantly, environmental historians draw on a very different set of concepts and literatures than other historians. Environmental historians stress how Western and westernized world views address nature and people's relations to nature, draw upon theories of cultural and environmental systems developed within anthropology and geography and incorporate a broad range of knowledge of environmental science. Environmental historians, in short, are writing history very consciously from an environmental perspective.

Donald Worster has edited a good cross section of articles which provide an excellent introduction to the field (*The Ends of the Earth: Perspectives on Modern Environmental History*, 1988). Worster also has written histories of water in the American west and of land management on the southern plains of America. Alfred W. Crosby has documented how European exploration, trade, and colonization resulted in the transfer of species, genetic characteristics, and diseases between continents (*The Columbian Exchange: Biological and Cultural Consequences of 1492*, 1972; *Ecological Imperialism: The Biological Expansion of Europe, 900–1900*; 1986). These transfers account for the vast majority of foods now eaten and of agricultural weeds and insect pests, the problems of exotic competition to indigenous species in "natural" environments, and a significant portion of health problems in the developing world. William Cronon (*Changes in the Land: Indians, Colonists, and the Ecology of New England*, 1983) and Carolyn Merchant (*Ecological Revolutions: Nature, Gender, and Science in New England*, 1989) have developed contrasting environmental explanations of history for a much smaller portion of the globe.

Third World scholars are also beginning to write environmental histories in the larger process of reassessing the meaning of development. Ramachandra Guha (*The Unquiet Woods: Ecological Change and Peasant Resistance in the Himalaya*, 1989) explains the broader historical and social significance of the Chipko (hug the trees) Movement. The village women who defended forests used by communities in northern India against commercial logging negotiated by the state, characterized as environmentalists or ecofeminists in the Western press, are a continuation of centuries of peasant protest against monarchial, colonial, and national control over resources. Madhav Gadgil, an ecologist by training, has written with Ramachandra Guha an environmental history for all of India which blends ecological interpretations of social structure with structural interpretations of environmental transformation (*This Fissured Land: An Ecological History of India*, 1993). Nancy Lee Peluso has elaborated an excellent history of shifting, weak forest control during precolonial, colonial, and the rise of the Indonesian state, resistance by local peoples to external control, and deforestation (*Rich Forests, Poor People: Resource Control and Resistance in Java*, 1992).

Once a field of study becomes defined, its own historical roots become identifiable. Donald Worster argues that environmental history started with Comte de Buffon's (Georges-Luis Leclerc, 1707–88) *Historie Naturelle*. Clarence Glacken (*Traces on the Rhodian Shore*, 1967) would certainly argue that people penned their perceptions and pontifications on people–environment relationships from the beginning of written history. All in the field would agree that George Perkins Marsh (*Man and Nature, or Physical Geography as Modified by Human Action*, 1864) wrote a classic book on European and North American environmental history. Like environmentalism itself, environmental history has strong roots in the influence of the frontier on American culture and vice versa. From this perspective, Frederick Jackson Turner, Walter Prescott Webb, and Bernard De Voto wrote classic environmental history.

The boundaries of environmental history, like its roots, are also varied. If histories written from an environmental world view are environmental histories, then many new chronologies of science fit the mold. Carolyn Merchant (*The Death of Nature: Women, Ecology, and the Scientific Revolution*, 1980) explains how the revolution to the modern scientific outlook diminished the inherent worth of both nature and women and supported a social structure which abused them. Donald Worster (*Nature's Economy: A History of Ecological Ideas*, 1977) and Sharon Kingsland (*Modeling Nature: Episodes in the History of Population Ecology*, 1985) describe the development of ecological ideas in a broad social context. Juan Martinez-Alier (*Ecological Economics: Energy, Environment and Society*, 1987) interprets the rejection of natural science understanding by mainstream economics from environmental and structural perspectives. While perhaps not environmental histories *per se*, they certainly complement the new perspectives being developed by environmental historians. Both Merchant and Worster have written in both fields.

Several scholars have developed ecosystemic arguments for how development occurs. Clifford Geertz documented how the development of Indonesian agriculture on Java, Bali, and Lombok differed from that on the outer islands. He argued that each was driven by population and productivity growth meeting a resource constraint. In the case of Inner Indonesia the constraint was overcome by intensifying paddy rice production while on the outer islands development consisted of expanding the area cultivated. Both the process of intensifying and extending were guided by the nature of the ecosystem and which furthermore helped determine the respective social structures (*Agricultural Involution*, 1963). Ester Boserup, a Danish economist, translated the specific arguments of Geertz and others into a general theory of development with greater emphasis on the role of population growth as a driving mechanism (*The Conditions of Agricultural Growth*, 1965; *Population and Technological Change*, 1981). Richard Wilkinson developed a similar argument for Western history overall. While many have documented the long history of cases where development results in ecological degradation or is stymied by resource constraints, Wilkinson reversed the cause and effect relationship, arguing that ecological disasters and resource shortages stimulate the new technologies and social orders we think of as development (*Poverty and Progress: An Ecological Perspective on Development*, 1973). Paul Colinvaux, an ecologist, has applied, unconvincingly by my reading, the concepts of niche and breeding strategy to explain the history of warfare between nations (*The Fates of Nations: A Biological Theory of History*, 1980). These works and related attempts to use biological explanations of social systems are considered in greater detail in Chapter 8.

My own modest effort at environmental history in this chapter is distinctive because I have tried to use an explicit framework that has not been used before. My own understanding of history developed through an early reading of the classics in environmental history, several courses during college in economic and geographic history, diverse reading since, and the recent environmental histories. For specific historical points, I have looked to John A. Garraty and Peter Gay (*The Columbia History of the World*, 1972) and D. B. Grigg (*The Agricultural Systems of the World: An Evolutionary Approach*, 1974).

The coevolutionary environmental history sketched in this chapter and environmental histories developed by others stress the reciprocal relations between social and ecological systems. Like other environmental histories, the coevolutionary approach I have sketched emphasizes the importance of value systems and knowledge systems. While environmental historians share a common concern that environmental systems have been degraded and social systems have not developed according to the modern project, there are differences in points of view with respect to the ways things have gone wrong. Many environmental historians tend to affix the blame on the maldistribution of power and distorted incentives they think are inherent in capitalist societies. In light of the analogous cultural and environmental destruction in socialist economies which are equally products of modernity, I affix the blame on the philosophical underpinnings of modernity itself. Since the coevolutionary framework itself is at odds with these underpinnings, I am perhaps more acutely aware of the tension. This difference is specifically elaborated in Chapter 6 and its bibliographic essay as well as generally throughout the book.

There are some very interesting parallels between the rethinking of history from an environmental world view and the rethinking of history from a feminist world view. Both perspectives address an imbalance in how history was perceived. Both address the dominance of men, in one case over women, in the other over nature, and how this dominance brought humanity to its current predicaments. Both projects are filling in an important mutual feedback ignored by conventional histories. Environmental historians are showing how the transformation of environments feeds back on social structure and the choice of technology and vice versa. Feminists are grappling with the difficulties of understanding the mutual feedbacks between the social construction of gender and social relations themselves (Riane Eisler, *The Chalice and the Blade: Our History, Our Future*, 1987; Mary O'Brien, *Reproducing the World: Essays in Feminist Theory*, 1989; Tamsin E. Lorraine, *Gender, Identity, and the Production of Meaning*, 1990). And ecofeminists are struggling with filling in both missing histories simultaneously (Irene Diamond and Gloria Feman Orenstein (eds), *Reweaving the World: The Emergence of Ecofeminism*, 1990). And just as those who held romantic, organic, or naturalistic views were belittled by those who held the increasingly dominant Newtonian world view during the nineteenth century, those who retain progressive views with their social determinism are belittling any appeals to nature and natural order among feminists (Janet Biehl, *Rethinking Ecofeminist Politics*, 1991).

CHAPTER 5

J. B. Bury's very scholarly *The Idea of Progress* (1920) is the classic historical work. Robert Nisbet has more recently provided a book along similar lines, but with much more emphasis on the nineteenth and twentieth centuries (*History of the Idea of Progress*, 1980). Both of these works document the long, rich, and varied history of how social and natural philosophers have believed in, advanced, used, and depended upon the idea of progress. Nisbet ties his history of progress much more closely to both Judeo-Christian beliefs and to the proven accomplishments of Western science while Bury is more agnostic on both. And though they were writing half a century apart, both conclude their books on the note that the idea of progress will continue to evolve. Yet at the same time, Nisbet is clearly very disturbed by the decline in the role of religion in forming values, the rise of materialism, and the decline in our faith in science.

One thing is strikingly clear. Neither Bury nor Nisbet take a critical stand or try to view the idea of progress from outside Western culture. Neither, for example, give much emphasis to the impact of the idea on other cultures. *Progress and Its Discontents* edited by Almond, Chodorow, and Pearce (1982) presents a far broader, better balanced, and more up-to-date discussion of what is happening to the idea of progress through the eyes of two dozen critical observers. This volume provides an excellent summary of the evolution of the idea and then pursues how it is perceived today in developing countries, in China, and in what was still then the Soviet Union, by philosophers reevaluating the history of science and technology, by scientists facing the challenges new technologies have wrought, by social scientists trying to understand modern politics, and by humanists trying to understand what is happening to religion and visions of utopia.

Robert H. Nelson (*Reaching for Heaven on Earth: The Theological Meaning of Economics*, 1991) traces how economic philosophy assumed the mantle of progress from classical and enlightenment philosophers and how beliefs about progress became embedded in the assumptions, models, and rhetoric of academic economists and economic policy makers. Nelson makes a very strong case that economics assumed the beliefs, myths and metaphors of the Judeo-Christian tradition, initially mostly for rhetorical purposes, and became a secular religion as ecclesiastical faith declined.

The idea that Western science is progressing toward truth has dominated the writings of epistemologists until recent times. The link between social progress and science requires that science progress. I find, for example, that the writings of Karl Popper, the preeminent philosopher of science of the twentieth century (*The Logic of Scientific Discovery*, 1934; *Objective Knowledge*, 1979) presume that science progresses and then explain how this occurs. More recently, however, philosophers are acknowledging that the advance of knowledge is not cumulative for knowledge is also being lost when it falls into disuse and the advance is also only along a narrow path which winds through the realm of all possible knowledge according to the needs of the time and the politics of public funding (Stephen J. Toulmin, *Human Understanding*, 1972). This winding pathway view is a much weaker image of progress than the image that science is steadily accumulating and will eventually encompass all possible knowledge in one coherent system.

The more traditional ideas about progress held most strongly in the Third World, especially Latin America (Crawford Young, "The Idea of Progress in the Third World" in the foregoing volume). While Third World peoples have discovered that the adoption of specific institutions and technologies from the West have had numerous unforeseen, unfortunate consequences, many still retain older ideas of progress from the West. The rapidity with which people from developing countries joined in the shaping of the international environmental movement that originated in the North suggests that they clung to the old ideas as long as they did for lack of anything newer. One of the most disturbing consequences of the Western vision of progress is that numerous Third World governments have waged campaigns against their own traditional peoples, rationalizing their actions in terms similar to those of the conquistadors of the new world (Bernard Neitschmann, "The Third World War," 1987; Susana B. C. Devalle, *La Diversidad Prohibida: Resistencia etnica y poder de Estado,* 1989).

The ongoing debate over the long-run scarcity of resources provides the sharpest example today of the dichotomy between true believers and doubters of progress in the North. The pessimists, typically environmental scientists, have repeatedly warned us of resource limits, the population explosion, energy shortages, the loss of biodiversity, and global climate change (Paul Ehrlich, *The Population Bomb*, 1968; Meadows *et al.*, *The Limits to Growth*, 1972; Norman Myers, *The Sinking Ark*, 1979; Paul and Anne Ehrlich, *The Population Explosion*, 1990). The optimists, typically economists, have argued that population growth will decline with development and new energy and raw material technologies will be found with development (Julian Simon, *The Ultimate Resource*, 1981). Nicholas Rescher (*Scientific Progress: A Philosophical Essay on the Economics of Research in Natural Science*, 1978) presents a more thoughtful, though still somewhat optimistic on net, assessment of the race between technology and resource scarcity. The position of economists is inherently contradictory since both neoclassical and marxist theories are built on the assumption of scarcity in the short run. If resources are scarce in the short run yet abundant in the long run, then economics ought to be putting all of its emphasis into how to make the long run shorter. While the debate between environmental and cultural determinists will be reviewed in detail in Chapter 7, it is important to place it in the context of our belief in progress.

Robert Ornstein and Paul Ehrlich (*New World, New Mind*, 1989) argue that we will only be able to overcome the environmental crisis by deliberately increasing the rate of our evolutionary consciousness of how we affect our environment. Orenstein and Ehrlich are arguing for the acceleration of cultural progress, albeit in a particular manner, to abate the devastation caused by earlier cultural "progress." They argue that, though we have large, reasonably well-wired brains, there are serious limitations in our "software," or patterns of thinking, which consistently get us into trouble. They offer biological-psychological explanations of how the software arose. What is missing, however, are cultural explanations of the selection for software as well as the nature of the interlinkages between brains, the structure of societies, which determine how we behave. This is stressed in my Chapter 8.

Perhaps this is the appropriate place to discuss the connotations of "development' and "progress." They are partially overlapping concepts. Development is the newer term and is associated with fairly specific instrumental concepts, while progress has a longer history and is associated with general beliefs about goals and processes. This difference is reflected in the previous two chapters. Chapter 2 dealt with current, specific challenges of sustainable development, whereas Chapter 5 provides background on the history of Western beliefs. Our ideas about progress might be thought of as earlier ideas about development which have survived history, become rarified, and which change more slowly. Each of us individually and cultures generally experience a tension between older beliefs and current ideas based on recent evidence. The line between these, however, is not especially clear. Yet past beliefs and current evidence seem dangerously at odds today, hence the need consciously to rethink our ideas about progress.

All social critiques are part of the discourse through which our image of the future becomes redefined. For this reason, it is not easy to draw the line with respect to which literature is relevant to our rethinking of the idea of progress. Certainly, however, the critiques from Latin America of traditional Western ideas of progress must be included. Latin America, like North America, was resettled and colonized by Westerners who, experiencing abundant resources and unlimited opportunity, stoked Western ideas of progress to greater fury than it ever raged in Europe. Unlike North America, however, Latin Americans neither broke their colonial bounds nor established societies more egalitarian than those of Europe. While belief in conventional ideas of progress still runs high in Latin America, its disillusioned intellectuals have also written the most strident critiques. E. Bradford Burns (*The Poverty of*

Progress, 1980) has analyzed the works of Latin American historians and writers to document the disenchantment with dependency, class society, the destruction of traditional societies, the loss of a sense of community responsibility, and the difficulties of sustaining their own cultures in the face of the onslaught of art, ideas, and gadgets from the North. Gabriel Garcia Marquez (*One Hundred Years of Solitude*, 1970) has written a farcical novel on how progress in Latin America has been indiscernible from a descent into hell. The views of Latin American scholars of development are well presented in a volume edited by Heraldo Munoz (*From Dependency to Development*, 1981). While the critiques of Latin American scholars are frequently marxist analyses of capitalism, many can also be seen as critiques of Marx's vision of progress.

The economic literature on development includes some other notable dissents. Many have critiqued economic development theory as being naive, a charge which frequently is attributable to excessive faith in conventional ideas about progress. Two books by Denis Goulet (*The Cruel Choice*, 1977, and *The Uncertain Promise*, 1977) document that "progress" is a difficult and inconclusive road. Deepak Lal (*The Poverty of "Development Economics,"* 1985) argues that development theorists were so convinced that progress was "natural," that they devised theory after theory attributing undevelopment to one or two barriers to progress which governments could easily remove through deliberate intervention (see also, P. T. Bauer, *Dissent on Development*, 1971). Fred Hirsch (*The Social Limits to Growth*, 1976) presents an excellent critique of the materialist treadmill in the developed world.

While many have questioned whether progress was actually occurring, Georges Sorel (*The Illusions of Progress*, 1908) provided an early attack on how the idea of progress is used and abused in politics and social theory. Sorel, a pragmatic French philosopher writing at the turn of the twentieth century, was mostly concerned that marxists had blindly adopted a false consciousness of capitalist society which protected the bourgeoisie through promises to the proletariat. He argued that as progress became everything that was good in history, and in effect history itself, no other standard of moral action would exist, and people would no longer be responsible for their actions. Sorel had explored the condition under which violence might be morally justified in earlier writings. On thinking about progress, he saw that violence could always be justified if whatever happens is progress. Sorel saw, in retrospect we can say foresaw, that the idea of progress could be used by supposed leaders of Marxist revolutions, just as well as the bourgeoisie, to mislead workers and delay real progress. Sorel identified the vacuity, and the dangers thereof, of the idea of progress.

Christopher Lasch (*The True and Only Heaven: Progress and Its Critics*, 1991) updates Sorel with a new twist on how belief in progress has distorted modern political thought. Lasch argues that the liberal, thinking minority fooled themselves, not the masses, with the idea of progress. Lasch documents the exceptions – Henry George, Max Weber, Georges Sorel, G. D. H. Cole, and others – who have run counter to the tide. Lasch argues that the progressive elite has misinterpreted popular movements which have been more concerned with community, loyalty, and pride of workmanship than with the acquisition of more and more things. He brilliantly reanalyzes social thought in early America and labor movements in the nineteenth century, showing how features which liberals had argued were retrograde oddities were really radical protests against progress. In keeping with his earlier work (*The Culture of Narcism*, 1979), Lasch continues to argue that our obsession with material progress displaced the possibilities for community development, cultural enrichment, and moral growth.

Articles in the press now commonly address how our faith in progress is eroding and what this means for the legitimacy of modern nations. *The Economist*, for example, linked the Chernobyl nuclear disaster to the demise of the Soviet Union in a lengthy article. One of many passages argued "For in the Soviet Union nuclear energy is a potent symbol of high technology and modernity. When Soviet citizens began to question the merits of nuclear energy, they were questioning one of the most basic assumptions of their system: that communism would lead them into the high-tech future, and that the high-tech future would be greatly better than the present" (Anon, "What Chernobyl Did," 1991).

While our belief in progress appears to have been naive, a positive image of the future gives a society hope and direction. Elise Boulding translated the work of Fred Polak (*The Image of the Future*, 1972) and has contributed herself to the literature (Futuristics and the Imaging Capacity of the West, 1978). Polak, writing from the Netherlands at the close of World War II, was concerned that the depression, war, and holocaust had left Europe and North America living day to day without a positive image of where they might be going. Elise Boulding, while decidedly more optimistic, pointedly identifies the pitfalls of not having an evolving moral, organizational, and technological vision. In this context, the idea of progress seems to have served this positive visionary role but somehow became twisted, as argued by Sorel, into a total concept of history. The same transformation seems to have occurred over the past half century to the word "development."

One image, or metaphor, that has arisen in the latter half of the twentieth century is acquiring considerable significance. The metaphor of the earth as a spaceship has had an interesting history. It was perhaps first elaborated by Adlai Stevenson in a presidential campaign speech in 1952.

> We travel together, passengers on a little spaceship, dependent upon its vulnerable reserves of air and soil, all committed for our safety for its security and peace preserved from annihilation only by the care, work and, I will say, love we give our fragile craft.

This metaphor was further developed simultaneously in the 1960s by Kenneth Boulding ("The Economics of the Coming Spaceship Earth," 1966) and Barbara Ward (*Spaceship Earth*, 1966) to argue that we must manage the earth as the nearly closed system that it actually is. Soon after, photos of the earth from space and from the moon brought the image into the homes of everyone with a television. It has been used frequently since on posters, magazine covers, and in advertisements (Yaakov Garb, "The Use and Misuse of the Whole Earth Image," 1985).

Adlai Stevenson went further and argued that the spaceship could not be maintained unless its crew more equally accommodates itself:

> We cannot maintain it half fortunate, half miserable, half confident, half despairing, half slave to the ancient enemies of mankind, half free in the liberalization of resources undreamed of until this day. No craft, no crew can travel safely with such vast contradictions. On their resolution depends the survival of us all.

While we have gained some of the benefits of thinking of the earth as a fragile spaceship, we have yet to adopt the metaphor of humanity as a disparate, unstable, rightfully mutinous crew. This step might help in the reimaging of the future as much as the spaceship understanding.

CHAPTER 6

Many have documented the rise of the Newtonian world view and its relation to modern thought and social organization (John Herman Randall, Jr. *The Making of the Modern Mind*; Leo Strauss and Joseph Cropsey, editors, *History of Political Philosophy*). The foregoing chapter greatly simplifies Western philosophy by stressing only the dominant trends which reshaped our social organization. Bertrand Russell (see, for example, his *The Scientific Outlook*, 1931) epitomized belief in the superiority of the "scientific outlook" and its eventual conquest of irrational understandings and prescriptions. Auguste Comte was the leading social philosopher arguing that science would both assist society in finding answers and help people organize rationally to act on these answers (*A General View of Positivism*, 1848).

Romanticism, a broad and opposing line of thought, was pursued in varying degrees by Rousseau, Kant, and Goethe, among many other famous philosophers. Romanticism stresses the ultimate unknowability of reality; speaks to the interdependence between perceiving, knowing, and what can be known; and glorifies, at least to mainline rationalists, the strengths of intuitive perception and artistic expression. Though romanticism has at times in some countries dominated philosophical thinking and certainly continues to influence our thought as individuals today, it has little appeal in scientific or public discourse. Indeed, views which are in opposition to the status quo or views contrary to the scientifically well accepted are frequently denigrated by referring to them as romantic.

The five dominant, publicly accepted metaphysical and epistemological beliefs provide starting points for the philosophical elaboration that was avoided in the chapter in order to highlight the central argument. Atomism in the natural sciences and individualism in the social sciences is rejected by those who belief in holism, sometimes also known as organism. Some holists also reject mechanism. In this alternate view, systems cannot be reduced to sets of comparable atoms, and relations may not be interpretable through underlying mechanistic principles. Rather, systems have properties of their own which emerge from the combination of parts and relations. These systemic properties might be explained, or at least some holists hope they can be explained, by universal principles, but holists hold that they will not be the same principles that explain the parts and individual relations between them. Marxist scholars contend that societies behave according to principles in addition to those which explain individual behavior. Organismal biologists contend that the functioning of whole animals cannot be understood by knowing solely about how organs or cells function. Both schools of thought, along the lines of thinking of Alfred North Whitehead, tend to eschew mechanical, cause-and-effect explanations and be more open to teleological explanations of system behavior (Morton O. Beckner, "Organismic Biology," 1967; W. H. Dray, "Holism and Individualism in History and Social Science," 1967; Ernst Nagel, "The Reduction of Theories," 1961).

Mechanistic models have unique equilibria for any combination of conditions. After mechanistic systems are disturbed, they return to their previous equilibrium when the initial combination of conditions once again prevails. Negative feedbacks bring the out of equilibrium system back into equilibrium. It is just these properties which give mechanistic characterizations of systems predictive power. Systems with positive feedbacks do not return to their previous equilibrium after a disturbance but keep on changing or go to a new equilibrium which is difficult to determine in advance. Development, of course, is better characterized by a positive feedback model, and economists have long informally contemplated growth in these terms. The mathematizers, or formalizers, of economics, however, have eschewed such models until very recently. Now, the most obvious positive feedbacks, such as the effect of one firm's location on that of subsequent firms are being "discovered" (W. Brian Arthur, "Positive Feedbacks in the Economy," 1990). Thus it is not only in public discourse that the philosophical premises underlying modernism are maintained, but also in formal economics.

Belief in universalism has spawned heroic efforts. Ludwig von Bertalanffy, Kenneth Boulding, and Anatol Rapaport, for example, established the Society for General Systems Research to pursue the commonality of some patterns of explanation across disciplines in the hope that the uncovering of further commonalities would result in a general systems theory (Ludwig von Bertalanffy, *General System Theory*, 1968). The search led to many interesting insights (C. West Churchman, *The Systems Approach*, 1969; Kenneth E. Boulding, *Ecodynamics*, 1978), but has not been fully accepted within the scientific community, probably because the standards of evidence, the nature of argument, and the way in which findings can be used are necessarily different for this line of inquiry than for the natural sciences.

Universalism is typically defended by noting that, if this belief does not conform to reality, then there are no universal principles, everything must be relative to particular times and places, and real knowledge would be impossible. And those who argue the complexities of different ecological and social realities are frequently accused of being relativists. But the number of principles needed to understand reality ranges from one to infinity with no clear demarcation between universalists and relativists. Furthermore, the accusation of relativism has carried with it a connotation of irrationality or inability to maintain logical explanations. The problem, however, is not that we cannot logically explain after the fact but that, if we have many theories from which to select, we cannot predict before the fact.

Objectivism has been criticized from so many perspectives that I think I am prudent to avoid references to the literature. My own coevolutionary view accepts that a society's values affect which ways of knowing prove fit and vice versa and the significance of this will be explored in later chapters.

Monism is strongly held by many scientists and philosophers. Physicists have searched for a unified field theory linking gravitational, electromagnetic, and strong and weak nuclear forces into one coherent explanation. Einstein hoped that such an explanation would eliminate statistical explanations – or in his own metaphor, "God playing dice" – from quantum mechanics ("Physics and Reality," 1936). David Bohm pushed monism to the limit in his exploration of the possible unity of all knowledge (*Wholeness and the Implicate Order*, 1980). Hermeneuticists, in contrast, do not believe in monism.

While I emphasized the dominant beliefs in this chapter, the dispersion of beliefs around the dominant ones provides the evolutionary basis for sustainable development and cultural pluralism. The diversity of beliefs is explored in greater depth throughout the remainder of the book.

Many philosophers have explored the mismatch between modern expectations for how science works and the reality of how science works. One of the most provocative was developed by Thomas Kuhn (*The Structure of Scientific Revolutions*, 1962). Kuhn introduced the idea of scientific paradigms and argued that the transition from one paradigm to another was a sociological phenomenon. A paradigm consisted of an agreed upon pattern of explanation and a list of most important remaining questions, or research agenda, to complete the pattern. The agreement as to which paradigm is the most productive and which questions the most important is presumed to follow strictly from empirical evidence and logical analysis. Kuhn described what all working scientists already knew but could not elaborate. The paradigm and agenda are reinforced through a complex system of camaraderie, invitations to lecture, acceptance of papers in journals, and financial support based on peer review. Individual scientists who disagree with the dominant paradigm are treated as oddballs at best, outcasts at worst. For example, numerous geologists between at least Alfred Wegener's article in 1915 and the 1960s, for example, could not convince their discipline of the theory of continental drift. In spite of decades of aspersions on the theory and a lack of research support, by the late 1960s so much brute, contrary evidence had accumulated to show there was no way that the existing paradigm could fit the "facts" that the discipline of geology very rapidly adopted the theory of continental drift (J. Bernard Cohen, "Continental Drift and Plate Tectonics: A Revolution in Earth Science," 1984). Kuhn documented how individual scientists who argue against conventional paradigms before sufficient evidence has accumulated are deprived of research funds, their articles are rejected in the confidential peer review process, and they are recognized as whimsical, unorthodox thinkers rather than as leaders in their field. While the sociology of science is now a well recognized field of study with a solid body of understanding (see Cohen, 1984), our best universities and research institutions still operate under the myth that scientists are open to any logical argument and empirical evidence. In fact, the sociology of knowledge in the sense it has been studied to date is extremely important.

One difficulty with the modern view is that science, contrary to Comte's vision of positivism, does not pursue its own objectives independently of society. Jerome R. Ravetz (*Scientific Knowledge and Its Social Problems*, 1971) documents how the organization of science necessarily intertwines with the organization of society as a whole. Our belief in the separateness of science and society only compounds the difficulties of supporting research and using scientific findings. Thomas A. Spragens (*The Irony of Liberal Reason*, 1981) looks at the mismatch from the perspective of modern expectations for rational society and concludes that, rather than thinking of societies as users of scientific knowledge, it would be better to think of politics as a part of the system of inquiry toward truth. In this view, politics might adopt more of the norms of science, particularly a critical, experimental stance. After a thorough review of Western epistemological tenets, Richard Rorty reaches the converse conclusion: scientists and the philosophers who study their methods know no more about how to inquire, let alone find truth, than poets or any other participant in the Western discourse (*Philosophy and the Mirror of Nature*, 1979).

The environmental problems which have arisen with modernism have been attributed by others to modernism's philosophical basis. During the 1980s, especially, numerous scholars traced the environmental problems of the twentieth century to an over acceptance of the Newtonian world view. Prigogine and Stengers (*Order Out of Chaos: Man's New Dialogue with Nature*, 1984) provide the best of the popular expositions on the rise of Newtonian thinking in the natural sciences and its inadequacy for understanding complex systems. Daniel B. Botkin (*Discordant Harmonies: A New Ecology for the Twenty-First Century*, 1990) provides an entertaining and thoughtful exploration of how the mechanical world view has distorted ecological thinking within and beyond academe. Carolyn Merchant (*The Death of Nature: Women, Ecology, and the Scientific Revolution*, 1980) and Morris Berman (*The Reenchantment of the World*, 1981) link Newtonian thinking to Western economic and social structure, arguing that Newton's mechanical world view facilitated capitalism and the exploitation of women, natural systems, and cultural systems. Feminists are now exploring in great detail how the beliefs of Western science and the practice of the same systematically excluded women and denigrated ways of knowing which have been attributed to women while men and science have been dependent on these ways of knowing (Evelyn Fox Keller, *Reflections on Gender in Science*, 1985; Sandra Harding, *The Science Question in Feminism*, 1986). J. Baird Callicott has linked the characteristics of modern agriculture to Western metaphysics ("Agroecology in Context," 1988) and analyzed

Western views of nature in the context of dominant scientific paradigms (various articles published in *Environmental Ethics*).

The literature on scientific knowledge and policy formation is already rich (Lasswell, *A Pre-View of Policy Sciences*, 1971; Lindbloom and Cohen, *Usable Knowledge*, 1979; Torgerson, "Between Knowledge and Politics", 1986; Haas, *When Knowledge is Power*, 1989). The number of investigations into the nature of environmental knowledge and public decision-making, however, is still limited. Three case studies offer insights. Wildavsky and Tenenbaum (*The Politics of Mistrust*, 1981) document the difficulties of building a national energy policy based on uncertain information in an environment of political mistrust. Brian Wynne (*Rationality and Ritual*, 1982) explores the interplay between experts, environmental information, and politics in the Windscale inquiry, an investigation into nuclear control and safety in Britain, again in an environment of mistrust. Christopher Bosso (*Pesticides and Politics*, 1987) shows how competing world views – environmental and industrial – interact with how the Environmental Protection Agency uses science in the regulatory process. Working across cases, Sheila Jasanoff (*The Fifth Branch: Science Advisors as Policymakers*, 1990) documents the general difficulties of using science to make regulatory decisions, arguing why science cannot live up to its own standards and the presumption of objectivity when associated with public decision-making. The International Institute for Applied Systems Analysis initiated its efforts into sustainable development through a series of background papers, many of which addressed the incongruencies between nature of scientific knowledge and our emerging perceptions of environmental problems (J. R. Ravetz, "Usable Knowledge, Usable Ignorance: Incomplete Science with Policy Implications;" P. Timmerman, "Mythology and Surprise in the Sustainable Development of the Biosphere;" and "Methods for Synthesis: Policy Exercises" Garry Brewer, 1986). All of these studies document how science is not working as Comte envisioned in the public decision-making process. John Dryzek (*Rational Ecology*, 1987) goes beyond the nature of science to a rich analysis of the incongruities between alternative modes of political decision-making and the underlying nature of environmental problems and concludes that radical decentralization may be the best option. Common themes in these works are the difficulties of rationally reaching a consensus in existing political structures and implicitly, or explicitly in the case of Dryzek, the plea for trust through stronger civil society. This theme will arise again in Chapter 12 on democratizing knowledge.

Perhaps it is important to reiterate that Comte's vision of social organization was adopted because it fit sufficient aspects of social organization, especially the distribution of power, at the beginning of the progressive era at the end of the nineteenth century. Specifically, the rise of technocratic federal agencies in the United States in the 1890s as well as the justification, for example, of stronger federal environmental regulations since the 1970s has been supported by industrial interests because regulation by diverse states who saw costs and benefits differently was making business difficult. One has similar worries with respect to the motives of business in promoting "free" trade agreements. In any case, the rise of technocratic social organization was coevolutionary; it did not simply arise with the gradual acceptance of Comte's vision but rather Comte's vision gradually complemented more and more other pieces in the historical unfolding (Richard Sylla, "The Progressive Era and the Political Economy of Big Government," 1991).

The new concern among philosophers and social scientists for communities, culture, contextuality, and contingency complements the image of a coevolutionary patchwork quilt. Yet the coevolutionary revisioning of this book certainly does not flow very directly from this new literature. Prior to Toulmin (*Cosmopolis: The*

Hidden Agenda of Modernity, 1990) I was only aware of one philosopher who turned a critique of the metaphysical and epistemological beliefs underlying modernism into a defense of cultural diversity (Paul Feyerabend, "Notes on Relativism," 1987). The patchwork quilt image developed in the last chapter comes from my own appreciation for diversity which has been stimulated by my contacts with other cultures and ecosystems; my background as an environmentalist; my sympathy for traditional peoples and reading of the journal *Cultural Survival;* my awareness as a Californian of the bioregionalist movement, though I am not read in this area; and my abhorence of bureaucratic and technocratic authoritarianism. Martin O'Connor ("Time and Environment," 1991) combines similar thoughts to my own after immersing himself among natural and social philosophers in France, exploring the cultural contradictions of development as exhibited between Maori and Westerners in New Zealand, and contemplating the history of economic thought and practice.

CHAPTER 7

Environmental determinism and cultural determinism have had a very long history. Discord and discourse between adherents of the two determinisms have been underway for millennia. I have only emphasized the clash between them in the text with respect to recent concerns over resource limits and the sociobiology debate. The discourse has developed very fine distinctions and the gray areas have been thoroughly studied. Thus, by stressing the extremes, one might argue that I have mistakenly followed popularized thought into a false dichotomy. On closer examination, for example, one finds that many thoughtful people have held both views simultaneously, applying one to one situation, the other to another, depending on the particular situation and time period involved as well as the audience to whom one is trying to speak. Let me acknowledge, furthermore, that dichotomies have long helped people emphasize a point. There are clear cases where people still rush to one extreme view or the other, for many reasons, as in the "limits-to-growth" and sociobiology debates. But my real point is that there has long not been, and the situation still begs for, a synthesis.

Clarence J. Glacken (*Traces on the Rhodian Shore,* 1967) chronicled the history of thought on culture and environment from early Greek and Roman times, through to the discourse between those with religious views and scientific outlooks during the Renaissance, and on to modern times. Glacken's analysis documents that the cultural and environmental determinism dichotomy was originally rooted in alternative interpretations of God's benevolence and empowerment of people. The rise of Western science both transformed and refueled the separate arguments, though God's benevolence and transfer of power have been appealed to by both sides well into this century. It is fascinating that the two opposing views have been so resilient and the debate between them has remained viable for so long even while the particulars have evolved.

Within the individual sciences and their associated professions, one determinism or the other has tended to dominate the culture except for anthropology and geography where a feud has been sustained. Let me emphasize that the separate determinisms have been reinforced and synthesis discouraged to a large extent because people within disciplines behave as cultures. Those who seek syntheses are typically weeded out of their discipline for no longer holding to the central tenets of the paradigm. Environmental determinism is generally stronger and reinforced among natural scientists while cultural determinism has reigned in the applied disciplines of agriculture and engineering. Social scientists now definitely favor and reinforce cultural determinism (Luten, "Ecological Optimism in the Social Sciences: The Question of Limits to Growth," 1980), though the social sciences had a good dose of environmental determinism at their start in the nineteenth century that lasted well into the twentieth. Economics provides a good example.

Thomas Malthus (1766–1834) argued that starvation, disease, and war were inevitable because the tendency for human populations to increase would always be greater than our ability to push back environmental limits. David Ricardo (1772–1823) built his theory of rent on the fixed attributes of land arguing that returns to good land would increase as population expanded and poorer quality lands were brought into production. William Jevons (1835–82) attributed the power of the British Empire to the use of coal that was fast disappearing. Only Henry Carey (1793–1879), arguing both from the perspective of the history of resource use by Westerners expanding their occupation across North America and from an understanding of how people could improve the quality of soil through good agriculture, contested environmental determinism. Within economics, environmental determinism effectively reigned until World War II.

In the midst of the Great Depression, however, a few U.S. economists became interested in the long-run balance between technology and resources in economic growth. Eventually empirically based arguments arose from this inquiry that refuted Ricardo's argument that resource rents would increase over time. Harold Barger and Sam Schurr (*The Mining Industries: A Study of Output, Employment, and Productivity*, 1944) documented that lower quality resources were not limiting mineral production, while T. W. Schultz ("The Declining Importance of Agricultural Land," 1951) argued that rent declines as a share of gross national product with development. Harold Barnett and Chandler Morse (*Scarcity and Growth: The Economics of Natural Resource Availability*, 1963) published an analysis showing that the labor and capital costs of extracting resources had declined precipitously during the preceding century. Economists' confidence in these findings led Carl Kaysen ("The Computer that printed out W*O*L*F," 1972) and Wilfred Beckerman ("Economists, Scientists, and Environmental Catastrophe," 1972) among others to roundly criticize the arguments made by Meadows *et al.* in *The Limits to Growth* (1972). So great was the conviction of the economists that their counterattacks lacked all sophistication. Beckerman repeatedly attacked the science of the scientists as being unscientific, because not all scientists concurred, yet his own argument was littered with items such as the following:

> Even though it may be impossible to mine to a depth of one mile at every point in the Earth's crust, by the time A.D. 100,000,000 I am sure we will think of something.
>
> (Beckerman, 1972: 338)

The economists' attack on the *Global 2000 Report* prepared by President Carter's Council on Environmental Quality (1980) was led by Julian Simon (*The Ultimate Resource*, 1981; Simon and Kahn, *The Resourceful Earth: A Response to Global 2000*, 1984) with arguments documenting past progress extended indefinitely into the future.

Since the energy crisis of 1974 and the subsequent increased concern with the loss of biodiversity, global climate change, and ultimately the sustainability of development, a small subset of economists who actually study the role of resources in the economy have become increasingly wary of cultural determinism. Their efforts to determine empirically whether resources are becoming more scarce or not have been better framed to pursue the intricacies of the problem. They have indeed found evidence that resources are limiting growth (Slade, "Trends in Natural Resource Commodity Prices: An Analysis of the Time Domain," 1982; Hall and Hall, "Concepts and Measures of Natural Resource scarcity with a Summary of Recent Trends," 1984). Within the profession at large, however, the earlier empirical analyses supporting the technological optimism of cultural determinism are still often cited. With respect to global climate change, the economist who has taken a leading role in the public discourse, William Nordhaus, has been more constructive than those who critiqued "Limits-to-Growth" two decades earlier. Nevertheless, Nordhaus has followed many of their precedents by chiding environmental scientists for not fully understanding scientific method, asserting that technology makes industrial nations relatively climate-proof, and arguing that economic analysis indicates little if anything should be done (Nordhaus, "Greenhouse Economics: Count Before You Leap," 1990).

Economists' analyses of resource scarcity suffer two logical flaws. First, their attempts to determine empirically from trends in resource costs whether resources are scarce assume that resource allocators – land holders, investors, and bidders in futures markets – already know whether resources are scarce. If they do not, their behavior will not generate trends in prices and costs which reflect the scarcity of resources. If they do know, economists could simply ask them (Norgaard, "Economic Indicators of Resource Scarcity: A Critical Essay," 1990). Second, economists' attempts to determine how resources should be allocated over the future have implicitly assumed that future generations have no rights to resources, that they should receive whatever this generation finds advantageous to save in order to sell to them. A different, yet equally efficient, allocation results when resource rights are distributed to future generations (Howarth and Norgaard, "Intergenerational Resource Rights, Efficiency, and Social Optimality," 1990).

In the 1970s Herman Daly and Nicholas Georgescu-Roegen challenged the resource economics profession with their own variations of environmental determinism. Their arguments, while only having a marginal impact within the discipline, have been interpreted by environmental scientists as the only evidence from within the social sciences of analyses rooted in reality (Ehrlich, "The Limits to Substitution: Meta-resource Depletion and a New Economic-ecological Paradigm," 1989). Herman Daly's introductory and concluding essays in two books he has edited (*Toward a Steady-State Economy*, 1973 and *Economics, Ecology, and Ethics: Toward a Steady-State Economy*, 1980) provide strong arguments for reducing the rate of resource use and pollutants released to the environment. Daly's ideas and the essays in his books by natural scientists are frequently the only exposure many economics students have had to any alternative reasoning beyond neoclassical dogma. Daly's book with philosopher John Cobb (*For the Common Good: Redirecting the Economy Toward Community, the Environment, and a Sustainable Future*, 1989) develops the moral arguments he had initiated in his earlier essays and the case for thinking of people as members of communities who care about each other. These extremely important arguments receive no more than a curious clause or two in the conventional economic literature.

Mechanistic determinism

Some environmental determinists premise their position on an interpretation of natural systems that admits their changing complexity and our limited ability to understand them. These premises indicate we must constantly monitor, interpret, and reinterpret through new patterns of thinking how we are interacting with our environment and maintain a large margin of error. Others, however, premise their position on the belief that environmental systems have identifiable limits, thresholds, or system states which can be identified and which if exceeded will entail consequences which no right-minded person or society would wish upon themselves or their heirs. These premises indicate that environmental rules can be specified for individual moral behavior, types of technologies that can be used, the rate of the flow of resources into the economy, and the rate of effluents from the economy. Adherents to this view will also admit that we cannot know the system perfectly hence margins of error are appropriate. To believe in limits is to presume that environmental systems are composed of unchanging parts in fixed relations, to posit that they are basically mechanical in nature, but with thresholds or break points beyond which their continued benevolent operation can no longer be assured.

Mechanistic determinists are thus asking environmental scientists to divine the limits of deforestation, soil erosion, carbon dioxide emissions, and toxic dumping beyond which sustainable development will not be possible. Define the rules and let's get on with the game. It is a familiar gambit in which players on both sides of the board, environmental and cultural determinists have chosen to participate. Natural scientists have already been asked by legislative bodies and administrative agencies pestered by people concerned with human health to determine acceptable levels of food additives, pesticides, and radiation. And natural scientists have complied, as if the relationship between the dosage of these factors and human health in fact could be known, was the same across large classes of peoples under a broad range of conditions, and had a clear break point below which there was little or no effect, above which the effect all of a sudden becomes clearly unacceptable. Impossible at worst, bad science at best, such socially constructed rules obviated more difficult political decisions or administrative rules, facilitating "progress" through the use of at least some food additives, pesticides, and radiation, among other things and better health through at least some limitations. And when the compromise is not politically acceptable, the "scientific" determination is soon sent back to the scientists for a rethinking.

Herman Daly has called for limiting the rate of throughput of raw materials and energy in the economy to slow resource use and for limiting the rate of environmental pollution in order to control environmental degradation. He argues quite cogently that throughput and pollution cannot continue to increase, that we may not be able scientifically to determine "correct" rates, but that we have to start turning the process around sometime. Daly, however, also popularized the term "steady-state economy" with its connotations of a machine running in equilibrium. More recently he has argued that markets allocate resources between uses pretty well, analogous to loading a boat evenly. But if we keep evenly loading the boat, it will evenly sink. Hence he argues for a plimsoll line to indicate the extent to which the boat should be loaded. His analogies to steady-state systems and to plimsoll lines are static limits which presumably can be determined by objective environmental criteria.

We need to use science as best we can. Mechanistic interpretations of complex systems are frequently very insightful. Only naive positivists think science should never mix with politics or never do the work of politics. But are we asking it to participate with politics in its best modes with respect to environmental questions? Have we asked science to make compromises at such a simple level, the setting of impossible standards too simply conceived, that we are unable to access the richer understandings that science has to offer to public decision-making? Are not our environmental and cultural problems today precisely due to the way science has interacted with politics at too simple a level? One interpretation of this book is

212

that it is an argument that we have not mixed science and politics effectively and an argument for how they might be combined better.

Herman Daly is among the first to admit that environmental systems rarely have thresholds beyond which they completely break down. Rather, systems are constantly adjusting to whatever stimulus they receive and changing their evolutionary course accordingly. Furthermore, if systems did have limits, the limits would depend upon technology, culture, and ecosystem characteristics. He realizes that the limits we now deem acceptable for air and water pollutants and for impurities in our foods are social constructs incorporating human values and social power. They are not scientifically determined thresholds above which drastic events begin to occur even though they are presented to the public in this manner. Daly, in effect, is presenting steady state and limits metaphors because he sees no other way to implement environmental management within existing understandings and institutions which have coevolved around these understandings. I think he is absolutely correct, and this book is a part of the effort to change those understandings and institutions.

It is easy to agree with Daly that we cannot keep using resources and assaulting the environment at the level we are now. He has been instrumental in helping get this point across. My concern is that his treatment of ecosystems as something that can be objectively defined apart from people and from which a fixed amount can be used in any time period is an inadequate model from which to derive policy. Inadequate metaphors and models have gotten us into the environmental and social difficulties we now experience and continue to impede the development of more sophisticated policies. Nicholas Georgescu-Roegen's critique of Daly (Energy and Economic Myths," 1975) is similar:

> The vision of a blissful world in which both population and capital stock remain constant, once expounded with his usual skill by John Stuart Mill, was until recently in oblivion. Because of the spectacular revival of this myth of ecological salvation, it is well to point out its various logical and factual snags. The crucial error consists in not seeing that not only growth, but also a zero-growth rate, nay even a declining state which does not converge toward annihilation, cannot exist forever in a finite environment. The error perhaps stems from some confusion between finite stock and finite flow rate. . . . And contrary to what some advocates (references to Daly) of the stationary state claim, this state does not occupy a privileged position vis a vis physical laws.
> (Georgescu-Roegen, 1975:367)

Nor, however, do I find Georgescu-Roegen's arguments convincing. And so let's move on to a fourth maladaptive determinism.

Entropic determinism

The second law of thermodynamics, the entropy law, challenged the idea of progress within decades of its derivation by Rudolph Clausius in 1854. According to the entropy law, the amount of energy available for work in a closed system only decreases. Since any action requires energy, any activity today is at the expense of potential activity in the future. This does not leave much hope for progress, and the entropy law has been invoked by pessimists ever since. Since the coevolutionary arguments presented in this book still hold hope for the future, a full elaboration of the second law is in order to understand coevolutionary potential.

The first law of thermodynamics states that energy and matter can neither be created nor destroyed. Matter and energy are equated through the well-known formula – $E = mc^2$ – of Albert Einstein. One can be converted to the other, but there is no way of creating or destroying one without destroying or creating the other. The first law suggests that we can never lose. Whatever we do, we will always have the same amount of matter and energy. Furthermore it appears that we can select the mix of material and energy since either can be converted to the other. If only the first law applied, there would be no such thing as a mistake since all problems could be readily corrected with nothing lost except time. If making mistakes ultimately had no costs, there would be little reason to write this book on the course of development.

The second law of thermodynamics explains why reality is so grim. Energy is not equally available for work. The entropy law, or second law of thermodynamics, states that in a closed system, one that is neither receiving nor losing energy or material, all physical processes reduce the availability of energy for further physical processes. When energy, which can also be thought of as stored work, is "used," it does not disappear, for that would violate the first law of thermodynamics or the boundary conditions of the closed system. But it does change form so that it is less available for further work. Physicists refer to this loss in availability as an increase in entropy. Energy with low entropy is more available for work than energy with high entropy.

For example, when coal is burned to generate steam to turn turbines to generate electricity, no energy is destroyed. But the energy in the original coal is greater than the energy in the electricity produced. The difference in energy between the coal and electricity it produces exists as heat that has been dissipated to the environment. This heat is not as accessible for further work as was its share of the energy in the original coal. The loss in the potential of energy for work can be reduced in conversion processes, but it can never be reduced below certain minimum levels. For work to be done, entropy must increase.

It is important to remember, however, that the second law of thermodynamics applies to closed systems, to systems that are not acquiring or losing energy or material.

Just as energy is not equally available for work, matter is not equally available for use. It is much easier, or perhaps we should say it takes less work, to make iron from ores that are 60 percent iron than from the dirt in the typical household garden made up of approximately 5 percent iron. Because of the relationship between concentration and work, the entropy law is also frequently associated with the concentration of materials. But concentration may not indicate usefulness, *per se*. Concentrating all of the books and papers in my office into one large pile in the corner, for example, would not increase their usefulness. Nor would concentrating the sugar and salt into one container be useful. So from concentration the definition has been extended to refer to the useful order or organization of things. Useful order or organization, however, depends on the users' information and needs. When the term entropy is used in this way, what started as a natural law in physics has lost all objectivity; it cannot be defined apart from people. Entropy used as order is only defined in the context of the knowledge, technologies, social organization, and preferences of people.

As in the case of energy, there seems to be a certain directionality to these material extensions of the entropy law. The iron ore we mine is much more concentrated than the iron that has dissipated as rust on our highways or even as cans in our garbage dumps. Concentrated things become less concentrated. To make them more concentrated again requires energy and deliberate effort, the costs of recycling. The books and papers in my office are constantly losing their useful order, and I am constantly fighting this entropic process. It is much easier to mix salt and sugar than to separate the two. Dye introduced into a glass of water dissipates evenly and never concentrates again on its own. Not only useful energy, but material stuff also seem to go in particular directions. Order tends to disorder.

All physical processes are subject to the first and second laws of thermodynamics. And since biological processes are driven by physical processes, they too are subject to the laws. Thus natural scientists are quick to catch social scientists who optimistically project into the future relations between development, resources, and technology that defy the second law. And social scientists frequently ask natural scientists the extent to which the law is true and whether or not new theory might replace it. Paul Ehrlich has responded:

> To wait for the laws of thermodynamics to be overturned as descriptions of everyday experiences on this planet is, literally, to wait for the day when beer refrigerates itself in hot weather and squashed cats on the freeway spontaneously reassemble themselves and trot away.
> (Ehrlich, "The Limits to Substitution: Meta-resource Depletion and a New Economic-ecological Paradigm," 1989)

Not only are resource limits and environmental pollution inextricably bound up with the second law, but its directionality also implies that things are only going to get worse. This has led to considerable fatalism. For the universe as a whole, it has been argued that energy becomes less and less available for work. This version has led those who view the universe as a magnificent mechanism, an elaborate clock, to conclude that the clock can only wind down. And if a stopped clock is not sufficiently descriptive of the end of the universe, imagine the monotony of energy uniformly distributed, matter disorganized, and temperatures near absolute zero.

During the 1930s, W. R. Inge, Dean of St. Paul's Cathedral, argued that the second law proved that all evolution and human progress was an illusion and that people should return to Christianity and seek citizenship in heaven. He subsequently authored two books on this theme.

> We have here no continuing city, neither we ourselves nor the species to which we belong. Our citizenship is in heaven, in the eternal world to which even in this life we may ascend in heart and mind. . . . Those who throw all their ideals into the future are as bankrupt as those who lent their money to the Russian or German governments during the war.

During the 1970s, Nicholas Georgescu-Roegen, an economist with prior training in physics, authored a book and numerous papers on entropy and economics. He argued that since all economic processes entail physical processes, all economic activity increase entropy. Higher levels of gross national product and continued growth only increase entropy ever faster, hastening the ultimate end. Progress is only temporary, at best. Sustainability a myth. Resource transformation today necessarily reduces the possibilities for resource transformation at some future date. The rate of entropy increase can be reduced per unit of economic activity by using energy and materials more efficiently, but such improvements can only forestall the inevitable somewhat.

While there is good scientific reasoning in Georgescu-Roegen's writings and probably even some good science in Pastor Inge's preachings, it takes only one error to reach a false conclusion. In fact, natural scientists had already pursued these same lines of reasoning and reached different conclusions. They extended concepts of thermodynamics to economic production throughout the nineteenth century and in the twentieth considered how entropy relates to the broader questions of the ultimate potential for development. Sir Arthur Eddington addressed the broader question at least as early as 1928, Joseph Needham in 1941, Erwin Schrodinger in 1944, Norbert Weiner in 1950, Harold Blum in 1951, and Ludwig von Bertlanffy in 1968. Ilya Prigogine covered the subject more recently in 1979 and there have, no doubt, been many others. The entropy alarm ringers have erred in one major way and several minor ways that are important for understanding why coevolutionary development is consistent with the second law.

First, and most importantly, the second law refers to closed systems. The earth is an open system receiving energy from the sun. For millennia during which much human advance occurred, the sun provided the only energy from which people drew their livelihood. The sun will shine for another 4.5 billion years or so. Economists and development planners are frequently quite rightfully accused of being short-sighted, but we need not go to extremes and begin to worry about billions of years. There are many more immediate concerns.

Economist Frank H. Knight deserves special mention for being among the few twentieth-century economists who was aware of the broader questions being pursued by natural scientists ("Statistics and Dynamics: Some Queries Regarding the Mechanical Anology in Economics," 1935 translation). Writing in 1930 on the use of mechanistic concepts in economics, he noted:

> Its [the sun's] flow perpetually maintains the disequilibria which cause the flow of water and air and hence the phenomena of life.'
>
> (Knight, 1935)

The second law helps us identify the importance of the sun for long term development. Without the energy input of the sun, the second law applies on earth, warning us that order ultimately proceeds to disorder in a closed system. The argument of the alarmists might then be redirected solely to the problem of the use of stock resources, to the use of hydrocarbon and uranium energy and to the use of the favorable ordering of minerals.

On the other hand, the second law only addresses direction. One does not need the second law to understand that resources used up cannot be used again, though it does help us understand the limits of recycling. The problem of stock resources is that we do not know how big the stock is. Similarly, the second law tells us nothing about how much order remains to be driven to disorder.

An additional argument waxes cosmological. To note that available energy is always dissipating begs the question of where did it come from in the first place. And to apply a law applicable to closed systems to the universe as a whole begs the question of from what is the universe closed.

Let's let the astrophysicists pursue the boundaries of the universe and whether the usefulness of energy is not being recreated somewhere, and simply resolve to use the second law correctly within the reasonable bounds of our solar system and the next thousand years or two.

The other social sciences

Let's consider the less dismal disciplines. To a large extent, both anthropology and geography evolved out of the observations of explorers and the related general theorizing of scholars during the age of discovery. And to a large extent such thinking was environmentally deterministic. Within anthropology, environmental determinism culminated in the writings of Fredrich Ratzel (1844–1904). By the late nineteenth century, however, anthropologists had accumulated sufficient field work to discover the rich variety of reality. The leading anthropologist, Franz Boas (1858–1942), turned from environmental determinism to possibilism, and others followed suit. The writings of Alfred Kroeber (1876–1960) and other great twentieth century anthropologists retained a strong interest in environmental influences, yet an emphasis on culture and cultural determinism has reigned (Leaf, *Man, Mind, and Science: A History of Anthropology*; 1979; Moran, *Human Adaptability: An Introduction to Ecological Anthropology*, 1979). As will be heavily acknowledged in the annotations to the next chapter, however, the more successful attempts at synthesizing cultural and environmental determinism have taken place within anthropology.

Geographers also were initially inclined toward environmental determinism and divided on the question at the turn of this century (Beck, "Environmental Determinism in Twentieth Century American Geography: Reflections in the Professional Journals," 1985). Ellen C. Semple (*Influences of Geographical Environment: On the Basis of Ratzel's System of Anthropo-Geography*, 1911), who drew her inspiration from Ratzel and clearly relied on his prestige, led what might best be described as a crusade for the continued recognition of the importance of the environment in geographic thought from the beginning of this century into the 1920s. Carl Sauer ("The Morphology of Landscape," 1925), though once a student of Semple at the University of Chicago, became a leading voice in documenting the influence of culture on the landscape, picking up a theme developed earlier by George Perkins Marsh (*Man and Nature: Or Physical Geography as Modified by Human Action*, 1864). Geographers, while making the case that people do affect their environment, have at least long questioned whether such sway will not ultimately account for their demise (William L. Thomas (ed.), *Man's Role in Changing the Face of the Earth*, 1956). After decades of intense debate, geographers seem uninterested in this issue at the very core of their discipline and have maintained a surprisingly low profile in the Western environmental discourse during the second half of this century.

The sociobiology debate was anything but low profile. Konrad Lorenz (*On Aggression*, 1966) argued that aggression and other behavioral traits appear to be genetic rather than learned in "lower" animals and may have a genetic basis in people. This speculation attracted considerable popular attention. Within academe, however, his arguments were dismissed by biological scientists because Lorenz also published as a behavioral scientist and by behavioral scientists because he also published as a biologist. Multidisciplinary scholars lack credibility because they so easily offend the assumptions adopted within individual disciplinary cultures. This was certainly the case when Edward O. Wilson (1975) published his treatise entitled *Sociobiology: The New Synthesis*. A very vocal group of biological scientists accused him of falsely stretching biological theory, while behavioral scientists accused him of not understanding the importance of culture (Sociobiology Study Group of Science for the People, "Sociobiology – Another Biological Determinism," 1976; Caplan, *The Sociobiology Debate: Readings on the Ethical and Scientific Issues Concerning Sociobiology*, 1978). At this level of the critique, both groups made valid points. What gave the debate high profile was that the critics argued that Wilson was motivated by social darwinist political beliefs which at best supported conservative policies with respect to the futility of fostering social justice and equality and at worst supported the eugenic policies of Hitler (Allen *et al.*, "Against Sociobiology," 1975; Caplan, 1978: introduction, and Wilson, "Academic Vigilantism and the Political Significance of Sociobiology," 1976: response to his critiques). There is, to be sure, a tension between biological understanding and our beliefs in free will, individual responsibility, and our potential for human betterment. Wilson pointed a large spotlight on an area others had wisely avoided. The sociobiology debate juxtaposed biological theory against our underlying Western beliefs which complement cultural determinism. This tension underlay earlier debates with respect to social darwinism that also split the scientific community along political ideologies (John C. Greene, *Science, Ideology, and World View*, 1981).

217

Elizabeth Carlassare ("An Exploration of Ecofeminism," 1992) has documented a similar division among ecofeminists. Some ecofemists argue that women have qualities, whether by biology or culture, which allow them especially insightful ways to interpret and resolve the environmental and social crises of our time relative to men. Other ecofeminists argue that all women's qualities have in effect been social constructions imposed by men and to argue that any of these constructions might be a basis for knowing and acting reduces the possibilities for the full liberation of women. The latter group, consisting of social and socialist ecofeminists, have labeled the former cultural ecofeminist and accused them of being essentialists and irrational. Those who have been so labeled, however, do not assume that label, find their accusers are too narrowly interpreting them, and are frankly disinterested in debating about which type of ecofeminism is right. This debate parallels the sociobiology debate and is equally maladaptive.

With respect to the sociobiology debate, Lorenz (*Behind the Mirror: A Search for a Natural History of Human Knowledge*, 1977) and Wilson (Lumsden and Wilson, *Genes, Mind, and Culture: The Coevolutionary Process*, 1981) quickly incorporated the scientific criticism of their initial effort into much more sophisticated syntheses. Lorenz developed a rich treatise on the role of learning, from amoebae to people, how learned knowledge is communicated, the role of cultural systems in learning and behavior, and the influence of all of these on what proves fit, and hence evolution. Lumsden and Wilson developed a sophisticated model of how cultural traits are passed from generation to generation and how evolution is really a coevolution between biological traits and cultural traits. Anthropologists (Durham, "Toward a Coevolutionary Theory of Human Biology and Culture," 1979) and biological scientists (Cavalli-Sforza and Feldman, *Cultural Transmission and Evolution: A Quantitative Approach*, 1981) also participated in the development of new syntheses. But the syntheses have been virtually ignored. Environmental and cultural determinism reign. Worse, Wilson's attackers continued to attack his original work well after he had remedied it (Lewontin, Rose, and Kamin, *Not in Our Genes: Biology, Ideology, and Human Nature*, 1984).

The rise and fall of social darwinism suggests that evolutionary explanations *per se* conflict with modern political beliefs concerning rational action, individual responsibility, and unfettered equality of opportunity. To be sure, there have been progressive writers who have elaborated evolutionary views while maintaining their moral integrity. Herbert Spencer was developing evolutionary explanations of social structures as Darwin was developing his ideas in biology, and their trains of thought later frequently intertwined with respect to the implications of evolution and evolutionary thinking for people. They held a progressive view, advocating that evolutionary thinking helps explain how people and cultures could evolve beyond raw individual competition for fitness. Thomas Huxley added ethical evolution to Spencer's sociology. Karl Marx considered evolutionary thinking in the vanguard of progress and considered dedicating *Capital* to Darwin. Highly progressive views have been elaborated throughout the twentieth century, perhaps most joyously by Pierre Teilhard de Chardin, a Catholic philosopher and paleontologist (*The Phenomenon of Man*, 1940; *The Future of Man*, 1964). Thomas Berry, another humanist Catholic philosopher, evokes the evolutionary optimism of Teilhard de Chardin while addressing the down to earth issues of environmental degradation and personal and social responsibility and the down to people issues of cultural and personal respect so lacking in modernity (*The Dream of the Earth*, 1988).

Kenneth Boulding is among the most notable and exciting of twentieth century progressive evolutionists (*Ecodynamics: A New Theory of Societal Evolution*, 1978; *Evolutionary Economics*, 1981; *The World as a Total System*, 1985). Boulding applies a keen sense of basic ecological and evolutionary theory to an interpretation of geological, biological, human, social, and conceptual histories. He treats these, however, as parallel histories operating under the same general principles, in keeping with his earlier interest in general systems theory, rather than as interacting histories. Boulding's thought ranges smoothly from epistemology to policy, synthesizing evolutionary systems thinking with modernity rather than accentuating the differences.

Peter Corning has attempted a grand evolutionary synthesis of the social sciences (*The Synergism Hypothesis: A Theory of Progressive Evolution*, 1983). This too-little recognized, highly detailed, indeed monumental, effort provides incredible insight into the complementarities between social science understanding and evolutionary thinking. The attempt at synthesis, however, reflects a drive for monistic coherence which betrays the real significance of our new understanding.

Historically, anthropologists, economists, and historians simply invoked the concept of evolution without attempting to develop a theory of the structures and processes of social evolution. Robert Boyd and Peter J. Richerson (*Culture and the Evolutionary Process*, 1985), an anthropologist and biologist respectively, have reviewed the literature on cultural evolution, especially that in psychology and economics. They documented that while the situation is steadily improving, more rigor and empiricism is sorely needed. Certainly my own efforts would be harshly judged by their criteria. Boyd and Richerson set out to develop the rigor, making a strong contribution with respect to what are the critical differences between biological and cultural evolution. But they clarify and add mathematical rigor by avoiding most of the exciting developments transforming evolutionary theory during recent decades. They retain the objectivism of people and their environments having separate evolutionary histories. Few besides Gregory Bateson have pondered the whole panoply from mind to nature as a necessary unity.

Within the protracted debates between the maladaptive determinisms and amidst the rising concern over the future of the human environment, many are confused about whether environmentalism is left or right and what is politically proper. Political ideology fueled the sociobiology debate in the U.S., but similar issues keep arising in Europe and in the South as well. From the right come charges that European Greens, after all, are but moderately transformed marxists while North American environmentalists are not only trying to resaddle the U.S. economy with the controls eased during Reagan's presidency but are striking for the heart of free economies through limiting the rights of corporations and individuals to burn fossil hydrocarbons. From the left come charges that Greens have abandoned their faith in the scientific progress that will ultimately drive capitalist economies toward communism; that the Greens have abandoned their concern with social justice within the current generation; and that Hitler and other despicable people including social darwinists believed in environmental determinism (Bramwell, *Ecology in the 20th Century: A History*, 1989). Fortunately, others are exploring the truth in between and chronicling how environmental concerns blended with social concerns are redefining the future of politics (Gorz, *Ecology as Politics*, 1980; Redclift, *Development and Environmental Crisis: Red or Green Alternatives*, 1984; Paehlke, *Environmentalism and the Future of Progressive Politics*, 1989; Tokar, "Radical Ecology on the Rise," 1990; Escobar with Thrupp, "The Unsustainable Paradigm of Sustainable Development," 1990; Chase (ed.), *Defending the Earth: A Dialogue Between Murray Bookchin and Dave Foreman*, 1991).

CHAPTER 8

Efforts to apply the ideas of ecology in the social sciences date back to 1915, when Robert E. Park used an ecological framework in a sociological analysis of urban environments. Sociologists continued to experiment with ecological thinking and developed their own strains of human ecology as a subdiscipline of sociology. Park and Ernest W. Burgess, drawing analogies from the work of the key ecological scientists who were also at the University of Chicago, developed the term human ecology in a textbook they wrote in 1921 (cited in Lee Freese, *Currents in the Stream: The Ideas of Human Ecology*, forthcoming). In 1923 the term "Human Ecology" was introduced into geography but apparently not significantly used by geographers again for decades (H.H. Barrows, Geography as Human Ecology). In 1926, R. D. McKenzie, a student of Park and Burgess drew upon the interactive concepts developing in ecology to describe social systems and scope out a new field of study (The Scope of Human Ecology). Robert E. Park further elaborated ecological metaphors of social systems in 1936 ("Human Ecology"). Amos Hawley ("Ecology and Human Ecology," 1944; *Human Ecology*, 1950) formally compared ecological systems in biology and human ecological systems. Since then, ecological metaphors have had a small and intermittent following within sociology, rural sociology, and natural resource sociology.

Sociologists have had explicit difficulty with homeostatic causal loop models of social systems because they seem to absolve both individual and class responsibility and negate directed strategies for change (see: Albrecht and Murdoch, 1985 and Swanson and Busch, 1985). Human ecology has, both rightfully and wrongfully, suffered many of the difficulties of social darwinism. Even Norbert Wiener, after elaborating cybernetics as a homeostatic loop causal model (*Cybernetics*, 1948) carefully crafted the moral use of this approach (*The Human Use of Human Beings*. 1950).

The largest repository of ecological thinking applied to social and ecological systems is clearly in anthropology. Anthropologists retain a healthy interest in how environments affect people as well as how people affect their environment. The subdiscipline of cultural ecology initiated by Julian Steward (1968, 1977) in the early 1950s is especially important. Steward and his students resolved much of the debate between environmental and cultural determinists within anthropology by stressing how cultural systems and ecosystems interact. The cultural ecology perspective, however, was initiated under conditions which limited its development. Steward assumed the intellectual burden of his teachers at the University of California at Berkeley, Alfred L. Kroeber and Robert H. Lowi, and tried to document the nature of the cultures of American Indians. Only tattered remnants of these cultures could be observed. Whatever dynamics existed prior to their destruction through the advance of Western civilization were difficult to contemplate. By necessity, Steward and his students tended to portray cultures to be, more or less, in homeostatic equilibrium with their environment. Thus the early literature in cultural ecology explained culture and environment, with the emphasis on culture, as an interacting system. The occasional references to the possible processes by which nature and culture came to "reflect" each other, morphogenetic causal-loop reasoning, were casual hypotheses at best (Marvin Harris, *The Rise of Anthropological Theory* 1968; Robert McC. Netting, *Cultural Ecology*, 1977; Murray Leaf, *Man, Mind, and Science*, 1979; and Emilio Moran, *Human Adaptability*, 1979).

Though cultural ecologists after Steward studied viable nonmodern cultures, they too described them as if they were homeostatic over at least decades (Roy A. Rappaport, *Pigs for the Ancestors*, 1968; William C. Clarke, *Place and People*, 1971). Homeostatic systems views of environment and culture can be simple or complex.

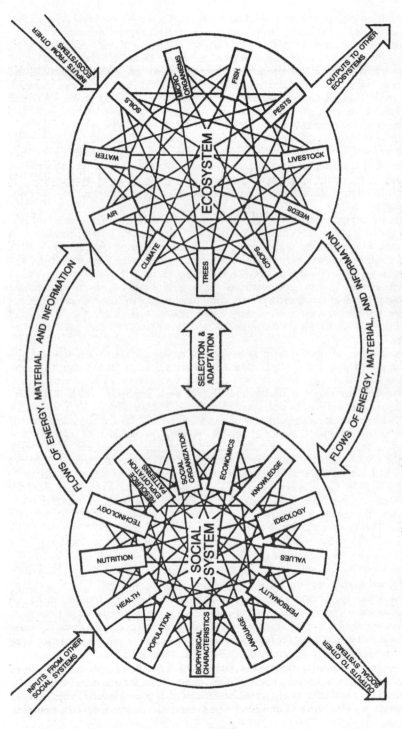

Figure B8.1 An illustration of key components and interactions of the cultural ecology approach

Source: Terry Rambo. 1988. "Conceptual Approaches to Human Ecology." Honolulu. East–West Environment and Policy Institute, Research Report 14.

The multiple connectedness developed by A. Terry Rambo (Conceptual Approaches to Human Ecology, 1983) and illustrated in Figure B8.1 represents one limit of the complexity of interactions considered by cultural ecologists. Rambo presents people and their cultural features and components of the environment as being in two highly complex systems which are connected through flows of energy, material, and information. Selection and adaptation, furthermore, occur across the two systems. Though most cultural ecology models are homeostatic, cultural ecology has had some influence on our understanding of the relationship between environment and development. Our current problems are explained as a breakdown in the equilibrium that traditional societies achieved with their environment. There are two difficulties with this approach. First, by concentrating on the idea of equilibrium rather than processes of change, the approach does not inform us of how to get to such an equilibrium. Second, the idea that society and nature should be in equilibrium is at odds with Western beliefs in progress and the more recent pursuit of economic development.

Ecosystem perspectives have become firmly rooted in organization theory, between the disciplines of sociology and political science. The interactions between bureaucrats, bureaucracies, legislatures, and interest groups, frequently with a technical component, have been thought of in ecosystemic terms. As in cultural and human ecology, the emphasis has been on the interactions of the social system rather than their evolution, but organizational ecologists have begun to incorporate evolutionary explanations. Furthermore, they have begun to incorporate organizational learning within their evolutionary explanations (Gareth Morgan, *Images of Organization*, 1986). In this sense, organizational theorists are further advanced than biologists.

The explanation of development as social and ecological system coevolution is a clear example of a morphogenetic causal-loop model where many mutual interactions can lead to changes in both the parts and the interactions between them.

Evolutionary thinking has undergone several very important additional interrelated expansions during the past quarter century. Paleontologists have long been struck by the apparent incompleteness of the fossil record, by the absence of fossils representing intermediate forms of gradually evolving species. Historically, this was attributed to the loss through erosion and other geological processes of the rock bearing the missing intermediate forms. Increasingly, however, this explanation did not seem to hold together with other evidence of geological history. In the early 1970s, Niles Eldredge and Stephen J. Gould advanced the hypothesis that the fossil record was not incomplete but that evolution proceeded in fits and starts ("Punctuated Equilibria: An Alternative to Phyletic Gradualism," 1972; "Punctuated Equilibria: The Tempo and Mode of Evolution Reconsidered," 1977). Species, they argued, evolved relatively little from the time they proved fit, even though the physical environment might change. The hypotheses that were advanced as to why evolution might be sporadic, including the possibility that embryological development imposed constraints on further evolution, seemed to conflict with accepted evolutionary theory. Their arguments stimulated heated debate, but within fifteen years evolutionary understanding had opened up to a whole new range of processes. Discontinuous equilibria mathematical models incorporating the interlocked nature of coevolving species helped evolutionists out of their lower order causal metatype mindsets (Roger Lewin, "Punctuated Equilibria Is Now Old Hat," 1986).

Selection in evolutionary theory has historically been described as a process of individuals with one trait outcompeting individuals of the same species without the more fit trait. Yet examples of apparent altruistic or cooperative behavior has clouded this explanation (William D. Hamilton, "The Genetical Theory of Social Behavior,"

1964). Richard Dawkins (*The Selfish Gene*, 1976) explained altruistic behavior toward siblings and others with whom an individual shares his genes as a means of enhancing the survival of the genotype even if it is at the sacrifice of the individual. Such behavior itself would logically be selected for because it enhances its own fitness. In the late 1970s, Robert Axelrod, a political scientist, discovered another explanation for cooperation which was reported in the *Journal of Conflict Resolution*. He set up a competition for the best strategy for use in a repeated Prisoner's Dilemma game. Anatol Rapaport of the University of Toronto submitted the most simple strategy, Tit for Tat, which proved superior to other strategies and when other players adopted that strategy as well, cooperation between the players evolved ("Effective Choice in the Prisoner's Dilemma," 1980; "More Effective Choice in the Prisoner's Dilemma," 1980). This finding was soon incorporated in the thinking of biology (Robert Axelrod and William D. Hamilton, "The Evolution of Cooperation," 1981) and also elaborated upon to explain phenomena as unbiological as the "live and let live" strategies that emerged during trench warfare in World War One (Robert Axelrod, *The Evolution of Cooperation*, 1984). Both biological and social scientists pursued the implications and expanded the theory in the subsequent years (Robert Axelrod and Douglas Dion, The Further Evolution of Cooperation, 1988).

While evolutionary phenomena were always recognized to be complex, the generalization that evolution tended in the direction of increasing the fitness of a species to its physical environment reduced the complexity to a simple cause and effect, or nonreciprocal causal model. In combination, the acknowledgment of coevolutionary, punctuated equilibria, and cooperative processes brought evolutionary thinking rather abruptly into a world of complex positive feedback processes during the 1980s. Such processes are now being simulated through interactive, self-replicating, evolving computer programs, a way of trying to understand the world far from the optimization techniques of mechanically described systems (M. Mitchell Waldrop, "Artificial Life's Rich Harvest," 1992). To further complicate matters, a few evolutionary theorists on the fringes were also thinking about how thinking and culture relate in the process of evolution (Konrad Lorenz, *Behind the Mirror*, 1977; Ronald H. Pulliam and Christopher Dunford, *Programmed to Learn*, 1980; L. L. Cavalli-Sforza and M. W. Feldman, *Cultural Transmission and Evolution*, 1981; Charles J. Lumsden and Edward O. Wilson, *Genes, Mind, and Culture*, 1981). Gregory Bateson (*Mind and Nature*, 1979) furthermore wholly contemplated how nature, culture, and thinking might be interrelated by evolutionary processes. The important point is that evolutionary thought increased in complexity dramatically and very quickly, compounding the already very difficult epistemological problems of this mode of reasoning (Michael Scriven, Explanation and Prediction in Evolutionary Theory, 1959; Elliott Sober, *The Nature of Selection*, 1984; Elliott Sober (ed.), *Conceptual Issues in Evolutionary Biology: An Anthology*, 1984; Robert J. Richards, *Darwin and the Emergence of Evolutionary Theories of Mind and Behavior*, 1987). While not all of the new ideas, patterns of explanation, and findings were accepted and incorporated into the thinking of evolutionists during the decade of the 1980s, an unusually large number were absorbed.

The transition in evolutionary understanding has occurred simultaneously, but I believe entirely independently, with a rapid increase in concern among biologists for the rate of loss of biological diversity. Management strategies to reduce the rate of extinction and the frequency of displacement of native species by exotics ought to be consistent with evolutionary theory and its implications for ecosystem structure. The consistency ought to be with respect to both the reasonableness of the objectives and the processes of management. In fact, while it is now clear that traditional management strategies for biological reserves are irrational, what is rational is unclear

(Reed F. Noss, "Can We Maintain Biological and Ecological Integrity?," 1990; Walter E. Westman, "Park Management of Exotic Species: Problems and Issues," 1990; and Bruce E. Coblentz, "Exotic Organisms: A Dilemma for Conservation Biology," 1990). Complex understandings do not lead to simple management rules.

There are specific examples of how evolutionary theory can be more rigorously applied to questions in the social sciences. Richard R. Nelson and Sidney G. Winter, going beyond earlier arguments of economists that markets select for profit maximization whether or not entrepreneurs are consciously optimizing, elaborated an evolutionary theory of how organizations learn (*An Evolutionary Theory of Economic Change*, 1982). Whether and how cultures might evolve toward increased fitness with their natural environments was explored by William Durham ("The Adaptive Significance of Cultural Behavior," 1976). During the 1980s, Durham assembled and synthesized theory, hypotheses, and evidence for the coevolution of genes and culture to explain human differences (*Coevolution: Genes, Culture, and Human Diversity*, 1991). While Durham acknowledges that biologists are beginning to think of evolutionary processes above the genetic level of individuals, he limits his own analyses to the coevolution between culture and the survival and dominance of genetic traits.

While progressive evolutionists abound, reactionary applications of Darwin's thought to the social world are still better known. Social darwinism is associated with the justifications of William Graham Sumner and others for *laissez-faire* and the superiority of the super rich and the justifications of Karl Pearson for colonialism (reviewed by John C. Greene, *Science, Ideology, and World View*, 1981, and Robert J. Richards, *Darwin and the Emergence of Evolutionary Theories of Mind and Behavior*, 1987). With morally reprehensible things that succeeded being "right" because they fit, right-wing social darwinism appropriately fell into scholarly disrepute. Thus, as the sociobiology debate also clearly documents (Arthur L. Caplan, *The Sociobiology Debate*, 1978), evolutionary thought applied to social systems has resulted in conflicts with our dominant world view – in how knowing, social organization, and values determine appropriate action – far more than in disagreements over understandings of process.

CHAPTER 9

I never expected my pursuit of development as coevolution to lead me to formalize an alternative construction of the cosmos. It ultimately proved necessary, however, when I reached the logical ends of the coevolutionary pattern of thinking. I found it impossible to share my findings with the vast majority of people unconsciously rooted in modern cosmology. Magoroh Maruyama pursued systems explanations to a variety of phenomena and discovered the same difficulty. This led him to identify alternative patterns of reasoning to which people ascribe, to ascertain the patterns' respective cosmologies, and to explore the difficulties of crossing between them ("Mindscapes and Science Theories," 1980). He argues that there are basically four causal metatypes in how people think:

1 *Nonreciprocal causal models*, in which causal relations may be either probabilistic or deterministic, but there are no causal loops.
2 *Independent-event models*, in which the most probable states of the universe or of an isolated system are states of random distribution of independent events, each having its own probability; nonindependent relations and nonrandom structures exist, but are less probable, tending to decay into more random, unstructured, homogeneous states.

3 *Homeostatic causal-loop models*, in which causal relations may be probabilistic or deterministic and may form loops; structures and patterns of heterogeneity are maintained by homeostatic causal loops.

4 *Morphogenetic causal-loop models*, in which probabilistic or deterministic causal loops can increase heterogeneity, generate patterns of mutually beneficial relations among heterogeneous elements, and raise the level of sophistication of the system.

Maruyama contends that people, even those trained as scientists, think predominantly in one of these four ways. Scientific models also fall into these four categories. Most people tend to use the first and second models of explanation. The third model includes the Newtonian mechanics adopted by neoclassical economics, drawn upon in some ecological explanations (Sharon E. Kingsland, *Modeling Nature*, 1985), and used generally in equilibrium models of systems. While this third understanding of causality exists in the public consciousness through popularizations of how economic, and to a lesser extent ecological, systems are thought to function, relatively few people regularly incorporate this model of causality in their own explanations of phenomena.

Coevolution occurs in the context of systemic relationships within both social and environmental systems. Thus ecosystemic thinking, as part of Maruyama's third causal metatype, is a critical step toward comprehending a coevolutionary model of development. This step is closely related with diverse attempts to develop a "human ecology," discussed further in the bibliographic essay to Chapter 8. My coevolutionary paradigm of development, however, is also clearly in Maruyama's fourth causal type in that it relies on morphogenetic causal loops. Maruyama argues that fourth causal metatype reasoning is both quite new and quite rare. He is perhaps correct with respect to both Western science and popular modern discourse, but Maruyama also acknowledges that traditional peoples seem to think in morphogenetic causal-loops. Alfred Whitehead and other philosophers and several psychologists in the late nineteenth and early twentieth centuries developed a critique of the Western world view under the general notion of "process philosophy." They argued that the Western world view had put too much emphasis on how things are, or at best how they became, and too little on how they are becoming (Milic Capek "Change," 1967).

The existence of creation stories in many cultures suggests that this fourth level of causality has not been especially rare in other times. The mix of spiritual and material in Western organic understandings of process prior to Newton also fit the fourth causal metatype better than the other three (Carolyn Merchant, *The Death of Nature*, 1980; Morris Berman, *The Reenchantment of the World*, 1981). Maruyama also ponders to what extent the dominance of current modes of explanation are cultural and gives examples of non-Westernized peoples who are fourth causal metatype.

In Chapter 6, I argued that the dominant epistemological and metaphysical assumptions of Western science that became institutionalized in Western culture during the late nineteenth and early twentieth centuries support the first three but do not admit the fourth. Morphogenetic causal-loop models do not facilitate prediction and control of the future, the determination of cause, or the allocation of responsibility. These are so critical to modernity that perhaps there is no point in even distinguishing between causal mindsets and culture.

And yet evolutionary thinking was clearly a part of Western thinking well before Darwin imprinted it with the idea of selection and it retains a recognized if troubled and troubling status within Western science today. In this sense, Maruyama's fourth causal metatype is neither especially new nor rare even in the West. Maruyama confronts this contradiction by arguing that even those people who seem to be able to "rise" to higher order causal explanations have a tendency to regress to lower levels. We strain to the higher levels, but we find ourselves frequently using lower level explanations. This dichotomy may be because we ourselves are more comfortable with the lower ones or because we are trying to communicate our ideas to a broad audience. This perhaps helps explain, for example, why evolution is still most frequently thought of as a process of species better fitting a fixed physical environment even though evolutionists have long known that other species are the predominant factors in each species environment. This portrayal reduces evolution to a nonreciprocal explanation of how species change with an end point, an explanation that a larger populace can understand and with which even the more scientifically trained are apparently more comfortable. Economist Herbert Simon, for example, elaborated on selection and rationality in decision-making, writing eloquently within a framework of directional evolution for 33 pages before he acknowledged his awareness of the implications of coevolution for his argument (*Reason in Human Affairs*, 1983: 37–74). As already argued in Bibliographic Essay 7, evolutionary thinking in the social science has had a rich and unusually difficult history. Again, our discomfort with fourth causal metatypes is quite likely due to the ways this mode of explanation conflicts with the modern belief that science allows prediction and control.

Hazel Henderson has also written extensively for lay audiences on paradigm shifts in the process of critiquing current social structures (*Creating Alternative Futures: The End of Economics*, 1978; *The Politics of the Solar Age: Alternatives to Economics*, 1981; and *Paradigms in Progress: Life Beyond Economics*, 1991). While Henderson presents intriguing ideas, her syntheses still reflect a drive for monistic coherence which betrays the diversity of our new understanding.

A most interesting but very difficult treatise has been written by Niklas Luhmann (*Ecological Communication*, 1989) based on concepts developed by Jurgen Habermas (*The Theory of Communicative Action*, 1984 and 1987). Luhmann envisages social systems and ecological systems in terms of the dynamics resulting from the signals, or communications, sent between their components. Environmental problems result when communication in the social system does not match that of the environmental system due to inadequate language and understanding that restricts perception and action and due to inappropriate timing. While both ecological and social systems are autopoetic, in that they recreate themselves through feedback loops, they also evolve or create new structures, in part due to their mismatch. Luhmann's representation of our cosmos complements this book in many ways.

Among the evolutionary social scientists described above, Luhmann is the only one whose cosmology and epistemology has both clearly and explicitly gone beyond modern constructions. Gregory Bateson (*Mind and Nature: A Necessary Unity*, 1979) and Konrad Lorenz (*Behind the Mirror: A Search for a Natural History of Human Knowledge*, 1977) also have explored the cosmological and epistemological implications of a coevolving world which includes minds. Most anthropologists, economists, and historians, however, have simply invoked the concept of evolution without attempting to develop a theory of the structures and processes of social evolution, let alone elaborating evolutionary cosmologies and epistemologies. The contradictions that result from pursuing evolutionary explanations of process with conventional understandings of methodology are well illustrated by Robert Boyd and Peter J. Richerson (*Culture and the Evolutionary Process*, 1985). Lee Freese has pursued the idea of ecological and social system evolution as well. His perspective, as a sociologist, adds a hierarchical structure between ecological and social systems that is absent in my own presentation while he argues how changes in resource availability set off autocatalytic, cumulative, and irreversible, i.e. evolutionary,

226

changes in social systems, whereas I argue that changes in knowledge, values, organization, and technology have parallel effects ("Evolution and Sociogenesis," 1988).

What we now understand as scientific rigor coevolved with lower level causal metatype reasoning on the relatively more durable bits of reality. Atoms and molecules reproduce their structures, forever for all we know, as do individuals among species, for periods of ten to a thousand generations. At this level the number of things to empirically verify is relatively limited and the rewards for doing so are high. But these relatively more durable bits of reality can organize in a large variety of ways, especially as people enter the analysis and their understanding, values, ways of organizing, and technologies become part of the patchwork quilt of evolving reality. These components reproduce their structures to some extent, but it is also helpful to think of them as changing through morphogenetic causal loop processes. Empiricism may still document and complement morphogenetic causal loop analysis, but with everything contextual across time and space, the number of things to empirically verify increases as dramatically as the rewards to doing so diminish. At the same time, the challenges of interpreting the broader implications of higher level causal models are substantial and rewarding.

Stephen J. Gould has provided us with a most accessible and entertaining challenge to universalism (*Wonderful Life: The Burgess Shale and the Nature of History*, 1989). Gould documents how paleontologists tried to fit the fossil evidence of past species into an evolutionary history which is progressive, from primitive to higher forms. The early twentieth-century classifications of fossils discovered in the Burgess shale in western Canada were "imagined" to fit existing phyla. More detailed work during the 1970s, however, showed that these classifications reflected the scientists' prior beliefs of paleontologists and the scientific community at large much better than the fossils themselves. The current interpretation is that there were more phyla in earlier times, some quite well elaborated, which simply no longer exist. For species in these phyla, evolution was by no means progressive. Most importantly, the broad pattern of species now visible is not universal. The progressive beliefs of modernity influenced paleontology, and the social dynamics of the discipline isolated those individuals who offered nonprogressive explanations. Gould stresses how the new interpretation of the Burgess Shale teaches us that we falsely saw universals in a history which is highly contingent. In this sense, his analysis is among the best within an emerging philosophy of science known as hermeneutics, or interpretative theory, wherein what we learn about ourselves as we study is as important as what we learn about the subject matter we study.

Hermeneutics stresses both the cultural contextuality and historical contingencies of events and the importance of the culture of the observer. At a particular point in history or from within a particular culture, explanation and truth may conform to a relatively few number of principles. From within a culture, universalism and objectivism may seem reasonable, except that principles change over time. For analyses of other times and of other cultures, the observer must be sensitive to both his or her own particular historical and cultural circumstances and that of the people being analyzed. At the same time, hermeneutic philosophers argue that what is important in interpretation is what is learned through the dialectic or exchange between the "interpreter" from his or her cultural position and the "interpreted" that results in new understandings for the interpreter and of the interpreted. The goal of interpretation is not some "objective" truth but learning about oneself in relation to other peoples and things (Robert Hollinger, (ed.), *Hermeneutics and Praxis*, 1985; Paul Rabinow and William M. Sullivan, (eds), *Interpretive Social*

Science, 1979; Richard J. Rorty, *Contingency, Irony, and Solidarity*, 1989; and Renato Rosaldo, *Culture and Truth*, 1989).

Interpretative theory developed within the realm of social, especially cross cultural, thought. Only a very hardened few who work across cultures do not discover that they have learned at least as much about themselves as about the culture they are studying. Similar self-realizations occur when we work across disciplinary cultures or between academe and an inner city community or a rural agricultural community. The emphasis of interpretive theory on learning about both the observed and the observer is also remarkably compatible with the scientific philosophy of many field biologists, especially those in the conservation biology movement. Ecologists who study tropical rainforests are rarely experts on agricultural systems, for example, but what they learn from forest ecosystems leads them to deep insights about our relation to nature and her response, insights which are different from those we acquire working in agriculture itself. "Deep ecologists," who argue that other species have a right to live, may also find hermeneutics a compatible philosophy in its acknowledgment of the legitimacy of the observed (Arne Naess, "Intrinsic Value: Will the Defenders of Nature Please Rise," 1983).

Biologists are also emerging from Newton's shadow and exploring their cosmological and epistemological underpinnings. Well-established biologists such as Ernst Mayr have become more reflective on the nature of biological knowledge, arguing for contingency and contextuality in particular (*The Growth of Biological Thought*, 1982). Marjorie Grene nicely summarizes the issues arising between the biologist's cosmology and epistemology compared to that of the eighteenth- and nineteenth-century physicist, emphasizing the importance of the researcher's prior perceptions and orientation, the history of events, the role of values in science, the social nature of science, and scientific pluralism ("Perception, Interpretation, and the Sciences: Toward a New Philosophy of Science," 1985). Gunther Stent connects hermeneutic philosophy and the practice of biological research ("Hermeneutics and the Analysis of Complex Biological Systems," 1985). The collection of philosophical essays in which Grene's and Stent's treatises appear has other articles which complement the theme of this essay (Depew and Weber, *Evolution at the Crossroads: The New Biology and the New Philosophy of Science*, 1985).

Hermeneutics is conceptually pluralistic in that it acknowledges that other cultures create their own social environments on their own belief systems. My own interest in conceptual pluralism certainly extends to this cross cultural, cosmos building, level. For the coevolutionary future I envision, learning across the cultural patches will be a hermeneutic process. At the same time, conceptual pluralism makes a lot of sense from within modern culture. Alternative patterns of thinking are different. Words have meaning within patterns of thinking, and what appear to be the same words will have different meanings in different patterns because they connect differently to other things (W. V. O. Quine, *From the Logical Point of View*, 1961; C. F. Presley, "Willard Van Orman Quine", 1967). Paradigms cannot be synthesized without losing the details and meaning of the separate paradigms. The richness of our knowledge can only be comprehended by knowing multiple paradigms. And, as Paul Feyerabend has so insistently made clear, if conceptual patterns of thinking are inherently different, then none can be better than another (*Against Method*, 1974). I have argued that the depth of our environmental crisis can only be comprehended, even solely from within Western culture, from multiple perspectives (Norgaard, "The Case for Methodological Pluralism," 1989).

Feminist scientists, philosophers, and writers are questioning the nature of Western science, the dominance of men in science, and the authoritative use of particular forms of science in modern societies (Carolyn Merchant, *The Death of*

Nature, 1980). While feminists first addressed the lack of women in science, they soon learned that the problem is systemic, that Western science, technology, and development are linked masculine projects. Along the way, feminist writers on science frequently address how atomism, mechanism, universalism, and monism contribute to beliefs in the possibilities for prediction and control. Evelyn Fox Keller has been especially effective at analyzing male, female, and science as interactive social constructions (*Reflections on Gender and Science*, 1985). Keller pleads for a science which becomes gender free science through the transformation of the very categories of male and female and thereby a transformation of many of the myths of good and bad science, a parallel transformation in our concepts of mind and nature, and an expansion of research strategies. Sandra Harding argues that science as presently constructed puts the cart before the horse, that the objectives of knowledge must be addressed ahead of and along with the pursuit thereof. Though their reformulations start in different places, each seeks to redress through a new coevolution the imbalance in what has been deemed worthy of study, how science works, and how science and men have reinforced each others status.

All areas of thought are contributing to our rethinking of the nature of modern science and its relationship to the modern conception of progress. Stephen Toulmin's collection of essays (*The Return to Cosmology: Postmodern Science and the Theology of Nature*, 1982) presents a fascinating exploration of the interplay between science, constructions of the cosmos, and images of the future. He argues in the last and most recent essay that the rise of biological thinking and environmental awareness is bringing both people and religion back into our conception of science. Toulmin (*Cosmopolis: The Hidden Agenda of Modernity*, 1990) provides an exceptional reanalysis of modernity's initiation in the sixteenth and seventeenth centuries and develops the implications of his argument nicely in his concluding chapters.

Theologians have emphasized individual philosophy over social and natural philosophy since the separation of church and state. Gerald J. Galgan (*The Logic of Modernity*, 1982), however, provides a detailed analysis of how Christian views that were critical to the Western concept of modernization eroded over time and left modernization without direction. A few theologians are also actively searching for a new social and natural philosophy. Thomas Berry is among the most outspoken theologians writing on our image of the future (*The Dream of the Earth*, 1988 and Lonergan and Richards *Thomas Berry and the New Cosmology*, 1987). His writings extend the scientific optimism and respect for nature of Pierre Teilhard de Chardin (see his *The Future of Man*, 1964) by incorporating new understandings of the nature of systems from physics and biology, by extending respect to other cultural values and ways of knowing, and by formulating a religious response to our environmental crisis.

CHAPTER 10

This will be an extremely short bibliographic note, not because of the paucity of material written on the Amazon, but because of an excess. To a large extent, the chapter stems from my direct experiences while working for the Ford Foundation, while acting as a consultant to the World Bank, and while on numerous excursions I made on my own into the area. Lastly, I have read so many senior theses over the past decade on the trials and tribulations of development in the Amazon that I have become convinced, falsely on the basis of a select sample, that anyone can access this literature and learn from it on their own.

For those who would like a few tips to get started, however, I recommend the following. Readily available references include Emilio F. Moran (*Developing the Amazon*, 1981), Stephen G. Bunker (*Underdeveloping the Amazon*, 1985), and Susanna Hecht and Alexander Coburn (*Fate of the Forest: Developers, Destroyers, and Defenders of the Amazon*, 1989). My own argument on the possibilities for coevolutionary development in the Amazon, extensively documented, is available in the academic literature ("Sociosystem and Ecosystem Coevolution in the Amazon," 1981).

CHAPTER 11

The critique of liberal individualism elaborated in Chapter 11 developed out of my own questioning of economics and periodic forays into the rich literature on social philosophy.

It is perhaps best to start with a recent treatise which reportrays the early development of modern social philosophy. Stephen Toulmin (*Cosmopolis: the Hidden Agenda of Modernity*, 1990) argues that there were two renaissances. The first rebirth of Western civilization, he argues, occurred in the sixteenth century and was a full, humanistic flowering of scientific, social and moral thought. Toulmin effectively maintains that this renaissance occurred before Protestantism became a political threat to the Catholic-dominated social order of Europe. The human tragedy and social chaos during the Thirty Years' War (1618–48) between shifting alliances of nobles and their Catholic and Protestant communities, however, sent intellectuals in search of new foundations for social organization. European history provides good reasons to be wary of cultural differences, much as do the shifting coalitions and cultural violence in the Mideast today. Toulmin's second renaissance was distinguished from the first by the deliberate use of philosophical strategies to build a rational basis for social order, strategies which allowed philosophers to avoid becoming caught up in the cultural conflict raging between Catholics and Protestants. In the midst of unstable allegiances, political repression, and the brutality of war, arguments for social order were best systematically reasoned ahistorically, starting with supposedly universal characteristics of individuals. The purity of Galileo's and Newton's atomistic-mechanistic reasoning provided hope for analogous models of a natural social order. The coincidence of these factors seem to explain why Hobbes and Locke construct theories of political order from the universal motives and rational behavior of individuals starting from "a state of nature."

Toulmin's explanation is exactly contrary to the conventional history of the rise of modern social philosophy which, true to progressive visions run backwards, attributed the seventeenth century transition in thought to an outbreak of better times and a flowering of intellectual freedom. On the contrary, it is probably better understood as a quest for abstract logical certainty in a period of real social chaos. Eventually, of course, the quest for certain, universal knowledge and avoidance of conditional, contextual arguments in social philosophy facilitated the erosion of cultural diversity which stimulated the quest. The same pursuit in natural philosophy analogously encouraged the misapplication of technologies across social and ecological systems. As we rethink the consequences of Western philosophy and science, Toulmin provides considerable insight by rooting it in cultural war and intellectual repression rather than in a flowering of civilization and scholarly freedom.

Among other important results to be highlighted in Chapter 11, the particular twists taken in Western philosophy during the seventeenth century left the dominant schools of social thought to this day sharing a common perspective on groups, communities, and cultures. There is nearly a consensus that individuals should determine the nature of groups. Any tendencies of groups to determine the nature of individuals is seen as a restriction on individual freedom, viewed as evidence that the individuals in the groups are irrational and out of step with progress, or, if the group is sufficiently "foreign," portrayed as a cultural curiosity. Individual liberalism operating within the rules of Western rationality continues to be justified, and with good reason given the prominence of both fascism and ethnocide in the twentieth century, as better than tribalism (Karl Popper, *The Open Society and Its Enemies*, 1966).

Milton Friedman's *Capitalism and Freedom* (1962) is already a classic example of liberal individualist argumentation. His arguments for the advantages of increasing the freedom of choice through the provision of publicly funded vouchers for use by parents to send their children to private schools of their choice, for example, have become a part of American conventional wisdom in merely three decades. Economists reach their general conclusions by basing every argument from the perspective of hypothetical individuals, ignoring the role of culture and class differences (Gary Becker, *The Economic Approach to Human Behavior*, 1976; Richard A. Posner, *The Economics of Justice*, 1981; Morris Silver, *Foundations of Economic Justice*, 1989). A whole realm of economists who think of themselves as public choice theorists in fact argue that collective action of any kind is irrational. Based on individualist rationality, those who claim to be working for the public good are really only seeking a better position for themselves (Geoffrey Brennan and James M. Buchanan, *The Reason of Rules: Constitutional Political Economy*, 1985; James M. Buchanan, *Liberty, Market, and State: Political Economy in the 1980s*, 1985 and *The Economics and Ethics of Constitutional Order*, 1991). Participating in democratic governance of groups is irrational since the probability that one's vote will change the outcome is rarely worth the time lost going to the polls. Economics, with its individualist rationality which denies the rationality of participating as a member of a group, is clearly the academic haven of liberal individualism. Dan Usher, speaking to the neoconservatives through their own neoclassical economics language, at least reverses the case, arguing for democracy and making the connections between how economies work and the maintenance of sufficient equity for democracy to work (*The Economic Prerequisite to Democracy*, 1981).

Interest in economic globalization increased rapidly during the 1990s as developing nations struggled to repay their debts and as the trade negotiations under the General Agreement on Tariffs and Trade (GATT) and the North American Free Trade Agreement (NAFTA) were coming to a head. Many of the critiques of the new global capitalism came through and expanded the discourse on sustainable development (Samir Amin, *Empire of Chaos*, 1992; John Cavanagh, John Gershman, Karen Baker, and Gretchen Helmke, *Trading Freedom: How Free Trade Affects Our Lives, Work, and Environment*, 1992; Jim MacNeill, Pieter Winsemius, and Taizo Yakushiji, *Beyond Interdependence: The Meshing of the World's Economy and the Earth's Ecology*, 1991; Arjun Makhijani, *From Global Capitalism to Economic Justice: An Inquiry into the Elimination of Systemic Poverty, Violence, and Environmental Destruction in the World Economy*, 1992; Chakravarthi Raghavan, *Recolonization: GATT, the Uruguay Round, and the Third World*, 1990). The environmental attack on free trade worried the World Bank sufficiently to counterattack (Patrick Low (ed.), *International Trade and the Environment*, 1992).

By my reading, however, the bulk of the exchange fails to address why more trade on a larger scale is more of a problem than a less trade on a smaller scale. My own efforts to address this along the lines argued in this chapter as a matter of how economic and ecological systems affect each other appeared in two papers ("The Rise of the Global Exchange Economy and the Loss of Biological Diversity," 1988; "Risk and Its Management in Traditional and Modern Agroecosystems," 1989).

Modern liberal individualism denigrates groups and denies how they affect individuals in a variety of ways:

1 people learn, both individually and collectively, through sharing their observations and lines of reasoning;
2 tastes or preferences – understandings about what is perceived as better and not – are acquired through participation in group discourse;
3 people enjoy social interaction *per se*;
4 these natural tendencies can be enhanced into an understanding of civic life which rewards virtuous behavior, improving life for all; and
5 a conscious civic life can be a morally higher form of existence, bringing out the best of what makes humans an exceptional species.

These ideas are familiar because they were never totally lost from Western thought. William M. Sullivan (*Reconstructing Public Philosophy*, 1986) documents how the American political debate at the transition from the eighteenth to the nineteenth century between Thomas Jefferson, on one side, and Alexander Hamilton, James Monroe, and John Jay, on the other, can be read as an argument over how to promote civic virtue over individual greed. Alexis de Tocqueville's analysis of America in the early nineteenth century noted the strengths of American communitarian behavior while fearing that this asset would eventually be lost. Max Weber, certainly one of the most insightful social scientists, characterized modern societies as being driven by a Western rationality that is apart from and overrides both bonds and differences rooted in local communal, cultural, and religious groupings. Weber "scientifically" elaborated, while he personally bemoaned, the implications of this characteristic of modernity. Appeals to civic virtue are still a part of political rhetoric, but they are received cynically by most Western social thinkers. These ideas and the validity they lend to groups, communities, and cultures have had little influence on Western social theory, analysis, or institutional design.

There is now, however, an identifiable resurgence of social philosophy and analysis working with precisely these concepts. Alasdair MacIntyre (*After Virtue*, 1981 and *Whose Justice, Which Rationality*, 1988) argues that concepts of justice are intertwined with how we reason and that both are cultural and historical artifacts. He argues furthermore that the moral quandaries of modern societies, the inability to agree upon moral and practical rationalities, are a product of having tried to separate rationality and justice from culture. MacIntyre's reasoning is exactly contrary to dominant modern liberal individualism. Robert N. Bellah heads a team including William Sullivan that has been undertaking a critical reportrayal and reconstruction of American concepts of self and community (*Habits of the Heart: Individualism and Commitment in American Life*, 1985; *The Good Society*, 1991). Alan Wolfe (*Whose Keeper?: Social Science and Moral Obligation*, 1989) has pondered the diminution of the social sciences to analyses of individual gratification in an exceptional comparative analysis of how people in the United States and Scandinavia actually do care about each other, the social institutions they have constructed, and the social consequences of alternative forms of caring. Amitai Etzioni (*The Moral Dimension: Toward a New Economics*, 1988) argues for rebridging economic and moral philosophy, returning to the issues of classical economics that were rooted in moral philosophy. Christopher Lasch (*The True and Only Heaven: Progress and Its Critiques*, 1991) critiques the dominant view of individualism in a historical analysis of the cultural "conservativism" of working people, arguing that people always have been interested in a sense of community. By Lasch's analysis, liberal, progressive, materialist interpreters of laborers and their interests have neither properly recognized how cooperative movements among workers differed from union efforts nor understood why unionization ultimately had so little impact. Jane J. Mansbridge (*Beyond Self Interest*, 1990) has assembled an excellent set of articles which question the tenet of individualism from the perspectives of each of the social sciences. Barry Schwartz (*The Battle for Human Nature: Science, Morality, and Modern Life*, 1986) has written a critique of individualism in economic ideology and the effects of this ideology on modern societies. Economist Herman Daly and theologian John B. Cobb (*For the Common Good: Redirecting the Economy Toward Community, the Environment, and a Sustainable Future*, 1989) argue that economic life must be understood as more than individual gratification to sustain the environmental systems on which we depend and to recreate the communities which can give new meaning to life.

The connection between sustaining the environment and this new critique of individualism and interest in community may be weak. And yet I think a possible way to replace global materialism and the gridlock of modern politics, both rooted in individualism, is through a new interest in communities. Perhaps this link, as weak as it is, is our best way out. Through communities of diverse types we can generate fresh values and new respect for working problems out together, at least at the community level. Rethinking modern social history and the importance and nature of communities as being more than the sum of materially greedy individuals should complement an understanding of global reculturization and community building. This new interest in the underpinnings of Western social philosophy, policy, and analysis may play a very significant role in reframing modern politics and social order and thereby how we interact with our envirnoment.

Many of the issues addressed in this chapter also arise in a tantalizing dialogue between Murray Bookchin and Dave Foreman (Steve Chase (ed.), *Defending the Earth*, 1991). Murray Bookchin, has argued for social orders like ecological orders, without hierarchy, to eliminate the exploitation of people – especially women, other cultures and other races – as well as nature (*The Ecology of Freedom*, 1982, *Remaking Society: Pathways to a Green Future*, 1990). Dave Foreman cofounded Earth First, is an environmental activist, and writes on deep ecology (*Confessions of an Eco-Warrior*, 1991). Their dialogue nicely explores and begins to constructively bridge the dilemmas between radical environmental and libertarian left thought.

A few readers will have noted how the section of the chapter on the relations between patches in the coevolving quilt parallel the environmental histories referenced in the bibliographic notes to Chapter 4. In this chapter I address the exchange of ideas rather than genetic material, but like the studies referenced earlier, the theme is that modernization has entailed too much exchange. In each case, homogenization rather than an enrichment of coevolutionary processes has occurred, leaving us with the risks of having "all of our eggs in one basket." J. A. Drake *et al.* provide an overview of the issues of introductions from a biological perspective ("Biological Invasions: A Global Perspective," 1989; see also Bruce E. Coblentz, "Exotic Organisms: A Dilemma for Conservation Biology," 1990).

A digression on the evolution of words

As history unfolds, words evolve new meanings, incorporating changes in concepts and linking to other new developments, such that from century to century they can have entirely new meanings. The evolutionary patterns of words parallel the changes of the times and both must be understood together. A threshold occurred in our realization of the nature of words when Wittgenstein, after long pursuing the idea that words had to have strict definitions, realized that words must be fuzzy. For Wittgenstein and philosophers since, this finding has meant that metaphysics could never be eliminated from the philosophy of political discourse (elaborated upon in Chapter 8 of Thomas A. Spragens, Jr. *The Irony of Liberal Reason*, 1981). Since Wittgenstein changed his own course and put a noticeable kink in the flow of philosophic thought, many have linked rhetoric to thought and then to social order. For example, the dichotomy between the humanities and the sciences, the idea that one was laden with values, the other objective, reinforced the idea of positivism and technocratic social structure. The association of values with the word humanities but not the word science has slowly been meeting its demise during the latter half of the twentieth century. This transition has been as difficult for the humanities as for the sciences (Wayne C. Booth, *Critical Understanding*, 1979). In an interesting synthesis of humanist and scientific thinking, Manfred Stanley (*The Technological Conscience*, 1978) argues that technology's tyranny over our lives is rooted in the words we use and the false consciousness we have developed more than in our physical dependence on modern technologies.

My awareness of the importance of the evolution of words in social philosophy and political discourse grows out of my reading of Albert Hirschman (*Exit, Voice, and Loyalty*, 1970 and *The Passions and the Interests*, 1977; and Samuel Bowles and Herbert Gintis (*Democracy and Capitalism*, 1986). They provide fascinating histories of the evolution of the use of key words – democracy, property, markets, rights, etc. – in the Western political discourse, how they changed and changed history, and how they might change again. The idea of rights, for example, has been used by land owners, commercial interests, capitalists, laborers, minorities, and feminists over time in different ways to accomplish different goals. The term acquired new meanings which inevitably conflicted with old meanings at each stage of its evolution. And the term is still evolving, is still undefined, and still has conflicting meanings.

The rise and fall of metaphors over time is at least as important to our changing political discourse as the evolution of particular terms. George Lakoff and Mark Johnson (*Metaphors We Live By*, 1980) make a strong case that they are both critical to understanding and the basis for creating new insights. Certainly Adam Smith's "invisible hand" is one of the greatest metaphors ever created. This metaphor may only invoke the sense of divine guidance to a few people today. In the nineteenth century, however, when Providence was frequently invoked and while scientific reasoning was the vanguard of progress, the "invisible hand" was a subtle way of appealing to the best of both. Donald N. McCloskey (*The Rhetoric of Economics*, 1985) provides numerous examples of rhetorical devices in a discipline which thinks of itself as coldly scientific.

The idea of development is evolving rapidly at the end of the twentieth century. It is changing as our understanding of environmental phenomena such as global climate change become better understood, as Third World peoples put their own imprint on the term, and as cultures repressed by westernization recapture their own sense of destiny. While it is challenging to try to define what development means today, the term will continue to evolve before any definitions we might decide are most appropriate today will see much use. In this book, I am emphasizing new ways of thinking about the changes that are taking place. The meaning of words like development will coevolve with the influence of these new understandings and with revisions in the idea of progress.

CHAPTER 12

Chapter 12 is simultaneously (a) a critique of processes associated with bureaucratic social order, and (b) a recommendation for reform based on knowing as a social process best facilitated by a return to broad democratic ideals. This combination, consistent with current experiments at mixing democracy and technical authority, is justified through the characterization of knowledge elaborated throughout this book. I argue that modern bureaucratic social organization has structurally and procedurally coevolved with atomism, mechanism, monism, and objectivism. This coevolution, I further argue, is maladaptive over the long term for dealing with the changing complexities of coevolving social and ecological systems. Paralleling this proposition, I also argue that our understanding of democracy has also coevolved with beliefs in atomism and objectivism, leaving democracy as being thought of almost solely as a process of making value choices with far too little emphasis on democracy as a process of collective learning.

The conventional dualist understanding is that bureaucratic social order is rationally superior, hence best for accelerating progress through the use of science. Democracy, on the other hand, is ethically superior and still necessary for making value choices. My counter-argument, based on recent shifts in epistemological understanding, is but one in a contentious century of analyses of the tensions between rational authority and democracy. Analyses rooted in the dominant epistemological beliefs of modernity, however, maintain dualist tensions with elaborate rationalizations as to why they must exist. Acknowledging that knowing is a social process which can be strengthened by democratic ideals provides opportunities for new resolutions.

As critique, my analysis portrays a healthy disrespect for centralized authority and its impact on individuals and communities, an attitude and set of concerns that have been expressed by many others. Henry Jacoby (*The Bureaucratization of the World*, 1973) provides one of the more brilliantly enraged analyses, arguing that the greater technological and geographic scales and complexities of human activities associated with modernization inevitably require a bureaucratic social order which stifles the individual. Though "necessary," at the same time he depicts bureaucracy as a spreading and deepening disease that steadily reduces individuality, restricts opportunities to make free choices, and diminishes the sense of self which comes with having been able to take responsibility for one's actions.

Disaffection with bureaucracy is not limited to academics who merely dream of a better world. Leon Trotsky, a key leader of the October Revolution in Russia, wrote a damning critique of how the high ideals, jubilation, and empowerment of a grass-roots-led revolution was so quickly squashed by the authoritarian efficacy rationalized as necessary by Stalin and the builders of scientific socialism (*The Revolution Betrayed: What is the Soviet Union and Where is it Going?*, 1937). Nearly five decades later, Maria Hirszowicz (*The Bureaucratic Leviathan: A Study in the Sociology of Communism*, 1980) poignantly documents how the contradictions of a bureaucratic order that dominated nearly every aspect of life was rationalized by science and belief in the march of progress toward the perfectibility of human goodness.

Capitalist development also presumed a strong role for bureaucracy. Development planning has consistently stressed the adequacy of bureaucratic development to support economic development (Joseph La Palombara (ed.), *Bureaucracy and Political Development*, 1963). In the midst of economic restructuring to promote market driven development during the 1980s, northern concern with the adequacy of bureaucratic development emphasized environmental regulations and enforcement. Guillermo A. O'Donnell (*Modernization and Bureaucratic-Authoritarianism: Studies in South American Politics*, 1973) describes the elusiveness of freedom to the once colonialized people of the South. The modern bureaucratic institutions established to drive development are controlled, more subtly than the historic control through class politics, by a new elite.

The concerns with bureaucracy portrayed by the left and the right, East and West, North and South are so widely felt and frequently expressed that all of social literature must address this theme to some extent. The most famous sociologist, Max Weber of Germany, advocated bureaucratic social order because it was clearly more rational than traditional social orders (*The Theory of Social and Economic Organization*, 1947 translation). Writing as early as the end of the nineteenth century, however, Weber also had to address his own fears, shared by scholars and laypeople alike, that modern bureaucracies rob people of their human dignity. Most of Weber's writings preceded the work of F. W. Taylor, who took the idea of scientific management to its logical extreme (*The Principles of Scientific Management*, 1911). Taylor and his followers clocked how long people took to accomplish different tasks, established standards, and showed how tasks could be optimally organized between workers. "Taylorism" was both much admired for being the scientific way of doing things and rightly critiqued for treating people like cogs in a giant people-machine. This image of science applied to the organization of people still drives the fears of Western and westernized peoples.

William T. Gormley, Jr. (*Taming the Bureaucracy: Muscles, Prayers, and Other Strategies*, 1989) presents, in my judgment, the best overview of the history of the tension between rational and democratic authority in the United States and the variety of attempts to control and direct bureaucratic power. Bengt Abrahamsson (*Bureaucracy or Participation: The Logic of Organization*, 1977) argues from a marxist perspective that bureaucracies are established to serve the interests of particular groups or classes, not the public, and that the problem is that even these special interests are not able to control bureaucracies. Judith E. Gruber (*Controlling Bureaucracies: Dilemmas in Democratic Governance*, 1987) provides a superior theoretical analysis of how various ways of controlling bureaucracies necessarily have undesirable or unexpected costs. John P. Burke (*Bureaucratic Responsibility*, 1986) presents an exceptional analysis of the legal and moral obligations that should guide administrators as they confront the contradictions between rational authority and democratic control. Many social scientists, however, accept bureaucracy and its ailments as inevitable and have grown so tired of critiques that they have become defensive (Charles T. Goodsell, *The Case for Bureaucracy*, 1983; Herbert Kaufman, "Fear of Bureaucracy: A Raging Pandemic," 1981).

The opening quote to Chapter 12 by Frank Knight ("Statics and Dynamics: Some Queries regarding the Mechanical Analogy in Economics," 1930) provides a simple entree to thinking systematically about social organization. Knight is one of several great economists to address matters of social organization beyond markets. Ronald Coase ("The Nature of the Firm," 1937) argued that firms exist when it is cheaper for people to enter into long term agreements to work together than to be brought together by repeatedly offering their services on the market. He introduced the term "transactions costs" which consist of the information, contractual, and enforcement costs associated with organizing people and resources through markets, the operation of a firm, or the maintenance of a bureaucracy. Herbert Simon, a Nobel laureate in economics though trained in psychology, wrote initially on the motives and decision-making strategies of bureaucrats (*Administrative Behavior*, 1947). Kenneth Boulding wrote broadly on the rise of democracy, markets, and progressive institutions relatively early in his career (*The Organizational Revolution*, 1953). William A. Niskanen, Jr. (*Bureaucracy and Representative Government*, 1971) presented an economic theory of why bureaucracies get out of control. Kenneth Arrow explored how the transactions costs of collecting and exchanging information affect organizational structure and capabilities (*The Limits of Organization*, 1974). Oliver E. Williamson (*The Economic Institutions of Capitalism*, 1985) has pursued organizational theory the furthest from an economic perspective. Though economists have stressed information in their interpretation of the division of activities between market, democratic, and bureaucratic decision-making, they have paid little attention to learning. In good Western tradition, economists have addressed the effectiveness of different forms of social organization as if information from different disciplines and from different contexts smoothly joined and that learning came through research, a separate activity, not a part of the process of fitting information together.

Some of the literature on bureaucracy acknowledges that organizations learn, typically too slowly. Organizations in this literature are portrayed as having knowledge and as being able to work toward solutions. The knowledge and decision paths are not simply a combination of those of the individuals in the organization. At the same time, the organization affects how individuals in the organization retain knowledge and patterns of reasoning and what they learn from experience (Gareth Morgan, *Images of Organization*, 1986; Peter J. Frost *et al.*, *Organizational Culture*, 1985). This literature confirms my own strong personal experiences working within the World Bank and among economists generally. Ernst B. Haas (*When Knowledge is Power: Three Models of Change in International Organizations*, 1990) provides an excellent study of international development organizations as culturally bound, yet as being able to learn incrementally or capable of forced learning in the process of confronting new interdependencies. Peter M. Haas (*Saving the Mediterranean: The Politics of International Environmental Cooperation*, 1990) presents an excellent case study of the difficulties of cooperation between governmental agencies. Both father and son develop and use the idea of epistemic communities to explain changes in environmental problem definition, cooperation, and action.

The literature on sociology of science stresses how the transition in scientific paradigms is affected by the social dynamics of disciplines and their interaction with the world beyond academe (Thomas S. Kuhn, *The Structure of Scientific Revolutions*, 1962). Jerome Ravetz has expanded on this view and emphasized the role of science in the policy process, noting that science is now big, multi-person, institutionalized science interacting with government and interest groups (*Scientific Knowledge and Its Social Problems*, 1971). More recently, Silvio Funtowicz and Jerome Ravetz have argued how the science of large scale environmental problems such as global climate change or nuclear waste disposal differs from conventional big science. Experiments cannot be run and much of the information underlying computer simulation models of macro-environmental problems can only be weakly known (*Uncertainty and Quality in Science for Policy*, 1990; "A New Scientific Methodology for Global Environmental Issues," 1991). Funtowicz and Ravetz argue that scientists cannot weigh the various uncertainties at different stages of their analyses to the satisfaction of the public and that the public must, and should, participate in the analysis.

The argument I develop in this chapter builds on my own efforts to understand how macro-environmental problems challenge the collective way we understand

(Norgaard, "Environmental Science as a Social Process," 1992), necessarily forcing us toward broader participation and the fuller use of democratic processes. While I have developed this theme on epistemological grounds, there is a substantial literature focusing on development in the South that makes the case for democratizing progress on the grounds that this would empower the poor and increase the effectiveness of project implementation. The early literature that critiqued top–down management framed largely by planners trained in the North is well argued by Robert Chambers (*Rural Development: Putting the Last First*, 1984), while diverse contributions are brought together by David C. Korten and Rudi Klaus (*People Centered Development: Contributions Toward Theory and Planning Frameworks*, 1984). Robert Chambers, Lori Ann Thrupp, and Arnold Pacey have edited a summary of experiences where farmers had participated in the design of research and development projects (*Farmer First: Farmer Innovation and Agricultural Research*, 1989). David Korten has more recently put a strong argument together for participation to alleviate poverty and attain sustainable development (*Getting to the 21st Century: Voluntary Action and the Global Agenda*, 1990).

The participatory development literature follows from the experience of Northern development experts working in Asia and Africa, and only to a lesser extent, in Latin America. On the other hand, Latin Americans themselves have a strong intellectual tradition of concern with grass roots empowerment from within their own cultural traditions. Paulo Freire has been at the center of this literature since the 1960s (*The Politics of Education: Culture, Power, and Liberation*, 1985 translation). Arturo Escobar has provided a strong historical, philosophical, and feminist addition to this literature ("Power and Visibility: The Invention and Management of Development in the Third World," 1987). Gustavo Esteva comes closest to practice ("Regenerating People's Space," 1987; "Development," 1992).

Within this milieu, interesting contradictions arise. The problem of systemic data collection over time and across regions and its transformation into information is currently undertaken within bureaucratic agencies. Agencies have the stability, interest, and resources to consistently collect and process data. At the same time, these strengths are closely associated with the culture of the agency, its disciplinary and professional patterns of thinking and its conventions and how they link most directly to particular worldly phenomena and particular private and public interests. Data are critical to the recognition of new problems and to democratic discourse with respect to their resolution, but our data are historically and institutional framed. Judith Innes presents an intriguing empirical analysis of efforts to derive and institutionalize new social indicators (*Knowledge and Public Policy: The Search for Meaningful Indicators*, 1990).

My brief summary of the changing role of economists in the policy process come from conversing with and reading Robert H. Nelson ("The Economics Profession and Public Policy," 1987), conversing with and reading Daniel W. Bromley (*Economic Interests and Institutions: The Conceptual Foundations of Public Policy*, 1989), from reading a volume edited by Joseph A. Pechman (*The Role of Economists in Government: An International Perspective*, 1989), and a quarter century of participation in the discipline.

At this point, I am quite frustrated because my ideas have evolved in the context of so many related literatures that I am not sure where I should go or when I should stop. Several books seem especially relevant, however. Murray Bookchin invokes a strong critique of central authority in favor of grass-roots empowerment, arguing that the hierarchical power structure of modern society needs to be replaced by interactive, interdependent relations between people analogous to our understanding of the interactions of species within ecosystems (*The Ecology of Freedom*, 1982). He argues, albeit with more conviction than persuasiveness, that such a social order would also interact with nature in a nondestructive fashion. What makes Bookchin interesting is that he selectively invokes progressive ideas from the left by appealing to freedom and equality but has beautiful tirades against big capitalists as well as against big technocrats in both capitalist and socialist societies. Robyn Eckersley (*Environmentalism and Political Theory: Toward an Ecocentric Approach*, 1992) accepts the social structure advocated by Bookchin and other ecosocialists but argues that a shift in world views from anthropocentrism to ecocentrism is necessary to make greater decentralization and participatory democracy work for the environment and future generations.

Rallying common traditions from left and right, Robert Bellah *et al.* close their book (*The Good Society*, 1991) with a prescriptive chapter calling for an attentive, generative, responsible, trusting, actively participatory democracy. Ann Ferguson, a feminist on the political left, appeals to democratic ideals and processes as a means to a respectful, sexually and conceptually pluralistic, society (*Sexual Democracy: Women, Oppression, and Revolution*, 1991). For the same reason I find the appeal to democracy by Samuel Bowles and Herbert Gintis exciting (*Democracy and Capitalism: Property, Community, and the Contradictions of Modern Social Thought*, 1986). Bowles and Gintis also abandon earlier visions of socialism as a form of social organization that is more scientifically rational and hence inevitable, acknowledge that capitalism continues to evolve, and then argue that capitalism's democratization should be its next evolution. Richard E. Sclove argues that technologies have as much influence on social order as any law ever passed by a legislative body and hence that the design and implementation of technologies should be democratized (*Technology and Freedom*, 1986). At a time when many recognize that the modern order has broken down, people from a variety of perspectives are finding that the ideals of democracy still provide fresh glue for building new social orders. The democratization of progress, in short, is a common theme.

The second proposition of this chapter, however, is that democracy has been reduced in modern practice to simply a method of adding up preferences through vote counting. This shrinking of its earlier, fuller meaning weakens its effectiveness when it is most needed. The proposition is well documented by the absence of reference to democratic debate and learning in the current literature on democratic theory. To be sure, treatises on democracy inevitably start with images of open democratic debate in ancient Greek city-states. The image of all being entitled to contribute and many in fact contributing to public understanding is still strong in our image of democracy. In fact, however, the democratic processes we experience in large nations with representative government have little to do with collective understanding.

On this experiential note, let me go one step further and point out that the term democracy as used politically by Presidents Reagan and Bush shrank to nothing at all. These men favored and touted democracy's emergence when it worked against socialism and ignored democracy that worked against capitalism (Samir Amin, *Empire of Chaos*, 1992). In no way do I want my appeal to democracy associated with their crass appeals or to others now so common in the mass ideological contortions of modern political communication. Nor do I want my vision tainted by neoconservative economic analyses of politics which treat people solely as selfish individuals, those who have been caught up in the tyranny of individualism (see the references mentioned in Bibliographic Essay 11).

And yet selfish individualism pervades liberal theory. Robert A. Dahl is certainly the reigning liberal academic writing on democracy (*Democracy and Its Critics*, 1989; *After the Revolution*, 1990). Dahl describes the pros and cons of democratic versus delegated decision-making, representative versus direct democracy, how the demos might best be defined for different situations, and how voting rules might best vary across circumstances, among a myriad of intricate topics. Knowledge is distinctly treated as something that is given. It may differ between people and between people and experts, lending one or the other greater efficacy if not legitimacy, but, in Dahl's analysis, democratic processes have little to do either with the sharing of knowledge or the collective creation of understanding. And no wonder, for in modern democracies, open democratic sharing and debate hardly exist.

Professor Dahl and other political scientists have addressed the balance between democratic, bureaucratic, market, and judicial decision-making (Anthony Downs, *An Economic Theory of Democracy*, 1957; Charles E. Lindblom, *Politics and Markets: The World's Political-Economic Systems*, 1977). They argue that it is rational to assign decision-making responsibility to the domain which most efficiently can handle the task. This, however, assumes that the domains are separate, that technocrats in bureaucracies are not using democratic processes to achieve a consensus understanding rather than sciences which naturally cohere to a predetermined truth. Harold D. Lasswell is unique among political scientists in that he accepted that scientists are not objective and could only contribute partial information to the policy process. This admission clearly weakens the conventional distinctions between science and politics (Harold D. Lasswell, *A Pre-View of Policy Sciences*, 1971; see also Funtowicz and Ravetz, 1990, 1991). Whereas conventional political theorists worry that the fact-value dichotomy does not hold, most still accept it as a basic premise of institutional design and critique. Without this distinction, the line between democracy and science necessarily blurs (for more on Lasswell see: Ronald D. Brunner and William Ascher, "Science and Social Responsibility," 1993).

The literature on democracy addressing the dynamics of voter opinion formation in the process of selecting representatives has some interesting applications to the problem of democracy and collective understanding. This literature has addressed the combined problems of the timing of primaries across states, whether candidates which may be preferred in one state are eliminated because they have been prematurely labelled as a loser in another state, and whether the process provides sufficient opportunity for informed deliberation. James S. Fishkin formalized these concerns into a recommendation for a "deliberative opinion poll" wherein representatives from across regions, selected randomly and asked to serve as on a jury, participate in a televised extended caucus with all prospective candidates early in the selection process (*Democracy and Deliberation: New Directions for Democratic Reform*, 1991). This approach was used experimentally in the 1992 presidential elections in the United States where many of the candidates met with representative people at the University of Texas in Austin. The thinking behind this approach is still based on "polling" and assembling opinions in a manner which is fair to the candidates and the issues to which they choose to speak. Yet it represents an innovation which seems open to further evolution when combined with the idea that learning and knowing are a collective phenomenon.

Interestingly, Jean-Jacques Rousseau in his early writings thought representation made more sense than direct democracy for it used people's time more efficiently and would be adequate to guard against the abuse of power. Through representatives, minorities might be in a better position to bargain for the small modifications which might resolve their concerns than under direct democracy where fine tuning could prove more difficult. Similarly, Alexander Hamilton, James Madison, and John Jay ("The Federalist Papers," 1787–88) argue that the purpose of government is first and foremost to guard the weak against the powerful and that representative government could do that better than direct democracy. But even Hamilton, Madison, and Jay acknowledged that debate between representatives responsible to the public will was the most effective way to uncover the facts. Similarly, Karl Popper (*The Open Society and Its Enemies*, 1966) favored democratic processes to prevent the concentration of power which might stifle competition in thinking and the suppression of knowledge which challenges the *status quo*.

In Rousseau's last essays, however, he argued that democracy was more than a matter of providing a passive guard against the abuse of power. The active exercise of democracy was a good thing in itself, for it regenerated the community spirit necessary to maintain commitment to democratic processes. The open debate of direct democracy facilitated sharing, learning, and the maintenance of a sense of democratic community. For open debate to occur, however, states had to be small for democracy to succeed in Rousseau's later vision (Richard Fralin, *Rousseau and Representation*, 1978). Carole Pateman (*The Problem of Political Obligation: A Critique of Liberal Theory*, 1979) proceeds along a path that complements Fralin's argument, again with frequent reference to Rousseau. She notes that democracy obligates people to participate for without participation democracy is a sham. From the perspective of individual rationality, assumed by Western liberal theorists generally and by economists religiously, it is illogical to participate since one's vote or contribution to debate is highly unlikely to affect the outcome and takes time that otherwise could be spent in economic activity. The mere existence of democracy, therefore, requires getting people beyond the individualist rationality otherwise assumed and encouraged by Western liberalism. Pateman reads Rousseau as arguing that people will only feel obligated to participate if the social values of the community reinforce their participation, that participation in the democratic process, so long as it is more than vote counting, leads individuals to abandon their position as individuals, that decisions will only be followed if people agree to them as members of communities, that participation reinforces the strength of the community, and that this series of mutually reinforcing phenomena are only possible if the state is sufficiently small for participation to actually take place. Pateman critiques liberal theory for assuming that democratic societies and adherence to democratically reached decisions are "natural" given reasonable equality. In fact, democracy and community have positive feedbacks which reinforce each other if working in the right direction and destroy each other if not. The combination of democracy and community in liberal theory, in short, is an unstable equilibrium which can only be maintained by a prior commitment to democracy and community, a commitment which is not natural and must somehow be embedded in culture and transferred from generation to generation.

The important point is that philosophers as well as the founders of newly democratic societies 200 years ago saw democracy as more than simply a matter of letting the people decide. All hint at democracy as a process of collective learning, and many saw democracy as a process of community regeneration.

J. Ronald Engel, a philosopher-theologian who has written extensively on ethics and the environment, argues that truth is evident in the creation, truth can be distorted to the ends of those in power, but so long as power is dispersed among all through democracy, truth will prevail ("Liberal Democracy and the Fate of the Earth," 1992). While I find this argument for democracy attractive, I have some difficulty with the initial premise, the evidence of truth in the creation. John Dryzek, a political theorist, has elaborated a more complicated argument on the process of democracy in reaching shared understandings, empowering people, building community, revisioning the state, and protecting the future (*Discursive Democracy*, 1990). Dryzek retrieves Aristotle's and Rousseau's image of democracy as community discourse, adapts Jürgen Habermas's idea of communicative action/rationality, and identifies remnants/forebears of what he calls discursive democracy in the practice of environmental and technological negotiation and in the discourses of new social movements. Dryzek's opening conceptual chapters and concluding revisioning chapters strongly complement the ideas I have tried to convey myself in this chapter. One of the most important distinctions Dryzek makes, echoed by Thomas McCarthy ("Complexity and Democracy: or the Seducements of Systems Theory," 1991) is that Habermas as well as Niklas Luhman (*Ecological Communication*, 1989) seem to assume that communicative action/rationality is predominantly a new, superior form of politics which would more effectively oversee existing bureaucracies using existing rationality. Dryzek and I, on the other hand, envision, albeit still weakly, a significant diminuation in the importance of the dominant rationality and its associated bureaucratic social structure. Thomas A. Spragens (*The Irony of Liberal Reason*, 1981) provides a complementary argument. Political discourse following enlightenment conventions of knowledge has supported technocracy, diminished our ability to address values, and ultimately proven impossible with respect to complex issues. As a consequence, modern politics has become irrational. Spragens argues that emerging understandings of how we know need to replace earlier conventions to revitalize politics.

Dryzek's earlier book (*Rational Ecology: Environment and Political Economy*, 1987) documents the failure of existing bureaucratic approaches to solving complex environmental problems and ultimately pleads that power must be decentralized to facilitate communicative rationality. And decentralization is the topic of the next chapter.

CHAPTER 13

I have tried to present a vision of multiple coevolving discursive communities as an alternative to modernity's monolithic hierarchical social structure. This vision formed in my own mind over a period of years through excessive thinking about coevolution as a process, while contemplating the structure of ecosystems, and by observing the rise of non-governmental organizations and the amorphous ways in which they work and interact. Both liberal and marxist scholars have critiqued bureaucratic processes, suggested alternative procedures, but not extended their thinking to the implications for structural reform beyond their prior advocacy for more markets or redistributions of power. Even though Western premises about science have dominated social structure for a hundred years in both market and socialist countries, structural solutions identified in the nineteenth century are still advocated at the close of the twentieth century.

Moving from process to structure is difficult because thinking about system scale and hierarchy is like thinking about many other things, but even more so. At a shallow level, thinking is easy. At only a somewhat deeper level, thinking becomes noticeably more demanding. The complexities of thinking about the structure of systems seem to increase even more rapidly than for other issues. One can easily imagine separate systems in different geographical regions. We commonly refer to centralizing versus decentralizing responsibility in political and bureaucratic systems, expanding trade between regions versus increasing their self-sufficiency, building stronger communities, and other issues involving changing the geographic dimensions in which human activities occur. Social systems, however, are a lot like ecological systems. The extent to which it makes sense to think about subsystems and how subsystems are defined depends on the objectives sought. Whether a community is more or less responsible, self-sufficent, or strong after a change in its relations with the rest of the world will depend on the nature of the future challenges that will confront the community.

Systems theorists refer to the "decomposability" or "separability" of systems as the extent to which one can successfully model subsystems, or clusters of inter-actions, independently of the whole system. Simple systems can readily be decomposed into subsystems of highly interconnected components which are only occasionally interconnected with components beyond the subsystem. Success at modeling the subsystems is measured in terms of the rate at which predictions break down, where the predictions are based on models of the subsystem which do not include interactions (connectance) with the whole system. As long as systems are sufficiently simple, one might compare the geographic, or other dimensions of scale, of the subsystems. As systems become increasingly complex, decomposition into sub-systems becomes more tenuous and predictions from models of the subsystems fail sooner due to the high connectance beyond the subsystem (W. S. Overton, "Decomposability: A Unifying Concept?," 1974; Garry D. Brewer, "Analysis of Complex Systems: An Experiment in Its Implications for Policy Making," 1975).

Decomposability is not a property that a system has or does not have for decomposability, except in the extreme case of completely separate systems, must always be defined with respect to some classes of connections. Decomposability is best defined as a function of the rate at which predictions breakdown over time. This has three implications. First, the extent to which we are comfortable thinking of a system as decomposable depends on the extent to which we are comfortable with the rate at which predictions breakdown. Second, predictions of different types of phenomena may breakdown at different rates hence the decomposability of a system will depend on what one wants to predict. And third, how one decomposes a system into subsystems, clustering the interactions, will depend on the types of predictions in which one is interested. Thus what started out as a theoretical attempt to objectively define scale and the nature of systems has rather quickly ended up depending on our subjective choice of the practical objectives we want to achieve and the risks we are willing to take that we will not achieve them.

Systems that are relatively more decomposable into clusters of high internal connectance and low external connectance are less likely to be affected by a disturbance than systems that are less decomposable with respect to the disturbance. Disturbances themselves are likely to have an impact initially on only a part of the system and to the extent that that part is relatively unconnected to the rest, the disturbance will have little impact on the whole. While systems that are highly interconnected throughout might have negative feedbacks, which quickly dampen the effects of a disturbance at any point in the system, sufficient negative feedbacks are by no means assured. From the perspective of system design, increasing decomposability may be easier than adding negative feedbacks. A practical implica-tion of this phenomenon, for example, is that it may be easier to assure global economic stability by putting more emphasis on regional trading blocs than to build all the necessary negative feedbacks into a global economy.

More generally, Western peoples facing unexpected positive feedbacks through their social and environmental systems have generally tried to identify and imple-ment additional negative feedbacks in the social system, thereby more complexly and tightly integrating the social system, rather than seeking to reduce or eliminate existing connections which account for the surprises. I cannot prove that this is true, but it does provide an explanation for the increasing complexity of modern social systems. Systems theory suggests we might better seek stability through increased decomposability of the system. The vision I have tried to portray of coevolving discursive communities, unlike the vision of an ever more perfect, more encompassing bureaucratic machine, puts as much emphasis on disconnecting as on connecting.

Ecosystems theorists concerned with structure initially investigated the properties of mechanical systems that return them to their initial state after a perturbation (Robert M. May, *Stability and Complexity in Model Ecosystems*, 1973; Stuart Pim, "The Complexity and Stability of Ecosystems," 1984). This work set off considerable controversy because it was clear that the mathematical representations of ecosystems that were analyzed were imagined by a mathematician and had little relation to the complex nature of real ecosystems that had evolved. Concerned with this problem, Peter John Taylor simulated on a computer the random evolution of ecosystems to learn how system properties including stability emerge ("The Construction and Turnover of Complex Community Models having Generalized Lotka-Voltera Dynamics," 1988). M. Mitchell Waldrop provides an excellent review of the work of Charles Taylor, Thomas Ray and others to build models of complex, evolving systems through computer simulation ("Artificial Life's Rich Harvest," 1992).

Some of the richest thinking about structure and process in ecosystems falls in the general category of hierarchy theory. Species with similar time periods over which they go through their life cycles are grouped into a hierarchical structure by length of time period. Dynamics at one level of the hierarchy may or may not affect the dynamics at another level of the hierarchy depending on the timing of events and critical periods at each level. This and other conceptions of hierarchy have been combined with food web and other ways of thinking about ecosystems and their properties to form a rich panoply of hypotheses about the relations between structure and process (T. F. H. Allen and Thomas B. Starr, *Hierarchy: Perspectives for Ecological Complexity*, 1982; C. S. Holling, "The Resilience of Terrestrial Ecosystems: Local Surprise and Global Change," 1986; R. V. O'Neill et al. *A Hierarchical Concept of Ecosystems*, 1986; Neo D. Martinez, "Artifacts or Attributes? Effects of Resolution on the Little Rock Lake Food Web," 1991, "Constant Connectance in Community Food Webs," 1992). These new lines of thinking about the structure and processes of ecosytems have led ecologists to reorganize their thinking about ecosystem management. Whereas earlier management ideas stressed establishing and maintaining the appropriate mechanical equilibrium, the new thinking stresses continual monitoring, learning, and adapting to a changing, inherently unknowable system (C. S. Holling (ed.), *Adaptive Environmental Assessment and Management*, 1978; Carl Walters, *Adaptive Management of Renewable Resources*, 1986). My own vision of coevolving discursive communities clearly builds on this transition in ecological understanding. Human systems need to learn and adapt their structure both as people's understanding of ecosystems changes and as ecosystems in fact change.

In the social sciences, concern with the relations between process and structure has found its expression in a multiplicity of forms with only a few analogs linking to the work in ecology. My acquaintance with the main themes of organization theory in the disciplines of political science and, to a lesser extent, sociology were reviewed in the previous bibliographic essay. It is important to note that much of the original thinking about how bureaucracies might be better structured came from Northerners looking at development in the South. While Northern social scientists tended to take their own social structures as given, change was relatively rapid and anything was deemed possible, or at least imaginable, in the South. Early analyses unabashedly documented how development bureaucracies were able to overpower and out-rationalize people acting through traditional institutions, thereby promoting development goals (Gayl D. Ness, *Bureaucracy and Rural Development in Malaysia*,

1967; Warren Ilchman and Norman T. Uphoff, *The Political Economy of Change*, 1969). Early apparent success, however, soon gave way to frustration as bureaucracies became ever stronger in capital cities and rural peoples found new ways to resist the new changes (James Scott, *Weapons of the Weak: Everyday Forms of Peasant Resistance*, 1985; Ramachandra Guha, *The Unquiet Woods: Ecological Change and Peasant Resistance in the Himalaya*, 1989; Nancy Lee Peluso, *Rich Forests, Poor People: Resource Control and Resistance in Java*, 1992). Development agency experts from the North and Southern elite formed an uneasy alliance with social scientists interested in local communities and empowerment in a search for ways to push the development agenda through somewhat contradictory efforts to break down barriers to central directed development imposed by local elites and supporting institutions and to empower local peoples prepared to join in development efforts (David K. Leonard, *Reaching the Peasant Farmer: Organization Theory and Practice in Kenya*, 1977; Leonard and Marshall (eds), *Institutions of Rural Development for the Poor: Decentralization and Organizational Linkages*, 1982; Bruce F. Johnston and William C. Clark, *Redesigning Rural Development: A Strategic Perspective*, 1982; Lenore Ralston, James Anderson, and Elizabeth Colson, *Voluntary Efforts in Decentralized Management: Opportunities and Constraints in Rural Development*, 1983; Milton J. Esman and Norman T. Uphoff, *Local Organizations: Intermediaries in Rural Development*, 1984). Those concerned with environmental planning in the South similarly pondered the structural linkages between global objectives and local implementation (Jeffrey A. McNeely and David Pitt (eds), *Culture and Conservation: The Human Dimension in Environmental Planning*, 1985; P. Jacobs and D. A. Munro (eds), *Conservation with Equity: Strategies for Sustainable Development*, 1987). While this literature richly identifies the difficulties of implementing the Northern objectives of either development or conservation through centralized structures and acknowledges the importance of local institutions, it only rarely acknowledges that local people can only be empowered when local people set their own objectives in the context of being full participants in the global process of knowing, bargaining, and choosing technologies. In short, this literature searched for a new instrumental rationality while retaining the objectives of the North.

Robert Chambers (*Rural Development: Putting the Last First*, 1984) and David C. Korten (Korten and Felipe B. Alfonso (eds), *Bureaucracy and the Poor: Closing the Gap*, 1983) acknowledged and began to work with the contradictions as Northerners. Korten rallied other Northern voices (Korten and Rudi Klaus (eds), *People Centered Development: Contributions Toward Theory and Planning Frameworks*, 1984). Chambers rallied local expertise in the South (Chambers, Arnold Pacey, and Lori Ann Thrupp, *Farmer First: Farmer Innovation and Agricultural Research*, 1989) and pushed the idea of participatory problem identification and research. And as central governments in developing countries became less and less able to meet expectations during the 1980s, Korten fostered the efforts of grass roots development groups and nongovernmental environmental organizations and began to document the rise of a whole new force for global change (*Getting to the 21st Century: Voluntary Action and the Global Agenda*, 1990).

A very similar phenomenon is occurring in the North. Established bureaucracies have not been able to address environmental problems which fall between their jurisdictions, as most do, by working up through their hierarchies to where they meet at the top. There are far too many environmental problems cutting across the federal agencies of the United States, for example, to have them all resolved in the Oval Office of the President of the United States and the halls of Congress. Rather, interagency working groups have been formed which have joined forces with representatives of nongovernmental organizations to reach agreements. Such ad hoc groups blend science and politics in free discourse, hire facilitators to get them past difficulties, and reach understandings including bargains which ultimately depend on the good faith of the parties involved (Connie P. Ozawa, *Recasting Science: Consensual Procedures in Public Policy Making*, 1991). While such *ad hoc* decision-making groups are becoming increasingly common, they have little formal basis in law and conflict with existing tenets of democratic procedure (Richard B. Norgaard, "Environmental Science as a Social Process," 1992).

Globally, discursive communities are also arising in response to social and environmental problems beyond the dwindling powers of existing formal institutions. Nongovernmental organizations are sharing understandings across national boundaries and increasingly acting together (Medea Benjamin and Andrea Freedman, *Bridging the Global Gap: A Handbook to Linking Citizens of the First and Third Worlds*, 1989). The United Nations and numerous governments and foundations facilitated the interaction between nongovernmental organization through a complex series of meetings in preparation to the United Nations Conference on Environment and Development in Rio in June 1992. While the future of these global discursive communities and their role in global politics is difficult to predict, many sense that a new age has dawned.

Most of the foregoing literature describes the emerging structures and advocates and facilitates their expansion. Social theorists have been slow to provide conceptual underpinnings to the coevolving communities that arise around emergent environmental problems. John S. Dryzek is an exception. He has argued that neither markets nor bureaucracies can resolve environmental problems because of their complexity and shifting boundaries (*Rational Ecology: Environment and Political Economy*, 1987). In a subsequent book, Dryzek goes on to argue how complexity can only be understood from multiple frames of analyses, frames in which scientific reasoning cannot be separated from the values particular models support, and hence the need for "discursive democracy" as elaborated in my previous chapter (*Discursive Democracy: Politics, Policy, and Political Science*, 1990). Though Dryzek objects to shallow democratic structures throughout the book and alludes to the possibility of discursive democracy as a dominant political form in the final chapter, he still seems to see discursive democratic processes as a way of controlling the false ambitions of bureaucracies. He sees it as a critical alternative to the abuse of power, perhaps fearful that if it becomes the dominant process that it too will be corrupted by power. While I acknowledge this problem, I think following through on the structural implications of the basic premises we share is the best way to begin to test them.

CHAPTER 14

To advocate a coevolving patchwork quilt of cultures while undercutting universal ideals through a coevolutionary cosmology is surely to risk the only hope we have for cross cultural justice, peace, and cooperation. While no doubt world order is based on power, orders based on military and economic power, even national and regional orders rooted in cultural fanaticism, invariably also appeal to the potency of universal ideals. The coevolutionary cosmology I have presented and cultural patchwork quilt I have advocated raise some deep questions with respect to appeals to universal human ideals to justify or to design social order. And yet I think I can argue that believing in diversity and describing change as coevolutionary do not deny that we might cultivate stronger bonds across cultures. The coevolutionary cosmology includes values, but it also stresses modes of connectedness which favor some values. It is this interplay of process and values which provide new hope.

Let me note at the outset that appeals to universal ideals have always struck me as being as vague as appeals to progress itself. Such appeals share the belief in the historical inevitability of a merging toward the best with the criteria for best being both undefined and somehow external to human history. The idea of a merger toward a set of highest ideals especially highlights the problem of from where the criteria of best might come. During the past century, furthermore, the appeals have been reduced to utilitarian idealism, to the maximization of material well-being through the advance of knowledge and control of nature, rather than to some higher human ethics (Frederick A. Olafson, "The Idea of Progress: An Ethical Appraisal," 1982). Serious efforts to identify universal human ideals typically reduce, when specifics are demanded, to the avoidance of pain and suffering (Richard Rorty, *Contingency, Irony, and Solidarity*, 1989) and the just sharing of the minimum pain and suffering remaining (Rawls, *A Theory of Justice*, 1971). But just as the vacuity of the idea of progress enhanced its potency and broaden its appeal, the absence of specifics with respect to universal ideals perhaps has been a strength.

However, to acknowledge history, let alone to tout diversity, is to question the idea of universality itself, regardless of about what, and erode the existing appearance of a universal ethical basis for intercultural justice, peace, and cooperation. Richard Rorty has explored how the abandonment during the twentieth century of metaphysics and, by analogy, of hopes for universal beliefs challenges the ethical bases for social order (*Contingency, Irony, and Solidarity*, 1989). The best I can do is interpret Rorty.

Contingency, in my interpretation of Rorty's analysis, encompasses all the realizations of Western philosophers who have abandoned the search for true descriptions of a universal reality and for ultimate justifications for ethical systems. All frames of reality and ethical arguments are human and therefore dependent on the historical contingencies of culture and language. The coevolutionary cosmology extends and clarifies some parts of this realm of thought in Western philosophy by providing a framework which readily highlights how culturally contingent descriptions and arguments themselves are a part of and affect a coevolving cosmos. Irony, by my reading of Rorty, refers to the realization of contingency by late twentieth century individuals while, at the same time, such a realization makes the descriptions and arguments of individuals in other cultures both enticing and a constant source of obfuscation and self-doubt. The irony is that descriptions and arguments are derived to clarify and justify, to root oneself, while acknowledging contingency is to both admit ultimate defeat in such endeavors, to wander rootlessly, and yet to acquire an awareness of the nature of humanity which itself is enlightening if not self-justifying and empowering. Again, pondering a coevolving cosmos and the possibilities for a coevolutionary patchwork quilt of cultures compounds these ironies yet leaves one with new understandings nonetheless. When I present the coevolutionary framework to my class, insisting that knowledge is within it, students typically ask whether the coevolutionary framework itself is within it and where we as observers/users of the coevolutionary framework fit. How can we be within it yet thinking about it and still have our thinking in it?

Without ultimate descriptions and arguments, yet ironically with general consciousness of the same, Rorty then goes in search for a basis of solidarity between peoples. What might be the foundation for compassion across peoples who are conscious of their consciousness, ironists in his terminology, as stemming from different areal contexts and historical contingencies?

The conventional portrayal of the problem is that recent philosophy, Rorty's included as well as my own coevolutionary cosmology and cultural patchwork quilt, leaves everything relative. The charge of relativism, however, only delivers a stunning blow when grounded to the hope of universalism. When not so grounded, it cannot even sting. As the hope for universalism fades, the circuit between them will be broken and no longer obfuscate our search for solidarity. Rorty rejects the existence of universal traits across individuals with which all would identify, or find solidarity, if they simply acknowledged their existence. On the contrary, certainly much of our repulsion on learning more about other cultures results from the further shattering of our already acknowledged belief that there is something universal about being human. Thus appealing to underlying universal characteristics of being human, regardless of our different histories, has increasingly been seen and will continue to be increasingly seen as false. Contingency is becoming increasingly accepted. Rorty believes morality can improve; he only wishes to disconnect the possibility for improvement from its historical philosophical rooting in universally shared understandings and values.

Yet even for Rorty, pain and suffering are real across cultures, and to feel obligated to reduce pain and suffering is the essence of being moral. Even in a contingent world, ethical ideals help us choose our destiny (Nicholas Rescher, *Ethical Idealism: An Inquiry into the Nature and Function of Ideals*, 1987). Abandoning metaphysics does not mean abandoning free will. Furthermore, Rorty does not reject people's ability to identify with some categories of people. There is such a thing as compassion across peoples. We regularly refer to "we" or "us" and "they" or "them," and in the process distinguish the limits of our compassion. The issue is how to extend our concept of the "we" across more peoples.

Rorty then argues that morality improves or not through literature and the arts. The writers of narrative, not philosophy, help us extend the "we" by helping us understand the histories of other peoples, helping us to get inside of their contingencies. And even while we necessarily fail in becoming them, we further reflect on ourselves and expand our own "we." Rorty, while acknowledging his Judeo-Christian history, has rediscovered the power of parables in his search for a secular expansion of a sense of "we."

Personal human practice at interaction with others is surely the best way to expand our human capabilities, an approach advocated in my own chapters critiquing individualism, advocating the democratization of knowledge, and encouraging coevolving discursive communities. Reaching beyond personal experience, Rorty is surely right. It is the humanities, not philosophy, that extend our sense of "we."

Perhaps little of this helps my readers get over a fear of a world of differences rather than of universals. But to the extent it does, further comfort might be found in the complementarities between a coevolutionary cosmology and Rorty's arguments that we need to look more to the humanities for solidarity. Just as Rorty short-circuited the charge of relativism, I need to point out again that the emphasis on competition in evolutionary thinking reflects the history of social thought, not ecological processes. Our false public consciousness of evolutionary explanations as supporting competition and even violence has left us at the mercy of our own conceptual history, unable to see cooperation in nature and to design social systems by analogy (Daniel Botkin, *Discordant Harmonies: A New Ecology for the Twenty-First Century*, 1990; George W. Salt (ed.), *Ecology and Evolutionary Biology: A Roundtable on Research*, 1984). The coevolutionary explanation, however, also has a positive contribution of its own. To date, modern philosophers have accepted contingency and contextuality but not described or explored its underpinnings. A coevolving cosmos is more than a mechanical world with random events, a world so complex as to be beyond comprehension, or a world sequentially teased by history. The coevolutionary cosmology builds on the diversity that, from a universalist perspective, threatens solidarity. Coevolution depends on differences and surprises and describes process behind our histories. A coevolutionary cosmology both helps us understand how differences arise between cultures and helps us respect differences with others for their possible contribution to our own unfolding and their importance to the maintenance of human history overall, for evolution relies on diversity. And just as abandoning a mechanical world view does not mean abandoning free will, accepting a coevolutionary world does not mean having and pursuing values is unimportant or impossible. Quite the contrary, our values can affect the coevolution of the cosmos. A coevolving world offers more hope for solidarity than not.

BIBLIOGRAPHIC POSTSCRIPT

The critique and revisioning elaborated in this book stems from an explanation of process that integrates people and nature through the coevolution of values, knowledge, organization, technology, and the environment. While this understanding of process emphasizes how each of these is influenced by the other, I have given far more emphasis to the coevolution between knowledge and organization than the full process. Some will find I severely slighted the interplay with technology, some will argue that I have not sufficiently documented how environmental systems have coevolved with people, but personally, I am most concerned that I have not written at least a chapter elaborating the interplay with values. The book is cosmologically driven to an end with clear moral implications, but I have not integrated how changes in values selected on changes in knowledge, social organization, or the environment in my critique of modernity and modern philosophy.

This deficiency is somewhat surprising given that my contributions to neoclassical economics during the past few years have been to incorporate intergenerational equity and environmental justice in our understanding of the use of resources over time. Nevertheless, I have not developed my thinking sufficiently with respect to values adequately to portray the complexities of how they affect the coevolutionary process and how such an integration affects numerous discourses in the history of modern philosophy. I continue to move in this direction, but the positivist academic and bureaucratic environments in which I work and through which I necessarily do much of my communicating have not facilitated my growth in this direction. As evidence of some development, however, let me include a statement on values and the environment which I hope represents a watershed in the history of relations between science and religion. At least it documents that I am actively participating in the coevolution of values and their relation to knowledge.

In May 1992, 115 prominent spiritual leaders, innovative religious philosophers, and leading scientists met in Washington, D.C., to draft and sign a declaration (Joint Appeal by Religion and Science for the Environment, Declaration of the Mission to Washington, 1992). Herman Daly and I participated, whether as scientists, apostates of the secular religion, or as representatives of the few economists addressing values and the environment remains unclear. The following appeal, though certainly not a new cosmology or new great life story, may be a significant turning point:

> We are people of faith and of science who, for centuries, often have traveled different roads. In a time of environmental crisis, we find these roads converging. As this meeting symbolizes, our two ancient, sometimes antagonistic, traditions now reach out to one another in a common endeavor to preserve the home we share.

We humans are endowed with self-awareness, intelligence and compassion. At our best, we cherish and seek to protect all life and the treasures of the natural world. But we are now tampering with the climate. We are thinning the ozone layer and creating holes in it. We are poisoning the air, the land and the water. We are destroying the forests, grasslands and other ecosystems. We are causing the extinction of species at a pace not seen since the end of the age of dinosaurs. As a result, many scientific projections suggest a legacy for our children and grandchildren of compromised immune systems, increased infectious disease and cancer rates, destroyed plants and consequent disruption of the food chain, agriculture damaged from drought and ultraviolet light, accelerated destruction of forests and species, and vastly increased numbers of environmental refugees. Many perils may be still undiscovered. The burdens, as usual, will fall most cruelly upon the shoulders of the poorest among us, especially upon children. But no one will be unaffected. At the same time, the human community grows by a quarter million people every day, mostly in the poorest nations and communities. That this crisis was brought about in part through inadvertence does not excuse us. Many nations are responsible. The magnitude of this crisis means that it cannot be resolved unless many nations work together. We must now join forces to that end.

Our own country is the leading polluter on Earth, generating more greenhouse gases, especially CO_2 than any other country. Not by word alone but by binding action, our nation has an inescapable moral duty to lead the way to genuinely effective solutions. We signers of this declaration – leaders in religion and science – call upon our government to change national policy so that the United States will begin to ease, not continue to increase, the burdens on our biosphere and their effect upon the planet's people.

We believe that science and religion, working together, have an essential contribution to make toward any significant mitigation and resolution of the world environmental crisis. What good are the most fervent moral imperatives if we do not understand the dangers and how to avoid them? What good is all the data in the world without a steadfast moral compass? Many of the consequences of our present assault on the environment, even if halted today, will take decades and centuries to play themselves out. How will our children and grandchildren judge our stewardship of the Earth? What will they think of us? Do we not have a solemn obligation to leave them a better world and to insure the integrity of nature itself? Insofar as our peril arises from a neglect of moral values, human pride, arrogance, inattention, greed, improvidence, and a penchant for the short-term over the long, religion has an essential role to play. Insofar as our peril arises from our ignorance of the intricate interconnectedness of nature, science has an essential role to play.

Differences of perspective remain among us. We do not have to agree on how the natural world was made to be willing to work together to preserve it. On that paramount objective we affirm a deep sense of common cause.

Commitment to environmental integrity and justice, across a broad spectrum and at the highest levels of leadership, continues to grow in the United States religious community as an issue of utmost priority – significantly as a result of fruitful conversations with the scientific community. We believe that the dimensions of this crisis are still not sufficiently taken to heart by our leaders, institutions, and industries. We accept our responsibility to help make known to the millions we serve and teach the nature and consequences of the environmental crisis, and what is required to overcome it. We believe that our current economic behavior and policies emphasize short-term individual

251

material goals at the expense of the common good and future generations. When we consider the long-term as well as the short-term costs, it seems clear that addressing this problem now rather than later makes economic as well as moral sense. We impoverish our own children and grandchildren by insisting that they deal with dangers that we could have averted at far less cost in resources and human suffering.

We affirm here, in the strongest possible terms, the indivisibility of social justice and the preservation of the environment. We also affirm and support the indigenous peoples in the protection and integrity of their cultures and lands. We believe the wealthy nations of the North, which have historically exploited the natural and human resources of the Southern nations, have a moral obligation to make available additional financial resources and appropriate technology to strengthen their capacity for their own development. We believe the poor and vulnerable workers in our own land should not be asked to bear disproportionate burdens. And we must end the dumping of toxic waste materials disproportionately in communities of low income and of people of color. We recognize that there is a vital connection between peacemaking and protecting the environment. Collectively, the nations of the world spend one trillion dollars a year on military programs. If even a modest proportion of this money were spent on environmental programs and sustainable economic development we could take a major step toward environmental security.

We commit ourselves to work together for a United States that will lead the world in the efficient use of fossil fuels, in devising and utilizing renewable sources of energy, in phasing out all significant ozone-depleting chemicals, in halting deforestation and slowing the decline in species diversity, in planting forests and restoring habitats, and in realizing worldwide social justice. We believe there is a need for concerted efforts to stabilize world population with humane, responsible and voluntary means consistent with our differing values. For these, and other reasons, we believe that special attention must be paid to education and to enhancing the roles and status of women.

Despite the seriousness of this crisis, we are hopeful. We humans, in spite of our faults, can be intelligent, resourceful, compassionate, prudent and imaginative. We have access to great reservoirs of moral and spiritual courage. Deep within us stirs a commitment to the health, safety and future of our children. Understanding that the world does not belong to any one nation or generation, and sharing a spirit of utmost urgency, we dedicate ourselves to undertaking bold action to cherish and protect the environment of our planetary home.

(Joint Appeal by Religion and Science for the Environment, 1992)

BIBLIOGRAPHY

Abrahamsson, Bengt. 1977. *Bureaucracy or Participation: The Logic of Organization.* Beverly Hills. Sage.

Albrecht, Donald E. and Steve H. Murdoch. 1985. "In Defense of Ecological Analyses of Agricultural Phenomena: A Reply to Swanson and Busch." *Rural Sociology* 50: 427–36.

Albrow, Martin and Elizabeth King (eds). 1990. *Globalization, Knowledge, and Society.* London. Sage.

Allen, E. *et al.*. 1975. "Against Sociobiology." *The New York Review of Books.* 13 November. (Letter signed by 15 activist scholars/professionals).

Allen, T. F. H. and Thomas B. Starr. 1982. *Heirarchy: Perspectives for Ecological Complexity.* Chicago. University of Chicago Press.

Almond, Gabriel A., Marvin Chodorow, and Roy Harvey Pearce. 1982. *Progress and Its Discontents.* Berkeley. University of California.

Amin, Samir. 1992. *Empire of Chaos.* Translated by W. H. Locke Anderson. New York. Monthly Review Press.

Anon. 1991. "What Chernobyl Did: Not Just a Nuclear Explosion." *The Economist.* 27 April: 19–21.

Archibold, Guillermo, Aurelio Chiarai, Brian Housseal, and Craig MacFarlane. 1985. "Culturas Indigenas y Areas Protegidas en Centro America. Proyecto de Estudio para el Manejo de Areas Silvestres de Kuna Yala." Serie Technica Informe Tecnico Numero 1. Panama.

Arrow, Kenneth. 1974. *The Limits of Organization.* New York. Norton.

Arthur, W. Brian. 1990. "Positive Feedbacks in the Economy." *Scientific American.* February. 92–9.

Axelrod, Robert 1980a. "Effective Choice in the Prisoner's Dilemma." *Journal of Conflict Resolution* 24: 3–25.

—— 1980b. "More Effective Choice in the Prisoner's Dilemma." *Journal of Conflict Resolution* 24: 379–403.

—— 1984. *The Evolution of Cooperation.* New York. Basic Books.

Axelrod, Robert and William D. Hamilton. 1981. "The Evolution of Cooperation." *Science* 211 (27 March): 1390–6.

Axelrod, Robert and Douglas Dion. 1988. "The Further Evolution of Cooperation." *Science* 242 (9 December): 1385–90.

Baker, Herbert G. and Paul D. Hurd. 1968. "Intrafloral Ecology." *Annual Review of Entomology* 13: 385–415.

Barbier, Edward B. 1987. "The Concept of Sustainable Economic Development." *Environmental Conservation* 14: 101–10.

Barger, Harold and Sam Schurr. 1944. *The Mining Industries: A Study of Output,*

Employment, and Productivity. New York. National Bureau of Economic Research.

Barnett, Harold J. and Chandler Morse. 1963. *Scarcity and Growth: The Economics of Natural Resource Availabiltiy*. Baltimore. Johns Hopkins University Press.

Barrows, H. H. 1923. "Geography as Human Ecology." *Annals of the Association of American Geographers* 13: 1–14.

Bateson, Gregory. 1979. *Mind and Nature: A Necessary Unity*. New York. E. P. Dutton.

Bauer, P. T. 1971. *Dissent on Development*. Cambridge, MA. Harvard University Press.

Baynes, Kenneth, James Bohman, and Thomas McCarthy. 1987. *After Philosophy: End or Transformation?*. Cambridge, MA. Massachusetts Institute of Technology Press.

Beck, Joanna E. 1985. "Environmental Determinism in Twentieth Century American Geography: Reflections in the Professional Journals." PhD dissertation, Department of Geography, University of California, Berkeley, 1985.

Becker, Gary S. 1976. *The Economic Approach to Human Behavior*. Chicago. University of Chicago.

Beckerman, Wilfred. 1972. "Economists, Scientists, and Environmental Catastrophe." *Oxford Economic Papers* v 24 (3): 327–44.

Beckner, Morton O. 1967. "Organismic Biology." In *The Encyclopedia of Philosophy* 5: 549–551. New York. Macmillan.

Bell, Daniel. 1973. *The Coming of Post-Industrial Society: A Venture in Social Forecasting*. New York. Basic Books.

Bellah, Robert N., Richard Madsen, William Sullivan, Ann Swidler, and Steven M. Tipton. 1985. *Habits of the Heart: Individualism and Commitment in Amerian Life*. Berkeley. University of California Press.

—— 1991. *The Good Society*. New York. Alfred A. Knopf.

Benjamin, Medea and Andrea Freedman. 1989. *Bridging the Global Gap: A Handbook to Linking Citizens of the First and Third World*. Cabin John, MD. Seven Locks Press.

Berman, Morris. 1981. *The Reenchantment of the World*. Ithaca, NY. Cornell University Press (Bantam Edition 1984).

Berry, Thomas. 1988. *The Dream of the Earth*. San Francisco. Sierra Club.

—— 1991. "The Ecozoic Era." Presented at the E. F. Schumacher Society Lectures. 19 October.

Biehl, Janet. 1991. *Rethinking Feminist Politics*. Boston. South End Press.

Bloom, Barry R. and Christopher J. L. Murray. 1992. "Tuberculosis: Commentary on a Reemergent Killer." *Science* 257 (21 August): 1055–64.

Blum, Harold F. 1968. *Time's Arrow and Evolution*. Princeton. Princeton University Press.

Bohm, David. 1980. *Wholeness and the Implicate Order*. London. Routledge & Kegan Paul.

Bookchin, Murray. 1982. *The Ecology of Freedom*. Palo Alto, California. Cheshire Books.

—— 1990. *Remaking Society: Pathways to a Green Future*. Boston. South End Press.

Booth, Wayne C. 1979. *Critical Understanding: The Powers and Limits of Pluralism*. Chicago. University of Chicago.

Boserup, Ester. 1965. *The Conditions of Agricultural Growth*. London. Allen and Unwin.

—— 1981. *Population and Technological Change: A Study of Long-Term Trends*. Chicago. University of Chicago Press.

Bosso, Christopher J. 1987. *Pesitcides and Politics: The Life Cycle of a Public Issue.* Pittsburgh. University of Pittsburgh Press.

Botkin, Daniel B. 1990. *Discordant Harmonies: A New Ecology for the Twenty-First Century.* New York. Oxford University Press.

Boulding, Elise. 1978. Futuristics and the Imaging Capacity of the West. *Cultures of the Future.* Magoroh Maruyama and Arthur M. Harkings (eds). The Hague. Mouton.

Boulding, Kenneth E. 1953. *The Organizational Revolution.* New York. Harper.

—— 1966. The Economics of the Coming Spaceship Earth. *Environmental Quality in a Growing Economy.* Resources for the Future, Baltimore. Johns Hopkins University Press.

—— 1978. *Ecodynamics: A New Theory of Societal Evolution.* Beverly Hills, California. Sage.

—— 1981. *Evolutionary Economics.* Beverly Hills, California. Sage Publications.

—— 1985. *The World as a Total System.* Beverly Hills, California. Sage Publications.

Bowles, Samuel and Herbert Gintis. 1986. *Democracy and Capitalism: Property, Community, and the Contradictions of Modern Social Thought.* New York. Basic Books.

Boyd, Robert and Peter J. Richerson. 1985. *Culture and the Evolutionary Process.* Chicago. University of Chicago Press.

Bramwell Anna. 1989. *Ecology in the 20th Century: A History.* New Haven. Yale University Press.

Brennan, Geoffrey and James M. Buchanan. 1985. *The Reason of Rules: Constitutional Political Economy.* Cambridge. Cambridge University Press.

Brewer, Garry D. 1975. "Analysis of Complex Systems: An Experiment and Its Implications for Policy Making." In Todd R. LaPorte (ed.). *Organized Social Complexity: Challenge to Politics and Policy.* Princeton. Princeton University Press.

—— 1986. "Methods for Synthesis: Policy Exercises." In W. C. Clark and R. E. Munn. *Sustainable Development of the Biosphere.* Cambridge. Cambridge University Press.

Bromley, Daniel W. 1989. *Economic Interests and Institutions: The Conceptual Foundations of Public Policy.* Oxford. Blackwell.

Brown, Becky, Mark Hanson, Diana Liverman, and Robert Meredith, Jr. 1987. "Global Sustainability: Toward Definition." *Environmental Management* 11(6): 713–19.

Brown, Timothy H. 1991. "Evolution of Pesticide Regulatory Policy. Chapter 2 in The Effects of Consumer Demand on Pesticide Regulation in the Market for Apples." PhD Dissertation in Agricultural and Resource Economics, University of California at Berkeley.

Brunner, Ronald D. and William Ascher. 1993. "Science and Social Responsibility." *Policy Sciences* 26: xx–xxx.

Buchanan, James M. 1985. *Liberty, Markets, and State: Political Economy of the 1980s.* New York. New York University Press.

—— 1991. *The Economics and Ethics of Constitutional Order.* Ann Arbor. University of Michigan Press.

Bunker, Stephen G. 1985. *Underdeveloping the Amazon: Extraction, Exchange, and the Failure of the Modern State.* Urbana Illinois. University of Illinois Press.

Burian, Richard M. 1985. "On Conceptual Change in Biology: The Case of the Gene." In *Evolution at a Crossroads: The New Biology and the New Philosophy of Science.* Cambridge, MA. Massachusetts Institute of Technology.

Burke, John P. 1986. *Bureaucratic Responsibility.* Baltimore. Johns Hopkins University Press.

Burness, Stuart, Ronald Cummings, Glenn Morris and Inja Paik. 1980. "Thermo-dynamic and Economic Concepts as Related to Resource-Use Policies." *Land Economics* 56(1): 1–9.

Burness, Stuart and Ronald Cummings. 1986. "Thermodynamic and Economic Concepts as Related to Resource-Use Policies: Reply." *Land Economics* 62(3): 323–4.

Burns, E. Bradford. 1980. *The Poverty of Progress: Latin America in the Nineteenth Century.* Berkeley. University of California.

Bury, J. B. 1920. *The Idea of Progress: An Inquiry into Its Growth and Origin.* London. Macmillan. (a 1932 edition was republished by Dover in 1955 from which I have quoted).

Buttell, Frederick, H. 1991. "Environmentalism: Origins, Processes, and Implica-tions for Rural Social Change." Presidential Address delivered to the annual meeting of the Rural Sociological Society, Columbus, Ohio, 18 August, 1991.

Callicott, J. Baird. 1982. "Traditional Western European and American Attitudes Toward Nature: An Overview." *Environmental Ethics* 4: 293–318.

—— 1985. "Intrinsic Value, Quantum Theory, and Environmental Ethics." *Environmental Ethics* 7: 257–75.

—— 1986. "The Metaphysical Implications of Ecology." *Environmental Ethics* 8: 301–16.

—— 1988. "Agroecology in Context." *Journal of Agricultural Ethics* 1: 3–9.

Capek, Milic. 1967. "Change." In *The Encyclopedia of Philosophy*. Paul Edwards (ed.). New York. Macmillan.

Caplan, Arthur L. (ed.). 1978. *The Sociobiology Debate: Readings on the Ethical and Scientific Issues Concerning Sociobiology.* New York. Harper.

Capra, Fritjof. 1982. *The Turning Point: Science, Society, and the Rising Culture.* New York. Simon and Schuster.

Carey, Henry Charles. 1858. *Principles of Social Science.* Philadelphia. J. B. Lippincott.

Carlassare, Elizabeth. 1992. "An Exploration of Ecofeminism." Paper submitted in partial completion of the Master of Science in Energy and Resources, University of California at Berkeley.

Carlson, E. A. 1966. *The Gene: A Critical History.* Philadelphia and London. W. B. Saunders Company.

Carnap, Rudolf. 1867. *The Logical Structure of the World: Pseudoproblems in Philosophy.* Translated by Rolf A. George. Berkeley. University of California Press.

Cavalli-Sforza, L. L. and M. W. Feldman. 1981. *Cultural Transmission and Evolution: A Quantitative Approach.* Princeton. Princeton University Press.

Cavanagh, John, John Gershman, Karen Baker, and Gretchen Helmke. 1992. *Trading Freedom: How Free Trade Affects Our Lives, Work, and Environment.* San Francisco. The Institute for Food and Development Policy.

Chaitanya, Krishna. 1983. "A Profounder Ecology: The Hindu View of Man and Nature." *The Ecologist* 13(4): 127–33.

Chambers, Robert. 1984. *Rural Development: Putting the Last First.* London. Longman.

Chambers, Robert, Lori Ann Thrupp, and Arnold Pacey (eds). 1989. *Farmer First, Farmer Innovation and Agricultural Research.* London. Intermediate Technology Publications.

Chase, Steve (ed.). 1991. *Defending the Earth: A Dialogue Between Murray Bookchin and Dave Foreman.* Boston. South End Press.

Churchman, C. West. 1979. *The Systems Approach.* New York. Delacorte Press.

Clark, William C. and R. E. Munn. 1986. *Sustainable Development of the Biosphere*. Cambridge. Cambridge University Press.

Clarke, William C. 1971. *Place and People: An Ecology of a New Guinean Community*. Berkeley. University of California Press.

Coase, Ronald H. 1937. "The Nature of the Firm." *Economica* New Series IV: 386–405.

Coblentz, Bruce E. 1990. "Exotic Organisms: A Dilemma for Conservation Biology." *Conservation Biology* 4(3): 261–5.

Cohen, J. Bernard. 1984. *Revolutions in Science*. Cambridge, MA. Harvard University Press.

Cohen, Mitchell L. 1992. "Epidemiology of Drug Resistance: Implications for a Post-Antimicrobial Era." *Science* 257(21 August): 1050–5.

Colinvaux, Paul. 1980. *The Fates of Nations: A Biological Theory of History*. New York. Simon and Schuster.

Comte, Auguste. 1848. *A General View of Positivism*. Translated by J. H. Bridges in 1865. Reprinted by Brown Reprints, Dubuque, IA, 1971.

Conway, Gordon. 1985. "Agroecosystem Analysis." *Agricultural Administration* 20: 31–55.

Corning, Peter A. 1983. *The Synergism Hypothesis: A Theory of Progressive Evolution*. New York. McGraw-Hill.

Cronon, William. 1983. *Changes in the Land: Indians, Colonists, and the Ecology of New England*. New York. Hill & Wang.

Crook, Stephen, Jan Pakulski, and Malcolm Waters. 1992. *Postmodernization: Change in Advanced Society*. London. Sage Publications.

Crosby, Alfred W. 1972. *The Columbian Exchange: Biological and Cultural Consequences of 1492*. Westport, CT. Greenwood Press.

—— 1986. *Ecological Imperialism: The Biological Expansion of Europe, 900 1900*. Cambridge. Cambridge University Press.

Dahl, Robert A. 1989 *Democracy and Its Critics*. New Haven. Yale University Press.

—— 1990. *After the Revolution: Authority in a Good Society*. New Haven. Yale University Press.

Daly, Herman E. (ed.). 1973. *Toward a Steady-State Economy*. San Francisco. W. H. Freeman.

—— 1980 (ed.). *Economics, Ecology, and Ethics: Toward a Steady-State Economy*. San Francisco. W. H. Freeman.

—— 1986. "Thermodynamics and Economic Concepts as Related to Resource-Use Policies: Comment." *Land Economics* 62(3): 319–22.

—— 1989. "Sustainable Development: From Concept and Theory Towards Operational Principles." *Population and Development Review* manuscript.

—— 1991. "Elements of an Environmental Macroeconomics." In Robert Costanza (ed.). *Ecological Economics: The Science and Management of Sustainability*. New York. Columbia University Press.

Daly, Herman E. and John B. Cobb. 1989. *For the Common Good: Redirecting the Economy Toward Community, the Environment, and a Sustainable Future*. Boston. Beacon Press.

Darling, F. Fraser and John P. Milton. 1966. *Future Environments of North America*. New York. Natural History Press.

Dawkins, Richard. 1976. *The Selfish Gene*. Oxford. Oxford University Press.

Depew, David J. and Bruce H. Weber. 1985. *Evolution at a Crossroads: The New Biology and the New Philosophy of Science*. Cambridge, MA. Massachusetts Institute of Technology Press.

Devalle, Susana B. C. 1989. *La Diversidad Prohibida: Resitencia Etnica y Poder de Estado*. Mexico City. El Colegio de Mexico.

Diamond, Irene and Gloria Feman Orenstein (eds). 1990. *Reweaving the World: The Emergence of Ecofeminism*. San Francisco. Sierra Club Books.

Dixon, John A. and Louise Fallon. 1989. The Concept of Sustainability: Origins, Extensions, and Usefulness for Policy. *Society and Natural Resources* 2: 73–84.

Downs, Anthony. 1957. *An Economic Theory of Democracy*. New York. Harper and Row.

Drake, J. A., H. A. Mooney, F. Di Castri, R. H. Groves, F. J. Kruger, M. Rejmanek and M. Williamson. 1989. *Biological Invasions: A Global Perspective*. New York. Wiley and Sons.

Dray, W. H. 1967. "Holism and Individualism in History and Social Science." In *The Encyclopedia of Philosophy* 4: 53–8. New York. Macmillan.

Dryzek, John S. 1987. *Rational Ecology: Environment and Political Economy*. Oxford. Basil Blackwell.

—— 1990. *Discursive Democracy: Politics, Policy, and Political Science*. Cambridge. Cambridge University Press.

Durham, William H. 1976. "The Adaptive Significance of Cultural Behavior." *Human Ecology* 4: 89–121.

—— 1979. "Toward a Coevolutionary Theory of Human Biology and Culture." In N. A. Chagnon and W. Irons (eds). *Evolutionary Biology and Human Social Behavior: An Anthropological Perspective*. North Scituate, MA. Duxbury Press.

—— 1991. *Coevolution: Genes, Culture, and Human Diversity*. Stanford. Stanford University Press.

Eckersley, Robyn. 1992. *Environmentalism and Political Theory: Toward an Ecocentric Approach*. New York. State University of New York Press.

Eddington, Sir Arthur. 1935. *New Pathways in Science*. Cambridge. Cambridge University Press.

Ehrlich, Paul R. 1968. *The Population Bomb*. New York. Ballantine.

—— 1989. "The Limits to Substitution: Meta-resource Depletion and a New Economic-ecological paradigm." *Ecological Economics* 1(1): 9–16.

Ehrlich, Paul R. and Peter H. Raven. 1964. "Butterflys and Plants: A Study in Coevolution." *Evolution* 18: 586–608.

Ehrlich, Paul R., Anne H. Ehrlich, and John P. Holdren. 1977. *Ecoscience: Population, Resources, Environment*. San Francisco. W. H. Freeman.

Einstein, Albert. 1936. "Physics and Reality." *The Journal of the Franklin Institute* 221(3). Reprinted in *Ideas and Opinions*. New York, Bonanza, 1954.

Eisler, Riane. 1987. *The Chalice and the Blade: Our History, Our Future*. New York. Harper Collins.

Eldredge, Niles and Stephen J. Gould. 1972. "Punctuated Equilibria: An Alternative to Phyletic Gradualism." In *Models in Paleobiology*, T. J. M. Schopf (ed.). San Francisco. W. H. Freeman.

Engel, J. Ronald. 1992. "Liberal Democracy and the Fate of the Earth." In Steven C. Rockefeller and John C. Elder (eds). *Spirit and Nature: Why the Environment is a Religious Issue*. Boston. Beacon Press.

Escobar, Arturo. 1987. "The Invention and Management of Development in the Third World." PhD Dissertation. University of California at Berkeley.

Escobar, Arturo with Lori Ann Thrupp. 1990. "The Unsustainable Paradigm of Sustainable Development." Manuscript.

Esman, Milton J. and Norman T. Uphoff. 1984. *Local Organizations: Intermediaries in Rural Development*. Ithaca, New York. Cornell University Press.

Esteva, Gustavo. 1987. "Regenerating People's Space." *Alternatives* XII(1): 136.

—— 1992. "Development." In *The Development Dictionary: A Guide to Knowledge as Power*. Wolfgang Sachs (ed.). London. Zed Books.

Etzioni, Amitai. 1988. *The Moral Dimension: Toward a New Economics*. New York. The Free Press.

Falk, Richard. 1988. "Religion and Politics: Verging on the Postmodern." *Alternatives* 13: 379–94.

Featherstone, Mike (ed.). 1990. *Global Culture: Nationalism, Globalization, and Modernity*. London. Sage.

Ferguson, Ann. 1991. *Sexual Democracy: Women, Oppression, and Revolution*. Boulder, CO. Westview.

Feyerabend, Paul. 1987. "Notes on Relativism." In *Farewell to Reason* London. Verso.

Fishkin, James S. 1991. *Democracy and Deliberation: New Directions for Democratic Reform*. New Haven. Yale University Press.

Foreman, Dave. 1991. *Confessions of an Eco-Warrior*. New York. Harmony.

Fralin, Richard. 1978. *Rousseau and Representation: A Study of the Development of His Concept of Political Institutions*. New York. Columbia University Press.

Freese, Lee. 1988. "Evolution and Sociogenesis, Part 1: Ecological Orgins; Part 2: Social Continuities." *Advances in Group Processes* 5: 53–89 and 91–118.

—— forthcoming. *Currents in the Stream: The Ideas of Human Ecology*.

Freire, Paulo. 1985. *The Politics of Education: Culture, Power, and Liberation*. South Hadley, MA. Bergin and Garvey.

Friedman, Milton. 1962. *Capitalism and Freedom*. Chicago. University of Chicago Press.

Frost, Peter J., Larry F. Moore, Meryl Reis Louis, Craig C. Lundberg, and Joanne Martin. 1985. *Organizational Culture*. Beverly Hills. Sage.

Funtowicz, Silvio O. and Jerome R. Ravetz. 1990. *Uncertainty and Quality in Science for Policy*. Dordrecht. Kluwer.

—— 1991. "A New Scientific Methodology for Global Environmental Issues." In Robert Costanza (ed.). *Ecological Economics: The Science and Management of Sustainability*. New York. Columbia University Press.

Futuyma, Douglas J. and Montgomery Slatkin with the assistance of Bruce Levin and Jonathan Roughgarden. 1983. *Coevolution*. Sunderland, MA. Sinauer Associates.

Gadgil, Mahdav. 1987. "Culture, Perceptions and Attitudes to the Environment." *Conservation With Equity*: Strategies for Sustainable Development. P. Jacobs and D. A. Munro (eds). International Union for the Conservation of Nature. Cambridge, U.K.

——, and Ramachandra Guha. 1993. *This Fissured Land: An Ecological History of India*. Berkeley. University of California Press.

Galgan, Gerald J. 1982. *The Logic of Modernity*. New York. New York University Press.

Garb, Yaakov J. 1985. "The Use and Misuse of the Whole Earth Image." *Whole Earth Review*. March. 18–25.

Garcia Marquez, Gabriel 1970. *One Hundred Years of Solitude*. New York. Harper and Row.

Garraty, John A. and Peter Gay. 1972. *The Columbia History of the World*. New York. Harper and Row.

Geertz, Clifford. 1963. *Agricultural Involution: The Processes of Ecological Change in Indonesia*. Berkeley. University of California Press.

Georgescu-Roegen, Nicholas. 1971. *The Entropy Law and the Economic Process*. Cambridge. Harvard University Press.

—— 1975. "Energy and Economic Myths." *Southern Economic Journal* 41: 347–81.

—— 1977. "The Steady State and Ecological Salvation: A Thermodynamic Analysis." *Bioscience* 27(4): 266–70.

Giddens, Anthony. 1990. *The Consequences of Modernity*. Stanford. Stanford University Press.

Glacken, Clarence J. 1967. *Traces on the Rhodian Shore*. Berkeley. University of California.

Goodland, Robert and George Ledec. 1987. Neoclassical Economics and Principles of Sustainable Development. *Ecological Modeling* 38: 19–46.

Goodsell, Charles T. 1983. *The Case for Bureaucracy*. Chatham, NJ. Chatham House.

Gormley, Jr. William T. 1989. *Taming the Bureaucracy: Muscles, Prayers, and Other Strategies*. Princeton. Princeton University Press.

Gorz, André. 1980. *Ecology as Politics*. Boston. South End Press.

Gould, Stephen J. 1989. *Wonderful Life: The Burgess Shale and the Nature of History*. New York. Norton.

Gould, Stephen J. and N. Eldredge. 1977. "Punctuated Equilibria: the Tempo and Mode of Evolution Reconsidered." *Paleobiology* 3: 115–51.

Goulet, Denis. 1977a. *The Uncertain Promise: Value Conflicts in Technology Transfer*. New York. IDOC/North America.

—— 1977b. *The Cruel Choice: A New Concept in the Theory of Development*. New York. Atheneum.

Greene, John C. 1981. *Science, Ideology, and World View: Essays in the History of Evolutionary Ideas*. Berkeley. University of California Press.

Grene, Marjorie. 1985. "Perception, Interpretation, and the Sciences". In *Evolution at the Crossroads: The New Biology and the New Philosophy of Science*, D. J. Depew and B. H. Weber (eds), Cambridge, MA. Massachusetts Institute of Technology Press.

Grigg, D. B. 1974. *The Agricultural Systems of the World: An Evolutionary Approach*. Cambridge. Cambridge University Press.

Gruber, Judith E. 1987. *Controlling Bureaucracies: Dilemmas in Democratic Governance*. Berkeley. University of California.

Guha, Ramachandra. 1988. "Ideological Trends in Indian Environmentalism." *Economic and Political Weekly* XXIII (3 December): 2578–81.

—— 1989a. *The Unquiet Wood: Ecological Change and Peasant Resistance in the Himalaya*. Oxford. Oxford University Press (also available through University of California Press, 1990).

—— 1989b. "Radical American Environmentalism and Wilderness Preservation." *Environmental Ethics* 11: 71–81.

Gutman, Pablo. 1985. "Teoria Economica y Problematica Ambiental: Un Dialogo Dificil." *Desarollo Economico* 25: 47–70.

Haas, Ernst B. 1990. *When Knowledge is Power: Three Models of Change in International Organizations*. Berkeley. University of California Press.

Haas, Peter M. 1990. *Saving the Mediterranean: The Politics of International Environmental Cooperation*. New York. Columbia University Press.

Habermas, Jürgen. 1984. *The Theory of Communicative Action I: Reason and the Rationalization of Society*. Boston. Beacon Press.

—— 1987. *The Theory of Communicative Action II: Lifeworld and System*. Boston. Beacon Press.

Hall, Darwin C. and Jane V. Hall. 1984. "Concepts and Measures of Natural Resource Scarcity with a Summary of Recent Trends." *Journal of Environmental Economics and Management*. 11(4): 363–79.

Hamilton, Alexander, James Madison, and John Jay. 1787–8. *The Federalist Papers*. [1982. Garry Wills (ed.). New York. Bantam].

BIBLIOGRAPHY

Hamilton, William D. 1964. "The Genetical Theory of Social Behavior: I and II." *Journal of Theoretical Biology* 7: 1–52.

Harding, Sandra. 1986. *The Science Question in Feminism*. Ithaca, NY. Cornell University Press.

Harris, Marvin. 1968. *The Rise of Anthropological Theory*. New York. Thomas Y. Crowell.

Hawley, Amos H. 1944. "Ecology and Human Ecology." *Social Forces* 22: 398–405.

—— 1950. *Human Ecology: A Theory of Community Structure*. New York. Ronald Press.

Hecht, Susanna and Alexander Cockburn. 1989. *Fate of the Forest: Developers, Destroyers, and Defenders of the Amazon*. London. Verso.

Henderson, Hazel. 1978. *Creating Alternative Futures: The End of Economics*. New York. G. P. Putnam's Sons.

—— 1981. *The Politics of the Solar Age: Alternatives to Economics*. Garden City, NY. Anchor Press.

—— 1991. *Paradigms in Progress: Life Beyond Economics*. Indianapolis. Knowledge Systems.

Hicks, John R. 1982. *Wealth and Welfare: Collected Essays on Economic Theory*. Cambridge, MA. Harvard University Press.

Hirsch, Fred. 1976. *The Social Limits to Growth*. Cambridge, MA. Harvard University Press.

Hirschman, Albert. 1970. *Exit, Voice, and Loyalty*. Cambridge. Harvard University Press.

—— 1977. *The Passions and the Interests: Political Arguments for Capitalism before its Triumph*. Princeton. Princeton University Press.

Hirszowicz, Maria. 1980. *The Bureaucratic Leviathan: A Study in the Sociology of Communism*. New York. New York University Press.

Holling, C. S. (ed.). 1978. *Adaptive Environmental Assessment and Management*. Chichester. Wiley.

—— 1986. "The Resilience of Terrestrial Ecosystems: Local Surprise and Global Change." In W. C. Clark and R. E. Munn (eds) *Sustainable Development of the Biosphere*. Cambridge. Cambridge University Press.

Hollinger, Robert (ed.). 1985. *Hermeneutics and Praxis*. Notre Dame, IN. University of Notre Dame Press.

Howarth, Richard B. and Richard B. Norgaard. 1990. "Intergenerational Resource Rights, Efficiency, and Social Optimality." *Land Economics*. 66(1): 1–11.

Ilchman, Warren F. and Norman T. Uphoff. 1969. *The Political Economy of Change*. Berkeley. University of California Press.

Innes, Judith E. 1990. *Knowledge and Public Policy: The Search for Meaningful Indicators*. Second Expanded Edition. New Brunswick, NJ. Transaction Publishers.

Jacobs, P. and D. A. Munro. 1987. *Conservation with Equity: Strategies for Sustainable Development*. Cambridge, UK. International Union for the Conservation of Nature and Natural Resources.

Jacoby, Henry. 1973. *The Bureaucratization of the World*. Berkeley. University of California Press.

Jasanoff, Sheila. 1990. *The Fifth Branch: Science Advisers as Policy Makers*. Cambridge. Harvard University Press.

Jevons, W. S. 1865. *The Coal Question*. London. Macmillan.

Johnston, Bruce F. and William C. Clark. 1982. *Redesigning Rural Development: A Strategic Perspective*. Baltimore. Johns Hopkins University Press.

Joint Appeal by Religion and Science for the Environment. 1992. Declaration of the Mission to Washington. Washington, D.C. 12 May.

BIBLIOGRAPHY

Kaufman, Herbert. 1981. "Fear of Bureaucracy: A Raging Pandemic." *Public Administration Review* 41: 1–9.

Kaysen, Carl. 1972. "The Computer that Printed Out W*O*L*F." *Foreign Affairs* 50: 660–8.

Keller, Evelyn Fox. 1985. *Reflections on Gender and Science*. New Haven. Yale University Press.

Kingsland, Sharon E. 1985. *Modeling Nature: Episodes in the History of Population Ecology*. Chicago. University of Chicago Press.

Knight, Frank H. 1935. "Statistics and Dynamics: Some Queries Regarding the Mechanical Analogy in Economics." In *The Ethics of Competition*. New York. Harper & Brothers. Reprinted in *On the History and Method of Economics*. 1956. Chicago. University of Chicago 1st German edition in 1930.

Korten, David C. 1990. *Getting to the 21st Century: Voluntary Action and the Global Agenda*. West Hartford, CT. Kumarian Press.

Korten, David C. and Felipe B. Alfonso (eds). 1983. *Bureaucracy and the Poor: Closing the Gap*. West Hartford, CT. Kumarian Press.

Korten, David C. and Rudi Klaus (eds). 1984. *People Centered Development: Contributions Toward Theory and Planning Frameworks*. West Hartford, CT. Kumarian Press.

Kothari, Rajni. 1979–80. "Environment and Alternative Development." *Alternatives* 427–75.

Krause, Richard M. 1992. "The Origin of Plagues: Old and New." *Science* 257(21 August): 1073–8.

Kuhn, Thomas S. 1962. *The Structure of Scientific Revolutions*. Chicago. University of Chicago Press.

Lakoff, George and Mark Johnson. 1980. *Metaphors We Live By*. Chicago. University of Chicago Press.

Lal, Deepak. 1985. *The Poverty of "Development Economics"*. Cambridge, MA Harvard University Press.

La Palombara, Joseph (ed.). 1963. Bureaucracy and Political Development. Princeton. Princeton University Press.

Lasch, Christopher. 1978. *The Culture of Narcism: American Life in an Age of Dimishing Expectations*. New York. W. W. Norton.

—— 1991. *The True and Only Heaven: Progress and Its Critics*. New York. W. W. Norton.

Lasswell, Harold D. 1971. *A Pre-View of Policy Sciences*. New York. American Elsevier.

Le Prestre, Philippe. 1989. *The World Bank and the Environmental Challenge*. London and Toronto. Associated University Presses.

Leaf, Murray J. 1979. *Man, Mind, and Science: A History of Anthropology*. New York. Columbia University Press.

Lele, Sharachchandra. 1989. "A Framework for Sustainability and Its Applications in Visualizing a Peace Society." Manuscript. Bangalore, India. Centre for Ecological Sciences.

—— 1991. "Sustainable Development: A Critical Review." *World Development* 19(6): 607–21.

Leonard, David K. 1977. *Reaching the Peasant Farmer: Organization Theory and Practice in Kenya*. Chicago. University of Chicago Press.

Leonard, David K. and Dale Rogers Marshall (eds). 1982. *Institutions of Rural Development for the Poor: Decentralized and Organizational Linkages*. Berkeley. Institute of International Studies. University of California.

Leopold, Aldo. 1949. *A Sand County Almanac*. New York. Oxford University Press.

Lewin, Roger. 1986. "Punctuated Equilibrium is Now Old Hat." *Science* 231(14 February): 672–3.

Lewontin, R. C., Steven Rose, and Leon J Kamin. 1984. *Not in Our Genes: Biology, Ideology, and Human Nature*. New York. Pantheon.

Lindblom, Charles E. 1977. *Politics and Markets: The World's Political-Economic Systems*. New York. Basic Books.

Lindblom, Charles E. and David K. Cohen. 1979. *Usable Knowledge: Social Science and Social Problem Solving*. New Haven. Yale University Press.

Lonergan, Anne and Caroline Richards. 1987. *Thomas Berry and the New Cosmology*. Mystic, CT. Twenty-Third Publications.

Lorraine, Tamsin E. 1990. *Gender, Identity, and the Production of Meaning*. Boulder, Co. Westview.

Lorenz, Konrad. 1966. *On Aggression*. London. Methuen.

——Konrad. 1970 (vol. 1) and 1971 (vol. 2). *Studies in Animal and Human Behavior*. London. Methuen, and Cambridge, MA. Harvard University Press.

—— 1977. *Behind the Mirror: A Search for a Natural History of Human Knowledge*. New York. Harcourt Brace Jovanovich. (originally published in German in 1973).

Low, Patrick (ed.). 1992. *International Trade and the Environment*. Washington, D.C. World Bank Discussion Paper 159.

Luhmann, Niklas. 1989. *Ecological Communication*. Chicago. University of Chicago Press.

Lumsden, Charles J. and Edward O. Wilson. 1981. *Genes, Mind, and Culture: The Coevolutionary Process*. Cambridge, MA. Harvard University Press.

Luten, Daniel B. 1980. "Ecological Optimism in the Social Sciences: The Question of Limits to Growth." *American Behavioral Scientist* 24: 125–51.

Lyotard, Jean-François. 1984. *The Postmodern Condition: A Report on Knowledge*. Minneapolis. University of Minnesota Press.

McCarthy, Thomas. 1991. "Complexity and Democracy: or the Seducements of Systems Theory." In Alex Honneth and Hans Joas (eds), *Communicative Action: Essays on Jürgen Habermas's The Theory of Communicative Action*. (Translated by Jeremy Gaines and Doris L. Jones). Cambridge, MA. Massachusetts Institute of Technology Press.

McCloskey, Donald N. 1985. *The Rhetoric of Economics*. Madison. University of Wisconsin Press.

MacIntyre, Alasdair. 1981. *After Virtue*. Notre Dame, IN. University of Notre Dame Press.

—— 1988. *Whose Justice, Which Rationality*. Notre Dame, IN. University of Notre Dame Press.

McKenzie, R. D. 1926. "The Scope of Human Ecology." *Publications of the American Sociological Society* 20: 141–54.

McNeely, Jeffrey, A. and David Pitt. 1985. *Culture and Conservation: The Human Dimension in Environmental Planning*. London. Croom Helm.

MacNeill, Jim, Pieter Winsemius, and Taizo Yakushiji. 1991. *Beyond Interdependence: The Meshing of the World's Economy and the Earth's Ecology*. Oxford. Oxford University Press.

Makhijani, Arjun. 1992. *From Global Capitalism to Economic Justice: An Inquiry into the Elimination of Systemic Poverty, Violence, and Environmental Destruction in the World Economy*. New York. The Apex Press.

Malthus, Thomas R. 1798. *An Essay on the Principle of Population*. London. J. Johnson.

Mansbridge, Jane J. (ed.). 1990. *Beyond Self-Interst*. Chicago. University of Chicago Press.

Marglin, Frederique Apffel and Stephen A. Marglin. 1991. *Dominating Knowledge: Development, Culture, and Resistance*. Oxford. Clarendon/Oxford University Press.

Marsh, George Perkins. 1864. *Man and Nature: Or, Physical Geography as Modified by Human Action*. 1965 issue by Harvard University Press edited by David Lowenthal. Cambridge, MA.

Martinez, Neo D. 1991. "Artifacts or Attributes? Effects of Resolution on the Little Rock Lake Food Web." *Ecological Monographs* 61(4): 367–92.

—— 1992. "Constant Connectance in Community Food Webs." *The American Naturalist* 140: 1208–18.

Martinez-Alier, Juan with Klaus Schlüpmann. 1987. *Ecological Economics: Energy, Environment and Society*. Oxford. Basil Blackwell.

Maruyama, Magoroh. 1980. "Mindscapes and Science Theories." *Current Anthropology* 21(5): 589–600.

May, Robert M. 1973. *Stability and Complexity in Model Ecosystems*. Princeton. Princeton University Press.

Mayumi, Kozo. 1991a. "A Critical Appraisal of Two Entropy Theoretical Approaches to Resources and Environmental Problems and a Search for an Alternative." In *Ecological Physical* . C. Rossi and E. Tiezzi (eds). Amsterdam. Elsevier.

—— 1991b. "Temporary Emancipation from Land: from the Industrial Revolution to the Present Time." *Ecological Economics* forthcoming.

Meadows, Donella H. 1972. *The Limits to Growth*. New York. Universe.

Merchant, Carolyn. 1980. *The Death of Nature: Women, Ecology, and the Scientific Revolution*. San Francisco. Harper and Row.

—— 1989. *Ecological Revolutions: Nature, Gender, and Science in New England*. Chapel Hill. University of North Carolina.

Moran, Emilio F. 1979. *Human Adaptability: An Introduction to Ecological Anthropology*. Belmont, CA. Wadsworth.

—— 1981. *Developing the Amazon*. Bloomington, IN. Indiana University Press.

Morgan, Gareth. 1986. *Images of Organization*. Beverly Hills, CA. Sage.

Munoz, Heraldo (ed.). 1981. *From Dependency to Development: Strategies to Overcome Underdevelopment and Inequality*. Boulder, CO. Westview.

Myers, Norman. 1979. *The Sinking Ark*. New York. Pergamon.

Nagel, Ernst. 1961. "The Reduction of Theories", Chapter 11 in *The Structure of Science: Problems in the Logic of Scientific Explanation*. New York. Harcourt, Brace & World.

Needham, Joseph. 1941. "Evolution and Thermodynamics." Reprinted in *Moulds of Understanding: A Pattern of Natural Philosophy*. 1976. New York. St. Martins Press.

Neitschmann, Bernard. 1987. "The Third World War." *Cultural Survival Quarterly* 11(3): 1–16.

Nelson, Richard R. and Sidney G. Winter. 1982. *An Evolutionary Theory of Economic Change*. Cambridge, MA. Harvard University Press.

Nelson, Robert H. 1987. "The Economics Profession and Public Policy." *Journal of Economic Literature* XXV(1): 49–91.

—— 1991. *Reaching for Heaven on Earth: The Theological Meaning of Economics*. Savage, MD. Rowman and Littlefield.

Nesbit, Robert. 1980. *History of the Idea of Progress*. New York. Basic Books.

Ness, Gayl D. 1967. *Bureaucracy and Rural Development in Malaysia*. Berkeley. University of California Press.

Netting, Robert McC. 1977. *Cultural Ecology*. Menlo Park, CA. Cummings Publishing Co.

Neu, Harold C. 1992. "The Crisis in Antibiotic Resistance." *Science* 257(21 August): 1064–73.

Nisbet, Robert. 1980. *History of the Idea of Progress*. New York. Basic Books.

Niskanen, William A., Jr. 1971. *Bureaucracy and Representative Government*. Chicago. Aldine.

Nitecki, Matthew H. 1983. *Coevolution*. Chicago. University of Chicago Press.

Nordhaus, William D. 1990. "Greenhouse Economics: Count Before You Leap." *The Economist*. 316(7662): 21–4.

—— 1991. "To Slow or Not to Slow: The Economics of the Greenhouse Effect." *The Economic Journal* (July): 920–37.

—— 1981. "Sociosystem and Ecosystem Coevolution in the Amazon." *Journal of Environmental Economics and Management* 8: 238–54.

—— 1986. "Thermodynamic and Economic Concepts as Related to Resource-use Policies: A Synthesis." *Land Economics* 64(3): 325–8.

—— 1988. "The Rise of the Global Exchange Economy and the Loss of Biological Diversity." In E. O. Wilson (ed.). *Biodiversity*. Washington, D.C. National Academy Press.

—— 1989. "Risk and Its Management in Traditional and Modern Agroeconomic Systems." In Christina Gladwin and Kathleen Truman (eds). *Food and Farm: Current Debates and Policies*. Monographs in Economic Anthropology. New York. University Press of America.

—— 1990. "Economic Indicators of Resource Scarcity: A Critical Essay." *Journal of Environmental Economics and Management* 19:19–25.

—— 1992. "Environmental Science as a Social Process." *Environmental Monitoring and Assessment* 20: 95–110

Noss, Reed F. 1990. "Can We Maintain Biological and Ecological Integrity?" *Conservation Biology* 4(3): 241–3.

O'Brien, Mary. 1989. *Reproducing the World: Essays in Feminist Theory*. Boulder, CO. Westview.

O'Connor, Martin Paul. 1991. "Time and Environment." PhD dissertation, Department of Economics, University of Auckland, New Zealand.

O'Donnell, Guillermo A. 1973. *Modernization and Bureauractic-Authoritarianism: Studies in South American Politics*. Berkeley. University of California, Institute of International Studies.

O'Neil, R. V., D. L. DeAngelis, J. B. Waide, and T. F. H. Allen. 1986. *A Hierarchical Concept of Ecosystems*. Princeton. Princeton University Press.

Olafson, Frederick A. 1982. "The Idea of Progress: An Ethical Appraisal." In Gabriel A. Almond, Marvin Chodorow, and Roy Harvey Pearce (eds). *Progress and Its Discontents*. Berkeley. University of California Press.

Ornstein, Robert and Paul Ehrlich. 1989. *New World, New Mind: Moving Toward Conscious Evolution*. New York. Doubleday.

Overton, S. H. 1974. "Decomposability: A Unifying Concept?" In S. A. Levin (ed.). *Ecosystem Analysis and Prediction*. Philadelphia. Society for Industrial and Applied Mathematics.

Ozawa, Connie P. 1991. *Recasting Science: Consensual Procedures in Public Policy Making*. Boulder, CO. Westview Press.

Paehlke, Robert C. 1989. *Environmentalism and the Future of Progressive Politics*. New Haven. Yale University Press.

Park, Robert E. 1936. "Human Ecology." *The American Journal of Sociology* 42: 1–15.

Pateman, Carole. 1979. *The Problem of Political Obligation: A Critique of Liberal Theory*. New York. John Wiley. (Republished by University of California Press, 1985).

Pechman, Joseph A (ed.). 1989. *The Role of Economists in Government: An International Perspective*. New York. New York University Press.

Peluso, Nancy Lee. 1992. *Rich Forests, Poor People: Resource Control and Resistance in Java*. Berkeley. University of California Press.

Perkins, John H. 1982. *Insects, Experts, and the Insecticide Crisis: The Quest for New Pest Management Strategies*. New York. Plenum Press.

Pezzey, John. 1989. "Economic Analysis of Sustainable Growth and Sustainable Development." Environment Department Working Paper No 15. Washington, D.C. The World Bank.

Pim, Stuart. 1984. "The Complexity and Stability of Ecosystems." *Nature* 307: 321–6.

Polak, Fred. 1972. *The Image of the Future*. Translated by Elise Boulding. Abridged Version. New York. Elsevier.

Popper, Karl. 1934. *The Logic of Scientific Discovery* (first English edition, 1959, New York, Basic Books).

—— 1966. *The Open Society and Its Enemies*. London. Routledge and Kegan Paul.

—— 1979. *Objective Knowledge: An Evolutionary Approach*. Revised Edition. Oxford. Oxford University Press.

Posner, Richard A. 1981. *The Economics of Justice*. Cambridge, MA. Harvard University Press.

Presley, C. F. 1967. "Willard Van Orman Quine." In *The Encyclopedia of Philosophy*, Paul Edwards (ed.) 7: 53–5. New York. Macmillan.

Prigogine, Ilya and Isabelle Stengers. 1984. *Order Out of Chaos: Man's New Dialogue with Nature*. New York. Bantam Books.

Pulliam H. Ronald and Christopher Dunford. 1980. *Programmed to Learn: An Essay on the Evolution of Culture*. New York. Columbia University Press.

Quine, Willard Van Orman. 1961. *From a Logical Point of View*. Cambridge, MA. Harvard University Press.

Rabinow, Paul and William M. Sullivan (eds). 1979. *Interpretive Social Science: A Reader*. Berkeley. University of California Press.

Raghavan, Chakravarthi. 1990. *Recolonization: GATT, the Uruguay Round, and the Third World*. Penang, Malaysia. Third World Network.

Ralston, Lenore, James Anderson, and Elizabeth Colson. 1983. *Voluntary Efforts in Decentralized Management: Opportunities and Constraints in Rural Development*. Berkeley. Institute of International Studies. University of California.

Rambler, Mitchell B., Lynn Margulis, and René Fester. 1989. *Global Ecology: Towards a Science of the Biosphere*. Boston. Academic Press.

Rambo, A. Terry. 1983. "Conceptual Approaches to Human Ecology. Research Report No. 14." Honolulu. East–West Environment and Policy Institute.

Randall, John Herman, Jr. 1976. *The Making of the Modern Mind*. New York. Columbia University Press (first published in 1926).

Rappaport, Roy A. 1968. *Pigs for the Ancestors: Ritual in the Ecology of a New Guinea People*. New Haven. Yale University Press.

Ravetz, Jerome R. 1971. *Scientific Knowledge and Its Social Problems*. Oxford. Oxford University Press.

—— 1986. "Usable Knowledge, Usable Ignorance: Incomplete Science with Policy Implications." In W. C. Clark and R. E. Munn. *Sustainable Development of the Biosphere*. Cambridge. Cambridge University Press.

Rawls, John A. 1971. *A Theory of Justice*. Cambridge, MA. Harvard University Press.

Redclift, Michael. 1984. *Development and the Environmental Crisis: Red or Green Alternatives*. London. Methuen.

—— 1987. *Sustainable Development: Exploring the Contradictions*. London. Methuen.

Rescher, Nicholas. 1978. *Scientific Progress: A Philosophical Essay on the Economics of Research in the Natural Sciences*. Pittsburgh. University of Pittsburgh Press.

—— 1987. *Ethical Idealism: An Inquiry into the Nature and Function of Ideals*. Berkeley. University of California Press.

Ricardo, David. 1817. *The Principles of Political Economy and Taxation*. London. G. Bell & Sons.

Richards, Robert J. 1987. *Darwin and the Emergence of Evolutionary Theories of Mind and Behavior*. Chicago. University of Chicago Press.

Rifken, Jeremy. 1980. *Entropy: A New World View*. New York. Viking.

Rockefeller, Steven C. and John C. Elder (eds). 1992. *Spirit and Nature: Why the Environment is a Religious Issue*. Boston. Beacon Press.

Roth, Paul A. 1987. *Meaning and Method in the Social Sciences: A Case for Methodological Pluralism*. Ithaca, NY. Cornell University Press.

Rorty, Richard J. 1979. *Philosophy and the Mirror of Nature*. Princeton. Princeton University Press.

—— 1989. *Contingency, Irony, and Solidarity*. Cambridge. Cambridge University Press.

Rosaldo, Renato. 1989. *Culture and Truth: The Remaking of Social Analysis*. Boston. Beacon Press.

Russell, Bertrand. 1931. *The Scientific Outlook*. New York. W. W. Norton Edition (1959).

Salt, George W. (ed.). 1984. *Ecology and Evolutionary Biology: A Roundtable on Research*. Chicago. University of Chicago Press.

Sauer, Carl. 1925. "The Morphology of Landscape." University of California Publications in Geography, v 2, pp 19–54, reprinted in *Land and Life: A Selection from the writings of Carl Ortwin Sauer*, John Leighly (ed.). 1963. Berkeley. University of California.

Schrodinger, Erwin. 1944. *What is Life?* Cambridge. Cambridge University Press.

Schultz, Theodore W. 1951. "The Declining Importance of Agricultural Land. Economic Journal" 6: 725–40.

Schwartz, Barry. 1986. *The Battle for Human Nature: Science, Morality, and Modern Life*. New York. W. W. Norton.

Schwartz, Peter and James Ogilvy. 1979. "The Emergent Paradigm: Changing Patterns of Thought and Belief." Values and Lifestyle Program, SRI International, Menlo Park, CA.

Sclove, Richard E. 1986. *Technology and Freedom: A Prescriptive Theory of Technological Design and Practice in Democratic Societies*. PhD Thesis. Political Science. Cambridge, MA. Massachusetts Institute of Technology.

Scott, James C. 1985. *Weapons of the Weak: Everyday Forms of Peasant Resistance*. New Haven. Yale University Press.

Scriven, Michael. 1959. "Explanation and Prediction in Evolutionary Theory." *Science* 130 (August 28): 477–82.

Semple, Ellen Churchill. 1911. *Influences of Geographic Environment: On the Basis of Ratzel's System of Anthropo-Geography* New York. Henry Holt.

Silver, Cheryl Simon with Ruth S. DeFries. 1990. *One Earth, One Future: Our Changing Global Environment*. Washington, D.C. National Academy of Sciences.

Silver, Morris. 1989. *Foundations of Economic Justice*. New York. Basil Blackwell.

Simon, Herbert A. 1947. *Administrative Behavior: A Study of Decision-Making in Administrative Organizations*. New York. Macmillan.

—— 1983. *Reason in Human Affairs*. Stanford, CA. Stanford University Press.

Simon, Julian. 1981. *The Ultimate Resource*. Princeton. Princeton University Press.

Simon, Julian L. and Herman Kahn. 1984. *The Resourceful Earth: A Response to Global 2000*. Oxford. Basil Blackwell.

Slade, Margaret E. 1982. "Trends in Natural Resource Commodity Prices: An Analysis of the Time Domain." *Journal of Environmental Economics and Management*. 9: 122–37.

Smith, Anthony. 1980. *The Geopolitics of Information: How Western Culture Dominates the World*. Oxford. Oxford University Press.

Sober, Elliott. 1984. *The Nature of Selection: Evolutionary Theory in Philosophical Focus*. Cambridge, MA. Massachusetts Institute of Technology Press.

—— (ed.). 1984. *Conceptual Issues in Evolutionary Biology: An Anthology*. Cambridge, MA. Massachusetts Institute of Technology Press.

Sociobiology Study Group of Science for the People. 1976. "Socio-biology – Another Biological Determinism." *Bioscience*. v 26 (March). Reprinted in Arthur L. Caplan (ed.). 1978. *The Sociobiology Debate: Readings on the Ethical and Scientific Issues Concerning Sociobiology*. New York. Harper.

Sorel, Georges. 1908. *The Illusions of Progress*. Paris (translated by John and Charlotte Stanley, Berkeley, University of California Press, 1969).

Southgate, Douglas D. and John F. Disinger (eds). 1987. *Sustainable Resource Development in the Third World*. Boulder, CO. Westview Press.

Speth, Gus. 1989. "Can the World be Saved?" *Ecological Economics* 1(4): 289–302.

Spragens, Thomas A., Jr. 1981. *The Irony of Liberal Reason*. Chicago. University of Chicago Press.

Stanley, Manfred. 1978. *The Technological Conscience: Survival and Dignity in an Age of Expertise*. New York. Free Press. (Reprinted by University of Chicago Press, 1981).

Stent, Gunther. 1985. "Hermeneutics and the Analysis of Complex Biological Systems." In *Evolution at the Crossroads: The New Biology and the New Philosophy of Science*, D. J. Depew and B. H. Weber (eds), Cambridge, MA. Massachusetts Institute of Technology Press.

Steward, Julian. 1968. The Concept and Method of Cultural Ecology. In David L. Sills (ed.) *International Encyclopedia of the Social Sciences*. New York. Macmillan. 4: 337–44.

—— 1977. *Evolution and Ecology: Essays on Social Transformation*. Jane C. Steward and Robert F. Murphy (eds). Urbana, Illinois. University of Illinois Press.

Strauss, Leo and Joseph Cropsey (eds). 1987. *History of Political Philosophy* (Third Edition). Chicago. University of Chicago Press (first published in 1963).

Sullivan, William M. 1982. *Reconstructing Public Philosophy*. Berkeley. University of California.

Sunkel, Osvaldo and José Leal. 1986. "Economics and Environment in a Developmental Perspective." *International Social Science Journal* 38: 411–28.

Swanson, Luis E. and Lawrence Busch. 1985. "A Part-Time Farming Model Reconsidered: A Comment on a Poet Model." *Rural Sociology* 50(3): 427–36.

Sylla, Richard. 1991. "The Progressive Era and the Political Economy of Big Government." *Critical Review* 5: 531–57.

Taylor, F. W. 1911. *The Principles of Scientific Management*. New York. Harper and Row.

Taylor, Peter John. 1988. "The Construction and Turnover of Complex Community Models having Generalized Lotka-Volterra Dynamics." *Journal of Theoretical Biology* 135: 543–68.

Teilhard de Chardin, Pierre. 1940. *The Phenomenon of Man*. New York. Harper and Row.

—— 1964. *The Future of Man*. New York. Harper and Row. Original edition in French 1959.

Thomas, William L., Jr. (ed.) 1956. *Man's Role in Changing the Face of the Earth*. Chicago. University of Chicago.

Timmerman, Peter. 1986. "Mythology and Surprise in the Sustainable Development of the Biosphere." In W. C. Clark and R. E. Munn. *Sustainable Development of the Biosphere*. Cambridge. Cambridge University Press.

Tokar, Brian. 1990. Radical Ecology on the Rise. *Z Magazine* (July/August): 12–18.

Torgerson, Douglas. 1986. "Between Knowledge and Politics: Three Faces of Policy Analysis." *Policy Sciences* 19: 33–59.

Toulmin, Stephen J. 1957. "Contemporary Scientific Mythology." Reprinted in *The Return to Cosmology: Postmodern Science and the Theology of Nature*. Berkeley. University of California. 1982.

—— 1972. *Human Understanding*. Princeton. Princeton University Press.

—— 1982. *The Return to Cosmology: Postmodern Science and the Theology of Nature*. Berkeley. University of California.

—— 1990. *Cosmopolis: The Hidden Agenda of Modernity*. New York. The Free Press.

Trotsky, Leon. 1937. *The Revolution Betrayed: What is the Soviet Union and Where is It Going?* New York. Pathfinder Press.

Turner, Bryan S. 1990. *Theories of Modernity and Postmodernity*. London. Sage.

Turner, R. Kerry (ed.). 1988. *Sustainable Environmental Management: Principles and Practice*. London. Bellhaven Press.

Usher, Dan. 1981. *The Economic Prerequisite to Democracy*. New York. Columbia University Press.

van den Bosch, Robert. 1978. *The Pesticide Conspiracy*. New York. Plenum Press.

von Bertlanffy, Ludwig. 1968. *General System Theory: Foundations, Development, Applications*. Revised Edition. New York. George Braziller.

von Hayek, Frederich August. 1974. "The Pretence of Knowledge." Nobel Memorial Lecture delivered December 11 and reprinted in *American Economic Review* (December 1989) 79(6): 3–7.

Waldrop, M. Mitchell. 1992. "Artificial Life's Rich Harvest." *Science* 257(21 August): 1040–42.

Wallerstein, Immanuel M. 1974. *The Modern World-System*. New York. Academic Press.

Walters, Carl. 1986. *Adaptive Management of Renewable Resources*. New York. Macmillan.

Ward, Barbara. 1966. *Spaceship Earth*. New York. University of Columbia Press.

Warren, Karen. 1987. Feminism and Ecology: Making Connections. *Environmental Ethics* 9: 3–20.

—— 1990. "The Power and Promise of Ecological Feminism." *Environmental Ethics* 12: 125–46.

Weber, Max. 1947. *The Theory of Social and Economic Organization*. New York. Free Press.

Weiner, Annette B. 1992. *Inalienable Possessions: The Paradox of Keeping-While-Giving*. Berkeley. University of California Press.

Wiener, Norbert. 1948. *Cybernetics: or Control and Communication in the Animal and the Machine*. Cambridge, MA. Massachusetts Institute of Technology Press.

—— 1950. *The Human Use of Human Beings: Cybernetics and Society*. Boston. Houghton Mifflin.

Westman, Walter E. 1990. Park Management of Exotic Plant Species: Problems and Issues. *Conservation Biology* 4(3): 251–60.

Wildavsky, Aaron and Ellen Tenenbaum. 1981. *The Politics of Mistrust: Estimating American Oil and Gas Resources*. Beverly Hills, CA. Sage.

Wilkinson, Richard B. 1973. *Poverty and Progress: An Ecological Perspective on Economic Development*. New York. Praeger Publishers.

Williamson, Oliver E. 1985. *The Economic Institutions of Capitalism*. New York. Free Press.

—— 1986. *Economic Organization: Firms, Markets, and Policy Control*. New York. New York University Press.

Wilson, E. O. 1975. *Sociobiology: The New Synthesis*. Cambridge. Harvard University Press.

—— 1976. Academic Vigilantism and the Political Significance of Sociobiology. *Bioscience*. v 26 (March), reprinted in Arthur L. Caplan (ed.) 1978. *The Sociobiology Debate: Readings on the Ethical and Scientific Issues Concerning Sociobiology*. New York. Harper.

—— (ed.). 1988. *Biodiversity*. Washington, D.C. National Academy Press.

Wolfe, Alan. 1989. *Whose Keeper: Social Science and Moral Obligation*. Berkeley. University of California Press.

World Bank. 1987. "Conable Announces New Steps to Protect Environment in Developing Countries." World Bank News Release No. 87/28, 5 May. Washington, D.C.

—— 1989. "Striking a Balance: The Environmental Challenge of Development." The World Bank. Washington, D.C.

World Commission on Environment and Development. 1987. *Our Common Future*. Oxford. Oxford University Press.

World Resources Institute and the International Institute for Environment and Development in collaboration with the United Nations Environment Program. 1988. *World Resources 1988–89*. New York. Basic Books.

Worster, Donald. 1977. *Nature's Economy: A History of Ecological Ideas*. New York. Cambridge University Press.

—— (ed.). 1988. *The Ends of the Earth: Perspectives on Modern Environmental History*. Cambridge. Cambridge University Press.

Wynne, Brian. 1982. *Rationality and Ritual: The Windscale Inquiry and Nuclear Dimensions in Britain*. Buckinghamshire, England. The British Society for the History of Science.

Ziman, John. 1968. *Public Knowledge: The Social Dimensions of Science*. Cambridge. Cambridge University Press.

INDEX

271